Health E{...}RSITY OF {...}AM *Week*

Second edition

This popular textbook provides a comprehensive but accessible coverage of health economic principles and applications. It provides an introduction for those with no previous knowledge of economics, but also more advanced material suitable for those with a background in economics. In this second edition, Barbara McPake and Charles Normand have incorporated developments in economic evaluation and the economics of health systems from recent research and experience while retaining an accessible approach and style.

The book starts with a section on basic economic principles as applied to health and health care, and goes on to discuss economic evaluation in health care, the economics of health systems and health care finance. Examples and illustrations are taken from a wide range of settings and world regions, reflecting the authors' belief that the same principles apply, and that it is useful to have some understanding of how different countries organise their health system. It provides an understanding of the performance of different health systems, from insurance-based approaches in the United States to the government funding that is common in Canada and most countries in Europe, and the mixed systems that operate in most low-income countries.

This book is ideal for students of public health and related courses, for health care professionals and those studying health economics at a more advanced level.

Barbara McPake is Professor and Director of the Institute for International Health and Development at Queen Margaret University, Edinburgh.

Charles Normand is Edward Kennedy Professor of Health Policy and Management at Trinity College, Dublin.

Health Economics

An international perspective

Second edition

Barbara McPake and Charles Normand

Routledge
Taylor & Francis Group

LONDON AND NEW YORK

First published 2002
Second edition 2008
by Routledge
2 Park Square, Milton Park, Abingdon, Oxon, OX14 4RN

Simultaneously published in the USA and Canada
by Routledge
270 Madison Avenue, New York NY 10016

Routledge is an imprint of the Taylor and Francis Group, an Informa business

Typeset in Times New Roman by
RefineCatch Limited, Bungay, Suffolk
Printed and bound in Great Britain
by TJ International Ltd, Padstow, Cornwall

British Library Cataloguing in Publication Data
A catalogue record for this book is available from the British Library

Library of Congress Cataloging in Publication Data
McPake, Barbara.
Health economics : an international perspective / Barbara McPake and
Charles Normand. – 2nd ed.
p. ; cm.
Includes bibliographical references and index.
ISBN 978–0-415–39129–0 (hbk) – ISBN 978-0-415–39132–0 (pbk) 1. Medical
economics. 2. Medical economics–Cross-cultural studies. I. Normand, Charles
E. M. II. Title.
[DNLM: 1. Economics, Medical. 2. World Health. W 74.1 M478h 2007]
RA410.M398 2007
338.4'33621–dc22
2007019057

ISBN10: 0–415–39129–6 (hbk)
ISBN10: 0–415–39132–6 (pbk)
ISBN10: 0–203–99524–4 (ebk)

ISBN13: 978–0–415–39129–0 (hbk)
ISBN13: 978–0–415–39132–0 (pbk)
ISBN13: 978–0–203–99524–2 (ebk)

In memory of Helen Agnes Elizabeth Normand 1922–2007

Contents

Illustrations

Tables

Boxes

Preface to the second edition

Experience as teachers and researchers in health economics has persuaded the authors first that applying even quite simple economic principles can provide very useful insights for health policy and practice; second that many of the principles are universal and can be applied in diverse settings; and third that it is useful for students to see the principles applied in different countries and to address different health policy issues. These beliefs guided the structure and content of the first edition. This second edition retains this approach, but has taken on board some useful feedback from students and teachers, and has drawn on insights from the recent research experience of the authors.

Using the first edition in our teaching, we were able to identify parts of the book worked very well and some that worked less well. We have updated material to include important developments in the discipline, and to reflect more accurately the current situations in the many countries visited over the course of the text. We have also revised or replaced sections to improve the focus and presentation.

Part I has changed little except to reflect more effectively the issues and situations that are frequently experienced in health policy. A good understanding of these basic pillars of standard micro-economics is required for understanding current developments, including critiques of the neoclassical approach.

Part II reflects several important changes and developments in economic evaluation. These include more sophisticated use of modelling and statistical techniques such as approaches to sensitivity analysis using estimates of uncertainty from variation observed in clinical trials or other sources of data, modelling techniques that extrapolate long-term costs and benefits from short-term outcomes, including the use of simple Markov models and Monte Carlo techniques, and the greater application of Bayesian approaches.

Part III has been updated to reflect the growth in empirical material that has applied institutionally oriented theory. The presentation of agency theory has been completely revised in response to difficulties students had with the previous approach.

Part IV is considerably expanded to reflect the growth in the literature on health systems reform and development, and the greater accumulation of evidence in relation to comparative health system performance. Comparison of the equity characteristics associated with different health systems is now facilitated by the application of common approaches across multiple settings and the publication of the resulting data by the World Bank. Similarly, the World Health Report has improved and made available its Human Resource Atlas, making possible comparison of some measures of efficiency of human resource use across health system contexts.

We hope the book will continue to make the contribution that it seems to have done over the past five years to the teaching of health economics in different countries and contexts. We hope that the improvements will improve the clarity and relevance of the book. We are very grateful for the feedback and suggestions that we've received about the book since its publication from our own students and other users. Please continue to let us know how helpful you are finding different sections, as a teacher or user.

B.M.
C.N.

Acknowledgements

The first edition of the text book was a joint output of the Health Systems Development and Health Economics and Financing Knowledge Programmes, both of which were financially supported by the Department for International Development.

In the production of the second edition, we are very grateful to Donna Carter Leay, for her assistance with the preparation of the manuscript.

We would also like to acknowledge a number of students and other users who pointed out to us errors and difficulties with the first edition. We hope they find these remedied.

1 Introduction
Health economics in international perspective

1.1 The role of economists in the health sector

Why do economists work in health? The health sector is not usually the first place people associate with economists. It is not supposed to be about money, profit, production and markets. Should it not be about medicine, nursing, caring and the difference between life and death? Surely, an economist has no wisdom to bring to bear here? Such views were virtually universal until quite recently but they demonstrate a limited understanding of the role and content of economics. In principle economists are concerned with better choices and in particular making the best use of existing resources and growth in the availability of resources. As economists started to work on problems in the health sector, the new discipline of health economics emerged. Many of the concerns in health economics are also those of other health scientists – how can we improve survival, quality of life and fairness in access to services? What economics brings is a different framework for analysing such questions. We think this framework offers important and useful insights.

Economists in all sectors are concerned with the allocation of resources between competing demands. Demands are assumed to be *infinite* – there is no end to consumption aspirations. Resources (like labour, raw materials, production equipment and land) in contrast, are always *finite*. Thus *scarcity* of resources (not in the sense of 'rarity' but in the sense of resource availability *relative* to demand) becomes the fundamental problem to which economists address themselves. Some readers will have difficulty with this description of the world. It is not necessarily 'true' but is, in a broad sense, a model on which economics is based. See Box 1.1 for further discussion of the nature and purpose of models, and of this one in particular.

In the health sector, such scarcity can be recognised in a host of questions that concern all who work there or use its services. Why has the volume of resources absorbed by the sector increased so fast over the last four decades worldwide? Why does it seem that no matter how many nurses and doctors are employed, new technologies adopted, new drug therapies introduced, even the rich countries of the world do not seem to be able to provide the highest quality of care for all citizens? Are we investing in the wrong kinds of health services? (Are we organising services so as to best improve the health of the population? Are we investing in technologies that have a low health output compared with alternative investments?) In poor countries, questions of resource scarcity are starker still. Can we afford, at all, universal access to high-cost services such as cancer care?

All societies must make choices as to how to allocate whatever resources are available to the production of health services, and how to distribute those health services

Box 1.1 Realism and the need for simplification: the use of models in economics

In teaching health economics, we have found that students often raise objections to the assumptions of economic models and the characterisation of all-pervasive scarcity on which economics is based. Others object to the concept of the 'rational economic man' that underlies demand theory (see Chapter 2) and the assumptions of the theory of perfect competition (see Chapter 6).

At least part of the concern comes from a misunderstanding of the role and usefulness of theories and models. Models are not intended to describe reality. They deliberately abstract from it, in order to simplify the relations between key variables so that we can see them clearly and analyse them. Models should never be 'realistic', they should always be simplifications. Models deliberately ignore variables we are less interested in, or consider to play only a small role, either by holding them constant or by setting them to zero. Economists use the expression *ceteris paribus* (all the rest the same) to indicate that all variables which haven't been included in the model should be assumed to be constant. By simplifying we aim to focus on the relationships we are interested in, examine the interactions between these variables, and avoid the 'noise' of the hundreds of other variables which will otherwise confuse those key relationships. An extreme position is that of Milton Friedman (1953), who has argued that a model is good if it predicts accurately. Its assumptions may bear no relation to reality. Friedman uses the example of leaves deliberately seeking to arrange themselves so as to maximise the sunlight each receives. The assumption of 'deliberating' leaves may be unrealistic, but a model based on that assumption predicts accurately the pattern of leaf growth and development on a tree. Others (for example, Hodgson 1988) consider that a model which predicts on the basis of very unrealistic assumptions fails to explain the relationships in question. We do not understand much about the process of leaf growth and distribution starting from this assumption. Explanation is often as useful a function of models as prediction.

Take the particular assumption that demands are 'infinite'. Are they really? Levels of consumption enjoyed in the rich economies of the world have grown beyond the imagination of previous generations – and of the 50 per cent of the world's population who live on less than US$2 per day today (*Human Development Report* 1999). The consumption levels of the richest in the world demonstrate that when resource constraints are low, people consume goods that would in other circumstances be considered of very low priority. If demand exists for psychiatric services for pet dogs, cars capable of speeds exceeding the maximum permitted on public roads, and dancing snowmen singing 'Jingle bells', where can limits be found? Observing some spectacles of consumption, one might conclude that increased wealth and command of resources increase greed and aspiration to consume even more.

In the health sector, one might reach similar conclusions based on the rapid development of technology, which makes available almost unlimited opportunities to extend and improve the quality of life. There seems no limit to the resources that might be consumed with the objective of improving the health of a population.

However, it is also clear that not all members of the world's population aspire to such levels of consumption. Many widely held systems of philosophical and religious belief from Calvinism to Islam eschew consumerism. And even if the levels of demand which might potentially be expressed are very large indeed, could they really be infinite? Is there not a maximum rate at which any individual could possibly consume resources?

The discipline of economics needs an assumption which is realistic enough to generate useful analysis and conclusions. What is unarguable is that the extent of demands on resources far outstrips the capacity of available resources to deliver, and does so to such a great extent that there is no prospect of ever meeting all demands with available resources. This is sufficient to make the economist's characterisation of all pervasive 'scarcity' a reasonable basis on which to proceed.

Of course, the current distribution of resources leaves some high-priority demands unmet at the expense of some of the low priority demands listed above. For the cost of the dancing snowman several people might have their sight restored through cataract surgery. In this insight lie the concerns of economists. Why do the current resource allocation mechanisms choose snowmen over cataract surgery? If we take the normative perspective that surgery is 'better' than snowmen as a starting point, what kinds of intervention might help us move towards a situation in which more demands for surgery and fewer demands for snowmen are met? These questions are the business of economics.

produced between those who want them. These choices are the subject of the discipline of health economics. Health economics (and economics in general) is often seen as having two branches: the *positive* branch, which is concerned with describing and explaining how such choices are actually made, and the *normative* branch which is concerned with judging which choices should be made. For example, a health economist might be concerned with health insurance coverage of a population. She might take a positive perspective. Why are there so many uninsured? What are the characteristics of those that are uninsured (are they unable to afford the cost of insurance premiums, or do they judge themselves unlikely to need health services)? From a normative perspective it is necessary to establish criteria according to which the situation can be judged. If equity of access to health services is one criterion, and ability to pay is a dominant explanation of non-coverage, the situation might be judged 'bad', and alternative interventions to reduce the problem evaluated.

There are two ways in which society can make choices about the allocation of resources to production in the health sector, and the distribution of the services that are produced among those that want them. A society can leave these decisions to the *market* – letting demand, supply and prices determine resource allocation, or it can *plan*, usually by giving its government the task of collecting resources from the population, allocating those to defined production activities and distributing the produced services among the population. The debate as to which approach is best has divided the world's population through the whole of the twentieth century, underlying the formation of political parties, *coups d'état*, and hot and cold war, and will not be settled in this volume! Societies worldwide have taken different stances on the question, and have evolved a wide array of mixes of plan and market in the attempt to reach a satisfactory choice as to how to produce and distribute health services.

Health economists have evolved different approaches to analysing and evaluating resource allocation in the health sector which reflect the plan–market dichotomy. In societies in which health services have been largely planned, the main activity of health economists has been the development and application of a set of tools which collectively make up the field of *economic evaluation*. Economic evaluation aims to consider whether appropriate services have been adopted in the health sector, or whether there is a mix of technologies and interventions which would better meet health sector objectives, such as the improvement of the population's health, or the equity of access to care. You might notice that in terms of the positive–normative dimension, this is an essentially normative activity. It requires the definition of objectives and asks: 'What should we do?'

Where there has been a greater role for the market in health sector resource allocation, more effort has been made by economists to understand that market to predict its pattern of development, and to analyse the implications of interventions such as regulation, subsidy of insurance coverage or the introduction of planned activities. Even in the most market reliant-health sectors, such interventions are always present. Understanding markets involves the understanding of demand (how consumers of health services express their preferences through their ability and willingness to pay), supply (conditions in input markets, cost, and how provision is organised, for example by one big firm or by many) and their interactions. This is essentially a positive activity – explaining what is happening and predicting the effects of introducing a change – but it can be normative. If it is decided that a particular effect is desirable, such analysis can be used to evaluate whether a change should be introduced.

As health sectors have evolved, especially over the last two decades, richer mixes of planning and markets have been developed in a large number of countries. In health sectors which have traditionally been planned, elements of market mechanisms have been introduced, for example through 'internal markets'. In health sectors which have traditionally relied to a greater extent on market mechanisms, more planning has been introduced – for example through more intrusive public regulation, or through the use of capitation payment mechanisms (consumers pay the provider a fee per year rather than per service) which shift risk on to providers and thereby pass on the planning role usually carried out by a public sector body. This has led to a certain cross-over of interests in the health economics fields. US health economists are now much more interested in the techniques of economic evaluation which can assist Health Maintenance Organisations (providers paid by capitation) in developing their strategies, and economists interested in the welfare state health provision of northern European countries are increasingly interested in the operation of markets and the implications of different kinds of regulation and other public intervention for market behaviour. On both sides of the Atlantic there is now interest in capturing the insights of economic evaluation to enable better planning by actors in the market place, and to better understanding how public intervention can improve outcomes associated with health markets.

These two traditions of health economics can be detected by comparing the outputs of health economists in northern Europe, Australia and New Zealand (largely planned health sectors), and the United States (where market forces have been allowed greater rein). Canadian health economics has perhaps been least categorisable, located in a health sector which is characterised by planned approaches to resource allocation, but strongly influenced by the academic environment of the United States. Some prominent contributions to health economics from Canada have provided a critique of US analysis.

Although most work in health economics has been produced in these regions, trends in health sector development affect those conducting economic analysis in the health sectors of almost all countries. It is no longer safe to assume that one is working in a planned environment, that an understanding of market forces is unnecessary, and that topics in economic evaluation provide the only useful tools required. Similarly, it is unlikely that the United States will ever return to the market conditions of the 1970s. Technology assessment, facility planning and the mandate of insurance packages are likely to feature for the foreseeable future, and economic evaluation will continue to play a major role in the operation of these.

It is therefore increasingly the case that, wherever their work takes them in the world, a health economist needs grounding in both branches of the discipline. This book is founded on that belief. It aims to explain basic health economics across the spectrum of the discipline and to demonstrate applications on a worldwide basis. The work of the two authors of this book covers a wide geographic span, taking in the UK, the United States, Canada and Australia, many of the countries of the former Soviet Union and Eastern Europe, Uganda, Zambia and Zimbabwe, Bangladesh, Colombia and Peru – in fact countries from all continents except Antarctica. Obviously, the problems faced by these different countries in trying to ensure that public health problems are thoroughly addressed and that all citizens receive high-quality health services are quite different – in type and degree. Nevertheless, the tools of economic analysis presented in this book have provided us with a good basis for seeking to understand and evaluate the problems encountered and the measures taken to respond to them irrespective of the context. We believe that contrasting experience of applying these tools in different countries is helpful in understanding issues and undertaking analysis in any particular country. The aim of this book is to provide an introduction to these tools and to show ways that the same approach can inform health policy in widely differing contexts.

1.2 Economics, health policy and equity

Economic analysis in health and health care is often undertaken with a view to help governments and other agencies better to achieve the goals of their health policies. An obvious requirement is to know what are these goals. Where explicit goals are specified it is common for two to dominate – improving the health status of the population and fairness or equity. Health economists have therefore focused on assessing how to maximise the impact on health and equity. In economics it is recognised that choices must be made – it is not possible to get everything you want. While some policies may offer the opportunity to increase both equity and health improvement, others require a choice between equity and health improvement – in other words we must sometimes choose to trade off efficiency (the achievement of better health) and equity (the fairer distribution of health).

Fairness and equity are difficult concepts, and a whole literature exists just on how they should be defined. As ideas they inevitably carry strong moral overtones. To be against fairness seems impossible almost by definition. To be openly in favour of widening gaps in health between the rich and the poor is understandably uncommon. Being clear about what is meant by equity or fairness is also uncommon, and it is important to define the concepts and desired outcomes more precisely. There can be many reasons why health and access to health care are unequal. Some people happen to be born with diseases or disabilities, or the predisposition to become ill. Some people are just unlucky, and become ill. Those without jobs or housing may live in risky or unhealthy conditions. Others take risks, such as rock climbing or smoking, and the outcomes may be bad. And some people would benefit from treatment or care but cannot find the resources to pay for it.

A significant part of this book is devoted to analysis of markets in health and health care, how they work, how they fail and what can be done to make them work better. Even if they work well, poor people are poor, and without help can afford only limited access to care. They are also more likely than richer people to have illness and disability. In most countries in the world there are government measures to reduce the disparity in access to care between richer and poorer people. Despite this the gaps remain between the health experiences of different groups – better health is enjoyed by richer people, by professionals and by women. Access to care does not reflect fully these differences.

In countries with government funding of health care, or some system of funding that is heavily regulated by government, it is common for there to be a system of allocating resources to take account of differences in needs in different parts of the population. The most common approach is for allocation to be based on population, weighted for need factors such as age, gender and morbidity. The allocations are then proportionate to the measures of need. This approach has done much to weight funding towards those with worse health. However, there are obvious problems, since it is not clear that the appropriate level of funding should be proportionate to a particular measure of need. This illustrates a difficulty in making operational a desire to create vertical equity (that is, the unequal support for unequals). The other common notion of equity is horizontal equity, the equal treatment of equals. In principle this is easier, since all that is needed is the same access to health or health care opportunities for people in the same situation. Putting it into practice is not so easy.

Economists often focus on the trade-off between efficiency and equity. Take the example of urban and rural populations and their different perinatal mortality rates. It is common for rural areas to have worse rates of such deaths, so it might be expected that the efforts of public health and health services would focus on reducing this difference. However, it is also likely that the cost of lowering the rate of perinatal deaths in rural areas will be higher (for example because service users are more costly to reach), so that a given expenditure might do more to lower the *number* of deaths if applied in the urban area. A real choice might be to lower the number of deaths by 100 if the focus is on urban areas but only by 80 if the same funds were spent on the rural programme. A difficult choice faces policy makers – spend the money on the urban areas and more deaths are prevented, but at the same time the disparity between urban and rural areas becomes wider. Of course we would all like to see both fewer deaths and less inequality, but for many spending questions we cannot avoid making this difficult choice between a more efficient intervention (i.e. fewer deaths) and a more equitable one. Is the additional fairness worth twenty deaths?

The example of perinatal deaths is based on a real choice that was faced by a health agency. It represents one of the most difficult dilemmas. There are also many occasions when there is no trade-off between efficiency and fairness, since people with worse health have more scope to recover with treatment. Take another example, based on experience in an urban area in England. Owing to differences in referral rates, people in the poorest part of the district had the highest rates of treatable coronary heart disease but were getting less treatment than those from more prosperous parts. In effect those with the least capacity to benefit were getting more, and those likely to benefit more got less. In this case the allocation of resources is inefficient (since more improvement in health could be achieved with the existing budget), and greater efficiency would also lead to greater equity. Being ill or at risk is a necessary condition for being able to benefit from treatment, so that it is often the case that those who can benefit most are those with low incomes and above-average morbidity. In some cases it is more expensive to treat poorer people, since they may need longer in hospital. There are also cases where there are higher costs of running a prevention programme for poorer people. For example, those choosing to attend for screening programmes tend to be those who are richer and have less disease. Recruiting those from poorer families may be important, since there is likely to be more disease detected, but it may cost more to organise such a programme.

These examples aim to shed light on several aspects of equity. There is no simple definition of equity. It is also important to consider equity in the health sector in the context of overall equity. Poverty leads to ill health, and constrains access to health care. Action to improve equity in access to health services can help, but tackles symptoms more than causes. To a large extent the problem of health inequalities is a problem of more general economic and social inequalities, and the solutions lie outside the health sector. There is some evidence that it is relative (rather than absolute) poverty that is associated with poor health, although recent studies cast some doubt on this. It is certainly the case that countries with great social inequalities have worse health on average than those that are more equal. The rapid changes in Central and Eastern Europe were associated with a rapid increase in income inequality and worsening of health.

It can be useful to distinguish within the health sector between structures that lead to unequal access to services and the failure of health systems to work as they are planned to. Countries with state funding or social insurance funding for health care normally aim to provide nearly equal access to important services. The rules normally state that care should be offered on the basis of need and not income or ability to pay. The reality is often different, since there may be user charges (whether official or unofficial), medicines may not be available at the hospitals, staff may be rude and careless with poorer patients, and buildings in a poor state of repair. The design may be for a system of equal access, but the reality is that those with more money get better access. This may be contrasted with systems that do not aim to provide equal access. In the United States access depends on income, employment, age and disease. Those who are employed and insured get excellent services. Those who are very poor or old get free or subsidised services. Those with renal failure may get free dialysis, but those with low-paid jobs and no insurance may be excluded from many parts of the system. Even if each part of the system were to work as planned, the system does not aim to provide the same health care opportunities to all users. This is not to argue the superiority of systems that aim to be equitable but which fail, but in such cases the solution may be to make the system work as planned. In a fragmented system such as in the United States any moves to greater equity are likely to require some changes in structures.

This book does not have a separate chapter on health equity or equity in access to care. However, many sections touch on these issues. The analysis of markets considers the consequences for who gets what access to what health opportunities. Economic evaluation may affect priorities and therefore access. In some cases better management and implementation of existing policy more fully will also reduce inequalities. The final section of the book, on health systems, addresses the implications of different health system structures for rationing principles. Where there is a trade-off between more health gain and more equality in health, those making policies must be clear: greater equity will be achieved only at the expense of worsening the overall levels of health. This may be deemed to be desirable, but equity, like most desirable ends, has a cost.

1.3 The structure of this book

Part I introduces basic micro-economics and its applications in the health sector. These topics – demand and elasticity, production and cost, perfect markets and market failure, provide the basic building blocks for any more sophisticated micro-economic analysis, whether of the operations of markets or the economic theory underlying topics in economic evaluation such as shadow pricing and willingness to pay as a means of valuing benefits.

Part II introduces economic evaluation. We have noted above that any normative economic analysis must start out with clear criteria by which to evaluate the goodness or badness of any proposed policy or change in current practice. This section starts with an introduction to welfare economics, which is the branch of economics which has developed the system of criteria on which economic evaluation is based. The rest of the section focuses on the philosophical and practical difficulties encountered in trying to evaluate policy and practice in the light of these criteria, and provides a running case study through which these difficulties are exemplified and explored.

Part III covers topics which enable a more sophisticated analysis of market behaviour and applications to the evaluation of market intervention such as regulation and contracting. On the basis of this section, the reader will start to understand the insights that can be gained from the application of market theory and analysis to health sector scenarios – whether in more or less planned health sectors.

Part IV provides an overview of the insights that economic analysis can provide into the understanding of health systems at a macro level. It starts with a review of the shape of health systems around the world and an overview of the performance characteristics associated with different systems. It proceeds to provide a framework for explaining the patterns of performance through an understanding of the resource allocation mechanisms associated with different health systems, and the nature of the institutions which finance and provide health services. It concludes with an introduction to health sector reform debates in which reforms are viewed as interventions aiming to reshape health systems, informed by an economic analysis of the strengths and weaknesses of alternative configurations.

The book is designed to be read in different ways. The aim has been to keep the text as readable as possible, and to use technical terminology only where necessary. Where possible the ideas are illustrated with examples taken from the authors' experience of applying economics to health and health care issues. A more technical approach is provided in parallel. Text boxes offer fuller explanation of some points, mathematical presentation of some of the theory and background to some ideas and individuals. The presentation in Part I assumes no previous knowledge of economics. The later parts build on this foundation. Readers with previous training in economics should find these quite accessible, but those new to economics should not attempt to read them without a reasonable grasp of the material in the first section.

Part I
Introductory health economics

2 The demand for health and health services

2.1 Demand and demand for health care

Medicine and health care have a long history of being treated as special. There are some obvious ways in which the way we interact with the health sector is different from our dealings with other providers of goods and services. Doctors advise us on what services we need and often also provide them. Some health services are used when we are very ill and may not be able to make sensible decisions. Some health care decisions are literally about life and death. In many cases interventions have very uncertain effects for any individual. Another problem is timing. In general we are healthier when relatively young and relatively rich. These are times when we are least likely to need health care, but most likely to be able to afford it. Perhaps the most important feature of our need for health care is that we seldom know in advance what we will need, when we will need it or how much we will need. Another interesting feature is that few of us actually want to use health services – we do so because we hope it will improve our health. Indeed, use of health services is often unpleasant. Most things we buy are more enjoyable to consume.

On the other hand not all health interventions are uncertain, few are really about life and death, and in many cases the intervention is well understood by the patient. For example, you have myopia, and need optometry services. You can calculate with almost perfect accuracy how often you need eye tests and, unless you sit on them, how many pairs of spectacles you will need for the rest of your life. For many people dental care is almost as predictable. There is no significant uncertainty in the need for many childhood vaccinations – the content and timing of immunisation are predictable.

Many health services are about comfort, mobility, feeling healthy and having good quality of life. Relatively little of what is done extends life to a significant degree. In an absolute sense health care is less necessary than many other necessities, such as food and clothing. This chapter introduces the economic theory of demand, and applies it to health and health care. The features of health that are special are explored.

There are several reasons why we should be interested in demand for health and health care. The first is to help us to predict likely reactions and behaviour. For example, if we charge people a fee for eyesight tests, what will be the effect on the number of people using the service? How will such a charge affect the frequency of use of optometry services? Second, knowing something about people's demand for health care may tell us something about how much they value services. This point will be explored in greater depth below.

2.2 Preference and indifference

The theory of demand is normally built up in two stages. First, we look at the patterns of preference or indifference between different goods or services. For example, do I prefer a twenty-minute phone call to my mother or twenty minutes of free internet access? Do I prefer one television set to one bicycle? Do I prefer a 20 per cent reduction in the size of classes at school or twenty sets of textbooks? Of course our preferences are complicated, and normally we want both the products or services offered. The best way to think about preference is 'Which would I choose?' The most reliable information comes from actual choices people have made, but at times we know only what they say they would choose. It is obvious that what people say may be affected by other factors, such as concern about what others will think.

Normally we like more rather than less. But the more we have of a service the less we value extra amounts. Take the phone call to your mother. After twenty minutes all the important news has been given. If offered another ten minutes it would allow more detail. It is not clear how much value would be put on an extra two hours. Similarly, when offered twenty minutes on the internet, this allows important information to be found. With subsequent minutes there may be enjoyable surfing, but most people would place a lower value on that. The normal response to the choice of the phone call and the internet access would be to say 'Can I have some of each?'

In order to understand more clearly the process of making choices it is useful to consider a very simplified example. You are caring at home for a relative with significant needs. With the help of family and friends you are able to provide all the care she needs, but it seriously limits your ability to leave the house, and for much of the time you cannot focus on other tasks and responsibilities. In order to encourage families to care for their own relatives a new government scheme provides families with funds that can be spent on buying extra help at home or on paying for short periods in residential care to provide respite for carers. At current prices you can afford to buy any of the combinations of home help time or respite care as shown in Table 2.1. Your preferences between these different combinations are given in the third column.

What is clear is that you prefer combinations that have a bit of each to ones that concentrate more on one or other type of support. We can imagine an experiment in which we vary the home help and respite care amounts to find combinations that are of equal value to you. This is illustrated in Table 2.2. Since you cannot choose between the different combinations you are said to be *indifferent* as between the different combinations. We can illustrate the data in Table 2.2 in a diagram, showing the combinations of home help hours and respite days between which you are indifferent. The points in Figure 2.1 are those between which you are indifferent. If we identify all the other combinations of respite days and home help hours between which you are indifferent

Table 2.1 Preference for combinations of home help hours and respite care

Home help (hours/month)	Respite care (days/month)	Order of preference
40	0	5
30	2	2
20	4	1
10	6	3
0	8	4

Table 2.2 Points of indifference

Home help (hours/month)	Respite care (days/month)	Order of preference
56	0	?
33	2	?
20	4	?
14	6	?
12	8	?

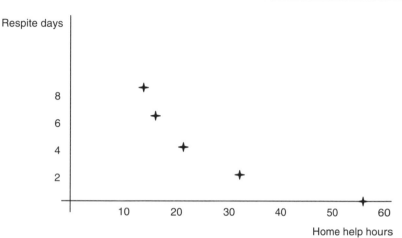

Figure 2.1 Indifference curve.

we can plot your *indifference curve*. There are reasons to expect that, for most individuals, for most pairs of goods, the indifference curve will have the shape outlined in Figure 2.1, that is, convex to the origin.

As we see in this example, the more you have of either service the less you value additional units. This is not surprising. If two goods are perfect substitutes for each other the indifference curve will be a straight line. If they are perfect complements, that is to say, they can be used only in fixed combinations, the indifference curves are L-shaped, as illustrated in Figure 2.2. For example, syringes and needles are needed in fixed combinations, and neither is useful without the other. For most people an effective treatment for a headache can be either ASA (aspirin) or ibuprofen, so they are near substitutes.

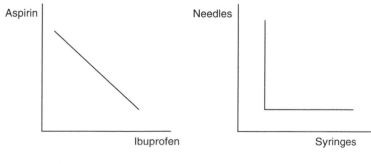

Figure 2.2 Perfect substitutes and complements.

For most goods and services we prefer more to less. Figure 2.1 showed combinations of home help hours and respite days between which you were indifferent, but you would prefer more of both. We can draw a series of indifference curves to represent sets of combinations between which a person is indifferent, as in Figure 2.3. Each of the indifference curves represents different levels of utility – since the person prefers more to less, all points on I2 are preferred to all on I1.

In this example the carer has a budget of €800 per month. The price of home help time is €20 per hour, and the price of the respite home is €100 per day. The carer wants to maximise her utility, so she will choose the combination of each that is within this budget but also on the highest achievable indifference curve. If the entire budget were spent on home help hours it would buy forty hours, and if it was all spent on respite that would allow eight nights per month. We can therefore draw a budget line that represents all combinations that are affordable at €800, as shown in Figure 2.4.

We can put the information in Figures 2.3 and 2.4 together to work out the best combination. Put another way, the best strategy is to choose the combination that allows the carer to be on the highest indifference curve. This is shown in Figure 2.5. The best combination is at point A, where the budget is used to purchase the most preferred combination of home help hours and respite nights.

The simplified example has only two services. We can of course think of the same process with three (where indifference curves become indifference surfaces, and budget lines budget planes). However, to retain the convenience of two-dimensional diagrams

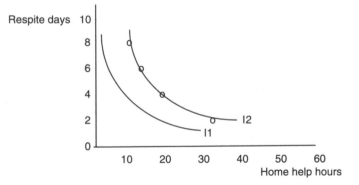

Figure 2.3 Indifference map.

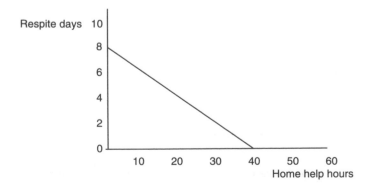

Figure 2.4 Budget line.

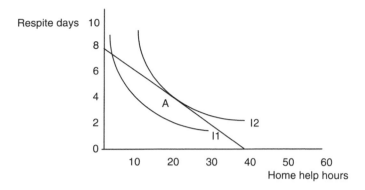

Figure 2.5 Indifference map with budget line.

we can simplify things by comparing a particular good or service to a composite good ('all other goods').

2.3 From preference to demand

In section 2.2 a two-stage decision process was described in which the consumer identifies her preferences between two services and then chooses, using this information and information on her income and the relative prices of each service. The analysis allows us to develop the theory of demand. Keeping all other factors constant, we can show that the effects on the choices made change as we vary the price of one good or vary income. Figures 2.6 and 2.7 illustrate the effects of a change in price or a change in income on the demand for home help hours.

In Figure 2.6, the price of home-help care has risen to €40 per hour. This halves the maximum number of home help hours that can be purchased but does not change the maximum respite nights; swivelling the budget constraint as shown. The carer chooses fewer hours of home help services at this higher price (ten instead of twenty) but makes a smaller reduction in the number of respite nights. But note also that in effect the person is also now poorer, in the sense that her money buys her less. We can analyse the effect of the price rise as having a *substitution effect*, which is the pure effect of the change in relative prices (i.e. a shift along I2 to the point where its slope matches that of the new budget constraint) and an *income effect*, which is the effect on demand of

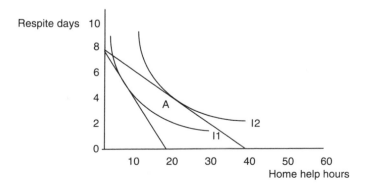

Figure 2.6 Changing the price of one service.

the person being poorer. Substitution effects are negative – the higher price leads to less consumption. Income effects are also normally negative, but may be positive in the case of certain goods.

From Figure 2.6 we can calculate the effects on the amount of each service that will be bought at each price (keeping income and the price of the other service constant). We could draw a series of budget constraints, each representing a value of the price of home help hours. From the information in Figure 2.6 we can identify quantities of home help hours that would be bought at different prices. These are shown in Figure 2.7. If we did this exercise a large number of times we would produce a *demand curve*, as illustrated.

In this model of demand, the quantity chosen is a function of the price

$$Q = f(P)$$

Those familiar with mathematical convention will notice that this diagram has been drawn with price on the vertical axis and quantity on the horizontal axis. This is the opposite of the normal convention in mathematics for the dependent and independent variable. Alfred Marshall, who first suggested this analysis in the nineteenth century, used the axes in this way, and the habit has stuck.

Figure 2.8 illustrates the effects of a fall in income on demand for each service. In this case the person chooses less of both, but there are times when a fall in income will lead to one good facing increased demand. This most often happens if, when income falls, people choose to decrease the consumption of luxury foods and consume more of basic ones.

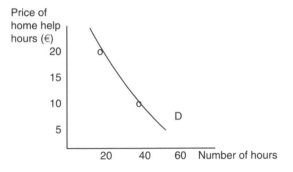

Figure 2.7 Demand curve.

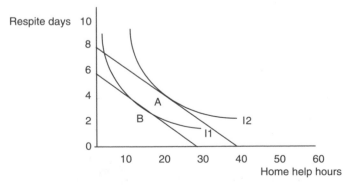

Figure 2.8 The effects of changing the budget constraint.

A fall in income can be represented by a parallel shift to the left of the budget constraint. In this case the effect is to shift choices to point B, where the person consumes less of both services. (In the case of a luxury good and basic good, the point of tangency could occur at a point where the demand for one good falls and the demand for the other increases.)

2.4 Determinants of demand

The analysis above suggests a number of determinants of demand for a service. First, individual tastes and preferences are important in determining the shape of individual indifference curves. These may be more or less stable – some things change with fashion, and others are more predictable. Second, the price of the good will influence the amount chosen. Third, demand will be affected by the price of other goods, both substitutes and complements. In general a fall in the price of substitutes leads demand for the service to fall, and a fall in the price of complements for it to rise. Fourth, the income of individuals is a determinant of demand. More formally we can express this as

$$D = f(P, P_s, P_c, Y, T)$$

where P is price, P_s is the price of substitute goods, P_c is the price of complement goods, Y is income and T is tastes.

We know that, in general, demand falls with price, increases with the price of substitutes, decreases with the price of complements, increases with income and increases as tastes and preferences increase.

What is illustrated in Figure 2.7 is the demand curve for one person. Clearly the overall demand for the good depends on the demand of all people who potentially are in the market. To get the community's demand curve we just add together the demand curves for all individuals. (The demand at each price is the total of all individual demands at that price, so the demand curves are summed horizontally.)

2.5 From demand to demand for health and health care

The example chosen to illustrate the basic theory of demand was taken from a social care setting. The question is to what extent the principles can usefully be applied to understanding demand for health and demand for health care.

The first point is that health has many dimensions. We enjoy it for itself, and use it to help us earn a living and to enjoy other goods and services. In order to produce health we can do a number of things – take exercise, eat healthier food, live in better housing, avoid contaminated water, stop smoking, have vaccinations, take part in screening for risk factors or early symptoms of disease, or have medical or surgical treatment.

Demand for health care depends in part on how much we value health – it is sometimes therefore described as a derived demand, since the real demand is for health, and the demand for health care is to help achieve the desired health. Of course many goods and services have this feature. The demand for cars might be described as the demand for hours of happy family motoring, or even the demand for access to different places.

In our behaviour we can observe trade-offs between health and other goods and services. When someone smokes they (presumably) enjoy the taste and the ending of the craving for an addictive substance. The decision to drive to near-by shops is a decision not to get the health benefits of some exercise. Crossing roads at pedestrian crossings reduces the chance of death or injury, but many people save themselves a few minutes and cross heavy traffic. Driving fast is exciting, saves time and increases the chance of death or injury. In these senses people constantly make a trade-off between consuming more health and consuming other goods which give utility. We may claim that our health is of paramount importance, but our behaviour does not always support the claim. By observing our choices of health-enhancing or health-damaging goods and services we can in principle impute the demand for health.

Perhaps a more important consideration is that health is not something that is very directly traded. We cannot easily buy it and sell it, and it is closely attached to us. In that sense it is a characteristic rather than a product. Since it is difficult to trade, and is in some senses part of us, it is different from phone calls or bananas.

Another important feature of health is that it is surrounded by uncertainty. Only some illness is predictable, and there is huge variation. We all know of lifelong smokers who live healthily into their nineties, and sensible people who follow the health promotion messages and get ill. Of course we can change the risks, but we cannot simply choose a good outcome. This further complicates matters.

Demand for health care is also affected by this uncertainty. In essence what we want to buy is access to care should we need it. This means that for some people the demand for health care is a demand for insurance offering guaranteed access to care should the need arise. Of course many other goods have this characteristic. A house being damaged by an earthquake or a freak hailstorm cannot be predicted, but we can insure against such eventualities. It is often claimed that health care is different from other goods because it is a necessity. To an extent that is true (although the proportion of

---

Box 2.1 The Grossman model of the demand for health

Grossman (1972b) developed a 'human capital' model of the demand for health in which individuals invest in their health on the basis of perfect knowledge of the relationship between their investment and its outcome.

The Grossman model assumes that health is produced using household inputs (such as tooth brushing) as well as by purchasing inputs (such as health care and the toothbrushes and toothpaste required for tooth brushing) from outside the household.

With perfect knowledge, households will choose to combine inputs such that the marginal productivity of each is equal. Marginal productivity of each input is diminishing so that each extra unit of health produced requires more inputs.

These assumptions can be used to generate a number of predictions. For example, with education, the household production function is assumed to be more efficient, predicting that more educated households will produce higher levels of health. With age, the rate of depreciation of health increases, making it increasingly costly to maintain a given level of health – predicting that health will decline continuously with age. Cullis and West (1979) note that this constitutes the individual 'choosing' the moment of death!

health care that is devoted to reducing premature death is relatively small in most countries). Many goods are necessities for life, and many are more important for this than health care.

A feature of health is that in some senses it is like a capital good. If you invest in better health it remains with you, and health-damaging behaviour can leave it permanently lower. In this sense we may want to draw on the insights of demand theory applied to capital goods industries, and look at decisions to invest in durable products. Perhaps the comparison should be with cars and houses rather than bananas.

Another test of whether health care can be considered to be the same as other services is how demand responds to changes in income or price. What is found in all studies is that, other things being equal, a rise in the price of health care reduces the amount consumed, and a fall in price increases use. Increased income is associated with higher demand for health services, and lower income with lower demand. Thus, in many important ways, demand for health and demand for health care are like the demand for other goods and other services. However, the great uncertainty, the limited information and the contexts in which health and health care are produced all make it a bit special, and the analysis later in this book explores many of the ways in which applying economics to health and health care can be challenging.

3 Demand, elasticity and health

3.1 Elasticity of demand

In Chapter 2 the ideas of preference, indifference and demand were explored. It was argued that demand is influenced by a range of factors, including income, tastes and preferences, prices of the good and prices of substitutes and complements. The demand curve was drawn showing how demand for the good or service may be related to price.

It is often useful to know more about how demand varies with price. Some services or goods are so necessary to life that we are likely to use them whatever the price. Others may bring benefits, but are less necessary or have more substitutes. The measure of how responsive demand is to price is known as the *price elasticity of demand*. In a similar way we can calculate the responsiveness of demand to income changes, and this is the *income elasticity of demand*.

3.2 Measuring elasticity

Many studies have estimated demand elasticities. It is often useful to know what will happen if prices rise or fall. Take the example of legalising the use of heroin. The current price of heroin is high, largely as a result of the prohibition of production, importation and distribution of the drug. If the drug were legalised it is likely that the price would fall, since it is very cheap to produce. It is very likely that consumption would rise in that case, since demand normally increases as price falls. The question of interest is 'How much is demand likely to rise in response to a fall in price?' Policy makers would be keen to know the answer to this before embarking on legalisation. It might be argued that, since heroin is addictive, users are not very sensitive to price. In other words demand is *inelastic*. But it would be useful to have estimates of elasticity before making the policy change.

Figure 3.1 illustrates the relationship between price and quantity of heroin demanded, per week in one market. From the information in Figure 3.1 we can draw up a table showing the relationship between quantity consumed and price. For example, at price €80, the demand would be 59 g. Table 3.1 shows all the combinations.

From the table what can be said about how responsive is demand to price? The fall in quantity seems quite large – the price rise from €20 to €80 reduces demand by 31 g. But really to answer the question we need to compare the *proportionate* changes. If price falls from €80 to €60, this 25 per cent fall leads to a rise in consumption of less than 7 per cent. This suggests that demand is not very responsive to price – what might be

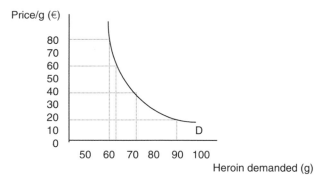

Figure 3.1 The relation between price and quantity of heroin demanded.

Table 3.1 Demand for heroin at different prices

Quantity sold (g)	Price per gram (€)
90	20
70	40
63	60
59	80

expected from the addictive nature of the drug. If we consider a fall in price from €40 to €20, this 50 per cent fall in price leads to a 29 per cent increase in demand. In this case we can see that demand is more sensitive to price changes at low levels of price, but is very insensitive at higher prices. This is important – we often find that the responsiveness changes at different levels of price.

Clearly this comparison of percentage increases in demand and decreases in price provides a measure of how much demand responds *proportionately* to price changes. This is the basis of the calculation of the price elasticity of demand. The normal way to calculate this is to divide the *proportionate change in the quantity* by the *proportionate change in price*. More formally

$$\text{Price elasticity of demand} = \frac{\text{Proportionate change in quantity}}{\text{Proportionate change in price}}$$

$$\varepsilon = \frac{\% \, \Delta Q}{\% \Delta P}$$

where ΔQ is the change in quantity and ΔP the change in price.

In the above example, when the price changes from €80 to €60

$$\varepsilon = \frac{\% \, \Delta Q}{\% \Delta P} = \frac{-7\%}{25\%} = -0.28$$

By the same calculation, when the price falls from €40 to €20, the elasticity of demand is calculated at −0.58. It is clear from the calculation that elasticity is just a number – it has no units. Note also that in these cases the price elasticity of demand is a negative number. In the above example percentages were used, but of course exactly the same answer comes if proportions are used instead.

The price changes in the above example are large (we are calculating elasticity over an *arc* in the demand curve). The calculations have been carried out on the basis of lowering the price. If instead the price were raised from €20 to €40, then the percentage rise is 100 per cent. In this case it therefore matters if we are calculating the elasticity on the basis of a rise or a fall in the price. There are two ways in which we can get round this. First, the percentage rise or fall can be calculated on the basis of the mid point of the change. If we did this we would get a slightly different estimate for elasticity:

$$\varepsilon = \frac{\%\,\Delta Q}{\%\Delta P} = \frac{-4}{61} \bigg/ \frac{20}{70} = -0.23$$

If we are dealing with large changes in price or quantity it is preferable to calculate elasticity in this way. However, the better solution is to consider smaller changes. We could consider changes in price of €1, and there would be much less difference between the calculation using the mid point and the calculation using the starting price to calculate the percentage.

We can easily rewrite the expression for elasticity in two parts – the ratio of the changes, and the ratio of the price and quantity:

$$\varepsilon = \frac{\%\,\Delta Q}{\%\Delta P} = \frac{\Delta Q}{\Delta P} \times \frac{(P2 + P1)/2}{(Q2 + Q1)/2} = \frac{\Delta Q}{\Delta P} \times \frac{(P2 + P1)}{(Q2 + Q1)}$$

where P1 and P2 are the initial and final prices, and Q1 and Q2 the initial and final quantities

The first expression approximates the slope of the demand curve. As we make the change in price smaller and smaller we can rewrite the expression for elasticity in terms of the slope of the demand curve and the ratio of price and quantity. Using normal calculus notation:

$$\varepsilon = \frac{\delta Q}{\delta P} \times \frac{P1}{Q1}$$

This expression is for the elasticity of demand for the good or service at the point P1, Q1 (and this is known as *point elasticity*). It is now clear that elasticity can vary along the demand curve, either because of changes in slope or as a result of the changing ratio of price and quantity. Even if the demand curve is a straight line, elasticity varies along the curve. This is important to note – a flatter demand curve is normally more elastic, and a steeper one less elastic, but elasticity is not the same as slope.

In the example above the elasticity of demand was calculated to be in the range from –0.28 to –0.58. In describing price elasticity of demand we normally describe the range 0 to –1.0 as inelastic – that is to say, demand responds to changing price by a smaller proportion than the change in price. When elasticity is –1 the proportionate changes in price and quantity are the same, a situation of 'unitary elasticity'. The range from –1 to –∞ is normally described as elastic. In this range the quantity demanded is highly responsive to changes in price.

3.3 Elasticity of demand and health promotion

Knowledge of price elasticity of demand can be useful for a range of policy decisions in health care and health promotion. An obvious example is the use of taxes to raise the price of cigarettes and discourage smoking. In this case several questions are relevant. First, if prices rise, to what extent will that achieve a reduction in smoking? Second, who will be dissuaded – will it be the young or the old, heavy smokers or occasional ones? What will happen to government revenue? Will the tax fall disproportionately on the poor?

Many studies have been carried out on the demand for cigarettes (Townsend 1987; Trigg and Bosanquet 1992; Stebbins 1991). Estimates vary, but the consensus is that the price elasticity of demand is around –0.5. Using this information we can make a number of judgements about the likely effects on smoking and tax revenue, and examine how the burden will fall on different population groups.

Let us assume that the current tax on cigarettes is an *ad valorum* tax (i.e. a percentage added to the selling price), and is set at 20 per cent of the selling price. What will be the effects of increasing it to 30 per cent of the selling price? Not all of this will be passed on to the consumer – the relative burden on consumer and seller depends on a range of factors. However, for simplicity let us assume that this tax is all passed on to the consumer. Since demand is inelastic, in order to produce any given percentage fall in consumption there must be a more than proportionate increase in price. Put another way, in order to produce a large reduction in smoking it is necessary to increase tax (and therefore price) substantially.

What happens to the tax revenue for the government? A simple example is set out in Table 3.2. The price increase is 8 per cent, and the fall in consumption 4 per cent. It can be seen from the table that spending has gone up despite the fall in consumption, and that tax revenue takes a larger share of the larger total spending. A simple rule of thumb is that, if demand is inelastic, a price increase caused solely by a higher tax *will always increase tax revenue*. It is sometimes suggested that governments are afraid to increase tax on tobacco for fear of losing revenue. They are almost certainly wrong. The example may understate the scope for government to increase revenue by increasing tobacco tax. In this example we have ignored the fact that normally some part of the tax is paid by the seller, so that government can increase its tax revenue from both buyers and sellers.

Studies of the elasticity of demand for tobacco have normally shown that demand is more elastic among young smokers, many of whom are recent starters. This means that the overall elasticity estimates are likely to imply that demand elasticity is even lower for older, more addicted, smokers. This would suggest that tax increases may be a good strategy for reducing smoking in younger people. However, although richer

Table 3.2 The effect of raising the tax on cigarettes

Variable	Before	After
Pre-tax price (€)	10	10
Tax (€)	2	3
Consumption (g)	100,000	96,080
Total spending (€)	1,200,000	1,249,040
Tax revenue (€)	200,000	288,240

people may display lower price elasticity of demand than poorer ones, the effect of the tax is likely to fall more heavily on poorer people. Poorer people spend a higher proportion of their income on tobacco, so the tax is *regressive*, that is, it takes a higher proportion of income from those who are poorer. Taxes are described as *progressive* if richer people pay a higher proportion of their income on the tax than do poorer people.

Another point to keep in mind is that price elasticity of demand normally varies at different prices. If we know that elasticity is −0.5 at the current price we can safely predict the effects of a relatively small tax increase. What is not so sensible is to make predictions of the effects of, say, a tax rise from 20 per cent to 80 per cent, which involves a move along the demand curve, possibly to a point where elasticity is much higher.

What can be said from this simple, although realistic, example? First, increasing tax on tobacco is likely to be an effective way of reducing smoking, but large tax increases will be needed to effect a moderate reduction. Second, the government is likely to enjoy an increase in the tax revenue as a result of the increase. Third, it is likely that this policy will be particularly effective in reducing smoking in new, relatively young smokers. Fourth, such a policy may have undesirable effects on the tax burden, since it falls disproportionately on poorer people. In some countries this is an even greater issue, since smoking rates are often higher in lower-income groups.

Low price elasticity of demand tends to indicate that the good is considered to be essential, and that there are few if any substitutes. Goods may be considered essential either because they are necessary to sustain life, or as a result of addiction. One indicator that a good is addictive is that it is not normally considered necessary to sustain life but nevertheless has a low price elasticity of demand.

High taxes on health-damaging goods may be effective in reducing consumption. We can do similar calculations to investigate the effectiveness of subsidies to encourage healthy behaviours. For example, it would be possible to exempt all fresh fruit and vegetables from tax to encourage more consumption. Sports facilities can be subsidised in order to encourage use. We cannot say whether these kinds of policy will be effective ways of encouraging healthier lifestyles without doing calculations of demand elasticity.

3.4 Cross-elasticity of demand

Price elasticity of demand is the most widely used measure. We can also measure other elasticities. For example, we can assess the *cross-elasticity of demand* between two goods – for example, how sensitive is the demand for needles to the price of syringes. Since they are complements, we would expect demand for needles to fall if the price of needles rises. If Pn is the price of needles, and Qs is the quantity of syringes, the cross-elasticity of demand can be expressed as

$$\varepsilon = \frac{\delta Qs}{\delta Pn} \times \frac{Pn_1}{Qs_1}$$

If goods are complements, as in this example, the value of the cross-elasticity of demand is negative. In the case of substitutes, the cross-elasticity of demand is positive.

For example, if the price of aspirin increases, we would expect a rise in demand for ibuprofen, since each can substitute for the other.

3.5 Income elasticity of demand

People on higher incomes can buy more of everything. Of course they do not do so – as income rises a person buys more of some goods, and less of some others. She may buy fewer bus rides and more taxi journeys, more housing and more expensive holidays. A good is said to be income-elastic if the *proportion* of income spent on the good rises with income. Income elasticity of demand can be positive (i.e. with rising income more is bought) or negative. Goods with positive income elasticity are described as *normal goods* and those with negative income elasticity as *inferior goods*.

Income elasticity is calculated from the relative change in demand for a good and the relative change in income. Formally, the formula for income elasticity of demand is

$$\varepsilon = \frac{\delta Q}{\delta Y} \times \frac{Y1}{Q1}$$

where Y is the original income, and Q1 the original quantity.

3.6 Elasticity and prices of health care

In the same way that we can use information on elasticity to inform policy on tax or subsidy to encourage healthier lifestyles, it can also be useful in developing policy on charging for health services. In most countries there are at least some charges for medical services, hospital care or drugs. If demand is inelastic, the effect of such charges will be to raise revenue with little effect on use. If it is more elastic, charges may deter people from using effective and useful care.

The evidence suggests that in general demand for health care is price-inelastic, so that there is only a small effect on demand from raising charges (Creese 1991; McPake 1993; Gertler *et al.* 1987). However, the evidence also shows that the picture is more complicated. Poorer people display more elastic demand than do richer ones, so a simple policy of charges will deter them more. This may justify exemption from fees for people on lower incomes.

A potential role for user fees is to deter people from making unnecessary use of services. If people face a charge for access they will think carefully about their need for care. However, again the evidence suggests that such a policy cannot be applied simply. The depressing fact is that the deterrent effect of charges seems to be the same for clearly useful and for probably pointless interventions (Newhouse, 1993).

Studies of the income elasticity of demand for health services suggest that the values are positive and greater than 1. In other words, demand for health care is income-elastic. As incomes rise the quantity of health care consumed rises *more than pro-portionately*. Goods with this characteristic are often described as luxuries, since richer people buy more. This does not imply that such goods are unnecessary, only that they are chosen in much larger amounts as income rises. This phenomenon may also explain the finding that countries that are richer not only spend more in total on health care but also spend a *higher proportion* of GNP on health services.

Overall the evidence from empirical studies of the impact of user fees suggests that they can be used to raise revenue without major deterrent effects on the use of services. However, it also shows that care has to be taken, since those on low incomes are most likely to be deterred, and are often those with the greatest needs. Understanding the patterns of elasticity of demand at different price levels and for different groups in the population allows policy to be developed to avoid some undesired effects.

Box 3.1 Estimates of elasticities of demand for health services in rural Tanzania

Sahn et al. (2003)[1] estimate the determinants of the demand for health services in rural Tanzania. Tanzania, like many low-income countries, has a highly pluralistic health care system (see chapter 20) where people choose from among different types of provider – in this analysis, public and private clinics, and public and private hospitals, or they choose to seek no care at all. The analysis of Sahn and his colleagues emphasises the importance of understanding this range of options so that own price elasticities (how the demand for a particular provider changes in response to its price) and overall price elasticities (how the demand for health care in total changes in response to a change of price of one provider) can be distinguished. The net effect of price changes on the decision to seek no care at all is the suggested outcome of greatest policy relevance.

This analysis also sought to consider the role of quality of care, as well as price and income. In analysis of health care markets, quality is often difficult to observe or measure, but at the same time an important influence on decision making.

The table shows the probability of rural Tanzanians choosing particular care options, and the own and cross price elasticities of demand between each of the options.

Own and cross price elasticities

	Probability of choice	Public hospital	Private hospital	Public clinic	Private clinic
No care	0.418	0.0757	0.0563	0.0536	0.0481
Public hospital	0.057	−1.8590	0.3345	0.0795	0.0713
Private hospital	0.05	0.4205	−1.6390	0.0795	0.0713
Public clinic	0.333	0.1116	0.0837	−0.3429	0.5826
Private clinic	0.142	0.1116	0.0837	0.6388	−1.6944
All	1	−0.0530	−0.0420	−0.0390	−0.0350

As expected, own price elasticities (on the diagonal) are negative, and cross-price elasticities are positive, indicating that the care options are substitutes. Own price elasticities are elastic for the three more expensive options (hospital care of both types and private clinic). This is probably because for each, there is a cheaper substitute available, whereas the user of a public clinic cannot respond by switching to a cheaper option when the public clinic price increases. Overall, the data imply a high degree of substitutability between options, so that when the price of one option increases, the main effect is on where people seek care, not on whether they do so. The cross elasticity for the decision to seek no care of a change in the price of any provider is never more than 0.1, implying that were the price of that provider to double, the number of people choosing to seek no care, never increases by more than 10%.

Nevertheless, it is important to distinguish between *inelastic* and *unimportant in policy terms* – a 10% reduction in care seeking may be catastrophic for some. Sahn and colleagues confirm that price elasticities are larger in lower income quartiles, reaching levels of -3. for the more expensive options in the lowest income quintile (the 25% of households with the lowest incomes).

Mean own price
elasticities by income
quartile

	Quartile 1	2	3	4 (highest)
Public hospital	−3.4576	−1.2552	−0.5320	−0.1344
Private hospital	−3.0454	−1.1060	−0.4745	−0.1205
Public clinic	−06186	−0.2445	−0.1114	−0.0310
Private clinic	−3.1610	−1.1412	−0.4740	−0.1165

They also confirm the importance of quality which had been measured only at the nearest public clinic. Interestingly, while the response of demand to quality in terms of drugs (availability) and environment (the availability of a toilet, water, and a covered waiting area) was positive only for the public clinic itself, the response of demand to quality of health staff was positive for all providers. This is probably because health staff work in more than one of the available provider types.

Sahn, D.E., Younger, S.D. and Genicot, G. (2003) The demand for health care services in rural Tanzania, Oxford Bulletin of Economics and Statistics, 65, 2, 241–59

4   Production, health and health care: efficient use of inputs

4.1 Introduction

Health services are very diverse. Some parts use technically skilled staff, sophisticated equipment and expensive consumables, while others require caring and human skills. Some are highly automated, and others are more like craft industries. Some require teamwork, while in others professionals work alone. They are provided in many different settings. This chapter considers the general approach of economics to production, and explores how this can help in understanding production of health and health care.

4.2 Efficiency in production

It is widely agreed that, given the scarcity of health care resources, it is important that services be produced efficiently. It is not always clear what we mean by efficient. Economists use a number of concepts of efficiency. At the most basic level we wish to ensure that the existing inputs are not capable of producing more services. For example, if ten staff are needed to produce a service and twelve are employed that is inefficient. But even if production is efficient in this narrow technical sense, it may still be possible to lower costs by changing to a different technology, or by paying less for the inputs. When economists think about production they focus on the fact that we almost always have choices of the technology used and the mix of inputs. The third sense of efficiency is getting the best value from the resources. In this chapter the first two meanings are relevant.

4.3 Factors of production and efficient use of resources

Production is the process of 'changing the form or arrangement of matter to adapt it better for the satisfaction of wants' (Marshall 1920). Marshall goes on to suggest that it is when we 'adjust matter to make it more useful'. By putting together materials, equipment and skills we provide a service or produce a useful product. Many different combinations are usually possible, and the choice of how to produce services should depend on many factors. The explosive growth of the Internet has led to many changes in the ways services are delivered – music no longer needs to be put on discs, and insurance can be bought electronically. News can be delivered on air, on paper or on line. Two important points emerge – first it is almost always possible to provide services in different ways, and the options open to us are constantly changing.

Production normally requires a range of inputs. (Various terms are used in economics to describe inputs – including factors of production and inputs. In this chapter the terms are used interchangeably.) There is a need for some or all of the following: buildings, equipment, vehicles, skilled staff, semi-skilled staff, energy and consumables. Once again, since paper is two-dimensional, we will simplify the analysis to take account of only two inputs – equipment and staff. Although this may seem to be too much of a simplification, it allows the principles to be applied. The analysis has some similarities to the analysis of indifference curves in Chapter 2.

Economists always think in terms of inputs to production being, to a greater or lesser extent, substitutes. We can choose to use more equipment (and relatively *capital-intensive* production) or more staff and choose a more *labour-intensive* process. We can choose to use more experienced staff, or use staff with less training but who are given more supervision or provide services following strict protocols. Tradition often dictates that certain professions do certain jobs, but if we go back to first principles it is not always obvious why this is the case.

The example in Figure 4.1 considers the options for providing immunisation services to a dispersed rural community. There are two options for transport – walking or cycling. In this example we define one unit of capital as one bicycle that is in working order for one week. Staff is measured as one person working for one week. In Figure 4.1 combinations of units of labour and units of capital are shown that can be used to immunise 1,000 children.

The example suggests that there is a trade-off between bicycles and staff, but that they are not perfect substitutes. (Research suggests that bicycles seldom give injections to patients!) In this example, when there are eight bicycles available there is no further advantage in having more. Intuitively this feels right. There comes a point when there is all the necessary transport, and what is needed is people to do the work. Equally, although we could provide the service with no bicycles, in order to reach the more remote areas we would need to send people on very long walks. Under these circumstances even one bicycle would make a great difference. Indeed, adding a second bicycle reduces the need for staff from ten to six.

This phenomenon is well known in economics. If we add more combinations of bicycles and staff we can show all the possible ways of providing the service as a curve, known as an *isoquant*, as shown in Figure 4.2.

The curve shows all the combination of staff and bicycles that allow the service to produce 1,000 immunised children. It is important to be clear what the isoquant means. Anywhere above (i.e. north-east of) the curve is feasible. Nowhere below the curve is

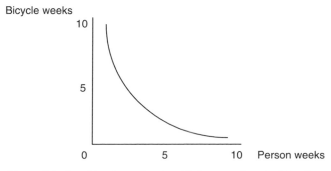

Figure 4.1 Combination of units of labour and capital for the immunisation of 1,000 children.

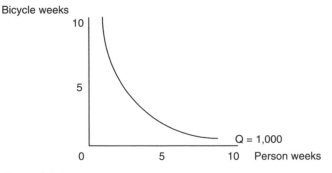

Figure 4.2 Isoquant.

feasible. In essence the curve represents the boundary of the feasible set of combinations of inputs that can produce an output of 1,000. Put another way, the curve represents the *technically efficient* combinations of staff time and bicycles that can produce 1,000.

The slope of isoquants is determined by the extent to which the inputs are substitutes for each other. As suggested above, this is likely to vary. The slope of the isoquant is a measure of the *marginal rate of technical substitution* between inputs. We could draw similar curves for 2,000, 3,000 and 4,000 children immunised. This is done in Figure 4.3.

These isoquants have all been drawn convex to the origin, suggesting that at all levels of output the two inputs become less substitutable as we move to higher proportions of one input. Knowledge of the shapes and positions of isoquants (the isoquant map) allows us to describe certain features of the service. For example, in some cases production uses less inputs relative to outputs at higher levels of output. This is known as *increasing returns to scale*. When there are increasing returns to scale the isoquants become closer together as output increases, as shown in Figure 4.4. If there are decreasing returns to scale, then the isoquants are more widely spaced as output increases.

We can show different production methods, or uses of different technologies, as different rays from the origin. Figure 4.5 shows relatively capital-intensive and relatively labour-intensive production.

4.4 Mix of inputs and diminishing marginal returns

In Figure 4.1 it was shown that there was no further advantage in more bicycles once eight were available. The argument was simply that, without people to ride them, no

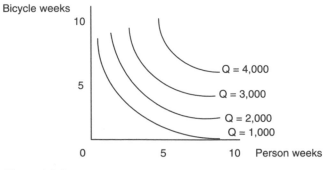

Figure 4.3 Isoquant map.

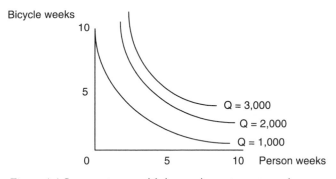

Figure 4.4 Isoquant map with increasing returns to scale.

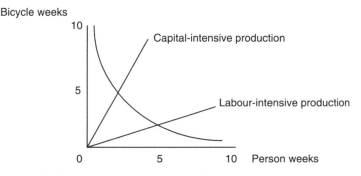

Figure 4.5 Rays of capital-intensive and labour-intensive production.

additional benefit come from more machines. In general we find that if we hold one factor of production constant, then increasing the other will increase output, *but at a decreasing rate*. One factor of production is considered to be *fixed* in the *short run* – see Chapter 5. This is illustrated in Figure 4.6a and 4.6b. In this example we hold the number of bicycles constant and observe the effects on output of increasing the number of staff. Similarly we explore the effects on output of changing the number of bicycles with the number of staff held constant. Holding the number of bicycles constant at three, four staff produce 1,000, six staff produce 2,000, but to produce 3,000 requires an additional four staff. For this given number of bicycles, the extra output (the *marginal product*) of each member of staff falls as the number of staff increases. This is not surprising, since there are fewer bicycles to go round, and more staff spend more time walking. In this case we hold staff constant at three. Using four bicycles it is possible to provide 1,000, and a further two bicycles allows this to increase to 2,000. A further three bicycles are needed to achieve 3,000. In this case we can calculate the marginal product of bicycles as we increase their number while holding person weeks constant.

This pattern is well known in economics, and is known as the principle (or law) of eventually *diminishing marginal returns*. Holding one factor of production constant, additional units of the other increase output, but at an eventually diminishing rate.

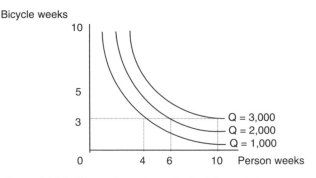

Figure 4.6(a) Decreasing returns to the labour factor.

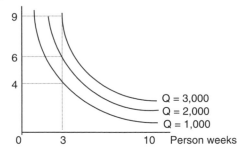

Figure 4.6(b) Decreasing returns to the capital factor.

4.5 Production, efficiency and health care

The basic economic theory of production can be useful in giving a focus to some issues in the delivery of health care. First, it emphasises that there are many ways to combine inputs to produce outputs. There is a tendency in health services for a belief to grow up that there is a 'best' or 'proper' way to do things. This can lead to inefficient choices about which technology to use.

Second, isoquants define the (efficient) boundary of the set of feasible ways in which health services can be produced. Clearly, most services, most of the time, are not completely efficient. The example chosen to illustrate production is very simple in comparison with most services. The service can be quite easily defined, and its production can be carefully planned and managed. In reality it is often not so simple. If we are running an emergency service, the product is not only treatment for those who have needs, but is also the readiness to provide care. This means that often the staff and facilities are ready for action but are not actually busy. This can be efficient, but defining efficiency in this type of circumstance is not easy.

It can also be difficult to be sure that apparently greater efficiency is not just lower quality of care. Once again, the problem is often of definition of what is the output. In the case of vaccination the service can be defined, and quality may not be a great issue. However, in long-term hospital or nursing care, differences in inputs may reflect (hidden) differences in output. There is no easy way to know if this is the case. Part of the problem is the tendency in health care for the output to be described in terms of processes or intermediate outputs. Where possible this should be avoided. Taking the immunisation example, output can be described anywhere on the spectrum from children immunised, cases of disease prevented, death or disability prevented, life years gained or welfare. If we define it in terms of achievement (for example, as life years gained) then poor quality of service will reduce this. However, if the output is described in terms of number of children injected with the vaccine, then there is more risk that what is in reality poor quality will appear to be efficient production.

Production theory raises a number of important issues in health care. For example, are there increasing returns to scale? When we think about health care production it is likely that there are few. Large hospitals are not really large, at least in the sense that they are composed of many (largely separate) departments. West (1997) suggests that hospitals are really sheds with workshops inside. This is explored further in Chapter 5.

4.6 Health care providers as multi-product firms

It has been suggested that hospitals and other health care providers produce a wide range of services. The analysis above shows how there is a degree of flexibility in the use of inputs, with different combinations of staff and equipment being feasible. Similarly, there is a degree of flexibility in what the hospital can produce. Some hospital inputs are very specific to particular services, but to a large extent the skills of health care professionals are generic.

If we imagine a hospital that produces two kinds of service (say stroke rehabilitation and geriatric assessment), there is scope within any given staff, buildings and equipment mix to switch between the two. However, since there are some specific skills and items of equipment, it is unlikely to be possible simply to substitute one stroke case for one assessment case. Figure 4.7 illustrates the likely pattern of output.

The slope of the curve in Figure 4.7 is the *marginal rate of transformation* between the two services – that is, the rate at which it is possible to switch from producing one to producing the other within any given level of resources available. This has been drawn in the diagram as being concave to the origin. The reason for this is that there is a mixture between generic and more specialised skills needed. If we move to one end of the curve, that is, to heavy concentration on one or other service, then it becomes increasingly difficult to switch production to even more of that service.

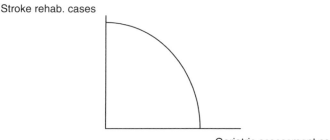

Figure 4.7 Transformation of production between two services.

4.7 Professions, skills and efficiency of production of health services

The emphasis of this chapter has been very much that there is scope for variation in the mix of factors of production, and that there is scope for switching between outputs. However, constraints on doing this often come from the very specific bundles of skills held by health care professionals. It is interesting to consider the extent to which this is a logical system or simply the accident of history. Changes in the technology of health care, and in the ways in which existing technologies are applied, tend to lead to a need to reconsider the packages of skills held by each profession or sub-profession. For example, as mental health services shift from institutions to the community there is a need for the professionals to combine assessment, treatment and practical skills if they are to provide the required support. Nurses have to deal with their patients' housing, financial and social problems as well as supporting the provision of medication. Similarly, it can often be efficient for nurses to be able to take simple x-rays, or for occupational therapists to carry out some (traditionally) nursing tasks. In many countries the roles of nurses are being widened, with some traditionally medical tasks being added. Some changes are driven by the desire of professions to enhance their position and status, but to some extent it is recognition that this offers more flexibility in the use of resources.

5   Cost of delivering health services

5.1 Production and cost

The theory of production in Chapter 4 suggests that inputs can be used in various proportions to produce health care services. Isoquants define the technically efficient combinations and form the boundary of feasible production possibilities. However, it is not enough to know that production is technically efficient – we want to minimise the cost of production of services. What is required is a way to identify the technically efficient combination of factors of production that minimises cost. We do this by adding a set of *isocost lines* to the analysis. (Points on the isocost line are points of equal cost.)

When we refer to minimising cost, this is defined as minimising the cost of any given quality and volume of services. It is always possible to cut costs by doing less or doing it worse. This may or may not be a good thing. However, reducing the cost of any given quality and quantity of services always allows more to be achieved with the given resources.

Figure 5.1 is based on the analysis of isoquants in Chapter 4. If we know the wage rate for staff and the cost per week to rent a bicycle, we can work out how much of each, or combinations of each, can be bought for any given budget. On each axis, the isocost line marks the maximum number of inputs that can be purchased from the budget if none of the other inputs is purchased. The slope of a budget line is the ratio of the factor prices (in this case the ratio of the prices of person weeks and cycle weeks). If the wage is £500 per week and bicycle rental price £250 per week, we can draw isocost lines (A, B, C in Figure 5.1, where A = £2,000, B = £2,500 and C = £3,000). If we wish

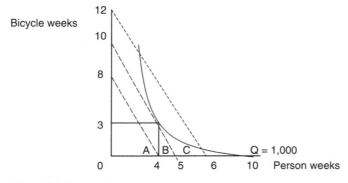

Figure 5.1 Isoquant.

to produce 1,000 vaccinations, it is not feasible on line A – that is to say, a budget of £2,000 is inadequate to produce 1,000 vaccinations even if it is used efficiently. Isocost line B is just feasible, and line C unnecessarily generous. In line B the budget is £2,500. The intersections with the axes are easy to calculate. If the entire budget were used on wages it would buy five weeks. If all were used on bicycle rental it would buy ten weeks.

In this example the lowest cost way of producing 1,000 vaccinations is to use three bicycles and four staff. At this point, the 'economically efficient' combination is determined (recall that all points on the isoquants are technically efficient – see Chapter 4, section 4.3). Presumably some people live within easy walking distance, so there is no great advantage in providing a bicycle for each member of staff. This is an important point – depending on the prices of bicycle rentals and staff, we can determine the lowest-cost way of providing the service. If the price of bicycles were to fall, then we would be likely to choose to provide each member of staff with transport. Equally, if wages fell substantially it might be cheaper to employ more people, and for them to walk to the nearer towns.

In the same way as the consumer chooses her consumption on the basis of preferences and relative prices, the lowest-cost way of providing services can be determined from the map of isoquants (representing different outputs) and relative prices of inputs.

We do not observe isoquants in everyday life, but a version of this approach is used in the statistical analysis of production in health care. In estimating production and cost functions we are effectively going through this process. The important points are that there are almost always choices in how we produce health care, and the lowest-cost method depends on selecting the cheapest of the efficient options.

5.2 Changes in technology

Isoquants represent efficient combinations of inputs to produce a given level of output. Underlying the isoquant is a given technology. It may be that as we increase output different technologies become available, so that the efficient combinations can change with volume of service. In the health sector this is particularly apparent in pathology, where automated systems may be efficient only if large volumes of samples are tested. Many technologies are 'lumpy', that is to say, machines come only in certain sizes, so that they may be efficient in use only if at least a minimum volume of service is provided. The isoquant map tells us about the behaviour of the technology in any particular case. Changing slopes mean that the relative productivity of different factors changes, and increasing or decreasing returns to scale are reflected in changes in the gaps between isoquants. However, in choosing the lowest-cost combination of inputs to use in production we need to remain aware also of any changes in the relative price of inputs.

There is constant evolution and development of health care technologies. This means that the efficient use of resources and the minimum costs of services are also likely to be changing constantly. Understanding the theory of production and costs can help remind us that budgets for particular services should not normally be left unchanged. It also helps focus on the fact that the potential for costs to fall with technical change varies between services, and across the board budget cuts fail to take this into account.

5.3 Changes in relative factor prices

To some extent the prices of inputs depend on workings of the market. The prices of equipment, drugs, buildings and consumables are determined largely by market forces. Demand for and supply of staff with particular skills may also play a major role in determining wages. However, there are often other factors that have important influences on the determination of prices of inputs. The operation of trade unions (including 'professional' associations) may raise wages. Professional organisations can be effective in restricting the supply of skilled staff, and thus can raise wages. Many countries have minimum wage laws that will affect the price of unskilled staff. However, in the long run supply and demand conditions are likely to be important determinants of these prices. For more detail of markets and how they can fail see Chapters 6–8.

In a growing economy there tends to be a rise in the wages of all workers. Cost of equipment normally falls over time (although this can be masked by increased sophistication and higher specification). Indeed, technical change is an important source of lower costs, and it should be remembered that in itself technical change *cannot increase the cost of producing a given output*. There is widespread confusion because new technology can be associated with higher health care expenditure through improving quality and by making available new opportunities to treat disease, but cannot increase the cost of a given service.

The result of technical change is lower costs of equipment for any given unit of output. This process occurs throughout the economy, leading to gradual increases in wages for all workers. This means that the relative prices of labour and other inputs change, with labour becoming relatively more expensive than other inputs. For this reason it is important to remember that the lowest-cost way of providing services is likely to change even when there is no change in the underlying technology. Once again, understanding that it is normally possible to make some substitution between equipment and labour means that what is efficient production is likely to change over time.

As technology has developed, some goods and services have become much easier and cheaper to make. In agriculture the development of systems that allowed oxen to be used greatly increased the productivity of farm workers, and the development of horse-drawn and mechanical technologies further increased it. In industry mechanisation, division of labour and new materials have allowed goods to be produced at much lower cost. However, some services are produced by 'handicraft' (Baumol 1995) industries, and these have more limited scope for technological progress and falling costs.

To some extent health care can be seen as such an industry. Although many elements of services have been automated, and new drugs and appliances can lower costs, a large part of most health service costs comes from staff who look after patients, and it is more difficult to get technical progress in that kind of work. The prices of handicraft goods generally rise over time relative those of other goods. Whereas the workers in industries with rapid technical change may obtain higher wages from sharing in the gains from higher productivity, in health care higher wages are likely to lead to higher costs of care. The increase in the relative cost of health care may therefore be seen as an inevitable feature of an industry that is more handicraft than mass-production in its technology.

5.4 What do we mean by cost?

It is never easy to answer this question. The classic answer is that economists use 'cost' to mean opportunity cost – that is, the value of the output of the resources in their best alternative use. That much is simple. But what determines the price we have to pay for inputs, and what is the value of the best alternative use of the resources? Indeed, what is the best alternative use of the resources? Health care systems are normally subject to many rules and regulations – often these are important sources of safety and protection to the users. But restrictions can also distort prices. In many cases the price of inputs (wages and prices, capital and consumable inputs) include an element of *economic rent* – that is, they are paid more than is necessary to make them available. For example, I may be willing to work for €70 per day but will happily accept €120 if it is offered. In that case the cost is €70, but in addition I accept economic rent of €50 per day. In principle such rent payments are not part of cost, but it is very difficult to separate the two.

More complicated issues arise with patented devices and drugs. Development costs are recovered through charging prices that are above the direct cost of producing the goods and maintaining the equipment. Without compensation for the investment in research and development in new product it is unlikely that many new drugs would be developed, and in many ways patent protection is an efficient way of providing incentives for innovation. But it does mean that the price charged is above cost.

The practical question of how we assess what is the opportunity cost is explored further when we discuss economic evaluation in Chapters 11 and 13. In this chapter the emphasis is on the normal determinants and patterns of financial cost.

5.5 Estimating cost functions in health care

The analysis of isoquants and isocost lines provides a framework for analysing the likely relationships between inputs to health care and the costs. Empirical investigation of the patterns of costs can be useful in understanding what is the lowest-cost way of providing services in different circumstances. An obvious question is whether there are *economies of scale*, i.e. does the unit cost of production of services fall with scale of production? If there are significant economies of scale in hospitals, then there are advantages in having fewer, larger hospitals. However, it is important to be clear why this might be the case. It is important to distinguish between the effects on unit costs of doing more of a given service (e.g. caesarean sections or cataract operations) and the effects on costs of being a larger hospital overall.

There is some evidence that the costs of relatively high-technology procedures fall with volume (e.g. Cronin *et al.* 1998), but much less that large-scale economies exist at the whole hospital level. In some cases it has been found that there are *economies of scope* – that is, by combining certain different services in the same organisation there will be savings. These are likely to exist if some equipment or staff can usefully be shared between the different services. The history of the development of health care infrastructure over the last fifty years shows that there has been a widespread belief in economies of scale, with a common pattern being the closure of small hospitals and redevelopment of services in fewer larger settings. Although this trend may be now reversing, it is still common to hear planners and clinicians referring to such changes as *rationalisation*. In the past most developments of health care infrastructure have been carried out without good evidence about the relationships of what is produced, how it is produced and at what cost it can be produced. Estimating cost functions for health care provision can allow better understanding.

Cost functions can be estimated by comparing data from different providers of care to explore the main determinants of cost. It is important in such studies to take account of case mix, and this can be very difficult. It is a constant problem that apparently similar cases in health care can have very different costs (Gray *et al.* 1997). There is a growing literature on cost functions in health care provision, and it is becoming clear that economies of scale are quite limited, but can be important in certain types of service. Case mix is normally very important. The evidence supports Baumol's assertion that health care has many of the characteristics of a handicraft industry.

The purpose of estimating cost functions is to discover more about the relationship between cost and the different ways in which services can be delivered. Figure 5.2 shows a possible pattern of total cost for a hospital or a service. It is worth noting that, since there are some fixed costs, at zero output there is a positive cost. This applies in the 'short run' only, since the 'long run' is defined as the period in which all factors of production can be varied – in other words there are no fixed costs. The cost relationships discussed below are those expected to apply in the 'short run'.

In this case total cost rises at a decreasing rate at lower output, and at an increasing rate at higher output. This suggests that at lower levels of output there are economies of scale, but these disappear and are reversed at higher output. For some purposes we are interested in the total cost of provision – for instance, if we are setting a budget for the service. However, for most purposes we are interested in two other measures – the cost of each unit of service (the *average cost*) and the cost of one more or less (the *marginal cost*). From the total cost curve here we can calculate the average cost. We can see that at lower output the average cost is falling, since with each extra unit of service all units become cheaper. However, as output rises this is reversed. This is shown on Figure 5.3.

From this pattern we can derive the average cost – it will be U-shaped in this case. We can also calculate the marginal cost. The marginal cost is the *additional cost of one more unit of service*. This can be described as the change in total cost divided by the change in output – and of course this just describes the *slope* of the total cost curve. This slope is positive all the way along the total cost curve, but the slope is initially decreasing, and

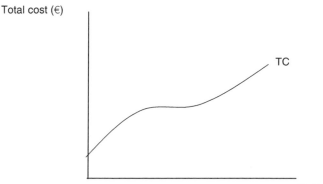

Figure 5.2 Total cost.

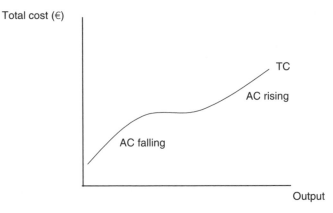

Figure 5.3 Patterns of average cost.

later increasing. Similarly the marginal cost curve therefore starts by falling, and then increases. The average and marginal cost curves are shown in Figure 5.4.

The observant reader will notice that the MC curve crosses the AC curve at its lowest point. This is not an accident. If the average cost is falling, it follows that the cost of one more unit of service (the MC) must be less than the average. If the average is rising, the cost of one more must be above the average. Thus the MC curve always intersects the AC curve at its lowest point. In this short-run analysis, the shapes of the cost curves reflect the 'returns to a factor' rather than the 'returns to scale', since, as discussed above, they reflect how costs change when one factor of production (or input) is varied while the other is considered fixed.

The normal interpretation of the cost of a treatment or operation is the average cost. For example, we might say that it costs €20 to immunise a child against the major infectious diseases, or say that percutaneous transluminal coronary angioplasty costs €2,000. As will be shown in Chapter 11, we need to be careful. Sometimes the relevant measure of cost is the marginal cost, since the policy question may be 'Should we do more?' Many serious planning errors have followed from confusing average and marginal cost.

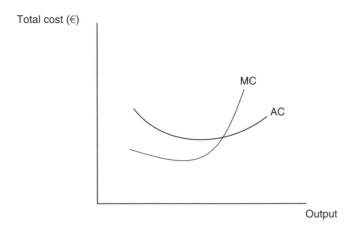

Figure 5.4 Average cost and marginal cost.

6 Basic market models

6.1 Demand, supply and equilibrium

Previous chapters have explained the logic behind demand and supply curves and have argued that, while health is often different from bananas or telephone calls, most of the differences are not unique to health. We argued that there were good reasons, both theoretical and from the observation of behaviour, to expect downward-sloping demand curves and upward-sloping supply curves in health markets. For example, where prices for health services are charged or are implicit (for example in distance and waiting times), we expect less health services to be demanded the higher they are. We also normally expect suppliers of health services – such as suppliers of pharmaceuticals or of skills and labour – to supply more as the price increases, *ceteris paribus* (although we will note important exceptions to that in the next three chapters).

Where we have downward-sloping demand curves and upward-sloping supply curves, the determination of price, output and the allocation of production and consumption should, in principle, be straightforward. Figure 6.1 illustrates the expected process. Demand and supply curves intersect at the equilibrium price (P*) and output (Q*) levels. The pressures exerted by demand and supply are expected to lead price to move towards P*Q*. Consider what would happen at any price away from this point. At P1, above P*, demand is QD1, less than supply QS1, suppliers are left with surplus goods to get rid of, and will have to lower the price to do so. At P2, below P*, demand is QD2,

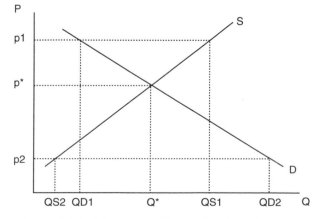

Figure 6.1 The interaction of demand and supply.

higher than supply at QS2. The result is a shortage of goods, and suppliers can increase prices and still sell what they want. Price can be stable only at the equilibrium point. At equilibrium, consumption is allocated to those willing to pay this price or more (those whose demands are illustrated to the left of the demand curve) and production to those willing to supply at this price or less (whose willingness is illustrated to the left of the supply curve).

This is a very simple model and, as much of the rest of the book will explore, does not capture the complexities of many real markets including health. However, it is an idea with enormous power to generate initial expectations about behaviour in markets which often turn out to be realised, even in health markets. For example, it suggests that if demands for dental services are increasing, *ceteris paribus*, prices of dental services are likely to increase, or that if the number of medical graduates rises faster than demand for medical services, new graduates are likely to find themselves accepting jobs with a lower remuneration package than before. These types of predictions often hold.

6.2 The perfect market model

An extreme set of simplifying assumptions lies behind the concept of the perfect market. It is best to think of a perfect market as you would think of a perfect square when studying geometry. It is not found in nature but it is an enormously useful tool to use to understand shapes which are. If you want to calculate the area of a complex shape it is useful to understand the principles behind calculating the area of a square. Similarly, if you wish to understand the operation of complex health markets, it is best to understand the operation of a perfect market which besides being perfect in its efficiency implications (as we shall see) is also perfect in its simplicity, like a square. It is safe to say that no perfect market exists, although we may be able to point to some markets which come quite close.

First, we need to step back and reflect further on what is happening behind the demand and supply curves. The indifference curve analysis of Chapter 2 emphasised that price determines the rate at which an individual can trade off the good in question with other goods he also values. At the point at which the budget constraint is tangential to the indifference curve, the individual's marginal rate of substitution of one good for another (the slope of the indifference curve) is equal to the price ratio (the slope of the budget constraint). Price then captures the value of the last unit of the good purchased (the marginal value) to the individual, in terms of whatever alternative good is considered. (When all choices have been made, the value of the last cent spent must be equal for each good purchased – assuming that an independent decision can be made over each cent.) Money therefore represents all other goods the individual values and knowledge of how demand changes as price changes tells us about how much individuals making up a market value each individual good at the margin.

If this seems too involved, a simpler way of arriving at the same conclusion uses the individual's demand curve. Whatever the price is, the utility-maximising individual will purchase those units of the good for which his utility values are higher than the price and will stop purchasing at the point where his values fall below the price. *At the margin*, he equates his value with the price. The individual's demand curve therefore measures his value of each additional unit of the good – or his marginal value. At the market level, all individuals are making the same assessment. It follows that demand curves are powerful tools for telling us about how individuals value the goods they purchase, and indicate the aggregate marginal value or marginal utility of goods in that market (see Box 6.1).

Box 6.1 Consumer surplus

The idea that demand curves 'reveal preferences' and are indicators of marginal values to consumers can be extended to produce the concept of 'consumer surplus'. Consumer surplus is defined as the value to a consumer of trading in the market at the given price. It is measured by the area under the demand curve and above the price line, since this sums the additional value to the consumer of each unit purchased (above the price, or marginal cost to the consumer of purchasing it).

The diagram represents Mrs Brown's purchasing decision and value for aspirin. The demand curve reveals the marginal value to her of each additional packet of aspirin consumed per year.

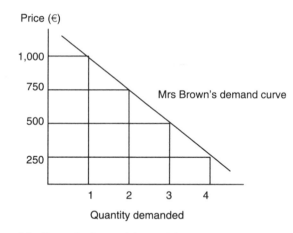

Mrs Brown's demand for aspirin.

Suppose the price is €500. Mrs Brown will purchase the first packet of aspirin (for which she would have paid up to €1,000; the second packet of aspirin (for which she would have paid up to €750) and the third packet (for which the €500 represents the most she would pay). However, she pays the going price – €500 – for all three packets. By interpreting the maximum she would have paid as her marginal valuation, we can identify a surplus value in the first packet of €1,000 – €500 = €500; and in the second packet of €750 – €500 = €250; and of zero for the third packet which cost exactly the most she was willing to pay. The total consumer surplus is equal to €500 + €250 + €0 = €750.

The example uses large units in relation to the total amount bought, and the area of consumer surplus is 'stepped' rather than smooth, and does not equal the area under the demand curve. Under these circumstances the demand curve is really stepped too – if the price fell to €375 Mrs Brown could not purchase a further half-packet of aspirin. Unless items can be bought in infinitesimally small quantities (e.g. dry goods by weight, liquids by volume), a smoothly drawn demand curve is really a stepped one. As the quantities considered get larger (either because we consider smaller units like individual aspirin for Mrs Brown, or because we consider markets involving large numbers of people) it becomes more accurate to draw a smooth demand curve, and more accurate to consider the area of consumer surplus as a triangle, underneath the demand curve and above the price line.

Consumer surplus has been used in cost–benefit analysis as a measure of the value of an intervention, and also underlies the use of 'willingness to pay' as a source of consumers' values.

On the supply side, we have seen that typical short-run cost functions are expected to take 'U-shaped' forms, reflecting diminishing marginal returns (see Chapter 4, section 4.4, and Chapter 5, section 5.5). Where the firm is a price taker (is not powerful enough to control the price but must accept the price given by the market), the firm's supply curve can be derived from the marginal cost curve. Total revenue is equal to the price multiplied by the quantity sold. In other words, it is the firm's income before its costs have been taken into account. Under price-taking circumstances, the given price indicates both the average revenue and the marginal revenue which is generated by selling one more unit of output. While the revenue to be gained from producing and selling one more unit of output is greater than the cost of producing that unit, a profit-maximising firm will produce it. If the marginal revenue is less than the marginal cost, a profit-maximising firm will not produce another unit. Such firms will choose to set production levels at the point at which marginal revenue equals marginal cost. In other words, the supply curve can be traced along the part of the marginal cost curve which is upward-sloping and lies above the average cost curve.

The following are the assumptions of the perfect competition model:

1   U-shaped, or upward-sloping, marginal cost curves in the short run (and also in the long run, see below);
2   profit-maximising firms;
3   no barriers to entry or exit from the market;
4   perfect mobility of factors of production;
5   the product being sold must be homogeneous (consumers cannot differentiate between the products of different suppliers);
6   large numbers of buyers and sellers;
7   perfect knowledge of market conditions on the parts of buyers and sellers;
8   no government intervention.

The firm operating in this environment has perfect knowledge and therefore knows its cost curves, and the prevailing price on the market. As explained above, it will choose to produce where price equals marginal cost. Consumers have perfect knowledge, are purchasing a homogeneous product (identical in every respect, including ease of access to each supplier) and will purchase from any supplier, up to the point where they equate price and marginal utility. There is no opportunity for an individual supplier to sell goods at higher than the prevailing price – consumers would all desert and go to other suppliers. There is no possibility of an advantage by undercutting the price because the firm can sell whatever volume it wants at the prevailing price. These assumptions produce price-taking behaviour. The market can reach equilibrium only through the entry and exit of buyers and sellers to and from the market in response to price movements (which are generated by the market, independently of individual buyers and sellers).

Figure 6.2 describes the process of reaching equilibrium from the perspective of any efficient (in the technical and economic senses – see Chapters 4 and 5) firm in this market. Firms expect to make normal profits which can be considered as the minimum return to capital necessary to induce the firm's entrepreneur to remain in the market. This normal profit is usually considered to be part of the cost of capital, included in the cost curves. Profits above normal profits are then made on each unit of production for which price (equal to marginal revenue) exceeds marginal cost. For example, at p1 the firm will choose to produce at q1, above-normal profit is made on each unit of production between q* and q1. Above-normal profit can be measured by distance ab per unit, which is the difference between price (also equal to average revenue) and average cost.

The availability of this abnormal profit attracts new firms to the market and shifts the market supply curve from S to S′ (Figure 6.3). This produces downward pressure on price, implying a new equilibrium at p2. The efficient firm will choose to produce at q2 (Figure 6.2) but now makes a loss. These losses drive firms out of the market, shifting the market supply curve back towards the left again. Equilibrium is implied at S″ and p* (Figure 6.3), where p* is equal to the minimum point on the efficient firm's average cost curve (Figure 6.2). At this point, all inefficient firms are driven out of business and only efficient ones can remain, earning only normal profit.

In this type of market, a number of conditions for efficiency have been met:

1   *Allocative efficiency.* Productive activity has been allocated to those products which consumers value in excess of their cost (marginal cost has been equated with marginal utility).
2   *Technical efficiency.* Technically inefficient firms have cost curves above those of the efficient firm in the example and have been driven out of business. All those remaining must be operating on isoquants (not above).
3   *Economic efficiency.* Economically inefficient firms have cost curves above those of

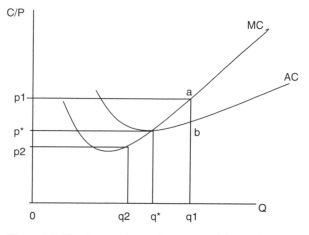

Figure 6.2 The firm under perfect competition.

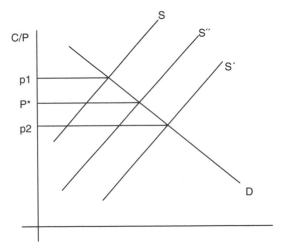

Figure 6.3 The industry under perfect competition.

the efficient firm in the example and have been driven out of business. All those remaining must be equating the marginal rate of substitution of inputs in the production process with the price ratios of those inputs.

4   *Scale efficiency.* Production has been divided between firms in such a way that each produces that proportion of total output consistent with operation at the minimum point of a short-run average cost curve.

If these conditions are met across the whole economy in a general equilibrium analysis, still further claims for efficiency can be made. Box 6.2 provides some further discussion of this.

Box 6.2 Perfect competition and general equilibrium analysis

The perfect competition model was based on a *partial equilibrium analysis*. It considered only one market in the economy, and the efficiency conditions listed at the end of section 6.2 would apply to that market only. If all markets in the economy are assumed to work on the same basis we can move from a partial to a *general equilibrium analysis*.

A general equilibrium analysis enables the analyst to focus on the linkages between markets. For example, each output uses inputs in its production, and these inputs are themselves traded in markets which for the purpose of this analysis are assumed also to be perfect. Review the efficiency conditions which conclude section 6.2. If they can be assumed true of input markets as well as of the market for the final product, we can conclude that inputs have also been produced at minimum cost, their production has earned their manufacturer only normal profit, and their price reflects the marginal cost of the last unit produced.

Now consider linkages between markets for substitute and complement goods which affect allocative efficiency. If substitute and complement goods are produced in perfect markets, they will also be sold at the marginal cost of technically efficient production, including only normal profit.

Putting all this together, at the margin, consumers are choosing between goods which are all valued at marginal cost – to the manufacturer of the specific good, and to the whole economy because each input has also been priced at marginal cost. The resulting equilibrium is Pareto-efficient (see Chapter 9). There is no reallocation of resources which could increase the welfare of one consumer without a cost to the welfare of another. This is often known as the *first fundamental theorem of welfare economics*.

In such a perfectly competitive economy, a number of marginal conditions are shown to hold, including:

1   *Consumption*. Consumers will consume at the point where their marginal rate of substitution between two goods is equal to the price ratio between those goods.
2   *Production*. Firms will produce at the point where the marginal rate of technical substitution between the two factors is equal to the ratio of the prices of those factors.
3   *Production sectors plans* are brought into line with the plans of consumers through the price signals of the market – which always indicate the marginal costs of production. Thus the market is co-ordinated as if by an 'invisible hand' – a term coined by Adam Smith in his treatise *The Wealth of Nations* (1776), which is seen by many as the foundation the discipline of economics.

However, conditions for perfect competition rarely prevail and in many cases are unlikely ever to prevail. In these circumstances it is important to understand the *theory of the second best*, which states that if there is an unavoidable distortion somewhere in the economy, then perfect competition in any one market may not be efficient. Consider again the market linkages discussed above. Suppose that one market which provides a substitute good to that under analysis is produced by a monopolist. (Review the monopolistic market model in section 6.3.) This implies that the price is above marginal cost. In choosing between the good produced in the perfectly competitive market, and that produced in the monopolistic market, consumers will equate marginal utility per rupee spent across the two goods. From the perspective of efficiency, they will buy 'too much' of the good produced at marginal cost under perfect competition, because the underlying costs of production have not been equated at the margin across the two goods. It would cost society less to achieve the same levels of utility for consumers by switching production towards the good produced by the monopolist where the marginal costs of production are lower. The result is no longer Pareto-efficient – a different allocation of resources could increase the welfare of at least one member of society without reducing the welfare of anyone else.

The same conclusion could be linked with a deviation from perfect competition in an input market, which distorts both the efficiency of choices made in production and the prices which determine choices in consumption. One distortion creates a series of further distortions throughout the economy, and Pareto efficiency can no longer be claimed, even for perfect competition, in any one market.

The implications of this are profound, from the perspective of the debate over the rights and wrongs of *laissez-faire* and interventionist approaches to market regulation. If there is an unavoidable distortion somewhere in the economy, it follows that it may be efficient to introduce other distortions to help counterbalance it. Note that this conclusion is independent of any concern for equity in market allocations which, as discussed in Chapter 9, is not a component of the Pareto criterion.

For example, if nurses are underpaid owing to monopsonistic (single buyer) purchasing arrangements, this will have implications for production choices which (if made efficiently from any individual provider's perspective) will use more of the services of nurses relative to other cadres of staff or of labour-substituting equipment than is efficient. If prices were then generated at marginal cost by the provider, they would be lower than without the nurse wage distortion leading to demand for more health services than was efficient. Thus it may be appropriate, for example, to set 'norms' for the inputs of different staff cadres which constrain providers from acting efficiently from their own perspective but aim to lead to efficient allocations from the perspective of the economy as a whole. In consumption markets, health services might be taxed to realign marginal costs so that consumers make efficient consumption decisions.

Given the wide range and number of deviations from perfect competition existing in any economy, precise measurement of the degree and implications of individual deviations within their own or related markets is not a feasible objective of economic policy. Rather, a more general point might be carried from this discussion to the debate over *laissez-faire* versus interventionist approaches to health policy. The introduction of deliberate distortions in the form of government interventions can be justified on grounds of efficiency, as a means to compensate for unavoidable market distortions elsewhere, as well as on other grounds, for example those of equity. We explore this point further in the context of regulation in Chapter 17.

6.3 The monopolistic market model

At the opposite extreme to perfect competition characterised by many sellers and price taking is monopoly, characterised by only one seller and price setting. Under the perfect competition model the firm, as a price taker, effectively faces a perfectly elastic demand curve: a tiny price increase will cause demand to fall to zero. Under monopoly, the firm's demand curve and the market demand curve are the same. The decision of the profit-maximising monopolist is represented graphically in Figure 6.4.

Under monopoly there is no supply curve because the supplier dictates price and sets price and output together. There is also no distinction between firm and market – the firm is the market. If all units of the good produced by the monopolist are sold at the same price (an assumption of this model), price equals average revenue. Marginal revenue can be derived from the demand curve, but is always less than average revenue because in order to sell one more unit of the good the monopolist must reduce the price charged for all the units sold. Just as did the firm under perfect competition, the monopolist maximises profit where marginal revenue equals marginal cost, and prices and produces at p1q1. However, this results in abnormal profit (average abnormal profit can be measured by the distance ab between the average revenue and average cost at the chosen production level).

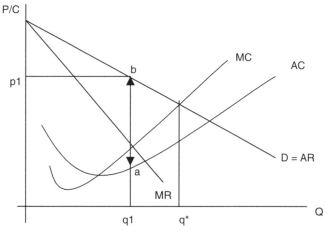

Figure 6.4 Monopoly.

In comparison with the perfectly competitive outcome, the monopolistic output can be deemed inefficient. A technically or economically inefficient monopolist will not be driven out of business. Profit maximisation implies a search for the most efficient ways of doing things but failure to achieve efficiency will not usually be catastrophic for the monopolist. Allocative efficiency is not achieved: units of output between q and q* are not produced, even though the marginal cost of doing so is less than the marginal utility placed by consumers on the additional units. The monopolist may operate at the minimum point of the short-run average cost curve, but only if this happens to coincide with the output level associated with equating marginal revenue and marginal cost.

6.4 From analytical models to policy

The reader may at this point be feeling a little detached from reality. Almost every assumption of the perfect market model is a rare or non-existent phenomenon. In some respects, the models themselves help to explain why that should be. Firms seek to make abnormal profits. Homogeneous products are a rare phenomenon precisely because it is in the interests of manufacturers to seek to differentiate their corn flakes or cola from everybody else's. Suppliers collude in order to avoid price taking. Information is jealously guarded rather than freely shared, and barriers are constructed against movement into markets in which abnormal profit is being earned by those benefiting. What are your expectations of the attitude of medical associations to the expansion of medical student numbers? No supplier wants to operate in a perfect market and earn only normal profit, and so suppliers seek ingenious ways to 'get ahead of the game' and more closely resemble monopolists. In their ability to cast light on these phenomena the models are already revealing their ability to perform as analytical tools – rather than to describe reality.

Nevertheless, some markets look a lot more like perfect ones, and others a lot more monopolistic. Within the health sector, the market for surgery might be concluded to be less perfect than the market for over-the-counter pharmaceuticals. We will explore the different ways in which markets fail or depart from the perfect model (see Chapter 8) – but already we can see that retailing pharmaceuticals involves many buyers and small firms competing with each other whereas much surgery takes place only in a few hospitals which are sometimes monopolies at local level; that on most estimations it is easier to become a pharmacist than a surgeon (and thus enter the market); that pharmaceutical products are more homogeneous (for example, you can buy generic aspirin or particular brands of aspirin at any pharmacy store) than surgical operations which are tailored to individual consumers, and so on.

If perfect markets are perfectly efficient, must it be true that few sellers are less efficient than many sellers in a market? Must it be true that attempts by government to intervene in markets are misguided? Such ideas seem to contradict common sense in health markets, where government intervention is popular and intuitively useful, and encouraging free entry to medical services – allowing anyone to practise medicine or nurse, regardless of their training – appears foolhardy. Fortunately, such ideas contradict economic theory too.

It is easy to fall into the trap of assuming that because perfect markets are efficient, and monopoly is inefficient, more perfect markets are more efficient than less perfect markets, and any move to impose measures which move a market closer to the set of conditions for perfect markets must increase efficiency. This leads to a great deal of confusion as to the purpose of the perfect market model. To repeat, it is not an attempt to describe reality, and it is not in itself capable of prescription. The theory of the second best provides a path through this morass.

Quite simply, the theory of the second best states that once there is a single imperfection in a market, the introduction of a second imperfection may increase rather than reduce efficiency. Once knowledge is not perfect, for example if consumers cannot judge which medical practitioners are competent and which are not, it may well increase efficiency to restrict entry into the market only to those who have achieved a minimum level of competence. If there are economies of scale which are exhausted only in the context of a few large producers[1] this may be more efficient than many small firms. It follows that the conditions for perfect markets have no normative implications. Box 6.2 provides a slightly more formal treatment of the theory of the second best.

Before converse confusions abound, it is equally important to point out that the theory of the second best does not imply that moving away from market perfection will necessarily increase efficiency either. Perfect government intervention is as rare as a perfect market. It is as important to be aware of government failure as of market failure. The model is a tool of analysis which cannot produce policy prescription in itself. There is no short cut to studying real conditions in a specific market and judging opportunities to increase efficiency (and other goals of health policy) in that light.

Note

1 In the long run the same logic applies – abnormal profit will be available if price does not fall to the minimum point of U-shaped long-run average cost curves and firms will enter or leave the industry accordingly. If economies of scale are exhausted at levels of output consistent with large enough numbers of sellers to ensure price-taking behaviour, the model continues to work. However, economies of scale are usually assumed to be exhausted at higher levels of production than this, and to be one of the factors which explain the existence of markets characterised by one or a few sellers. If so, perfect competition can be assumed to imply the absence of economies of scale in the long run.

7 Supplier-induced demand and agency

7.1 The information problem

This chapter focuses on what is probably the most important deviation found in health markets and some other markets, from the standard set of assumptions of the demand model proposed in Chapter 2 – the information problem. The standard model assumes that consumers are sovereign, or are the best judges of their own interests. This point may have passed unnoticed in thinking about the health economist's decision to phone his mother or surf the net. While his mother may be an exception, most people will not believe they understand the economist's interests better than he does himself in this respect. As soon as we enter health markets a range of objections to this perspective implicitly and explicitly arise.

Consumer sovereignty is challenged by the widespread idea that consumers should not be left to suffer the consequences of poor investment decisions in health, and should be required to make provision for likely health service needs. Hence, almost all countries require citizens to purchase insurance, or do so for them through the tax system (see Part IV). Similarly, a range of health-risking behaviours are usually proscribed by law – some drugs are almost universally outlawed for recreational use, and diving into the sea from Brighton pier is prohibited; and some health-promoting behaviours are required, such as immunisation in some countries. These rules can be interpreted as requiring socially responsible behaviour (protecting society from the self-interested behaviour of individuals), a standard explanation of rules in any society, but they seem also to contain an element of policy makers knowing best. This knowing best may involve a belief in superiority of judgement in some cases (you may well understand the risk of recreational use of heroin but we still will not allow you to damage yourself), an attitude termed paternalism. More commonly, it involves the belief that the information held by the rule maker is superior to that of the ruled (you do not understand the risks of recreational use of heroin and must be protected from your ignorance).

This is one type of information problem encountered in health markets. More generally, there are many important areas of specialised knowledge involved in the seeking of health status improvement which are not involved in the seeking of a banana.[1] As a result, it is inefficient for each consumer (the principal) to seek out all the relevant information and understanding herself, and we observe the widespread use of agents such as doctors, physiotherapists, pharmacists, opticians and nutritionists, employed (directly or indirectly) by the consumer to make purchasing decisions on her behalf. This phenomenon is known as agency, and occurs to different degrees in many fields:

the law, car mechanics, financial investment, education and numerous others. Almost everywhere there is a professional there is an agent in disguise.

In some cases of agency, including much but not all of its occurrence in health markets, the agent is also the supplier of the service. This means that demand and supply are not completely separable and gives rise to the possibility that agent-suppliers will abuse their role as agents in order to pursue their profit-seeking role as suppliers. The combination of *information asymmetry* (one party to a transaction has more information than the other), *bounded rationality* (not all contingencies can be foreseen and accounted for) and potential for *opportunism* ('self-interest seeking with guile') is a problematic combination for standard economic organisational forms to handle (Williamson, 1975) and no doubt contributes to an explanation of some of the unusual institutions which arise in health markets such as medical ethics and self-regulatory bodies. It also gives rise to the *potential* for that much debated phenomenon in health economics: supplier-induced demand.

7.2 Perfect agency

Before turning to discuss whether or not we can establish that health professionals[2] induce demand, or exploit their role as agents, it is useful to consider exactly what we might expect of a medical practitioner who is working as a perfect agent. What would the objectives of a doctor acting as a perfect agent in recommending and supplying health services be? Possible candidates include:

1   To maximise the health status of the patient.
2   To maximise the utility of the patient.
3   To maximise the health status or utility of the whole society.

Lack of clarity in this is expressed in a wider debate about the role of doctors in society which pervades much more than health economics textbooks. The first option, maximising the health status of the patient, confines the doctor to her appropriate professional sphere but risks paternalism, which may not be the intention. For example, it suggests that, were it to be effective, doctors should browbeat patients to give up smoking, rather than just ensure they are well informed of the risks.

The second option, maximising the utility of the patient, might suggest that the primary role of doctors should be to provide information to patients and, as far as possible, leave patients to make their own decisions. This seems to accord with many current ideas. Objections to this definition of role are more likely to relate to patients not wanting (or, in our terms, losing utility from) the making of fateful decisions than to argue that patients might in turn maximise the wrong thing (for example, give insufficient weight to health status).

The third option, maximising the health status or utility of the whole society, responds to the growing awareness of the inevitability of rationing in health markets – awareness that to provide a service to one patient may entail denial of another patient. Attitudes to this objective are likely to be health system-dependent. Doctors employed privately by the patient have a much clearer duty to that individual patient, and any rationing implications for others are at least indirect and may not arise if it is simply a question of that patient deciding to spend less of their own resources on other goods. Doctors employed in a public system are potentially the agent of both the state and the individual patient. Some health systems impose this role on doctors much more than others. If drugs are in very short supply, the doctor cannot but consider those given to one patient as lost to another – perhaps an hour later in the same clinic. In less constrained circumstances, budget constraints may operate at hospital level, which at least imply that the use of resources by one doctor in the hospital at the beginning of the year may mean their unavailability to another doctor's patient at the end of the year. In other situations, the 'down the line' implications of a decision made by one doctor may only ever be understood in the abstract – an unknown patient in another part of the system who might benefit from a budget surplus at year-end is affected.

This leaves even the best intentioned doctor in an unenviable position in attempting to clarify their own role. It also leaves health economists with some, perhaps easier to live with, difficulties. If we cannot clearly define perfect agency, we are in a difficult position when it comes to identifying departures from that standard.

7.3 Supplier-induced demand

Supplier-induced demand (SID) refers to a specific type of agency imperfection and implies that, in order to promote her own interests, the doctor recommends care the perfect agent would not recommend. The idea therefore implies a definition of perfect agency and also the identification of motivation. Inappropriate advice motivated by imperfect information, for example, is usually not considered SID. Concern with SID can be traced to early contributions to the health economics literature, most famously Roemer's Law: 'a built bed is a filled bed' (Roemer 1961). Correlations between supply and utilisation are not difficult to establish across health services but are not in themselves evidence of causal effect. Patients may cross borders to where services are more plentiful, hospitals and doctors may choose to locate in areas where demand is high, unmet demands may be high where fewer services are provided, markets may simply find equilibria! The explanation that demand is induced where supply exceeds the level it would otherwise attain requires a stronger test.

SID implies the shifting of the demand curve. A doctor who aims to encourage more patients to visit her surgery by reducing her fees (in other words is aiming to produce movement *along* the demand curve) is acting only as any other supplier of goods may act. If profit maximisation is her goal, she may equate marginal revenue and marginal cost in setting her price without being said to have induced demand. The problem with attempting to observe the shift of the curve is that demand curves themselves cannot be observed, only equilibrium points. This makes it very difficult to distinguish between normal market demand and supply movements, and market behaviour which implies that suppliers have shifted the demand curve.

Consider Figure 7.1. One way of looking for SID is to follow what happens in a health services market when the supply of doctors increases. In a standard market (Chapter 6, section 6.1), we would expect a shift in the supply curve to result in a new equilibrium at lower fee per visit and higher number of doctor visits provided (Figure 7.1a). However, if doctors are able to shift the demand curve, they will be able to protect themselves against lower fees. They may be able to do so, partially, by shifting demand curve D to D1; wholly, by shifting the demand curve to D2; or may even shift the demand curve as far as D3, in which case fees would increase (Figure 7.1b). However, the observer can observe only point A, and alternative points B, C and D, and not whole demand curves. If points A and B are observed, the pattern is consistent with the

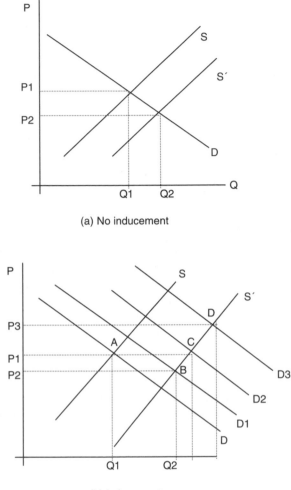

(a) No inducement

(b) Inducement

Figure 7.1 The difficulty of identifying supplier inducement: (*a*) no inducement (*b*) inducement.

normal market behaviour of Figure 7.1a: fees per visit have reduced and the number of visits has increased. Only if a point to the left of point C is observed, such as D, is it clear that the market is not normal: supply of doctors increased but so did fees per visit.

Looking for situations in which a movement from A to D seems to have been caused by an increase in the supply of doctors is known as *the fee test of inducement*, attributed to Reinhardt (1978). It should be noted that the test is a specific rather than sensitive one: many cases in which demand is induced will fail the test, but when the test is passed there is at least something odd about the market and inducement is a strong candidate to provide the explanation.

It will not surprise you to learn that the evidence about inducement is mixed and that most reviewers of this literature conclude that SID is an unproven hypothesis (McGuire *et al.* 1988; Folland *et al.* 1997; Mooney 1994). Two attempts to identify presence of SID are discussed in Box 7.1.

Box 7.1 Trying to find supplier-induced demand

There are many difficulties in identifying supplier-induced demand. Many studies have attempted the identification by looking for association between the supplier-to-population ratio and levels of utilisation. As discussed in the text, there are many alternative explanations of association besides supplier-induced demand.

Wilensky and Rossiter (1983) try to resolve some of these identification problems by separating physician and patient-initiated visits within total utilisation. Many explanations of association between demand and supply – felt need, cross-boundary flow, supply responding to demand levels – are associated with patient decision making. If demand is induced, it would therefore be expected that the proportion of physician-initiated visits would be higher than if it is not.

For the population in this study (14,000 households interviewed across the United States between 1977 and 1978), 39 per cent of all ambulatory visits were physician-initiated and 52 per cent patient-initiated (the remaining 9 per cent were referrals from elsewhere, or of unknown initiation). However by defining all diagnostic tests, prescription drugs, surgical procedures and hospitalisations as being physician-initiated, about 90 per cent of expenditure was physician-initiated.

Wilensky and Rossiter applied regression analysis to these data, and data relating to the supply of physicians (the physicians or surgeons per 100,000 population in the county or small area in which the patient resides). The likelihood that a visit would be physician-initiated, the number of physician initiated visits and the expenditure on such visits were significantly positively correlated with physician supply, which would seem to support the inducement hypothesis. However, evidence of inducement in relation to surgery, total physician-initiated expenditures and physician fees was absent.

Most studies of supplier-induced demand, like that of Wilensky and Rossiter have focused on the situation in the United States, where fee-for-service reimbursement is an important mechanism for paying for services, especially at ambulatory level. In most other countries the problem is less likely to arise. For example, in the UK medical care is not reimbursed on a fee-for-service basis, and the preconditions for supplier-induced demand are absent. Some have argued that the incentives in the UK system favour 'supplier-reduced demand' (e.g. Roberts 1993). However, dentists are reimbursed on a fee-for-service basis under a fixed price system, and a study of dental practice (Birch 1988) suggests that similar problems can be identified.

Birch (1988) identifies another problem with trying to identify inducement in data relating to undifferentiated visit numbers. As the number of suppliers increases, the 'shadow price' (or real cost to users) of access to care falls because a larger number of suppliers is likely to reduce distances to the nearest supplier, and queues and waiting times are likely to fall. This can be represented as a shift in the demand curve. In these circumstances, Reinhardt's fee test of inducement (see main text) fails. A shift in the demand curve caused by a falling shadow price cannot be distinguished from a shift caused by inducement.

However, it is the shadow price of the visit which has fallen, and not of the services provided during the visit. Therefore inducement can be tested by considering the 'content per visit': the volume of treatments recommended per visit. If no inducement takes place, content per visit should decline as the shadow price falls, since marginal attenders would be likely to require a lower volume of treatment. Birch's finding that cost per course of treatment (given fixed prices) is correlated negatively (and highly significantly) with population per dentist therefore suggests inducement.

In contrast, Grytten *et al.* (2001) apply a similar test to primary care physicians in Norway where, as with UK dentistry, fees are set centrally and one payer dominates. They argue that where there is a scarcity of physicians the choice to work longer or more intensively meets unmet demand, rather than induces demand. Their hypothesis of an income effect – the higher is 'non-practice' income (household income that does not derive from the physician's practice, including spousal income and interest on private investments) the less work load will the physician take on – is corroborated by their research: consultations per physician (but not treatment items per consultation) were higher for physicians with lower non-practice income. However, this relation failed to hold in areas of high physician density, suggesting that inducement does not occur.

7.4 Imperfect agency

Perhaps the issue need not be as complicated as these attempts to prove that demand curves shift. Much depends on the source of our concern. Most of us are likely to believe that medical advice should be given on the basis of the best scientific evidence available and may in recent years have reluctantly come to accept that expenditure control or reasonable budget limits imply rationing and the need for the use of cost-effectiveness criteria rather than effectiveness evidence alone. In public health systems this focus on demand rather than on need may also seem peculiar. From either perspective, we do not want our doctors to be influenced by the profit motive when they give us advice.

It is clear enough from much less complex studies that doctors are human, and fall short of this ideal. All that needs to be tested is whether advice or interventions change when the economic rewards associated with different types of advice and interventions change. There is an abundance of evidence from many different parts of the world that this is the case. When fee-for-service reimbursement is used, more services are provided than when systems of reimbursement that reward on a per-case or per-patient covered basis are used (see Box 7.2).

All this implies that we have a situation of imperfect agency. Medical science is imprecise, but that is not the source of the problem, or at least not the whole source. When advice responds to economic incentives, doctors cannot be applying their best guess about the best possible treatment all the time. It may be that uncertainty is exploited to play safe when incentives are set to reward higher levels of activity. Doctors may order multiple diagnostic tests with low likelihood of important findings, or operate now when a 'wait and see' policy has a low risk of exacerbating the problem. The opposite may be decided and slight risks taken when incentives lean the other way. The right decisions are difficult to identify, but it is clear that if economic incentives intervene, best guesses, consideration of the risk-intervention trade-off the patient

Box 7.2 Provider reimbursement

Changing the remuneration system of general practitioners in Copenhagen
Mooney (1994) reports a study of a change to the remuneration system of general practitioners in Copenhagen from capitation to fee-for-service, which took place in October 1987 and brought these general practitioners into line with the reimbursement system in the rest of the country. Fees were paid for all types of contacts with patients and for diagnostic and certain curative services.

The table shows the results of a survey of the activity of a group of doctors affected, in March 1987 (before the change) and in March 1988 and November 1988 (after the change). The table shows dramatic responses in terms of the provision of additional services for which fees were paid, and reduction in referral which not only did not pay but would in some cases have substituted for paying services.

Number of contacts and activities in a week and number of enlisted patients in March 1987, March 1988 and November 1988 for seventy-one doctors in Copenhagen city

Activity	March 1987	March 1988	November 1988
Contacts	9,942	11,387	10,618
Diagnostic services[a]	536	768	896
Curative services[a]	99	201	203
Referrals to specialist	1,276	1,176	1,002
Referrals to hospital	251	226	176
Number of enlisted patients	122,223	125,412	125,536

[a] Services for which an additional fee is paid.

Source: Mooney (1994).

This evidence suggests that while fee-for-service is associated with higher levels of provision of services by those receiving fees, it also reduces their referral of patients elsewhere. Mooney draws attention to the fact that over 20 per cent of referrals to specialists and nearly 30 per cent of referrals to hospital made under capitation appear to have been unnecessary, at least according to the implicit criteria adopted after the change.

Changing payment, reimbursement and patterns of care in Vietnamese hospitals
Sepehri *et al.* (2005) analysed the effect of reforms to the financing system governing public hospitals in Vietnam. During the 1990s, among other changes in the system, health insurance was encouraged, and user fees were introduced. Public hospitals were reimbursed on a fee-for-service basis, either by patients through the user fee system, or by insurers (at higher fee rates). By 1998 16.1 per cent of the population were insured. Between 1994 and 1998 the share of fee and insurance revenues in total hospital income increased from 17 per cent to 45 per cent, and staff bonuses derived from these revenues amounted to 30 per cent of total staff income in 1996.

Both numbers of service contacts and treatment intensity per service contact increased rapidly over the same period, and large differences emerged in total

annual contacts, admission rates and lengths of hospital stay across socio-
economic quintiles and between the insured and uninsured. It is difficult to
separate demand and supply effects in these data, although, as with estimating
supplier-induced demand, treatment intensity is less easy to explain by demand
pressures.

prefers, and trading off risk, effectiveness and cost are not the only considerations in
the decision-making process.

This is not all bad. Recognition of imperfect agency gives policy makers important
opportunities to influence the behaviour of doctors, especially where doctors identify
their role in terms of the first two definitions of perfect agency (concerned only with the
individual patient) and policy makers are concerned to bring influence to bear on
behalf of society as a whole. The same evidence relating reimbursement method to
doctor behaviour shows how powerful a tool the reimbursement system provides
to seek improvements in the cost-effectiveness of the treatment pattern recommended
and provided. Few health policy makers now ignore this opportunity.

Notes

1 Although we might again emphasise here that health services may not be as 'special' as they
  think they are. After all, the banana may be sought for its health status-inducing effects. To this
  extent, the material of this chapter is as relevant to bananas as to health care.
2 The discussion of the rest of this chapter applies to most health professionals with respect to
  many of their duties. The term 'doctor' is used throughout as a simplification and because
  most attention has been given to the doctor's role.

8 Market failure and government

8.1 Introduction

In Chapter 6 the perfect competition model was explained, and it was emphasised that the model aspired to be a tool of analysis rather than a description of reality. In this chapter that tool will be used further. Some of the major ways in which health markets diverge from the model will be explored and the model will be used to address the efficiency implications of these divergences. Mostly, the analysis involves only demand and supply curves, but it is important to remember that in a perfect market, demand curves are marginal utility curves and supply curves are marginal cost curves (review sections 6.2 and 6.4 if necessary).

It is important to remember that divergences from perfect markets are not necessarily bad things in themselves – positive externality is a good example (see 8.2 below). Divergences merely imply that efficient outcomes will not be forthcoming if the market is left to freely determine price, output and the allocation of consumption and production. Of course, perfectly efficient outcomes are likely to be out of our reach by any means. Once a divergence is identified, the challenge is to find a strategy which responds to the resulting inefficiency and will perform better than leaving the market to its own devices. In many cases there may be no such strategy, especially if the resulting inefficiency is not great. Government intervention is recommended only if likely government failure to intervene perfectly is less than the market failure under assessment.

8.2 Externality

Externality has been defined as 'a side-effect of either consumption or production which is not traded on the market or taken into account in setting a price' (Knapp 1984). In other words, consumers and producers either are not affected or do not bear the full brunt of the effects of their consumption or production.

The standard example of *negative* externality is pollution, usually (but not always) a side effect of production. A producer such as a manufacturer of clothing releases dyestuffs into a river. This results in tangible costs. The water company has to use additional filtering procedures to produce water of drinkable quality. The ecosystem of the river is damaged and fishing is affected. None of these costs automatically impacts on the clothing manufacturer – his marginal cost curve is not affected and the costs imposed are not internalised in transactions between the clothing manufacturer and those who buy from him

Externalities can be negative or positive and can arise in production or consumption.

On the consumption side, the consumer of a radio programme in the garden on a sunny afternoon does not internalise the annoyance cost experienced by his neighbour who wished to read quietly. However, the neighbour on the other side may have enjoyed the programme – a positive externality on the consumption side!

There are many externalities affecting health markets. The ones which are likely to be most important are positive ones. There are clear externalities in the treatment and prevention of infectious disease. If one person's TB is treated and cured, others are not infected. If vaccination is received by the majority, the unvaccinated minority may also be protected.

The second type of positive externality which may be important in health is known as the caring externality. It would appear that we are far more likely to care whether others receive health care or not than we are to care whether others drive prestigious cars or eat out at restaurants regularly. Newspapers respond to their readers' concern over accounts of those needing health care who are unable to access it, and often mount related appeals. Charitable institutions in the health field abound. The good Samaritan provided health care to a stranger. All this implies that many benefits have a positive externality on the consumption side when others receive health services.

Both these types of externality occur in consumption, or on the demand side. They imply that the individual purchaser of health care does not consider all the benefits associated with the purchase, only those received by himself personally. His demand curve captures his personal marginal utility, but not all the marginal utilities in society as a whole which are affected by his purchase decision. We can imagine that, besides the individual's personal demand curve, there is a marginal utility curve for the whole of society which lies everywhere to the right of the individual's curve.

In Figure 8.1 the individual (Mr Pink) is willing to trade a certain amount of other goods represented by a price for a doctor's visit (for example), and in the rest of society others would also be willing to trade some amount for Mr Pink's visits too.

We assume that there is an upward-sloping supply curve equal to marginal cost. At point A the free market solution is described – the equilibrium between the supply curve (MC) and Mr Pink's demand curve (Di). The price is €10 and the number of doctor visits purchased is four per year. However, the *efficient* solution is at B, where Mr Pink continues to buy doctors' visits up to the point where all the values in society become equal to the cost (six visits per year). To see why this is so, consider the fifth visit. The

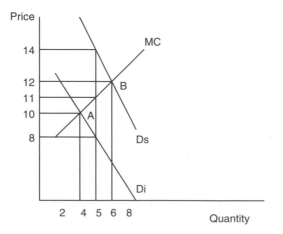

Figure 8.1 Positive externality on the demand side.

marginal cost of this visit is €11 (from the marginal cost curve), but the marginal value of the visit to Mr Pink is only €8. He will therefore not purchase it. However, in society as a whole there is an additional value of €6 for Mr Pink buying the visit – in total (adding Mr Pink's and others' values for the visit, as is done in the societal marginal value curve Ds), €14. From this perspective the visit is a good buy, but the purchase will not be made in a free market. Only if institutions are created which distort the free market can the efficient solution be made possible.

At this point, we can consider strategies which aim to move the market towards the efficient solution. The problem is the presence of values which are not translated into willingness to pay in the market. We might use charitable institutions to solicit from the public, money to subsidise doctor visits. We might impose such subsidy through a tax system. These solutions are also beset by inefficiencies. Both involve administrative transaction costs. Charity encounters free-rider problems – although the Samaritan cared about the stranger, he might have waited to see if someone else would pick him up. Tax systems may involve compulsorily extracting payment from those who do not care – subtracting more from their utility functions than they gain.[1]

Uncertainties apply to both strategies. Either charities or government may over-subsidise relative to the extent of the inefficiency and too many doctor visits may be utilised. In the example, free doctor visits would result in over-utilisation relative to the efficient point, at eight visits per year for Mr Pink (he would purchase all visits which for him had a marginal value greater than €0). If we are going to provide free services, we should try to estimate how many visits, or how much health education, is appropriate in the sense that social values are higher than cost. In the case of the doctor visits, we would have to ration Mr Pink to that number of visits and set up rationing systems which try to ensure that the visits made are the most appropriate ones. Ultimately, we must estimate the areas of inefficiency involved, estimate whether intervention of any sort is likely to improve on the market outcome or make it worse and, if we believe that intervention can increase efficiency, plan the strategy likely to maximise the impact. Economic evaluation (see Part II) offers one set of methods for tackling this complex task. In many circumstances it is impossible to apply such methods and a more intuitive way of tackling the problem is needed. A policy maker's guess at what is affordable may be an implicit judgement of society's values.

Equivalently, negative externalities might be addressed by banning or taxing the relevant activity. However, zero activity will only by coincidence equate to the efficient level of activity, and even in principle, a ban may therefore create more inefficiency than it solves. Policing bans may also be expensive, and poorly policed bans may be the most expensive of all – potentially giving rise to criminal modes of behaviour and inability to exert any controls whatsoever.

In principle, taxes can be assessed by asking what is the appropriate tax to ensure that external costs are imposed on the producer so that she then equalises social marginal cost with social benefit. A tax which tries precisely to internalise a negative externality (i.e. is at every level of production equal to the relevant external cost) is known as a Pigovian tax, after the economist A. C. Pigou (1877–1959). Setting taxes at the appropriate level involves the same difficulties as setting subsidies – can the external costs be measured and allocated to the appropriate producers?

With respect to all these strategies market failure has to be balanced against government failure and an assessment of whether or not the best intervention improves on the market outcome has to be made.

8.3 Public goods

When I eat a banana, I use it up – nobody else can ever eat that banana. It is *rival*. If I am selling bananas, I can give them to those who pay, and refuse them to those who don't. Bananas are *excludable*. Public goods are characterised by *non-rivalness* and *non-excludability*.

Non-rivalness means that one person's consumption of a good does not prevent another also consuming it. A theatrical performance is non-rival to the extent that, once provided for one person, it costs nothing to provide it to others up to the seating capacity of the theatre. Non-excludability means that it is not possible to exclude non-payers from consuming. Once a street has been cleaned, it is not possible to prevent anyone who uses the street from enjoying the benefit. Non-excludable goods are also usually non-rival, but non-rival goods are quite often excludable. It is quite easy, and indeed usual, to exclude non-payers from a theatrical production.

Environmental health services and public health education campaigns are examples of goods which are both non-rival and non-excludable and are therefore close to being pure public goods. Positive externality in consumption implies a degree of non-rivalness and although the two types of market failure are usually separated, it may be more useful to identify degrees of public goods characteristics.

Figure 8.2 suggests a representation of degree of public goods characteristics of a few health-related interventions on a two-dimensional map of non-rivalness and non-excludability. Cancer treatment is both rival and excludable and therefore a private good. Immunisation is also relatively easily excludable (although there are advantages in providing the service to groups of people at once moving it slightly to the left in comparison with cancer treatment on the ease of exclusion axis). Much of the benefit of immunisation is captured by the immunised individual but, to the extent that benefits are captured by others, non-rivalness is implied.

Non-rivalness creates market failure because it causes the marginal cost of supply of the good to drop to zero for each additional person provided with it after the first. Although it is possible to exclude non-payers, it is inefficient to do so. Consider

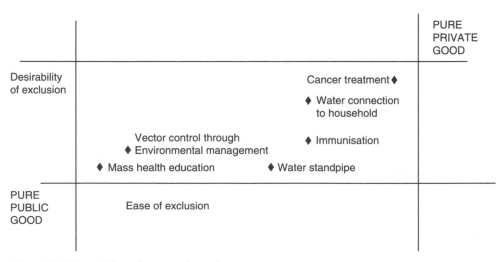

Figure 8.2 The public–private good continuum.

Source: Bennett (1991), p 70.

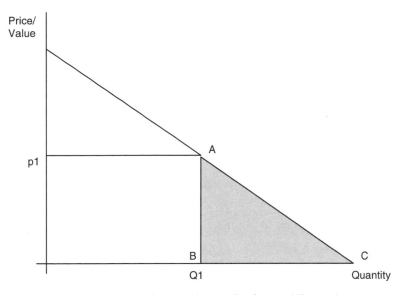

Figure 8.3 The welfare loss from setting a price for a public good.

Figure 8.3, which might represent the situation of a theatrical production. The marginal cost curve coincides with the x axis because, after the first person, the marginal cost of additional provision is zero. The private demand curve for tickets (Dp), as usual, can be used to estimate the value of tickets to individuals. If the price is greater than zero (for example, p1), there will always be some people who would value a ticket (would pay more than zero price) but would not pay the price charged. Providing free tickets to these people would create more value in society than it would cost. There is therefore an opportunity to increase social utility which is not seized. The inefficiency in comparison with a zero price can be represented by shaded triangle ABC. (Theatre companies try to capture some of this lost efficiency by pricing differentially in the form of student and pensioner discounts and same day tickets – students, pensioners and those not determined to book in advance may set a lower value on tickets than average – but the attempt is inevitably imperfect and some areas of inefficiency remain.)

Non-excludability implies severe difficulties in organising a market in the good concerned. In many cases, the total cost of providing the good will exceed the willingness to pay even of the individual who sets the highest value on it. No one person may value mosquito control sufficiently to be willing to fund a whole area's programme. Under these circumstances the good will not be provided at all by the market.

Since non-rivalness is an extreme form of positive externality on the demand side, health policy strategies responding to a recognition of public goods characteristics echo those discussed to deal with positive externality in section 8.2. However, if marginal costs are truly zero, there is a stronger likelihood that free provision of the good in question, as opposed to a limited subsidy, is the appropriate strategy, and if non-excludability also applies, this is the only feasible course. It should be remembered that public provision implies taxation and uncompensated losses to those who do not value the public good. Overall, the total benefit to be derived from the service in question must exceed the total value to society before there is even a potential gain from public provision.[2]

A non-government option in the case of non-excludable public goods is for individuals to voluntarily club together to purchase the good. However, free-riders will wait for others to do so, and may falsely claim zero values in the hope of avoiding payment – the expressed willingness to pay cannot be relied upon to reflect society's true willingness to pay and, at the margin, provision of the amount of the good which would equate marginal value and marginal cost cannot be attained.

Public provision might answer both non-rival and non-excludable characteristics of public goods.

Where values are more difficult to measure, recourse to criteria such as whether the public good benefits are non-trivial and the costs of provision relatively affordable may yield the best judgement possible as to whether public provision is likely to be warranted. Even if it were in theory possible to eliminate a disease agent such as the rat population, if enough resources were directed to the problem, it is not necessarily efficient to do so. The conclusion that it is impossible to do so might be read as meaning that the opportunity costs of doing so would be unreasonably high.

8.4 Monopoly and oligopoly

Many components of the health sector are natural monopolies – they exhibit features which tend to limit the number of suppliers in the market. Competitive markets require the entry of small contenders for a share of the market's business, and opportunity for such small firms to become established. A number of factors militate against this. High fixed costs imply that only those firms which can call on substantial resources from capital markets will be able to make the initial investment necessary to start in business. (In contrast, if variable costs are relatively high, a business can start small and expand as its business does.) Sunk costs – investments in specific assets which cannot be moved from one market to another – are a particularly off-putting type of investment for a market entrant: if entry proves to have been a mistake, very little of the investment is likely to be recoupable, especially if the entrant's own failure in the market suggests limited capacity for market expansion. These arguments are especially relevant to more sophisticated and high-technology services which require large capital investment, often of a sunk nature – for example, diagnostic services such as x-ray and CT scans, and operating theatres and equipment. More generally, the provision of hospital services as a whole encounters this constraint. Only very large markets (larger cities) offer the possibility for more than a few hospitals to compete.

Economies of scale also militate against the entry of many firms to a market. If the minimum efficient scale is large in relation to the total demand for the service, only a firm which captures a high proportion of market business will be able to operate at that scale. This acts as a barrier to entry to other firms. Even if the dominant firm's price is high, reflecting its profit level, it can always reduce the price for long enough to drive a new contender out of the business again. Unless the new contender can immediately start to operate at the same scale as the dominant firm, it will be unable to enter. The barrier to entry is similar to that presented by high fixed costs.

Chapter 6 explored the inefficiency implicit in the abnormal profit levels associated with monopolistic markets. Strategies to deal with the inefficiencies caused by monopoly and oligopoly are unlikely to focus on trying to increase the number of providers, since the causes of monopoly and oligopoly often suggest that larger numbers of providers would be even more inefficient. Rather, strategies are likely to focus on public provision and regulation. The latter subject is discussed in Chapter 17.

8.5 Other sources of market failure

Considerable attention has already been given to imperfect knowledge and agency, which as suggested in Chapter 7 are possibly the most important sources of market failure. In addition to failure resulting from agency itself, Chapter 7 suggested that imperfect knowledge causes the relationship between the demand curve and marginal value to be questioned. We can still rely on the demand curve to indicate the patient's best guesses as to her marginal values of different services, but we can no longer rely on those best guesses to be her true marginal value. For example, in the early 1960s there was a high demand for the drug thalidomide in pregnancy. Later information as to its link with certain congenital malformations reduced that demand to zero. The true marginal values (presumably highly negative) of antenatal thalidomide use were not represented by 'ignorant' demand curves. For types of services for which imperfect knowledge is likely to be greatest, demand curves may have little relevant information from an efficiency perspective.

A different type of uncertainty, with different implications, arises from the individual's inability to predict her demands. Health service costs can be large and time-concentrated. From the individual's perspective they should therefore be planned and saved for, but the added complication that they are uncertain means that savings may still be inadequate. Health insurance ensures that contribution levels will prove adequate, even where costs for health service needs prove to be above average. However, health insurance also causes the market to fail. The two main ways in which it does so are through moral hazard and adverse selection. Moral hazard arises when consumers face zero prices at the time of use: their utilisation decision does not take account of marginal cost. Adverse selection arises where low-risk individuals are able to opt out of the risk pool. As a result, average risk rises, causing the cost of insurance to rise and further lower-risk individuals to opt out. Ultimately it may be impossible to organise a market in health insurance, or at least one which does not exclude a large proportion of those needing to access health services.

As with monopoly and oligopoly, insurance arrangements arise in response to the underlying inefficiency causing characteristic. Sensible strategies therefore do not try to imitate perfect markets by trying to remove insurance arrangements but are more likely to regulate the insurance market. Compulsory insurance or social insurance is a regulated arrangement which addresses adverse selection, for example (see Chapter 23). Insurance agencies themselves can address some of the problems through specific contract forms. For example, the no claims bonus is an attempt to mitigate moral hazard (see Chapter 14 on contracts).

8.6 Merit goods and equity

Many believe that health services are special, or 'merit', in other words, that those in need have a basic right to medical care and that rights imply that no one should face financial or other barriers to the use of health services. This argument can be seen as an absolutist one – not amenable to consideration of degrees of efficiency and equity implicit in different market arrangements but leading directly to the policy prescription that health services must be offered free at the point of use.

Absolutist arguments are always difficult to sustain, however. If all goods are not merit, it is difficult to identify the boundaries without recourse to relative standards. If health services are merit because they relieve pain or even extend life, perhaps those health services which do neither (some types of plastic surgery might provide an example) should be excluded. Recognition that even the most prosperous societies could allocate their entire GNP to health interventions with life-extending and pain-relieving potential (however minute or unlikely) suggests that the scale and likeliness of such potential have to be taken into account. These considerations tend to suggest that more relativist rationales for health policy are required.

For example, some would argue that the principal objective in organising a market for health services is not efficiency but equity. Hence markets fail in that even perfect markets make no special claims with respect to equity. This is a very persuasive argument, but it warrants some further examination.

First, it is not sensible to exclude efficiency considerations altogether. Production of health services has to take place, or there is nothing to share round equitably. *Ceteris paribus*, even the most avid egalitarian would prefer more to share round than less. Concern that productive resources are not just wasted, and in fact are used to produce the most health care possible, for any given distribution must be important in any schema.

Second, a set of misunderstandings can arise from the normative rather than analytical use of the perfect market model. If we believe that efficiency dictates that the perfect market should be imitated as closely as possible – in other words, if we don't understand the theory of the second best (see section 6.4 and Box 6.2), there are clear conflicts with equity. This can leave some to intuit a fundamental conflict between equity and efficiency: a zero-sum game in which every unit of equity gained is at the expense of efficiency, and vice versa. In this case a choice between efficiency and equity must be made which is ideological rather than technical.

Once the theory of the second best is admitted, however, there may be substantial overlap between the dictates of efficiency and equity. The concepts of allocative efficiency and equity can in practice, and even conceptually, be difficult to unravel. Concern that resources should be allocated according to where they can most efficiently produce health will direct those resources to the greatest need (at least where need is defined as the capacity to benefit).

On a specific set of definitions allocative efficiency and equity may be almost identical. For example, Mooney (1983) suggests a list of possible definitions of equity. According to this list, equity may imply equality of: (1) expenditure *per capita*; (2) inputs *per capita*; (3) inputs for equal need; (4) access for equal need; (5) utilisation for equal need; (6) marginal met need; (7) health. If need is defined as capacity to benefit, definitions (3) to (5) coincide with allocative efficiency (if capacity to benefit is per unit of input, unit of access or unit of utilisation, respectively).

Between these extreme viewpoints, situations can be identified in which allocative efficiency and some definitions of equity conflict. If need is defined in terms of extent of health problem rather than capacity to benefit, the productivity of health resources varies in situations of equal need. For example, if Mr Pink responds better to a health intervention for the same health problem than Ms Brown, allocative efficiency would allocate more resources to Mr Pink, whereas equity would indicate an equal allocation.

Notes

1 This implies that Pareto optimality cannot be inferred – see Chapter 9.
2 Or a potential Pareto improvement – see section 9.3.

Part II
Economic evaluation

9 The theoretical bases of economic evaluation

9.1 Adding up costs and benefits: the need for a conceptual basis

We all personally make decisions on how to allocate our limited resources for our families and ourselves. If we are 'utility maximisers' (see Chapter 2) we aim to maximise our expected welfare by choosing to buy the goods and services that should achieve this end. To do this we check that there is no alternative mix of goods we could consume that would increase our welfare. Once this is achieved we cannot increase our welfare simply by changing the mix of goods and services we consume. For the formal treatments of efficiency in production and exchange see Boxes 9.1–3. By analogy, when a decision is made on behalf of society to provide some services collectively, the aim may be to maximise the welfare of the whole of society, and in a similar way to ensure that no change in the mix and pattern of consumption of goods and services would increase overall welfare.

But what works easily for the individual does not so obviously work for collective decisions. If we try simply to compare different options by adding up the costs and the benefits we immediately run into the problem of comparing benefits to different individuals. Does a cataract operation to restore my sight offer more benefit than one that restores the sight of a keen reader, an artist, a farmer or a mother? Are benefits greater from supplementing iodine in the diet (and avoiding damage to intellectual skills) or

---

Box 9.1 Efficiency in exchange

In a world of two individuals and two goods, individuals will trade the goods in order to maximise utility. They will do this until the marginal rate at which they are willing to substitute the goods (the *marginal rate of substitution*, MRS) is equal to the ratio of the prices of the goods. Thus, for efficient exchange, for any two individuals and any two goods

$$MRSa, b^{n, m} = Pa/Pb \; \forall a, b, \forall n, m$$

where a, b are goods, n, m are individuals, Pa and Pb are prices of goods a, b and $\forall$ means 'all'. What this is saying is that, for all pairs of goods, and all pairs of individuals, the marginal rate of substitution is the same.

Box 9.2 Efficiency in production

In a world of two factors of production, say equipment (K) and labour (L), production is efficient when the cost of the inputs is the lowest possible. Keeping output constant, we can vary the proportions of equipment and labour. The rate at which we can substitute K for L for a given output is the *marginal rate of technical substitution* (MRTS) between K and L. The lowest cost of production will be when no further substitution leads to a reduction in cost, that is, when the MRTS is equal to the ratio of input prices.

This principle applies to all inputs. For production at minimum cost, the MRTS for all pairs of inputs should be equal to the ratio of the input prices.

Formally the marginal rate of technical substitution between inputs x and y is equal to the ratio of the prices of x and y for all pairs of inputs:

$$MRTS_{x, y} = P_x/P_y \; \forall x, y$$

where inputs are x and y, and the prices of inputs are P_x and P_y.

Box 9.3 Efficiency in production and exchange

Where production takes place in an economy, the rate at which it is possible to switch production between any two goods a and b (the *marginal rate of transformation*, MRT) must equal the ratio of the prices of goods for efficient production and exchange:

$$MRT_{a, b} = P_a/P_b$$

Thus for efficiency in production and exchange:

$$MRS_{a, b}^{\, n, m} = MRT_{a, b} = P_a/P_b \; \forall a, b, \; \forall n, m$$

---

from measures to control the transmission of malaria? How much extra is it worth paying for a new treatment with no additional impact on survival but fewer side effects? Should we give priority to life-extending treatments over those that enhance quality of life? An individual can, in principle, answer these questions for herself, and decide on priorities for her treatment. But as soon as there are two or more people involved, we face the difficulty of comparing different people, with different likes, wants and needs.

In some senses this dilemma cannot be resolved – there will always be differences between individuals, and it is likely that views on what should be the priority will depend in part on personal circumstances. However, it is important that some principles are applied to the issue of how we make decisions on the use of resources. One obvious starting point is the body of theory on the economics of welfare.

9.2 Markets, microeconomics and Paretian welfare economics

In most societies most goods and services are allocated through market processes. Some markets work well, and can be very efficient mechanisms to match available goods and services to those that need them and want them (see Chapter 6). Using market mechanisms may remain the best available option even when the conditions for perfect markets are violated (Chapters 7 and 8). The great strength of markets is the way they use information. There is no need to gather and analyse the data on who wants what, and who wants to provide what services. Buyers and sellers bring the necessary information with them to the market, so it is available when and where it is needed. But when markets fail badly, for example due to problems of monopoly, limited information or externalities, we need to find other ways to make collective choices. What happens in a well functioning market can give us some guide to how this should be done.

To achieve the aim of obtaining the greatest benefit to society from health interventions, certain conditions must prevail. An important one is that the processes of production of services must be efficient. There are two main ways in which production can be inefficient – using unnecessarily large amounts of all inputs, and using inefficient combinations of inputs. For example, if we employ ten people to do a job that can easily be done by six, it is just wasteful. Technically, under these circumstances, production is at a point off the cost curve (sometimes known as X-inefficiency (Leibenstein 1966)). More subtly, if highly paid and expensively trained doctors do work that could be done by other staff, that is inefficient. If we use expensively equipped facilities for work requiring only basic equipment, that is also likely to be wasteful. There may also be cases where production is inefficient because the technology used is not the one with lowest costs. If three individual vaccines are used where a combination vaccine is available (costing slightly more), it may be more efficient to pay more for the drugs, but less for staff. Conversely, it may be more efficient to employ a larger number of staff who are equipped with bicycles than to employ fewer who drive cars.

There are really two steps in finding the lowest-cost process of production (see Chapters 4–5). First we need to identify technically feasible ways of producing the desired outcomes. Second, we apply information on the cost of the different inputs in order to find the lowest-cost method. In a country where staff are relatively cheap, but equipment is expensive, it is likely to be more efficient to use relatively labour-intensive processes (for example, in laboratory work we might choose processes involving examination of slides by skilled staff rather than automated processes or use of pattern recognition equipment). The process of searching for the best combination of inputs should continue until no further changes can be found that would lower the production cost. Formally this is when *the marginal rate of technical substitution* between any pair of inputs equals the ratio of the costs of the inputs (see Box 9.2 and Chapters 4–5).

Having ensured that services are being produced efficiently, a second requirement for efficiency is to choose to provide those services that will maximise welfare. This again involves comparing the benefits of different services and their relative cost. For example, consider the available life-extending interventions in the field of HIV. There are options for primary prevention, either personal health promotion activities or by reducing the risk of transmission by the treatment of other sexually transmitted diseases. There are potential interventions, which can improve the health and extend life for people who are already seropositive, such as treatment of TB. There are treatments that aim to control the virus directly using combinations of drugs. Unless we assemble detailed information about the effectiveness of each of these in a particular country it is not self-evident which should be given priority. In a simple case we might define output of health services as years of life gained. We could then choose the combination of these interventions that would maximise this for any given overall expenditure. At that point, no further changes in the mix of interventions will increase output. More formally, the marginal rate of transformation between all pairs of interventions is the same (see Box 9.3).

But we are not interested only in interventions that extend life for people with or at risk of HIV. We need to choose the best ways of achieving not only health gain for this disease, but also the maximum health gain overall. Again a useful starting point is the likely choices we each make. An individual chooses to consume combinations of goods and services that maximise her welfare. In principle she will switch between different services until further switching cannot increase her welfare. Imagine she has a range of chronic conditions (such as arthritis, coronary heart disease, diabetes and asthma) and has access to only limited funds to buy services. She would choose the combination of surgery, physiotherapy, occupational therapy, drug treatments, assistance with personal care and home modifications that she would expect to have the greatest overall impact on her health and quality of life (within her limited resources). She would choose more of a service if the extra would have a bigger impact on her health than any other use of the resources. Formally this means that her marginal rate of substitution between any pair of goods is equal to the ratio of the prices of the goods (see Box 9.3 and Chapter 2).

Finally, we have to choose the extent to which we allocate our limited resources to health compared with other goods. Although it is tempting to believe that health care is always the most important good, we can observe that people do not act as if this were so. People take risks with their health by smoking; mountain climbing; driving faster than necessary and even crossing roads they could avoid. In so doing they are indicating that they value the associated benefits more than the cost of the associated risk. At this level, too, the rational utility-maximising individual would choose to equate the marginal rate of substitution between health goods and other goods.

When people interact in a market they trade until no further trades increase their welfare. They will take their income and the goods they already own (their *initial endowments*), and buy and sell till they have maximum benefits from what they consume. In a perfect market, with all individuals aiming to maximise their welfare, we see the best use of resources *for any given initial distribution of wealth and incomes*. At prevailing prices all individuals have their chosen combination of goods and services. No one can be made any better off without someone else being made worse off. Formally we have a situation where the *marginal rates of substitution* between all pairs of goods for all pairs of individuals are equal and are equal to the *marginal rate of transformation* between all pairs of goods and the *ratios of prices*. In production the *marginal rate of technical substitution* between all pairs of inputs for all goods and services is equal and is the *ratio of the prices of inputs* (see Box 9.3).

In one sense we can describe this state of affairs as optimal. If we accept the initial income distribution, then we have a situation in which all individuals have maximum welfare. Simply by carrying out voluntary trades people convert their initial endowments, which may include many goods they do not like, into their desired consumption. Those who like holidays spend more on holidays; those who want transport buy bicycles or cars; those who want more housing or food choose those. No one can be made better off without someone becoming worse off. This circumstance is described as a *Pareto optimum*, after the Italian sociologist and economist Vilfredo Pareto (1848–1923), who first formalised the concept.

It is easy to see the limitation of the notion of a Pareto optimum, since in many instances it may not seem like a very nice state of affairs. If one person starts off owning half the assets in a country, and all others live in grinding poverty, there can still be a Pareto optimum, despite the hardship and misery. But before being too dismissive it is interesting to think about situations that are not Pareto-optimal. If further voluntary trade would give people more preferred combinations of goods and services, then their welfare will be improved when they trade. If I am a vegetarian, I gain no welfare from meat, and would be better off selling the meat and buying more or better vegetables. Voluntary trades of this kind make at least one person better off, and no one worse off. This is known as a *Pareto improvement*. There is a strong intuitive appeal to the suggestion that if one person is better off, and no one worse off, then society as a whole is better off.

Perfectly functioning markets move us automatically towards a Pareto optimum. Collective decisions are normally taken in circumstances where markets have for some reason failed. When making these collective decisions a possible choice rule is to seek out Pareto improvements. This will increase welfare, in the Paretian sense, for any starting point (in terms of income distribution). Many economists argue that if we do not like the current income distribution we can change it by tax or subsidy, but once that is done we will act only when we spot an opportunity to effect a Pareto improvement. To many economists this forms a conceptual justification of cost–benefit analysis, the underlying framework in economic evaluation.

9.3 Developments of welfare economics, social welfare functions and cost–benefit analysis

In the real world of collective decision making it is not always easy to find Pareto improvements. When we build a road there are winners who benefit from better transport and those who lose from pollution and danger. When we develop a vaccination programme there are many who are saved from disease but some that are harmed (and a few who may be killed) by the vaccine. When we develop computing skills in teenagers some will help solve problems of world poverty and some will become hackers or write viruses. Almost no activity can be guaranteed to be without losers. Strictly applied, the criterion that no one may be worse off means that almost no decisions can be made. Taking this to *reductio ad absurdum*, if eradication of malaria could be achieved only if Bill Gates had to pay €20 in taxes against his will, we could not justify doing it on Paretian grounds. When taxes are used to pay for services, then there are likely to be losers, since few people enjoy paying taxes. On this strict interpretation, any programme that uses any tax finance cannot constitute a Pareto improvement.

Most people would judge that it is reasonable for there to be some losers if the gains to those who benefit are sufficiently large. We need some basis for judging the relative importance of the gains to the gainers and the losses to the losers. One approach is to ask those who gain to compensate those who lose. If they do this, and are still better off, it shows that their gains exceed the losses to those who lost. In effect the compensation means that there are no longer any losers, so there is a Pareto improvement.

An apparently small step is to argue that even if they do not compensate the losers, if they *could* do so and still be better off, then there is a *potential* Pareto improvement, and this justifies a decision. Sadly there is a problem with this argument. Since there are losers, then some sections of the population now have lower incomes. It was demonstrated by Scitovsky (1941) that there can be cases where the changes in incomes from doing a project lead to a paradox – the potential Pareto improvement can be used to justify a change, and also to return to the starting point (see Box 9.4). This is most likely

---

Box 9.4 The Scitovsky paradox

By definition a Pareto improvement occurs when at least one person is made better off and no one is made worse off. By extension it is argued that a potential Pareto improvement occurs when it would be possible to make at least one person better off with no one worse off, but the compensation to the losers is not actually paid.

What Scitovsky was able to show was that there are circumstances in which the potential Pareto improvement criterion could be used to argue both for a change and conversely for a return to the original position. This is clearly worrying if the potential Pareto improvement is used as a rule for resource allocation.

A simple example illustrates how this can happen. For a fuller account of why this occurs see Quirk and Saposnik (1968). Imagine the hypothetical case of two people who have hypertension, but the drugs to control it are very scarce. In their cases both thiazide diuretics (TD) and beta blockers (BB) have some effect. For these patients combination therapy has proved more effective at controlling their hypertension than either drug alone. Given the severity of their problems, they are both recommended to take one standard dose of each, and failing that to take double the standard dose of one.

Suppose an intervention enabled a change in the world so that scenario 2 applied rather than scenario 1.

	Juan	Maria
Scenario 1		
TD	Two standard doses	None
BB	None	One standard dose
Scenario 2		
TD	One standard dose	None
BB	None	Two standard doses

Juan would lose from the intervention and Maria would gain. However, Maria could compensate Juan for his loss by giving him one of her BB doses and still be as well off as she was under scenario 1. On this basis the compensation criterion would approve the intervention.

However, suppose the intervention instead enabled a change in the world so that scenario 1 applied rather than scenario 2. Now Juan would be better off and Maria worse off – but this time Juan could compensate Maria for her loss by giving her one dose of TD, maintaining his own welfare at the scenario 2 level while improving Maria's.

This hypothetical example shows that, unless the compensation is actually paid, there is a risk that a change in either direction can be justified on the basis of offering a potential Pareto improvement. To ensure that the change is really equivalent to a Pareto improvement we need additionally to check that this 'reversal' will not occur.

to happen when the project has a large effect on the distribution of incomes. It is not clear how likely it is that this will happen, but it is a warning that the apparently modest development of the idea of a Pareto improvement to a potential Pareto improvement may undermine the welfare economics basis of the analysis. In practice, most economists are aware of this problem, and are concerned if the effect of a project is to harm some people significantly. Most of the time the Scitovsky paradox is treated as a theoretical nicety.

The cost–benefit framework can be justified as the application of the idea of the potential Pareto improvement. When the gains to those who gain exceed the losses to those who lose, then the benefits exceed the costs. The justification does not require decision makers to compare the welfare of individuals, only to ensure that the winners *could* compensate the losers fully and still be better off than before the change.

The Paretian framework tries to avoid the need to make direct comparison of the welfare of different individuals. However, many of us are willing to do this. A case can be made that it is more important to provide treatment for mothers, people who are working and supporting families, medical scientists on the brink of important new insights, film stars who bring pleasure to millions or presidents and prime ministers than for people who are single, childless, unimaginative and lack political ambition. At times of shipwreck the tradition is that the first priority for scarce lifeboat places goes to women and children. In preparations for nuclear war, priority is to be given to senior politicians and leaders. It is interesting to think about our feelings about these types of priority. Many people would agree with the priority for children and those with dependants, but perhaps fewer would put film stars and politicians above others (see Box 9.5).

The potential Pareto improvement criterion is based on individuals and their welfare. In effect the approach is to define the welfare of the community as being made up of the welfare of individuals. The perspective does not rule out the possibility of people gaining utility from benefits to others – their utility functions might well include welfare gains to others as arguments, but it does rule out the possibility that the welfare of society is different from the sum of individual utilities. Other perspectives are possible, involving notions of a common good that are more than simply the sum of welfare of individuals (see Box 9.6). If the utility of any individual rises (with no fall for anyone else) it increases social welfare in the Paretian sense, but this framework does not allow us to quantify the change. In other words, we can say a little about the direction of change of social welfare if particular individuals are better off, but we can say nothing about the extent of the change. More technically, the Pareto framework specifies a social welfare function where social welfare depends on individual utilities. Social welfare increases with increases in the welfare of individuals, but otherwise the shape of the function is not determined. This has two limitations. First, we have no clear basis on which to compare the effects on social welfare of utility gains to different individuals. Second, even if we are able to derive ordinal rankings of welfare implications of different population health profiles, we cannot value them.

Box 9.5 Welfare economics and income distribution

Paretian welfare economics aims to answer questions about how to maximise welfare from a given income and wealth distribution starting point. In thinking about health care priorities decisions on the use of resources may change the distribution of income and wealth.

It is possible to argue that economic efficiency (in the Paretian sense) and issues of distribution should be considered separately. Many economists argue that if we do not like the current distribution of income we can take measures to change it, such as taxing the relatively rich or subsidising the poor. The advantage of this approach is that it allows us to use information about people's demands and choices as measures of their welfare.

In all situations, redistributing income and wealth is not as simple as issuing edicts, since tax and subsidy régimes affect incentives. In the case of health interventions there are still further problems. A particular issue is that in general ill health is concentrated in parts of the population that are relatively poor. This may mean that the greater health needs of the poor would be assessed as relatively unimportant, since their ability, and therefore willingness, to pay is lower than for (fitter) richer people.

Also, the willingness of richer people to subsidise poorer ones may depend on what is being provided. They may be willing to pay taxes to help people restore their health but not to allow them to increase spending on gambling. Rich people might be willing to subsidise access for poor people to decent housing but not to allow more smoking. Thus the availability of tax funds to provide subsidies may depend on the use to which they are to be put. This can make it even more difficult to use the general tax system to sort out issues of income and equality.

See Chapter 12 for discussion of how issues of income and equity are sometimes taken into account in economic evaluation.

Box 9.6 Social welfare functions

'Social welfare' has been defined as 'whatever is good, or whatever ought to be maximised' (Ng, 1983). A social welfare function (SWF) implies that a single set of welfare values can be assigned to any specified state of the world.

We have already encountered the Paretian SWF which is based on a vector of individual welfare values (or 'utilities') and applies the criterion that social welfare improves only if each value changes in a non-negative direction. The compensation criterion amends the Paretian SWF and implies the ability to *aggregate* the individual welfare values in the SWF. Both approaches are 'individualist' and 'utilitarian' in that they base their estimation of the well-being of society on utilities from individuals' perspectives.

However, aggregation presents complex issues which are avoided by the Paretian SWF. Suspicion of inter-personal comparisons of utility are long-standing and characterise the 'new welfare economics' (in comparison with the 'old welfare economics' of Pigou). Many believe that, while it is possible to order an individual's utilities, it is not possible to measure them 'cardinally' (against a natural zero) or to compare them between individuals. If this is the case, aggregation is impossible.

The 'revealed preference' approach proposed by Samuelson (1938) seems to offer a way forward. This approach argues that, in making choices between goods, individuals reveal their marginal valuations of each. Although unlabelled, the approach has already appeared in this volume – for example, underpinning the notion of 'consumer surplus' in Box 7.1. It is tempting to conclude that consumer surpluses can be aggregated to produce a measure of total utility – or a SWF.

Economic evaluation, when it uses 'willingness to pay' measures, or seeks equivalents to perfect market prices, adopts this approach – but in doing so, as in the case of the Paretian SWF, it has ignored issues of income distribution and the underlying problem of inter-personal comparison of utility. Proposals to 'weight' the results according to income level cannot be derived from the underlying rationale of 'revealed preference' on which the SWF is based. They can only effectively be arbitrary judgments of how 'society' might want to re-weight those preferences.

Some argue that the attempt to derive the SWF from the aggregation of individual welfares is misguided. Social welfare is more than the sum of its parts. A 'communitarian' approach claims the existence of an explicit or implicit 'social contract' and a community-based notion of the common good (for example, see Reich 1995). This notion provides a standard by which to order alternative states of the world.

In contrast a Marxist approach rejects the existence of a unique SWF. Stewart (1975), for example, argues that individuals do not just differ in their tastes but in their interests, which are embedded in class. These cannot be reconciled, averaged or substituted: 'To select projects in such a way that net benefits are maximised is meaningless until we have defined whose benefits we are talking about.'

A society may wish to be more specific in valuing different health profiles. For example, we may wish to impose the condition that particular gains to any individual will be considered of equal value. In this case we are saying that for the purposes of analysis we assume that the utility of an additional year of life, or of a year of good eyesight, or of a year without pain from angina, are given the same value, regardless of who is the individual. In this case, for any category of treatment or care, we would maximise welfare by maximising the health gain (measured as years gained, years of good sight, etc.).

In principle there is no reason to choose any particular social welfare function. Some people argue for equal access to care regardless of, for example, age. In effect they argue that the welfare gain depends only on how many treatments were provided for people who have any treatable problem. There is an obvious disadvantage in specifying social welfare in this way. A procedure to remove a cataract would produce ten more years of good eyesight in an average seventy-year-old than in an average eighty-year-old. By taking age into account in setting priorities, assuming all other factors are the same, we increase the output if it is specified in terms of years of enjoyment of the improvement. At least in extreme cases we would normally find this argument compelling. Most people would choose twenty years of extended life in preference to twenty days, or ten years of better eyesight over ten days. It is common for the measurement of benefits to take account of duration of effect but to assume that any given benefit is of equal value regardless of who is receiving it. Thus it is not age *per se* that is being used as a criterion, but rather duration of benefit, which is likely to be associated with age in the treatment of non-life-threatening conditions.

A liberal 'Rawlsian' approach suggests that only improvement in the welfare of the member with the worst starting position constitutes an increase in the SWF. This also implies the ability to make inter-personal comparisons. This philosophy might be judged to underpin Robert Chambers's approach to decision making in rural development projects of '*Putting the last first*' (Chambers 1983).

9.4 Limits to welfare economics: the extra-welfarist approach

This brief discussion of the framework of theoretical welfare economics has demonstrated that Paretian welfare economics can provide a theoretical framework for economic evaluation, but also that there are problems in deriving clear rules from this framework. To many economists it is absurd to agonise over the application of a framework that in any case offers limited guidance for many real-world decisions and for judging the merits of different choices. In many countries there is a clear consensus in favour of policies and changes that have winners and losers, and it may be more fruitful to spend time eliciting values in the population that can then set the rules for economic evaluation.

Dissatisfaction with conventional welfare economics has led some leading researchers to reject Paretian ideas as a basis for economic evaluation. The main drive to develop alternative frameworks is normally associated with Amartya Sen (Sen 1979). Culyer and others (e.g. Culyer 1989) have vigorously promoted these alternative 'extra-welfarist' ideas and approaches in application to health.

Some important implications follow from a move away from a welfarist basis for economic evaluation. Culyer argues that the objective to be maximised should be health rather than utility. Instead of attempting to devise measures of changes in utility, we have the (slightly simpler) task of measuring changes in health. He proposed the use of quality-adjusted life years as the measure of health. On the face of it this may not seem very different from taking a welfarist approach – many welfarists would also advocate this measure of outcome. In practice, many of the problems associated with utility and revealed preference (see Box 9.6) remain unsolved. The debate around the question of age (see above) has many dimensions in common with the debate around income weights in relation to revealed preference-based measurements. Nevertheless, without the constraints of attempts to remain within a welfare economics framework a wider range of information might be considered to be legitimate. Hurley (1998) offers a useful discussion of the similarities and differences between welfarist and extra-welfarist approaches, and how these may be important in application to economic evaluation in the health sector.

Existing guidance on the application of economic evaluation has always emphasised strongly the importance of making assumptions and judgments explicit, and this is stressed strongly in the development of extra-welfarists' approaches. For example, we may wish to give higher weighting to benefits to women with children, or to people who have uniquely valuable skills. A case can be made for favouring workers over non-workers or, as happens in many countries, those who have been injured in the service of their country. It is perhaps poignant that both the United States and Vietnam give special access to health care to former soldiers. This can be interpreted as saying that benefits should be allocated partly on the basis of former contributions to national defence. There is nothing necessarily right or wrong in such judgments, but it is important to know what they are if we are to make sense of the results of any analysis. For example, in assessing antenatal screening programmes it is important to know whether termination of pregnancy is thought of as a legitimate clinical intervention or is considered to be murder. The same framework can be applied, but the criteria for assessing benefits would be very different.

Economists often assert that the two important dimensions of health care outcomes are length of life and quality of life. But many people would argue that there are other important issues, such as previous behaviour, previous suffering or religious belief. So long as the judgements are clear and explicit, they can be included in the analysis, and any recommendations can be shown to depend on these values.

It can be argued that the practice of economic evaluation is not significantly affected by whether its justification is derived from the body of theory in Paretian welfare economics or is based on a set of values and criteria taken from outside that framework. However, the interpretation of the results, and the acceptability of some criteria, may depend on the approach taken. Theoretical debates are not best resolved by voting or numbers. However, it is probably the case that the majority of health economists believe that economic evaluation has its foundations in Paretian welfare economics, and that this offers a justification for the measurement of cost and benefits. It can be helpful to understand how much and how little we can say on the basis of Paretian principles, since it helps in interpretation of the results of any evaluation.

9.5 Time value of money and discounting

The discussion on the theory that supports economic evaluation has focused on choices between individuals and between services. Another important dimension is time. It is widely asserted that the value of a cost or benefit is not the same if it occurs at different times, and we need therefore to take this into account.

Try an experiment with your colleagues. Ask one of them to buy you a bicycle now. In exchange, in twenty years' time you will give that person a bicycle of the same quality. It is unlikely that anyone will agree to this (apparently fair) deal, and it is interesting to think why. Several factors may come into play. First, your colleague (or indeed you) may not be around in twenty years, and she may not be fit enough to cycle. She may refuse because she expects to be richer in twenty years' time, and would therefore prefer to borrow from you. She may just prefer to have things now to getting them later. The exact reasons for refusing this offer may be complex, but the general preference for now rather than later is found in all countries.

Given that we give a different value to goods and service today or in the future, we cannot add up costs and benefits that occur at different points in time *without adjusting them to take into account this time value of money*.

9.6 Interest rates, time preferences and discount rates

The time value of money is reflected in the existence of positive interest rates. When borrowing money we have to pay back the original sum, and also pay interest to compensate the lender for having to wait for the use of the money. Interest rates may vary depending also on other factors, such as risk. Looking at the level of interest rates over time, there is tendency for rates in real terms (i.e. after allowing for any inflation) to be around 3–4 per cent for low-risk loans.

If we know the interest rate (say 5 per cent) we can make comparisons of sums of money in different periods. €100 today would be worth €105 in one year and around €128 in five years. The important point is that these different sums of money have the same value at the start. We can show this more formally, that the value of €1 after n years at y per cent interest is

$$€ (1+y/100)^n$$

Normally we replace the description of interest in percentage terms with the equivalent decimal, so that 10 per cent is 0.1. We can then write the formula as

$$€ (1+r)^n$$

where r is the interest rate expressed as a decimal.

This is just the working of compound interest. We can easily reverse the process. The value today of €100 five years' time is €100/128, which is just over €78. So we can say that the present value of €1 in n years' time at interest r is

$$€1/(1+r)^n$$

Box 9.7 illustrates five different ways of financing a new vehicle.

In economic evaluation some costs or benefits often occur at the same level for several years. Instead of calculating the present value for each year, we can use an annuity factor, which is just the sum of the different present values. The present value of €1 per year for N years, starting next year, is calculated as

$$PV = \sum_{n=1}^{N} 1/(1+r)^n$$

This is also known as the annuity factor for N years at interest r.

Tables of values of discount rates are available, and it is easy to set up programmes on a computer to calculate present values. In economic evaluation we must identify the year in which costs or benefits fall, and then discount to ensure that all sums are in present value. It is sometimes also convenient to calculate the cost of a project in terms of *annual equivalent cost*. The best way to think about this is to consider it as the rent that would be charged by an efficient not-for-profit supplier. A present-value sum can be converted into an annual equivalent cost by dividing by the annuity factor.

9.7 Choice of discount rates for costs and benefits

Discounting of costs and benefits aims to make them comparable over different years. There has been some controversy as to whether it is appropriate to discount all costs

Box 9.7   Five ways of paying for a vehicle: an illustration of the time value of money

The effects of interest payments and discounting can be seen clearly in the decision about how to finance a new vehicle. If a new van costs €10,000 we can in principle pay for it in at least five ways. First, we can simply pay today, and the funds paid will be €10,000. Four other options have very different 'headline' prices. In all these examples the interest rate is taken to be 10 per cent.

The first option is to set aside funds ten years before the purchase, and allow them to accumulate. At 10 per cent we would need to set aside €3,855.

The second option is to save a certain amount each year for ten years, allowing interest to accumulate on the saved amount and the van to be bought at the end. In that case we would need to save €570 per year (a total of €5,700).

The third option is to pay in instalments over ten years after the purchase. In that case the amount payable per year would be €1,627 (a total of €16,270).

Finally, in the fourth option we might agree to pay ten years from now, and we would be charged €25,937.

What is important to note is that in an important sense all these sums of money have the same value – in all cases they describe the cost of a new van to be delivered today. However, in terms of the number of euros paid, there is a difference of over €22,000. When interest has to be paid, or when it is received on balances held, it matters significantly *when* the money is paid over.

and benefits (Parsonage and Neuberger 1992; Cairns 1992). Part of the concern comes from the fact that discounting of health benefits can produce some surprising results. The discounted value of benefits in fifty years' time can be almost zero, which means that many health promotion interventions seem very poor value. For example, if we discount benefits in year 50 at 5 per cent, the value is reduced by about 90 per cent. It is interesting to consider why we accept the principle of time value of money but do not always feel comfortable with the results of it.

Economic theory would suggest that, in equilibrium, we would adjust our lending and borrowing so as to have the optimal flow over time of costs and benefits (within the constraint of our wealth and income). This implies that at any given interest rate we choose how much to save and how much to borrow. Since interest rates are positive, over a lifetime we consume more if we consume later. It has been observed that our behaviour is not always consistent with discounting costs and benefits at the same rate. We may have a different view of discounting benefits in terms of better health and less pain than we do of a need to pay money at different times.

There are several reasons why we may not be consistent (in addition to the possibility that we are just stupid). Markets, which deal with rights over time, are often distorted in various ways, and may therefore not be in equilibrium. Also it is possible that we do not treat benefits in different years as independent events. A schoolchild may enjoy the prospect of a long summer holiday and the apparently infinite period of happiness before returning to the drudgery of schoolwork. This is in some ways separate from the actual enjoyment of each week of holiday. Similarly, we may get reassurance and pleasure now from the knowledge that we are likely to have a healthy old age, or that we will receive palliative care if close to death, or that we are protected from the risk of hepatitis and its effects. In a technical sense, what seems to be happening is that the individual's utility in the current year is affected by the expected utility in future years, and that knowledge about future events and health influences the quality of life today. In the simple formulations of outputs of health services the benefits of an intervention change quality of life in particular years, and these gains are summed to derive the overall benefit. In principle there is no reason why we should not take into account effects of knowledge about future health states on utility – it just is not normally done. There is a need for more work to gain a better understanding of the effects of knowledge and anticipation on the utility gains from health interventions. There is a fairly clear consensus that both costs and benefits should be discounted in economic evaluation, and that the discounting should be at a common rate.

There is less consensus about the rate that should be used to discount costs and benefits. In principle the rate chosen should reflect the social opportunity cost. In a well functioning capital market that will be the same as the rate of interest for low-risk borrowing. In most countries it would be around 3–5 per cent. Many countries specify the discount rate to be used in public or quasi-public economic evaluation. For example, in the UK the recommended rate was for many years 5 per cent, and was increased to 6 per cent. The World Bank has generally used a higher rate. In order to ensure some consistency in the reporting of economic evaluations, the guidelines in the *Journal of the American Medical Association* recommend reporting results with costs and benefits discounted at 3 per cent as well as any other (nationally recommended) rate. The effect of using a higher rate is to give relatively little weight to costs and benefits in the distant future, so it can significantly affect the choices made.

9.8 Do these theoretical disputes undermine economic evaluation?

In judging the merits of the different possible theoretical bases for economic evaluation, it is worth distinguishing between unresolved debates about theory, and proceeding without a theoretical basis. All good science is based on clear and explicit theory. For example, most clinical research (and almost all good clinical research) draws heavily on statistical theory, and theoretical models of biological processes, which are crucial to understanding disease processes. These theoretical frameworks are not true in any absolute sense, any more than quantum physics or postmodernism is true, but they provide useful frameworks for understanding the problems and designing the empirical work. In a similar way, it is important that economic evaluation is carried out and interpreted within clear and explicit theoretical frameworks, which guide the conduct of the research, and assist in its interpretation. The existence of disputes over the theoretical basis of economic evaluation is similar to disputes between classical and Bayesian statisticians. The position adopted by the analyst may affect in detail how the evaluation is carried out and interpreted, but adherents of the different schools of thought can accept the legitimacy of the alternative approaches.

An understanding of the theoretical issues can be useful in understanding what the results of economic evaluation mean, and the extent to which there remains a need for policy judgments to be made. Since we have no absolute basis for making interpersonal comparisons of welfare, it can be quite legitimate to specify some groups for whom benefits should be more heavily weighted. In this sense economic evaluation provides guidance to decision makers but does not remove the need for interpretation and judgment. However, economic evaluation should not be seen as just another argument to feed into the decision-making process. The reason is that the evaluation attempts to assemble all (or at least most) of the relevant information. If we are not careful, some arguments will be counted twice. If the cost–effectiveness ratio already includes a valuation of a benefit this same benefit should not be counted again when decision-makers are making political judgements.

Consideration of the difficulty of agreeing a clear theoretical framework for economic evaluation reminds us of how difficult the choices really are. It is unusual for any development or change to have no losers. Careful thought needs to be given to the losers and the losses. Is it likely that the overall benefits outweigh them? It is common for there to be groups whose needs will not be met, and we need to be confident that we have done our best to prioritise services that will yield the greatest benefit. The fact that the theoretical issues are difficult is not a reason to run away from them.

10 Issues in the measurement of costs

10.1 How should costs be measured?

There are really only two practical problems in economic evaluation – measuring costs and measuring benefits. Superficially, measuring costs appears to be easier than measuring benefits. In almost all organisations there are some attempts to measure costs, if only for the purposes of financial control and accountability. But measuring costs accurately is often very difficult, and there are important conceptual and practical problems to overcome.

All good students of economics know that cost is the opportunity forgone, and in economic evaluation the aim is to measure opportunity cost (see Chapter 5). While it is not usual practice to seek to identify a specific opportunity forgone and its value, if markets function well, input prices reflect the value of their next best use. However, an economic evaluation will adjust prices where specific market failures are identified (see Chapter 8). For example, where there are externalities, an economic evaluation will seek to measure those costs that are not internalised in the transaction, and where there are price distortions resulting from controls, monopolist or monopsonist influence on the market, an economic evaluation will seek to find the shadow price – the one that would prevail in the absence of those distortions.

This implies that cost estimates produced for economic evaluation may not be applicable to some other purposes. For example, if a health service manager is interested in the financial implications of the introduction of a new service, or even the maximum effect (in health or welfare terms) achievable for a given expenditure by the health service, a modified analysis of this would need to be carried out.

The justification for the choice of opportunity cost is that it takes into account the costs of all members of society, as they impinge on the social welfare function (see Chapter 9), and so is consistent with the attempt to measure benefits in the same way. Alternative conceptions of cost, which are not consistent with benefit measurement, can lead to illogical conclusions. Box 10.1 provides some examples. Nevertheless, if we believe that health services are 'under-funded' relative to other parts of the economy (see Chapter 21 for further discussion of this idea), we might mean that money in health service hands has a higher value than elsewhere. This would justify a lower estimate of costs, since the losses in welfare from reduced spending elsewhere in the economy would be lower. Before making this tempting judgement, it is worth bearing in mind that 'under-funding' is hard to demonstrate and that Box 10.1 contains a powerful argument for consistent treatment of costs and benefits. On that basis, this chapter will largely focus on opportunity cost-based

Box 10.1 Opportunity costs or health service costs?

Suppose we are interested in maximising the health effects achievable from the health service budget. This implies that we are not interested in costs to patients, or in adjusting financial costs to reflect underlying social costs. We are interested in whether or not AIDS treatment is better carried out in patients' homes or in hospitals and we discover that the matrix of costs and benefits applies.

Costs and benefits of home-based versus hospital-based AIDS treatment (000 pesos per patient month)

Cost or benefit	Home-based care	Hospital-based care
Cost to the health service	10,000	10,000
Cost to patients	5,000	8,000
Value of health benefits to patients	18,000	20,000

The analyst who ignores patient costs will conclude that hospital-based care is producing health benefits from the health service budget more efficiently than home-based care. This is concluded on the basis that, although costs to the health service are the same, patient benefits are higher under hospital-based care. However, not only is hospital-based care less efficient from a societal perspective than home-based care, but patients' net benefits are lower (12 million pesos compared with 13 million pesos). This means that despite better health effects from the hospital-based programme, patients would prefer the home-based one – they would choose to sacrifice the marginal health effect to avoid the costs associated with a hospital stay. It should be remembered that these might be extreme, perhaps involving inability to work and support a family.

Furthermore, considering costs and benefits inconsistently can sometimes produce an analysis that can be interpreted in multiple ways, undermining the objective stance that is the goal of the approach. For example, immunisation imposes financial costs on the health service. In rare cases, it also imposes serious health costs on patients. If we treat these as costs in this framework, we will ignore them – the only costs we are interested in are financial costs to the health service. If we treat them as a reduction in health benefits, they will be included. Clearly, it is possible that the results of our evaluation will be affected by which we do. Most would argue in this case for accounting for these effects as reductions in benefit. But if we include these patient costs in our analysis, what about other possible patient costs? Milder but more common immunisation side effects? The burden on home carers and the associated stress? The financial losses associated with a long absence from work, which may have implications for a family's health status? It becomes clear that what is apparently a simple framework is prone to serious problems. Drawing a line between health and non-health effects is not straightforward. Justifying why only those items on one side of the line should count is even less so.

Adjusting financial costs for social costs has the same logic as including patient

> costs. We are trying to enquire after the impact on the whole of society, not just a particular budget. The potentially illogical results of trying to avoid this step are equivalent.

analysis, but will make occasional points relevant to a greater focus on health service costs.

To measure opportunity cost, we need to know the context in which choices are made. Good costing exercises start from a clear understanding of how current or potential services operate, what resources are used solely for particular groups of patients, which are shared, and how the staff actually spend their time. For example, in one study that was assessing the cost of a long-stay mental health facility, it was found that the staff actually spent most of their time caring for a small group of patients with the most serious problems. This meant that very little direct support was provided for the majority of residents. The actual use of the staff resources, and therefore the way in which costs varied between different groups of residents, would not have been observed if costs had been calculated only from accounting data. It is likely that costs would have been assessed as being the same for all residents in the facility.

A good understanding of current provision can also help to identify whether there is any spare capacity, which might allow the service to be expanded at low cost. It can be important to assemble information about technology and organisational structure at different scales of provision. It is hard to assess the costs of new developments accurately without quite detailed knowledge of the technology, management and human skills needed.

Some costs are fixed, some can be changed but only slowly. Some elements of cost can be easily observed and are obviously related to a particular activity, but others, especially buildings and land, senior staff, equipment and administration, may not vary directly with the level of activity, and it may be difficult to apportion these costs.

The simplest approach to calculating costs lists all the inputs into a service, multiplies each by the unit cost, and thereby calculates total cost. This can present an accurate account of the direct costs of a particular service, although overhead costs may be hard to apportion. A drawback of this approach is that it does not demonstrate clearly how costs are likely to behave in the event of changes in scale, case mix or technology. There is therefore an argument for trying to estimate cost functions from information on costs and outputs in a larger number of service providers (see Chapter 5). These data are analysed using statistical methods to identify how costs vary with the level and mix of output, and to identify the factors that affect costs.

It is quite common for costing exercises to use a mixture of approaches, since there are usually constraints on access to appropriate data. In some studies a cost–function approach is used to calculate the unit costs to be applied to activity data.

Costing is not a simple technical exercise – it is too important to leave to accountants alone. Understanding the services provided as well as the financial data and analysis is important. Some examples may help. Many health interventions exhibit economies of scale, so that increasing the output may allow a lower-cost service to be developed. In these circumstances the average cost based on current services will overestimate the costs of expansion. Most emergency services exhibit economies of scale due to the possibility of using the capacity more intensively. An example is neonatal care (O'Neill *et al.* 2000). Since the need for such services is inherently unpredictable, most centres aim to keep at least one cot free at any time. The proportion of empty cots is therefore lower when there are fewer, larger centres. In cases like these it would be very misleading to cost services at the average if changes in the scale of provision were being contemplated. Other services are less likely to show significant scale economies, such as palliative care for people dying of cancer, and many parts of primary and secondary care. In such examples, the advantages of centralisation are often balanced by the disadvantages to patients of greater geographical distance between home and facility.

It may take time to adapt to higher levels of output, so scale economies may not be realised instantly. The technology used may be lumpy (e.g. bits of equipment come only in certain sizes, so that expansion beyond a certain threshold requires a large additional investment). New approaches to the provision of certain services may involve a large change in the scale of provision.

Tradition plays a large part in how services are organised. Many patterns of care owe more to historical accident than careful and rational planning. This means that it is important to understand what inputs are really necessary. For example, immunisation schedules may be rationalised, grouping a number of vaccines within a single administered dose. Among the reasons for doing this might be a more efficient use of staff time, but it is unlikely that staffing levels of an immunisation programme will be immediately adjusted. After some time, it might be apparent that there is a little more slack in the immunisation programme than in another programme, and staff might be reallocated.

There are several reasons why costs of care for different patients may vary. First, there may be characteristics of the patient that lead to longer hospital stays or more interventions, and therefore higher costs. Second, hospitals may use different technologies for some services, and this can lead to variation in cost. For example, local hospitals in rural areas may not have specialised equipment, and may therefore have to use more labour-intensive techniques. This may be sensible given the small caseload for such services, but for a particular patient the unit cost may be higher than in a hospital using a different technology. Third, the providers may have different levels of X-efficiency, and so any given service will have a different unit cost. For example, there may be more staff employed than is necessary to provide the services.

If we are seeking the opportunity cost, in principle we should be interested in identifying the lowest feasible cost of providing a given service. Differences that are explained by patient characteristics must be taken into account. It is less obvious how we should treat different clinical policies – normally they vary most where the evidence is weakest, and we often do not know if lower-cost practices reflect greater efficiency or lower quality. In principle the opportunity costs should not allow any X-inefficiency (technical inefficiency), so we should try to identify the cost in an efficient care provider.

Technically, cost that results from inefficiency is not a part of opportunity cost, since simply by using the resources efficiently it is possible to increase welfare – no opportunities need be forgone for the use of those resources. However, if we are convinced that it is impossible to eliminate X-inefficiency within a particular time scale, then it may be appropriate to include some element of inefficiency in the estimates of cost. What we are saying in this case is that in practice these are the minimum costs of providing the programme, in the short term at least.

Identifying the appropriate concept and measure of cost can be particularly difficult when economic evaluation is carried out as part of clinical trials and studies. Patients recruited into a study are normally heterogeneous, and some variation in costs is likely.

Normally they are not completely typical of patients who are likely to receive the treatment. Large trials normally recruit patients from many centres, and clinical policies and efficiency will affect the assessed cost. To assess the cost-effectiveness of a new intervention we need to calculate the costs for those patients likely to be provided with the service, in the ways and places they are likely to receive the service. It is important therefore to know how costs vary with such factors as age, sex, disease severity, co-morbidities, case mix and scale of provision. To do this properly we need large enough samples of patients for variations to be understood, and for it to be possible to calculate confidence intervals for the estimates of cost. Since little is currently understood about the patterns of costs and these factors, it is not yet easy to estimate *ex ante* the sample sizes needed for costing studies, but it is clear that in some cases the variations are large. There has been widespread criticism of the lack of data on confidence intervals in economic evaluation studies (Barber and Thompson 1998), and a range of methods is often applied to estimate these. Issues in estimation of confidence intervals are considered in section 10.2.

Ideally, costing studies calculate unit costs of services from a range of settings, but this is not always feasible. Where a range of different providers show very different unit costs, and these are not explained by characteristics of patients or effectiveness of treatment, there is an important question of which estimate should be used. Since opportunity cost is the objective, there is a case for choosing the lowest observed estimate of unit costs, as discussed above. However, differences in unit costs by institution may not only reflect differences in technical efficiency, as this perspective suggests. Since interventions are administered through a given infrastructure, there is a need to match the ideal infrastructure for this particular intervention and the ideal infrastructure for the health system as a whole. This intervention may be most efficiently delivered in medium-sized health centres, whereas others are most efficiently delivered in small or large ones. Additionally, health infrastructure as a whole has to balance technical efficiency questions from a health service perspective with patient access costs. Patterns of human settlement do not present standard problems capable of producing a single 'best' solution to health unit size.

On the assumption that the most important determinant of cost variation between units is technical efficiency, some costing studies use data envelopment analysis (DEA) or stochastic frontier techniques, which aim to show costs of the most efficient care providers (Vitaliano and Toren 1994; Rosko and Proenca 2005). Both these approaches aim to estimate cost functions in terms of the lowest observed costs rather than as the average of those observed. DEA is a non-parametric technique, and simply joins up the lowest cost observations to describe the function. Since there is likely to be measurement error there are advantages in using a method that takes this into account. Stochastic frontier analysis estimates the frontier accepting that points on this will be measured with error, so that some observed levels of efficiency may not in fact be achievable.

Using these techniques the relative efficiency of different hospitals can be estimated by comparing observed cost with the lowest observed cost for a comparable provider. A typical measure of relative efficiency is the ratio of the cost of a service to the cost of the lowest-cost observed service.

As with all statistical methods of estimating costs, the concern must be to ensure that differences in case mix and quality are properly controlled for, so that the lowest observed cost is genuinely an example of greater efficiency and not simply the result of easier cases or poor quality. With that proviso, there are many advantages in frontier methods to estimate cost. The estimate of cost is the lowest for a comparable provider and should therefore contain less X-inefficiency than the average provider. Thus the frontier estimate can be viewed as being closer to opportunity cost than the average unit cost for all providers. Of course, such techniques can only identify relative efficiency, since the comparison is with the most efficient observed provider, and not with one that is necessarily efficient in absolute terms.

The costs we are aiming to estimate will usually be associated with adding a new service, or expanding an existing service. Where we are expanding an existing service, whether increasing the level of activity within a unit, or expanding the service from one set of units to others, information derived from cost functions can be very helpful. When a cost function is estimated it can be used to identify costs at higher or lower levels of output, and with different mixes of cases. By comparing the costs at the present level of activity with the costs at the level after implementation of an expanded service, we can obtain estimates of additional (or incremental) cost. The incremental cost is a similar concept to marginal cost, but in this case the change in service volume may not be small.

Where we are adding a new service – which is not yet provided anywhere in the health system – existing cost data are probably not very useful, and we are likely to be evaluating experimental provision (as where the economic evaluation is attached to a clinical trial – see below), or building up a hypothetical picture of costs. Nevertheless, our interest is still in incremental cost. Whereas, when we are expanding an existing programme, economies of scale cause divergence between average and incremental cost, when we are introducing a new programme, economies of scope may cause this divergence (see Chapter 5).

In principle a focus on incremental cost is useful, since in assessing options we really want to compare differences in costs and benefits between options. When costs are estimated using measures of changes in activity and a vector of (average) unit costs, the estimated costs or savings are likely to be over- or underestimates of incremental cost. It is, of course, possible to make adjustments to the unit cost vector to reflect any economies of scale or scope, and therefore to derive estimates that are closer to incremental cost. If we know the change in output associated with a development, the incremental cost (calculated from a cost function or from a hypothetical model of a new activity) can be used in the cost vector in place of average cost.

There is continuing controversy about the best estimates of incremental costs. In the short run capital costs are not relevant to measuring incremental costs, since there will be no change in capital (and other fixed) costs. If the current service has excess capacity, there may be little or no need to invest in new facilities and equipment, and there may be no need for additional staff. Under these circumstances the incremental cost will only include consumables. However, in the long run all efficient services will adapt capacity to that which is most efficient. Changing the volume of a service will therefore mean that the fixed costs will change in the long run. For this reason, many economists argue that the correct basis for calculating incremental costs includes any changes in capital and other fixed costs. In many cases this means that the short-run average cost (which includes an allocation of fixed costs) is a better proxy for long-run incremental cost than the short-run incremental cost.

In circumstances of economies of scale and scope, divergence between average and marginal or incremental cost applies to the long term. For example, where the underlying cause is 'lumpy' investment requirements, or 'indivisibilities' (units of investment are large), there will be no long-term reconciliation between the two meas- ures of cost. In these circumstances, it is clearer that adjustments for incremental cost have to be made, although there is debate over the extent to which long-run economies of scale and scope exist.

When average cost is being used as an estimate of long-run incremental cost, it is important to check that the change in activity is unlikely to lead to a major change in the most efficient technology of provision. For example, if a new universal vaccination programme replaces a smaller selective one, the whole organisation of the service, and probably the equipment and staff in use, will change. Average costs are unlikely in these circumstances to be a useful basis for estimating the incremental costs of the additional services. In general, for small changes in the volume of a service it is safe to use short- run average cost as a proxy for long-run incremental cost unless the technology is such that there is spare capacity in the current provision, and the service can be efficiently expanded without additional investment.

10.2 Sources of variation in cost measures, confidence intervals and assessing sample sizes for costing

There are many reasons why costs vary for the same service in different locations, and some of these were discussed in section 10.1. There is a useful analogy here with the measurement of the effectiveness of different treatments in clinical trials and studies. The statistical principles for judging the comparative effectiveness of different interven- tions are widely accepted (if not completely uncontroversial). Before the start of a clinical trial there is a calculation of the sample that will be needed to give a particular probability of demonstrating a given difference of effect with a given level of statistical significance. Clearly this calculation is dependent on assumptions about the likely dis- tribution of effects, and this assumed variability in effect for any given treatment is one factor in determining the sample size needed. In the case of clinical trials it is normal for the basic unit to be the patient. In most studies patients are allocated to different treatments (using random allocation if feasible), and variations coming from different facilities or staff skills matter little, since in each site the patients are allocated at random. A problem arises in cases where randomisation has to be by hospital or district rather than by patient, since local facilities or skills may play important roles. There can be similar problems in assessing costs. Since costs for a particular patient depend on disease severity, co-morbidity, hospital size, location and efficiency, it is not clear whether we need a large sample of patients or hospitals in order to assess the range within which costs are likely to lie.

There is a growing understanding of the ways costs vary as a result of differences in patient characteristics. Many costing studies, particularly in clinical trials, calculate costs for each patient, and this gives data on the degree of variability. Such evidence can give a basis for the calculation of sample size that will allow costs for each category of patient to be assessed with reasonable reliability. When economic evaluation is being carried out alongside clinical trials or studies, this should be done. Some studies have shown that the distribution of service use is highly skewed in certain patient groups, especially in mental health and in cases where some patients receive treatment involving high-technology equipment (Gray *et al.* 1997).

It is usually desirable, but not always feasible, to assess unit costs of services from many different hospitals. In terms of interpreting the results of economic evaluation there are two reasons to be interested in understanding variation in cost between facilities. First, it may be that a particular service or intervention is cost-effective only if provided in a low-cost facility. Knowledge of the structure of costs can allow judgments to be made about where such developments should be located. A good example could be haemoglobinopathy screening. Given the large economies of scale in testing, the service is likely to be cost-effective only if testing can be centralised. Second, unless we know the variation in unit costs in different facilities, there is a risk that the assessment of cost-effectiveness reflects the chance that the evaluation was done at a lower rather than at a high-cost location. This is somewhat analogous to drawing conclusions about the efficacy of a new treatment from case reports or small studies.

There is increasing evidence to suggest that failure to assess costs in a wide range of settings can lead to misleading results (Grieve *et al.* 2005; Thompson *et al.* 2006). In particular there can be inaccurate estimates of the degree to which costs are varying due to differences between patients and differences between hospitals or centres. In the future it may be recognized that accurate estimation of costs requires many centres and appropriate multi level modelling to identify the real sources of variation.

If costs are assessed in only a few centres, it can be impossible to explore the range of likely costs using conventional statistical methods. It is still useful to present evidence of variation in unit costs, but confidence intervals for cost variation are possible only if it is possible to include in the study data from a large enough range of providers to allow the distribution to be analysed. We should remain interested in the consequences of any errors in estimates of cost, and we should try to ensure that strength of recommendations reflects our level of confidence in the estimates.

10.3 Using sensitivity analysis on costs

While it is desirable where possible to calculate mean costs and confidence intervals around the mean, since variability may be related to location of services, it is often impossible to do this. In these circumstances it is still desirable to explore the consequences of variation in costs. This is best done by sensitivity analysis. There are two ways in which sensitivity analysis can be used. First, a range of plausible assumptions can be tested out (such as ± 15 per cent), to see if this is likely to affect the conclusions of the analysis. If there is some basis for judging plausible levels of variation this is appropriate. An alternative is to start from the other end, and ask the question 'What size of variation in cost would be needed to change the conclusions?' If the conclusion remains the same with even quite large variations in cost, then this may be grounds for accepting the results as robust. This does not avoid the need for an estimate of what levels of variation are 'large', or unlikely to be encountered in the implementation of the changed or new programme.

10.4 Costing in economic evaluation

The normal approach to calculating costs in economic evaluation is to estimate the number of cost-generating events for each patient, and to multiply this matrix of different events for different patients by a vector of unit costs. As suggested above, this unit cost vector may be calculated using a range of methods, from accounting or budget data or estimates of cost functions. In many cases simple approaches have been considered to be adequate, and most studies do not take into account changes in costs with time or technical progress. It was argued at the start of this chapter that costing requires understanding of circumstance as well as technique. It may be quite acceptable to assume that costs for a particular service will remain stable over time. Equally, there are some instances in which such an assumption leads to serious errors. For example, for most surgery in industrialised countries, the length of hospital stay has fallen consistently, and this trend seems likely to continue and to be capable of exploitation in other countries. Failing to take this into account may lead to overestimates of the costs of surgical options in the future. New technologies may reduce in price over time, and may be the subject of learning, suggesting that health workers' skills may develop in such a way that they use the technology more efficiently. Patients and potential patients learn more about the service and how to use it, contributing to reduced costs. For example, a new technology such as the treatment of bed nets with insecticide to combat malaria may require aggressive marketing at first but rely on word of mouth later once its uptake has reached high levels. Costing studies should take all these factors into account.

Costing cannot be an exact science, but costs estimated using sensible approaches by people who are well informed about context are more likely to reflect the true forgone opportunities.

Box 10.2 Economic evaluation of renal services for older people (I)

You are in charge of policy on acute health service development for older people in your region. Recent press comment has been highly critical of the current policy of rationing access to certain renal services for older people. At present haemodialysis (HD) and peritoneal dialysis (PD) are available only to people who develop end-stage renal failure before the age of seventy-five. In order to make a better choice on what, if anything, to do about this situation you commission an economic evaluation. The stages of this evaluation are considered here in Chapter 10, and in Chapters 11–14.

Since this service exists only in other districts you have to use information from elsewhere to estimate costs. You have found three districts that provide a service for older people, but in two cases this is in the context of a trial of a new form of peritoneal dialysis.

What follows are extracts from the report by the economic evaluation team and questions you have raised for discussion with them. Brief responses from the consultants are also given.

Costs of dialysis were calculated on the basis of a detailed assessment of the use of resources by each patient in three dialysis services. Details of service use were collected from the hospitals providing the services, and from interviews with the patients to find out more about the use of services in other hospitals, and use of primary care and social care.

Question. I can see that the information from the dialysis centre is likely to be quite accurate, but what about data from patients? Can they really be relied upon to give accurate information about other services used?

Consultant. This is a good point. Studies have shown that patient recall can be quite accurate over a relatively short period – indeed, in this study we compared what patients said about their use of the hospital (where we also had information from medical records), and we found that there was close correlation between data from patients and data from the medical records.

Costs to patients, families and friends were also assessed. In principle costs were included regardless of who paid. In the case of the clinical trials, the makers provided some equipment free, but a cost was nevertheless included for this. As instructed we tried to assess the full opportunity cost.

Question. I don't quite understand this point – if the equipment is free then surely it is free!

Consultant. No. All resources have an opportunity cost. The fact that it is paid in this case by the equipment manufacturers makes no difference. The decision to develop a service should depend on the balance between opportunity cost and the benefits of the new service.

Once a full list of services used had been gathered the next step was to calculate unit costs. For equipment the unit cost was assessed by assessing the cost of new equipment, its likely useful life, and from this was imputed a rental equivalent cost (the annual equivalent cost). The assumption was made that equipment would be used to 90 per cent of its capacity, allowing for servicing and repairs.

Question. I can understand that to add up capital costs and running costs it is useful to treat equipment as if it were hired – this allows you to add capital costs and running costs all in terms of cost per year or cost per patient treated. I'm more worried about the assumption of 90 per cent use. Is that realistic?

Consultant. This is always difficult. My advice is always to work closely with professionals who actually understand using the equipment. In addition to needing to account for maintenance, there is also some variability in needs of patients. We got round this by doing a sensitivity analysis on the level of use – you'll remember, this appears later in the report.

It was decided to calculate the unit costs of dialysis from information from the three hospitals. Information on whole-time equivalent staff by grade was collected, taking account of the sharing of staff with other services. In one case we were able to compare staff costs before and after an expansion of the service, so it was possible to calculate the incremental cost of providing services for the additional patients. This gave a lower estimate than that from those hospitals that had no records of previous staffing levels. An attempt was also made to count only staff actually needed to provide the service, and to exclude those that are needed to support the research projects.

Question. What difference did you find between the three centres, and how do we know which is right?

Consultant. Ideally data on unit costs would be available from more centres, and it would then be possible to calculate costs using statistical methods. In this case we just had to use our judgement. One centre seemed more expensive, and it looks as if this was due to a long tradition of weak management and overstaffing, so we used staffing levels from the average of the other two. Not very scientific, perhaps! However, we did carry out a sensitivity analysis on the staffing costs. We were more concerned that one centre was much larger, and we expected to find lower staffing due to economies of scale, but there was no sign of that.

The pattern of costs differs greatly between haemodialysis and peritoneal dialysis. In the former case there is expensive capital equipment, but the consumable costs are relatively low. Staff costs for haemodialysis are also higher than for peritoneal dialysis, since peritoneal dialysis is mainly delivered at home by the patient and family. Family time off work was costed at the average national wage, but for non-working family members half of this was used. Peritoneal dialysis patients have high costs early in their dialysis as they were being prepared and trained. Prices (net of discounts) for consumables were used as a proxy for costs.

Question. This makes it likely that the choice of haemodialysis or peritoneal dialysis will be quite sensitive to wage levels and costs of consumables. Should we really make these decisions on cost grounds?

Consultant. See the comments later in the report. Yes, since the cost of consumables is so high for peritoneal dialysis it is likely that the choice will be sensitive to this and to wage costs. There is some evidence that consumables are priced so as to leave the overall cost of the two technologies the same.

Two important findings about costs emerged. First, dialysis patients are very low users of primary care services – perhaps not surprising, since they see doctors and nurses regularly. It was also found that patients requiring nursing home care cost nearly twice as much in total as those living at home. The full cost of their care has been included.

Question. Surely we should include only those costs directly related to dialysis and related treatment? People get primary care because they need it, and the same could be said of nursing home care.

Consultant. It is always difficult to decide the boundaries. In our view both these costs should be included. The benefit side of the equation is years of life (of whatever quality) gained. The full cost of this benefit is the overall cost of all services. The low cost of primary care means that the difference in cost between those with and those without renal failure is less than the cost of dialysis, but really we should be asking how much we get for how much. Some of these issues are taken up later in the report.

11 Measuring benefits in economic evaluation

11.1 The different types of economic evaluation

The practice of economic evaluation in health care takes a number of forms, and most of these are defined in terms of the ways in which benefits are measured. It is easy to be confused by the terminology used. Drummond *et al.* (2005) did their best to make things clear with detailed definitions of the hierarchy of types of evaluation from those comparing costs alone to full cost–benefit analysis, where all costs and benefits are measured in money terms. Several problems result from this attempt at standardisation. First, since practitioners normally ignore the suggested classification, terminology is normally used 'incorrectly'. For example, the *Journal of the American Medical Association* published guidelines for economic evaluation that use the term cost-effectiveness analysis for what the Drummond classification would describe as cost–utility analysis. Second, this approach may lead to a tendency to see the different ways of measuring benefits as being different types of analysis, when in reality they are variants on a theme. Benefit measurement is normally difficult and placing a value on benefit is very difficult. The choice of type of evaluation to use is normally made on the basis of how difficult it is to obtain data that will allow benefits to be measured or valued.

When benefits are traded in the market a value is put on them automatically, since the buyer must consider that they are worth at least what she paid. Sometimes it is possible indirectly to assess the value people place on benefits from their behaviour. For instance, even when they do not pay directly for a service, they may be willing to take time off work and travel, so there is a 'price' on the service. But often it is really not feasible to put any sensible money value on the outputs of health interventions. It may, however, be possible to compare them in some standard unit, such as years of healthy life gained or improvement in activity of daily living scores. Sometimes it is difficult even to find proxies for output or outcomes, and all that can be compared is the volume of services, but this type of measure is difficult to interpret.

The best way to think of the different economic evaluation techniques is as a spectrum, with cost–benefit analysis at one extreme, where benefits are valued, through cost–utility studies with benefits measured in some standard unit, to cost-effectiveness analysis, where outcomes are defined in natural units. If the outcome is assumed the same for all options, then the analysis simply seeks to identify the lowest-cost delivery of the service. The decision on what type of analysis to use may depend mainly on the resources available for the study. Assessing values and utilities is expensive and controversial, and many people prefer to leave the benefits in years of life gained or some specified improvement in health status.

It is a mistake to think of the different methods of economic evaluation as different approaches. Rather, they should be seen as variations in what is desirable and feasible. All methods have their logic in the cost–benefit approach, and the differences come mainly from the judgment about how best to assess benefits.

1   In *cost–benefit* analysis costs and benefits are assessed in money terms. This allows all types of service to be (in principle) compared, but it is often difficult to measure benefits in this way.
2   *Cost-utility* analysis adopts an index of benefit that is common across different types of service. The most commonly used is the quality-adjusted life year (QALY).
3   Where the units of outcome can be described and measured in natural units only, the approach is *cost-effectiveness* analysis. Outcomes may be measured as (for example) years of life gained, number of children immunised or days of palliative care.
4   *Cost-minimisation* analysis is appropriate if the outcome is the same for all options, and the question is simply: what is the lowest-cost way of achieving the outcome?

Rather than a free choice as to what technique to use, it is better to think of the problem as being: 'How constrained are we in the measurement of outputs?' Often the desirable analysis would use outcomes measured in money terms or utility scores, but the data that would allow this cannot be accessed. (Source: Drummond *et al.* 2005.)

11.2 Measuring and valuing outputs

Advocates of attempts to assess benefits in financial or utility measures stress that, without a standard and comparable system of measurement, it is difficult to compare outcomes of different types of intervention. For example, comparing probably life-extending interventions, such as dialysis or ORT, with (mainly) quality-of-life-improving ones, such as cataract surgery, normally involves comparison of outcomes that are in different dimensions. This makes people reluctant to make explicit comparisons. However, somehow the value of the different benefits must be compared if evaluation is to be used for setting priorities. This can be done as part of the political decision-making process, and many would argue that this is how it should be done (Carr-Hill 1991). However, it is also argued that it is much better to set in advance the way in which benefits will be compared (Williams 1991). As a society we might agree in advance on the relative value of, say, thirty additional years of life for one person and better vision for 300 people who will expect to live for another five years.

Specialists in quality-of-life measurement understand that there are many dimensions of quality, and some measurement instruments deliberately avoid having a single overall score. Even on the different domains (such as physical abilities, pain or psychological well-being) it is possible to argue against overall scores. For example, whether improved mobility is more or less important than continence depends in part on the lifestyle of the person involved. And attitudes to a given set of circumstances may not be stable over time. Tolerance of disability can increase with experience and adaptation. It is inevitable that any system that derives single-figure scores for complex effects will ignore important subtleties, and will destroy some important detail in the data. But no simple way exists for making comparisons of multiple dimensions.

Measures of quality of life can be designed to meet the needs of a particular patient group, or can attempt to be more generic. Disease or patient group-specific measures have the apparent advantage of deriving more detailed and sensitive data on those dimensions of health that are most affected by a particular disease. For example, instruments used in palliative care will emphasise pain control, and a range of objectives in terms of psychological and spiritual well-being. They are also likely to take into account the impact of an intervention on informal carers. Outcomes measured in this way have a lot of meaning in terms of the particular service, but are of little use in making comparisons between disparate services. In general there is a trade-off between using measures with meaning in a particular context and using ones that allow comparisons to be made. The ideal for comparisons is a single index number which can be applied to health gains of all types. Such an instrument is less sensitive for making detailed comparisons within a particular service. However, implicitly or explicitly, comparing a malaria control programme and cataract surgery involves judgments about their relative importance, and this may be helped by the use of a common system of measuring benefits.

Measuring benefits in money terms has particular attractions for decision making. There are two main advantages. First, since the same unit or measurement is used in all cases, all potential developments can be compared on the same basis. Second, it is in principle possible to make judgements not only on relative priority, but also on whether or not something is worth doing at all. On the basis of the 'potential Pareto improvement' rationale, if the costs exceed the benefits, a project should not go ahead, even if it is the best of the projects under consideration in the analysis.

11.3 Valuing benefits in money terms

The demand curve for any good or service is the schedule of willingness to pay. This can be interpreted as the self-assessed benefits to consumers (after all, you would not buy something if you did not value it at least at the price). At the margin, the last unit consumed will be valued by the consumer at what she had to pay for it (i.e. the benefit is equal to the price for the marginal user). Of course there are objections to using estimates of willingness to pay as measures of benefit, not least because willingness to pay is closely related to ability to pay. But in a well functioning market, for any given distribution of income, we can say that the willingness to pay represents the users' own measure of benefits.

A feature of most circumstances in which economic evaluation is used is that there is an element of market failure. Under these circumstances the benefit to the marginal user may not be equal to the price. For example, an element of a service may be in short supply relative to market willingness to pay, with the result that the marginal user may be rationed out, despite a willingness to pay the going price. Also, since consumers are not fully informed, their willingness to pay may not reflect their preferences fully. Observed prices for those who do pay for services may also be misleading as a guide to willingness to pay. Often only a small proportion of the provision of a service is traded, so that observed trading may be only by an unrepresentative sub-group in the population. In practice it is therefore seldom reliable to use information on prices paid for services to estimate willingness to pay (see Box 11.1).

An alternative to observing directly the willingness of individuals to pay for health care is to ask them how much hypothetically they would be willing to pay for treatment or for a defined improvement in health. There are many ways in which this can be done,

Box 11.1 Willingness to pay and measurement of benefits

The analysis of demand for health and health care in Chapter 2 showed that the quantity of a good demanded depends on price. In Box 7.1 we extended that concept to argue that consumers 'reveal their preferences' through the demand curve, and outlined the concept of consumer surplus. That concept relied on the idea in the diagram.

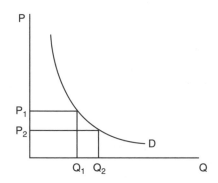

When the price is P_1, the individual chooses Q_1, This means that the person assessed that the benefit to herself of the last unit of consumption was exactly equal to the price P_1. The demand curve can be interpreted as a schedule of willingness to pay for individuals. To maximise their utility, each person equates the marginal willingness to pay to the additional cost of buying the service. If price falls to P_2 the individual will buy more, not because the willingness to pay has changed but because of additional units which are valued above P_2 but below P_1

Just as the individual should equate marginal willingness to pay (marginal benefit) to marginal cost to maximise her welfare, so too should a society with this objective equate willingness to pay for a service with the marginal cost.

and many studies have attempted to derive estimates. Although in principle information on people's declared willingness to pay is very valuable, there are several reasons for doubting if the estimates will be robust. First, it is difficult for people to detach themselves from existing institutional arrangements – if a service is currently available without charge to the user, she may say she is willing to pay nothing, since she believes she should get it free. Second, if the respondent knows that the information will be used to set priorities for service development, she has an incentive to overstate the willingness to pay and, if it is to be used to set fees, to understate it. As with other methods of assessing benefits, there is the problem that if the respondent needs the service she will naturally want the assessed willingness to pay to be high, and if she has no need it may be difficult to think about what would be the willingness to pay for treatment of a hypothetical need.

Willingness-to-pay calculations currently play only a small part in the practice of economic evaluation, but the inherent attraction of the approach keeps researchers interested in developing it (Olsen *et al.* 2005). There has been some recent interest in eliciting views on preferences using techniques from marketing and applied psychology, especially discrete choice modelling (Ryan *et al.* 2006). This approach can be interpreted as being based on the theoretical work of Kelvin Lancaster (1966), which suggested that demand for goods is a function of their characteristics. By observing a large number of choices between services with different characteristics (including price) we can potentially assess the value placed on each characteristic. Early evidence suggests this approach will have uses mainly in understanding better the value patients place on details of how services are delivered, but it may come to be used more widely in assessing willingness to pay.

11.4 Standardised measures of outcome and utility scores

If it is not feasible to measure benefits in money terms, it may still be possible to compare very different health gains related to treatment for different needs. If a common system of measuring outcomes can be used, then the costs and benefits of different interventions can be compared. This is the reason why attempts have been made to devise measures that combine the different dimensions of health gains into a single score. It allows comparison between the costs and health gains of different interventions, although it cannot directly help us to assess whether or not an intervention should be provided.

The economic theory of demand uses the concept of utility (see Chapter 2). Rational consumers spend their income so as to gain the maximum utility from it. The task is made more difficult by the fact that some benefits are uncertain. Spending on a health care intervention may or may not effect the desired health gain, and in some circumstances may actually lead to a deterioration in health status. This is common in other sectors, and there is a well established body of theory on the problems of choice in the face of uncertainty or risk.

The general expectation in economics is that a person's utility rises with consumption, but probably at a decreasing rate. In other words, as someone consumes more of a service her utility rises, but each subsequent unit of consumption has less and less impact on utility. This is known as 'diminishing marginal utility'. It is interesting to consider this against a number of possible measures of health gains. If we give equal value to a year of life gained, irrespective of by whom, and the circumstances of the recipient, then we are implicitly saying that the value of that gain in terms of utility is constant. More formally, the utility function of all individuals is identical, and is a linear function of the number of years lived. This conflicts with the usual expectation of diminishing marginal utility.

Further, to argue that years of life should be weighted according to their quality appears at first sight an uncontroversial technical improvement. For any individual, it is clear that a year of life at high quality is better than a year at low quality; any intervention which produces the first will be preferred to one which produces only the second. However, when applied as a means of determining priorities between individuals the proposal is more contentious. It implies, for example, that it is a lower priority to extend the life of a disabled person than it is a fully able-bodied person. This type of problem does not arise in most economic evaluations because the beneficiaries are anonymous at the time of evaluation. They can be assumed all to be in perfect physical condition other than with respect to the need under evaluation. However, where an intervention is specifically designed to extend the life of those suffering from a quality of life-affecting disability (for example, cystic fibrosis), the question cannot be avoided and requires an explicit judgement to be made. More generally, the issue arises with services for the elderly who are more likely to have coexisting pathologies and disabilities.

The commonly used measures of health gain in economic evaluation are the quality adjusted life year (QALY) and the disability adjusted life year (DALY). They both make some adjustment for the different circumstances of different individuals, but otherwise assume that gains are of equal value. There is no direct adjustment to account for diminishing marginal utility of health gains. In effect they assign equal value to measured improvements in health.

Interpreting the meaning of these measures is not straightforward. There is a fuller discussion below about the ways in which the adjustments are made to allow for diminished quality of life in these measures, but at this stage the interesting question is what a QALY means – how we interpret the unit we have constructed. If it is used as the basis for setting priorities, then implicitly the QALY score is used as if it is a measure of social welfare, and it is common for this to be the interpretation. We have already seen in Chapter 9 that the extra-welfarists reject this interpretation of the QALY and it can be argued that such measures are interpretable as utility or welfare only on some rather restrictive assumptions.

A simple illustration is the issue of risk. Since the effect of treatment for an individual is not known, what is being chosen is at best a known mean and distribution of gains, and is at worst uncertain (i.e. we do not know the mean and distribution of the likely gains). The degree of risk may significantly affect the attitude of people to a likely but risky gain. In principle it is possible to derive QALYs that are adjusted for risk aversion, and to allow for diminishing marginal utility of health status improvement, but this is complex and costly. In most cases the data simply do not exist to do it. The important point to bear in mind is that an increase in the number of QALYs can be interpreted unambiguously as a welfare gain only if we know the relationship between health status, risk, distribution of gains and social welfare. Attempts to negotiate the problems of interpreting QALYs and to remain more closely rooted in utility theory have generated a continuing debate.

The debate about the meaning and interpretation of QALYs is important, especially when they are used to inform important priority setting issues. There are also important practical issues in how the weighting of years for quality of life is best done. Some hypothetical questions are easier to answer than others. If people are asked to choose which they would prefer, a longer spell in a state of diminished health or a shorter one in good health, then most could answer. This allows at least an ordinal ranking to be derived.

11.5 Measuring health gains and utilities

Tools for measuring health gains and utilities attempt to take into account the size of potential benefits, the likelihood that benefits will be realised and when they will occur. In economics it is normally assumed that consumers maximise utility. In a world of certainty this is relatively straightforward, but when faced with risky alternatives (as will always be the case in health interventions) it is more complicated. If the distribution of possible outcomes is known, then the patient can maximise expected utility. However, other strategies may be adopted when outcomes are genuinely uncertain (such as adopting a maximin strategy, where the person takes steps to ensure that the worst conceivable outcome is as good as possible).

There is much debate about the extent to which the different approaches to measuring health gains do or do not represent maximisation of expected utility in the sense of the formal Neumann–Morgenstern formulation. Von Neumann and Morgenstern's proposition is:

> Consider three events, C, A, B, for which the order of the individual's preferences is the one stated. Let α be a real number between 0 and 1 such that A is exactly equally desirable with the combined event consisting of a chance of probability $1-a$ for B and the remaining chance of α for C. Then we suggest the use of α as a numerical estimate for the ratio of the preference of A over B to that of C over B.
>
> (Neumann and Morgenstern 1947)

QALYs and 'healthy years equivalents' (HYEs) are both attempts to measure outcomes that reflect the benefits of longer life and better quality of life, but proponents of the HYE approach claim the two-stage procedure proposed for HYEs gets closer to being a representation of expected utility maximisation (Gafni and Birch 1997). Several contributors to the debate have demonstrated that under certain conditions the two measures can be shown to be identical (Morrison 1997).

Various methods are used to combine length of life and health-related quality of life to form health gain or utility scores. In some cases a combination of methods is used, first to describe the different outcomes in more generic ways, and then to value these. For example, we can describe the outcome of cataract surgery in terms of visual acuity or in terms of months of ability to undertake certain tasks. The latter has the effect that it is easier to compare this to benefits from quite different interventions, such as accident prevention or supply of hearing aids. The trade-offs between greater complexity with more sensitivity, and simplicity with less power to discriminate, was discussed above (section 11.2). Box 11.2 shows the classifications of one of the simplest systems, the EUROQOL EQ-5D. Users of this instrument convert different states of health into scores on these five dimensions, and then apply weights for these different combinations that have been derived separately.

Deriving a weight for quality of life can be done in several ways. One is to ask people directly to assess the value of a year in a state of diminished health. Another is to use visual analogue scales, where people are asked to rate their quality of life by choosing a point on a scale that most nearly describes how they feel about their health. A general problem that always occurs in these situations is interpreting what people really understand by the different points on a scale. However, it does at least provide an ordinal ranking of health states.

Economists have often argued for the use of the standard gamble technique to value health states, mainly in the belief that it comes closest to applying Neumann–Morgenstern expected utility theory. The method is conceptually simple. A given health state which will persist for t years is compared with a gamble between perfect health for t years and certain death. The perfect health occurs with a probability p, and death with a probability (1 – p). The experiment is to vary the values of p until the person is indifferent between the health state and the gamble. The value of the probability is the measure of how the health state is valued as compared with perfect health.

Box 11.2 Economic evaluation of renal services for older people (II)

For the first part of this case study see Box 10.2

EUROQOL EQ-5D

This is one of the simpler systems of classifying health states, and is intended mainly to be used as a standard instrument alongside other measures. Combinations of the five dimensions have been valued, using a number of methods. The health states are defined not in terms of a single score, but rather as the different combinations.

Mobility

1   No problem with walking.
2   Some problem walking about.
3   Confined to bed.

Self-care

1   No problem with self-care.
2   Some problems washing or dressing self.
3   Unable to wash or dress self.

Usual activities

1   No problems with performing usual activities (e.g. work, study, housework, family or leisure activities).
2   Some problems with performing usual activities.
3   Unable to perform usual activities.

Pain/discomfort

1   No pain or discomfort.
2   Moderate pain or discomfort.
3   Extreme pain or discomfort.

Anxiety/depression

1   Not anxious or depressed.
2   Moderately anxious or depressed.
3   Extremely anxious or depressed.

Attempts to derive weights for the different combinations have come both from population surveys and from the use of a visual analogue scale for self-reported quality of life alongside the five dimensions. Time trade-off has been used to rate the different profiles.

   If we wish to rate the change from cataract surgery we might find changes in mobility, self-care, usual activities and possibly anxiety and depression. For example, the profile might change from 22212 to 11111. This might improve the quality of life from say 0.8 to 1.0.

In practice it is not always straightforward to carry out standard gamble experiments, since it is not easy for people to understand and think in terms of probabilities. In addition to coming closest to applying Neumann–Morgenstern expected utility theory, the standard gamble approach has been argued to introduce risk into the evaluation, since the comparison is made between certain and uncertain outcomes.

There have been several attempts to derive quality-of-life weights for use in economic evaluation from health status measured using generic instruments such as SF36 (Brazier *et al.* 1998). SF36 is a commonly used questionnaire that assesses both physical and psychological dimensions of health-related quality of life. It has thirty-six questions, and was developed from the longer Medical Outcomes Study quality-of-life measure (Ware and Sherbourne 1992). It has the advantage that it has been used in many different circumstances, and benchmarking data are available for many diseases. Most such tools are designed to rank health states, but not normally to produce a cardinal score. However, since health states can be ranked, it is then possible to ask people to place a value on each. In most cases the aim is to place health status and the related quality of life on a scale running from 0 for death to 1 representing full health-related quality of life. The advantage of this approach is that these instruments are widely used, and thus comparison with other evaluations may be possible (if other features of the two evaluations are sufficiently similar).

Time trade-off approaches ask a person to indicate indifference between longer periods in poorer health and shorter ones in full health. For example, I might put the same value on four years of life in full health and eight years with severe pain. In doing this I would be saying that the value of a year with severe pain was approximately half that of a year of full-quality life. An advantage of such approaches is that the questions asked directly address the relationship between the two main objectives of most health interventions – to extend life and to improve its quality. Standard gamble approaches have the advantage that they also put the decision about trade-offs into the context of the riskiness associated with different patterns of interventions. Respondents are asked to choose between different combinations of likely outcomes and the risk associated with these.

Of course it is possible to argue endlessly about what is meant by full quality of life, especially as many aspects of health status are affected by ageing. It is also possible to argue that factors other than health status are important, since some people are unable to convert healthy life into good quality of life. However, it is normal to consider quality of life in the context of what health status a reasonably fit person of that age might hope for, and to ignore all aspects of quality of life that are not caused by illness and/or modified by treatment and care.

Although many advocates of QALYs question whether they really measure utility, their use tends to imply this is the case. An alternative interpretation is that the QALY is simply a standard measure of outcome that can usefully be used to compare different interventions with very different types of effect. On this interpretation its use to guide decision making is to provide quasi-objective information about the patterns of outcomes and their impact, but not necessarily to provide a basis for recommending particular priorities.

The disability-adjusted life year (DALY) is a more modest attempt to weight years for quality, where the main adjustment is for the effects of illness on disability (see Box 11.3). DALYs have been widely used in assessing the global burden of diseases and in identifying priorities in low and middle-income countries. Different diseases were

Box 11.3 The composition of a DALY

The Disability-adjusted Life Year (DALY) is used in two ways – to calculate the 'global burden of disease' by estimating the extent to which disease causes loss of life and disability in geographically defined populations; and as a generic measure for use in cost-effectiveness analyses. The measure combines an estimate of the duration of time lost due to premature death, a weight representing the social value of time lived at different ages, a weight for disability and a discount rate. Treating all these components together, the DALY formula is complex, but it consists of a series of relatively simple stages:

1   The duration of time lost owing to premature death is calculated using the 'standard expected years of life lost'. This uses a standard mortality table approximating life expectancy in rich Western economies which produces a life expectancy for each age cohort. Deaths in each age cohort are deemed responsible for the loss of this amount of life expectancy. Mortality tables associated with rich Western economies are deemed appropriate for all countries because they are argued to measure the potential length of life, rather than the actual one, and therefore to be a better indicator of the gap between potential and actual life, which global burden of disease measurement aims to capture. It is admitted by the authors of the measure that a different approach would be more suitable for use in economic evaluation because an intervention to prevent or resolve a specific health problem will not resolve others a population is susceptible to in the future.

2   A weight representing the social value of time lived at different ages is calculated so as to reflect different social roles of different age groups, and the dependence of some age groups on others. It is argued that 'The concept of dependence and social role is broader than formal sector wage productivity and is not linked to total income levels'. Nevertheless, many interpret this weight as a productivity weight, and although it is not used to discriminate between individuals of different income levels, it is otherwise not dissimilar.

Disability weightings

Class	Description	Weight
1	Limited ability to perform at least one activity in one of the following areas: recreation, education, procreation or occupation	0.096
2	Limited ability to perform most activities in one of the following areas: recreation, education, procreation or occupation	0.220
3	Limited ability to perform activities in two or more of the following areas: recreation, education, procreation or occupation	0.400
4	Limited ability to perform most activities in all of the following areas: recreation, education, procreation or occupation	0.600
5	Needs assistance with instrumental activities of daily living such as meal preparation, shopping or housework	0.810
6	Needs assistance with activities of daily living such as eating, personal hygiene or toilet use	0.920

3   Disability is weighted according to the table. The classes of disability were defined without reference to empirically based description of disability states, and weights were calculated on the basis of the opinions of a group of independent experts. Note that, in contrast to the QALY, these weights work negatively – the higher the score, the worse the health state.

4   Finally, discounting is conducted for all components of the calculation at 3 per cent on the basis that this is 'consistent with the long-term yield on investments'.

The authors of the DALY do not claim to be consistent with any specific conception of a social welfare function, rather they argue that the four components 'have enjoyed wide consensus with the groups involved in the study'.

Source: Murray and Acharya (1997).

compared in terms of their effects on DALYs lost, and in terms of the cost-effectiveness of treatments in terms of DALYs gained.

The most obvious criticism of the DALY is the bias against health improvements that reduce pain, improve survival and quality of life but do not significantly affect disability. The calculation of the DALY also builds in adjustment for the social value of time lived at different ages, and the timing of benefits from discounting, both of which reduce the transparency of the measure. DALYs have been widely used in comparisons of health programmes for low-income countries, and there must be some concern that they lead to a bias against interventions of benefit to old and very young people. This reflects a judgment that members of these age groups also benefit from health benefits to those of working age, owing to their dependent status. Those involved in the development of DALYs claim that they do not aspire to be a measure of utility, but their use in setting priorities means that they are used in ways that imply correspondence with social welfare.

11.6 Whose views should count?

A general problem with any system of valuing health states for the purpose of setting priorities is to determine whose views should count. It is not really possible to understand fully the impact of a disease or disability without having experienced it. However, those with a disability are interested parties, and may not be expected to take a fully detached view. An interesting example of why this may matter is the weighting given by different groups to disability that requires the use of a wheelchair. Those with direct experience may consider the problems to be less severe than those who simply observe – although the reverse is also possible.

Similar issues arise in giving information to people who are asked to score or weight health states. It is difficult to give such information in sufficiently neutral ways that it does not also encourage a particular interpretation. Democratic principles might suggest that elected politicians, who in other contexts are the decision makers, should do the scoring. This is not always a popular suggestion. When opinions are sought from the general population there are several typical findings (Bowling *et al.* 1993). In general, low priority is given to services for older people, and to certain groups of people deemed to have brought problems on themselves, but this is not entirely consistent. Low priority is normally indicated for HIV and other mainly drug-related or sexually transmitted diseases, but the same prejudice does not seem to prevail against smokers who develop smoking-related diseases. There is also typically enthusiasm for children's services and those treatments that use high technology. Some studies have found that the public favour using health-gain information for setting priorities, but like also to have other criteria for rationing. It is important to understand that the weightings given to health states and therefore the priorities for interventions will depend in part on whose views are sought, and how the views are aggregated.

11.7 Measuring and describing outputs in natural units

The advantage of using utility scores as measures of outcome is that this allows comparisons between programmes with different types of outcome. However, it may not always be helpful to do this, and the conversion of information on outcomes into utility scores involves losing some of the meaning. It is therefore often sensible to compare options only in terms of the costs and outcomes measured in natural units. For example, if we are considering TT vaccination we can assess the number of cases averted, and would have a picture of the significance of this achievement in terms of treatments and ultimately deaths avoided. In screening for congenital dislocation of the hip we can (in principle) measure the number of cases averted. It is also easy to interpret a case averted, since it leads fairly directly to less disability, fewer operations later in life and less pain. In either case, the cost per case averted at the margin could be used to inform policy on what service, if any, to provide. However, if we measure the outcome as number of suspect cases identified, or number of doses of vaccine administered, this is more difficult to interpret, given that only a small proportion of cases testing positive will in fact become disabling, even with no treatment, that a small proportion of those vaccinated will be exposed to the disease, and that some of those vaccinated will not be protected.

In general we should avoid using measures of process unless they can easily be interpreted in terms of useful health gains, or there really is no possibility of data to provide a better basis of outcome measurement.

An advantage of using natural units to measure outputs can be the greater ease of making judgments about the value of such effects. QALYs allow comparison between interventions but lose some of the richness of the full description of benefits. In areas such as continuing care, where the objective might be to provide better quality of life for elderly people, or in palliative care, when dignity and spiritual well-being are important, it may be difficult to convert the complex descriptions of the outcomes into measures of utility without losing important details. In this case measuring in natural units may be preferable. In cases of infectious diseases there may be particular interest in bringing the numbers vaccinated above a threshold that achieves herd immunity. Cases averted may therefore be a sensible objective for a cost-effectiveness analysis.

A good rule is to try to use measures that as far as possible reflect outputs and not just processes of care. It should be an objective not to provide care, but really to improve quality of life. If we take the analogy of an airline, it could describe its output as happy holidays enjoyed, passengers carried or aircraft kilometres flown. The first is hard to measure, but is the real output. The second may be a good proxy if data on the first are not available, but the third is clearly not an objective in itself.

11.8 Comparing costs when outcomes are the same

There are some occasions when the objective of a programme is clearly identified, and the question is only how best to do this. Under these circumstances the appropriate analysis is simply to compare costs. No additional useful insights are gained from looking at the benefit side. The danger of this approach is that the objective may not, in fact, be so easy to specify. Policy makers may believe that the objective is to ensure universal vaccination against a particular disease, but their real objective should be to avoid cases of the disease, and universal coverage may not be a cost-effective option. Clearly this approach does not require the analyst to worry about measurement of outcomes or benefits, but it is important to worry about the assertion that the outcome is determined, and that the only remaining question is the method of achieving it.

11.9 Taking into account income and equity

Measures of outcome or health gain do not normally take distribution and equity explicitly into account. Gains are normally assessed as being of equal value regardless of who receives them (although quality of life of individuals may be used in assessing benefits). Several approaches to taking distribution into account explicitly have been proposed. One option is to weight benefits to give greater importance to those for poorer people. Another is to add a rule such as not supporting any change that makes distribution less equal, or that makes poorer people worse off.

It is difficult to think clearly about issues of equality and fairness in health care. The effect of a rule on special treatment of poorer people may be to lower the average level of health. To what extent are we willing to have worse health on average in order to have it more equally distributed? Would we accept a higher infant mortality rate in order to have it equal between urban and rural areas? Are we concerned mainly with reducing deaths in childhood, or do we also care about which deaths we avert?

Since poorer people have more disease, in some cases this means that they also have the greatest opportunities for health gains. Many simple and highly effective interventions reduce disease burden in poor people, many of whom have worse health and use health services less than richer people. A policy of supporting interventions with the largest benefits might in this case also be weighted towards poorer people. Unfortunately, although richer people are often less sick, they sometimes have more capacity for improved health, so this argument may not hold. This may be because richer people comply more fully with the treatment, or it may be because their general level of health is better, and they therefore are more likely to respond well to treatment and recover quickly. Additionally, rich people can be easier to reach. At least in some contexts, the poorest live in the most remote areas and interventions reach them only at high cost.

There is a large literature on appropriate ways of defining equity, equality and justice. A common principle is 'do to others as you would have them do to you'. Perhaps the most elegant formulation of this idea is that associated with John Rawls (1971). A feature of his analysis is that it does not require people to care about each other – his approach works even when people are selfish. His analysis started from how people would rate different distributions of income when they know the different possible distributions but do not know which share they would get. This 'justice as fairness' is a reflection therefore of what people consider just when behind a 'veil of ignorance'

Box 11.4 Economic evaluation of renal services for older people (III)

For the first two parts of this case study see Boxes 10.2 and 11.2.

Measuring benefits in services for ESRF
The framework of analysis in this report is cost-effectiveness. The costs of dialysis are compared with years of life gained in this group. As can be seen from the early results from the clinical trials, survival was over 90 per cent in each year for those selected for dialysis. Since those denied dialysis die quite quickly, we can use years on dialysis (adjusted to account for expected survival without treatment) as a proxy for survival. The main results are presented as cost per year of life gained.

In addition there was an assessment of quality of life using two instruments – a renal services measure known as KDQOL and a generic measure (SF36). This allowed some assessment of the quality of the life years that were gained.

Question. Why did you not combine these two dimensions – if you know life extension and quality of life, surely you can calculate QALYs?

Consultant. Yes, in principle that is possible. The particular instruments were not designed for this, and perhaps in retrospect it would have been good to use also a measure designed for calculating QALYs. The attempts to use SF36 to calculate QALYs have been only partially successful. I can see that for the purpose of comparing expansion of renal services with other priorities it would have been helpful to have an estimate of QALYs. The role of KDQOL is a bit different – it may be more useful for comparing the different dialysis modes.

No attempt was made to measure willingness to pay or other monetary measure of benefit. This would have required more work, and many people find the idea offensive.

Question. But surely this is in principle the best way to measure benefits? In this case it's pretty clear that people would be willing to pay a lot – after all, just look at the alternative!

Consultant. You have a point, but we would be more likely to measure ability to pay than willingness to pay. Few older people could afford the full cost of dialysis. The doctors would have refused to co-operate with the study if they thought we were assessing benefits in money terms. However, I can see that there would be interesting results.

about how they would fare. When faced with this situation people tend to opt for treating people in some sense according to their needs.

A common issue in discussing equity and fairness is the extent to which account is taken of differences in needs and differences in likely capacity to benefit. An attractive (if not very operational) principle is to treat equals equally, and unequals unequally. If someone has much greater problems, most fairness principles would give them more than those with lesser problems. However, there is no consensus about how to define fairness when different people, with similar problems, have very different capacities to benefit. For example, two people with angina would both benefit from surgery, but the non-smoker would benefit more. It may be that the symptoms of the smoker are worse. The utilitarian response is to make priorities of services that maximise health gain, and this is the usual perspective in economic evaluation. This perspective may maximise improvements in health, but it does not mean that the scale of the suffering *per se* is a criterion.

A further set of issues in equity is whether we should strive for equality in health, or only some measure of equity in health care or in access to health care. Many would argue that we cannot force people to be healthy or to consume care, and we should not strive for equity in use, but only for equity in access to services. There is a lot of evidence that people are uncomfortable about seeing people with serious ill health being denied treatment that would help them. This is particularly the case when they have other problems or deprivations. There is no simple way of incorporating equity weightings into economic evaluation. One approach is simply to describe in some detail the distributional consequences of different options and allow decision makers to apply their judgment.

11.10 Synthesising evidence from existing studies

It is increasingly understood that it is risky to rely on evidence from a single study, and choices of treatment now often rely on evidence from combining studies using meta-analysis and systematic reviews. It is increasingly common for economic evaluations to derive estimates of benefits (and sometimes of costs) from such reviews. It is also increasingly common for the analysis of this evidence to be placed in a decision analysis framework. More detail of these approaches is provided in Chapter 12.

12 Practical steps in economic evaluation

12.1 Asking the right questions

The discussion of problems in the measurement of costs and benefits aims to make people cautious in the use and interpretation of economic evaluation studies. However, much can be learned from careful and sensible use of economic evaluation of health interventions. The most important starting point is to ensure that the evaluation is concerned with the right, or at least sensible, questions. Several principles are important. First, the objective should normally be defined in terms of achievement that matters rather than well intentioned effort. The objective should always be to get as close as possible to 'output' while recognising that that is often difficult. Different ways of reducing infant mortality can reasonably be compared. Different ways of providing continuing care to terminally ill people may be subjected to evaluation. The point is to be clear about the objectives. In the first case we want low infant mortality, and in the second we want good-quality care. In contrast, we can only set the number of appendicectomies as an objective if we are sure that more would be better – in other words, that the current rate of the procedure means people are suffering or dying for want of this treatment. If such is not the case, one can still evaluate whether or not there are lower-cost methods of achieving the same rate of appendicectomy, but one needs to be very careful not to fall into the 'more is better' way of thinking.

It has been argued that the best way of describing objectives is in terms of achievement. It is also important that evaluation is carried out without a clear prior view about the answer. It is common for economists to be asked to carry out an economic evaluation study to show that a service is cost-effective. Often attempts are made to avoid even considering options that are considered by clinicians or managers to be unacceptable. While being realistic about what can be achieved in the highly political context of much decision making in health, it is important to try to ensure that a wide range of alternatives is considered in the evaluation exercise.

12.2 Choosing the perspective for economic evaluation

Economists usually argue that the appropriate perspective for economic evaluation is societal. They argue that a cost is a cost whoever pays, and similarly benefits should be included regardless of who receives them. It is inappropriate to choose an option simply because it shifts costs from formal health services to families, or because the harm done is not taken into account. A societal perspective means that the evaluation tries to include all costs and benefits, whoever pays or receives them.

It is difficult to make a coherent argument in principle against this perspective. Any serious case for looking only from the point of view of a government, insurance company or hospital has to be on practical or pragmatic grounds. For example, it may be shown that the spill-over of costs to other parties is small, and it makes no sense to spend resources on costly calculations that are unlikely to affect the outcomes. It is less clear that it makes sense to take a more restricted perspective (say that of the government or insurance fund) if there are significant shifts of costs to patients and families and these have not been taken into account (see Box 10.1).

Managers in commercial organisations typically are concerned to pursue commercial goals, and this means that they do their best to make profits for shareholders (and in most countries are legally obliged to do so). Any evaluation carried out by such organisations is likely to take the perspective of the best interests of the shareholders. But in the context of government-mandated systems of health care the best outcomes will come from evaluation of options for change from a broader societal perspective.

12.3 Measuring costs in economic evaluation

The most common approach to measurement of costs is to record all services provided for each patient, and then to convert this into cost by multiplying by estimates of the unit unit cost of each service. If the economic evaluation is alongside a clinical trial, this allows both point estimates and standard deviation of costs to be assessed. In turn this means that results can be quoted with confidence intervals. As is discussed in Chapter 5, there are difficulties in estimating unit costs, and they may vary with several factors such as the volume of production. There are also issues in what should be included if we are aiming to assess the additional cost of additional services.

It is not always easy to record all events, and it is sometimes necessary to use a range of sources of data. For example, it may be necessary to draw on data from deployment of staff, clinical records, patient diaries, direct observation or published sources to assess the number and type of services. It can be an exercise in detective work to find all the relevant information.

Deriving a list of unit costs can also be difficult. Financial data are often poor in the health sector, and the observed prices (if any) may not be good indicators of opportunity cost. The normal starting point is financial accounts and budgets. These are devised for purposes of planning and accountability, but may nevertheless be suitable sources of information. If these data are provided at an aggregate level (for example, hospital ward or health centre), and are to be used to compute unit costs, it is important to be clear that:

1   The services delivered are similar for different patients.
2   Fixed costs are included only if they will change with the change in services
3   Apportionment of shared costs is appropriate, and included only if the change in service changes the shared costs.

It is also important to be confident that using a single measure of unit cost is reasonable. In particular it is worth checking that there are no significant economies of scale or scope. If there are it may be necessary to adjust the unit costs for different levels or volumes of service. Unit costs may change over time, and it is important to use recent data if they are available.

Although it is common for a single set of unit costs to be used, it may be better to develop a separate cost vector for each care provider if there are reasons why they may differ. Also, it may be important to explore the combined variability of use of services and unit cost of services, so that costs can be quoted in terms of means and confidence intervals, taking all relevant variation into account. If a study involves many different sites it may be best to derive the set of cost weights from data on costs in the participating providers. Cost functions may be estimated to give a better understanding of the level and pattern of unit costs. Although many early economic evaluation studies estimated costs based on averages for all patients at a single centre, this is no longer considered best practice, and the results of such studies are now often treated with caution. Nevertheless, economic evaluation studies cannot be better than the data on which they are based, and even when these are imperfect they may provide a much better basis for choices to be made. The important consideration is that the analyst is aware of the limitations of estimates produced in that way, and communicates a suitable level of caution in interpreting findings to decision makers.

12.4 Measuring benefits in economic evaluation

The first step in assessing benefits is to ask two related questions – what approach to measuring benefits would be desirable, and what is feasible? In most cases there will be more than one dimension of benefits – longer life, better health, higher productivity or reduced risk. It is useful in the first instance to identify the main objectives of the intervention, and what implications they have for measurement. For example, a malaria control programme may aim to reduce deaths and the harmful effects of disease, and this may justify assessing benefits in some detail. On the other hand, if the service is cataract surgery in older people, the outcome may be adequately described in terms of years of eyesight restored.

When the benefits are defined in terms of simple natural units they may need no substantial economic work. However, if utility scores are used, there is a need to ensure that the necessary data are collected, normally using a standard method, as discussed in Chapter 11. It is common for there to be gains in life years and gains in quality of life. The example in Box 12.1 illustrates how the two can be combined.

12.5 Using data from reviews of evidence

It is increasingly common for economic evaluation studies to be based on the combined evidence of existing studies (or to be a combination of existing and new evidence). This is particularly the case when evidence is being considered for licensing new products or providing evidence for approval for subsidised provision of treatments. To a large extent this has involved the use of Bayesian techniques to combine and weight the evidence. A body of literature is emerging providing guidance on these approaches (e.g. Willan and Briggs 2006), and this is a rapidly developing field. A related and interesting literature is assessing the need for new research on the basis of analysis of the existing body of work (Claxton and Sculpher 2006).

12.6 Presenting the results of economic evaluation studies

The most common format for presenting the outcome of economic evaluation is to show the incremental cost-effectiveness ratios (ICERs) of moves from the *status quo*

Box 12.1 Calculating QALYs from data on longer life and better quality of life

In this group of patients percutaneous transluminal coronary angioplasty (PTCA) has the effect of extending life by one year and improving quality of life from an average of 70 per cent to 90 per cent. The life expectancy of the patients in the absence of PTCA is five years.

QALYs are gained in the following ways. First, for each of the next five years the quality of life is improved by twenty percentage points. Without treatment the person would have 3.5 QALYs (that is, 0.7×5 years). With treatment there is an addition of one QALY (0.2×5 years). In addition there is one year at 90 per cent of full quality of life, which gives a further 0.9 QALYs.

Therefore the total effect of the intervention is to produce 1.9 QALYs.

If the benefits are to be measured in terms of money, some method must be used to identify either willingness to pay or some other appropriate monetary valuation of benefit.

It is important to present the outcomes measured in terms of both means and the confidence intervals around measures of benefits as well as costs.

(do nothing option) through better but more expensive options. The ICER is the extra cost of the additional service divided by the extra outcome of effectiveness. Where an option costs more and achieves less than another, it is said to be dominated. Since the ICER would be negative it is not presented in the table of ICERs. Box 12.2 gives an example.

Box 12.2 Presenting options in terms of ICERs

Three options are being considered for developing an eye service. In the table they are shown in comparison with the current provision. Clearly we should not choose option 2, since it is dominated by option 1. Two questions arise. Should we do option 1? If yes, should we go further and do option 3?

Incremental cost-effectiveness ratios

Option	Cost (€)	Additional years of sight
1	2,000	100
2	3,000	90
3	4,000	160

The ICER for a move from the *status quo* to option 1 is 20. For the further move to option 3 it is 33.3 (that is 2,000/60, the additional cost of 3 compared with 1, divided by the additional gains).

In some senses option 1 is more cost-effective, since the ICER is 20 compared with 33.3. However, we might still consider that it is good value to pay €33.3 for each additional year of sight. This raises an important point. The ICER is a picture of the relative cost-effectiveness, but it is not true to say that we should choose the option with the lowest ICER. For each best way of increasing benefits we ask whether the ICER represents good use of resources. The question facing policy makers is, how much more will be achieved for how much more? The ICER answers that question.

This contrasts with the situation where the outcomes are identical or where the costs of the intervention are identical. In such cases there is a simple decision rule – the most cost-effective option is the one with the lowest ICER.

If the ICER for an intervention is known (or at least the likely distribution of the ICER) it is possible to compare it with a threshold level (ceiling ratio) above which interventions are considered to be cost-effective. For example, in a particular country it might be considered that a year of eyesight gained is worth at least $5,000, so that any intervention that achieves a year at or below this cost is considered cost-effective. Any such threshold must be related to the budget constraint, so that applying such a rule will lead to a set of priorities that maximises the overall health gain. Put another way, the threshold value of cost-effectiveness should represent the socially agreed opportunity cost of resources to be spent on health.

Where there is significant uncertainty about the evidence on cost-effectiveness there is a need to present the evidence to decision makers in a way that allows them to make choices based on the likelihood that an intervention would be considered cost-effective. The most common approach is to derive cost-effectiveness acceptability curves (CEACs), which show the likelihood that an intervention will be considered to be cost-effective at different cost-effectiveness thresholds. Clearly the probability that an intervention will be considered to be cost-effective rises as the threshold rises. Figure 12.1 illustrates a CEAC. The figure suggests that, if a year of eyesight gained is worth $5,000, there is about a 90 per cent chance of cataract surgery being cost-effective.

As the presentation of results of cost-effectiveness studies has come to include estimates of the degree of uncertainty surrounding the estimates there has been increasing concern about the use of ICERs. The main issue is that since ICER is a ratio, there are difficulties in estimating the confidence intervals. An alternative approach is to estimate the net benefit statistic. The net benefit calculation is shown in Box 12.3. Essentially this calculates the collective surplus for an intervention, given the costs and willingness to pay for the benefits. It is therefore possible to calculate the net benefit only if the decision makers' threshold willingness to pay is known. The advantage of this approach is that the key statistic is no longer a ratio. It is likely that the net benefit approach will become more common in the presentation of cost-effectiveness evidence.

Some useful discussion of the alternative ways of presenting findings is provided in O'Hagan and Stevens (2002).

12.7 Transferring the results of an economic evaluation

Results of economic evaluation are dependent on a wide range of highly local factors and, as we have discussed quite extensively, cannot be relied upon to be similar when one unit is compared with another in the same health system, and even within the same town. Nevertheless, inside a single health system, a number of factors are more

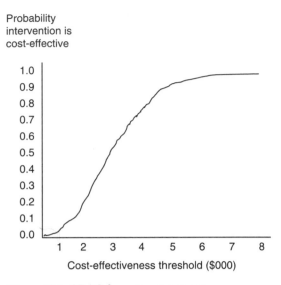

Figure 12.1 CEAC for cataract surgery.

Box 12.3 Calculating net benefit

Set the cost of treatment for individual i to be Ci and the effectiveness of the intervention for individual i to be Ei. If the community willingness to pay coefficient is K, the net benefit for individual i is

Net benefit $= KEi - Ci$

Since the wiliness to pay coefficient K is expressed in monetary terms, this calculation shows net benefit in money. It is equally possible to show net benefit on the effectiveness scale.

The net benefit for individual i is part of a distribution of the net benefit for all individuals who would benefit from the treatment.

---

similar than outside it. There are considerable international differences in the practice of medicine itself which are often even greater than those differences inside a single system (Wennberg and Gittelsohn 1973, 1982): doctors trained in different health systems are likely to prescribe different drugs and procedures for the same condition. A hospital stay for treatment of a given condition cannot be assumed to involve the same inputs. Official laws, regulations, guidelines and protocols vary from country to country.

Health systems are characterised by different levels of resource availability (see Chapter 20) which imply that components of care regimens offered within one health system will not be offered within another. Different prices apply, and this implies not only that costs differ for an identical package of care, but that the most economically efficient way of delivering care varies (see Chapters 4 and 5). For example, where labour is cheap, more efficient production techniques will be more labour-intensive.

Health systems are organised differently, meaning that the context in which care is received varies. For example, specialist doctors take responsibility for much primary care in the United States and France; generalist doctors play the same role in Canada and the UK; paramedical workers take much of this responsibility in developing countries. A procedure carried out as day surgery in one system may involve a several-day stay in hospital in another, and it may not be the result of inefficiency in the latter case. To convert in-patient surgery to day surgery may imply the use of a more sophisticated technique, or rely on the availability of systems supporting patients in their homes that may not be available in some health systems. In general, day surgery may be more technology- and less labour-intensive, making it more appropriate for an economy with high labour costs. Similarly, mass campaign programme modes of delivery of immunisation cannot be expected to have similar costs to programmes that operate through the routine health system – but choice between the two approaches depends on various health system characteristics.

Population characteristics also affect results. An immunisation programme is more costly to deliver in the remote hill settlements of Nepal than it is in the densely populated cities of Bangladesh. Effectiveness depends on the underlying disease conditions – cost-effectiveness ratios for anti-malaria interventions cannot be transferred to Oslo! More generally, an expectation that prevalence is an important correlate of cost-effectiveness is frequently appropriate, though this may not apply to treatment of relatively rare conditions.

Since the importance of the different comparability problems briefly surveyed is likely to vary between interventions, it follows that the ordering of cost-effectiveness need not be transferable from one country to another either. Differing levels of the general price index will affect cost-effectiveness measures but not their order. Every other difference cited above is likely to affect which interventions are most cost-effective. As was discussed, a difference in labour costs may affect the relative cost-effectiveness of in-patient and day surgery. Differences in underlying disease patterns and in health system configurations can affect whether it is most cost-effective to combat malaria using specific treatment regimens, preventive measures such as insecticide-treated bed nets, spraying for mosquitoes or using malaria prophylactic drugs. This point is equally applicable to the choice of rehabilitative regimens following heart attacks. Both depend on the distribution of underlying aetiologies in the population, the economically efficient use of inputs in the context of divergent relative prices; the availability and cost of community-based support services and even the cultural acceptability of alternative treatments such as exercise or bed nets.

All this suggests that looking to the international literature for evidence of cost-effectiveness relevant to choices to be made in a specific country is best avoided. Where it is not feasible to expect that local cost-effectiveness estimates will be available, transferring expectations of relative cost-effectiveness needs to be done with great care, considering each of the important sources of variation discussed above and whether or not differences between the target country and the source country are likely to be sufficient to change the conclusion regarding relative cost-effectiveness levels. Clearly, the use of actual ICERs converted at current exchange rates, to make incremental choices, is likely to be highly misleading in all but extremely similar conditions.

Lastly, measures of effectiveness such as the QALY and DALY, and the health status measurement surveys they are based on, are argued by some to be culturally specific. While the EUROQOL has been adapted and translated for use in a large number of

European countries, it has been argued that people's perceptions of what constitutes health varies between cultures, and therefore any instrument aiming to measure health status must also do so. The KENQOL (Fox-Rushby *et al.* 2000; Bowden 2001) is an instrument developed on the basis of research into perceptions of health in rural Kenya. A KENQOL–EUROQOL comparison illustrates the potential extent of the problem. Even countries which consider themselves closer to those for which the EUROQOL was developed might question whether minor adaptation and translation are sufficient to capture the potentially different perception of what constitutes health, and what matters most within that. This perspective undermines the quest for internationally comparable cost-effectiveness data. The interest in making international pronouncements on health priorities underpins both the EUROQOL and the DALY. If Swedish, French or US perspectives on what constitutes health and what components of health matters are most used to identify priorities in Turkey, Thailand or Tajikistan, we have to ask the question 'Whose priorities are identified?'

12.8 Non-statistical sensitivity analysis

The aim of economic evaluation is to support decision making. The data that are used in the analysis may be inaccurate for many reasons – there may be bias or measurement error, or the data may be taken from experimental conditions that will not be replicated in normal service conditions. Calculating confidence intervals is useful in helping decision makers to understand some elements of uncertainty. However, where this is not or cannot be done, and where there are other sources of uncertainty that are not described in the confidence intervals, it can be useful to test the results of economic evaluation for their sensitivity to certain types of error.

The practical steps in sensitivity analysis are simple – the values of the relevant variables are varied by different amounts to see if the changes in the observed ICERs are likely to change the order of the options or change the decision to or from any intervention. The process requires knowledge of the services, understanding of the likely sources of error or uncertainty, and the likely size of any errors.

It is sometimes best to present the sensitivity analysis in terms of the robustness of the findings. For example, it may be found that even with an error of 30 per cent in the value of the estimated cost, the decisions would be unchanged. Equally it might be found that an error of 5 per cent would change the order of options. This type of sensitivity analysis allows the analysts and decision makers to judge whether errors are likely to be in a range that would change the outcome, and in some cases is the basis of a decision to do further research with a view to improving the estimates, if the current degree of uncertainty makes decisions difficult.

12.9 Long-term costs and benefits

Economic evaluation can draw the data on costs and benefits from current practice, experimental evidence, observational studies and some knowledge about developments and changes in technology. However, many interventions have long-term effects on costs and benefits that cannot be adequately assessed within the current data. In these circumstances it is necessary to use modelling techniques to make the best assessments of long-term effects.

The simplest forms of modelling for long-term effects use current knowledge of events or probabilities of events, and simulate the future on this basis. A common approach is to use Markov models (which allow the probabilities associated with possible future states to be dependent on the condition of the previous time period) to explore future scenarios. In all cases the principles are the same – current knowledge is used to make the best estimates of future costs and future benefits.

It is often objected that modelling introduces extra uncertainty, but not to look at likely future costs and benefits means that serious bias can undermine the findings of economic evaluation. Where there is great uncertainty, sensitivity analysis can be used. There are particular risks of bias if the measured benefits include long-term effects (such as additional years of life, which will be lived decades hence), but the analysis does not include estimates of the resources needed in the future to support that benefit. It is common to find economic evaluations that have included as benefits years of life gained, but have not included the corresponding long-term costs of care.

12.10 Useful guidance on economic evaluation in health care

The aim in this chapter has been to outline the underlying theory and issues in the application of economic evaluation. It should give readers sufficient understanding to assess the meaning and quality of reports and published studies. It does not aim to be a definitive guide to the practice of economic evaluation. Several books of guidance exist (e.g. Creese and Parker 1994; Gold *et al.* 1996; Drummond *et al.* 2005). In addition, there are various sets of national guidance in many countries, which specify how studies should be carried out, and what rates should be used for discounting. It is important to ensure that any economic evaluation carried out is at least done in the knowledge of local guidance and recommendations. In addition it is useful to look at guidance provided by certain journals – in some cases it is necessary to present the results of economic evaluation studies in a particular way.

There is particular importance in following guidance on best practice when the evaluation is carried out as part of the case for licensing or reimbursement of a new drug or treatment. In these cases the evidence will be accepted only if it complies with best current practice. However, as with all techniques, the best practice is evolving, and it is important to draw on the available guidance, but not necessarily to accept it all.

13 Economic evaluation as a framework for choice

13.1 A framework for choice

Economic evaluation provides a framework within which a range of evidence can be assembled. In some senses this makes economics seem arrogant, since findings from many other health sciences can be brought together within the economic framework. This does not imply that the economic framework is more important, but simply that the role economic evaluation plays is to help to interpret diverse information and provide a framework for choice.

There are several reasons why it is useful to bring together evidence within the framework of economic evaluation. First, it helps us to ask the right questions. The issue is normally not 'Does it work?' but rather 'Should we do it?' The question should be 'Do the benefits of this service or intervention justify the costs?' Not all costs and benefits are easy to measure. This has been a major issue in the preceding chapters. It is nevertheless useful to ensure that they are all listed, and taken into account. Similarly, it matters when costs and benefits occur, and this should be taken into account.

The concept of cost used by economists is appropriate for decision making on behalf of society – the opportunity forgone – reminds us that the inefficient use of resources harms real people in real ways. Apologists for inefficient use of resources can be confronted with the full implications of such inefficiency. For example, a decision to allow scarce health care resources to be used for low-priority uses is a decision to allow more people to die, more people to become or remain disabled and more people to suffer avoidable pain. Third, the framework helps to ensure that measurement is consistent, and the same assumptions are used throughout. It is important that measured differences reflect real differences, and are not simply an artefact of the measurement process.

By being more explicit the perspective of the analysis should be clearer. Economists normally advocate taking a societal perspective, so that all costs and benefits are included, irrespective of who pays. Thus a decision to close local services to reduce costs to the hospitals may be shown to increase costs if patients have to travel further. Shorter hospital stays may reduce hospital costs, but may also increase costs for primary care, social services, informal carers, family, friends and the patient herself. A societal perspective considers the effects on all of these. If another perspective is taken, then this can be clearly stated and the results interpreted accordingly.

The main argument for economic evaluation is therefore that it helps us to see the whole picture. Decisions taken on partial information are likely to be flawed, and it is important to know at least what information should have been used.

13.2 Using economic evaluation to assess existing policies

Any analysis of current health sector services will identify things that are clearly high priorities, services that were previously useful but which should now be discontinued, and some that should never have been provided in the first place. Economic evaluation can help to distinguish these. There is considerable inertia in health service provision, not least because many people come to have an interest in continued provision of particular services. It is important always to remember that there is no good reason to continue to provide a service just because it has always been there – it is just more difficult to make change. It is no less ethical to discontinue a service than it is to decide not to provide it in the first place. A careful assessment of the costs and benefits of the services can help to determine whether it should be given priority over other potential uses of resources.

Measuring the costs and benefits of existing services can be relatively easy, since there are activities and outcomes to observe. This can give opportunities to measure the resources used and how they improve health. However, there are also some common difficulties. If a service has existed for a very long time, it is sometimes almost impossible to tell what would happen if it did not exist. A good example is screening for congenital dislocation of the hip in newborn babies. There are grounds for doubting whether this programme actually reduces the number of people with disabilities in the long run, but since Western countries have been doing it for years it is difficult to assess what would happen without the service.

It is often easier to get agreement to carry out economic evaluation of possible service developments than to revisit the priority of existing programmes. There is no inherent reason why we should accept current provision, especially where technological change may have reduced the need for some services. There is marked variation in the extent to which countries have seized opportunities to use less invasive surgical techniques and reduce the need for in-patient rather than day case surgery. While as was emphasised in Chapter 12 some of this variation may reflect differences in marginal rates of substitution between inputs, it cannot be seriously doubted that some variation reflects inertia in some of those countries that have been slower to adapt. Careful evaluation of existing practices can identify services that should no longer get priority.

13.3 Evaluation of potential policies and developments

Ideas for development of health policies and services have complicated origins. Often the early developments come from an inspired (or misguided) enthusiast, and what starts as an experiment can quickly become a routine service. Recent awareness of scarcity of resources has helped to raise questions of priorities and appropriateness, but it is naïve to ignore the fact that new ideas normally already have supporters among potential providers and patients.

Policy makers are not always detached and clear-thinking. Faced with demands for a new service, they may prefer positive findings in an evaluation, or may want the analysis to be negative in order to legitimise inaction. The analyst should be aware that in some cases policy makers are commissioning the evaluation in the hope of a particular outcome and not simply to inform the choice. Requests for analysts to find particular results are normally subtle, but good evaluation starts from a neutral position. Even the title of a study can be important. For example, the request may be to carry out an economic evaluation of a proposed new primary care facility in a particular town. This already restricts consideration to a particular way of expanding the service (excluding options of mobile services or services provided in the home) and alternative siting of the facility. Sometimes the initiative comes from the existence of a building, and a desire to put it to some use, rather than from the needs of people for services.

It is very common for proponents of services to try to limit the options that are considered, and for the choice of alternatives to favour their preferred option. It is normally wise to ensure that the options favoured by interest groups are included in any evaluation, but it is also wise to include options that do not have significant support but may offer better value. Historical promises often colour the thinking of the public and policy makers, however misguided these promises may have been. It is very common for schemes for major new facilities to have been agreed many years before, followed by a sequence of financial crises or policy reviews that delayed the start. Press reports describe decisions not to proceed as cancellation, and referral for evaluation as prevarication. These are the real circumstances in which options for new services are often evaluated, and the analyst needs to be aware of such issues and context. But it is important to remember that previous mistakes, ill considered promises and vocal advocates are not in principle reasons for making bad decisions about the future use of resources.

13.4 What the results of an evaluation mean, and what they do not mean

The results of economic evaluation can be presented in several ways, normally reflecting the ways in which it has been possible to measure benefits. In some cases this allows a single number to be presented, representing the net benefit of a particular choice. For example, if the benefits of a project have a value of €2 million and the costs a value of €1.8 million, the net benefit is €0.2 million. Each potential option can be assessed, and the one with the largest net benefits would normally be chosen. In many cases the measurement of benefits will be in terms of some non-financial measure, so that alternatives may be compared in terms of the ratio of costs to effectiveness. Thus we might compare the cost per year of life gained, or simply the cost per fully immunised child.

Care must be taken in the interpretation of cost-effectiveness ratios, since there are circumstances in which we would not choose the lowest. Take, for example, the case of screening for chlamydia in asymptomatic women in Canada. There is a choice between non-culture tests, with low cost (Ca$20) and sensitivity of around 70 per cent, and culture tests, with much higher cost (Ca$50) and sensitivity of over 80 per cent. If we compare the cost-effectiveness ratios in a high to medium (10 per cent) prevalence population, it costs Ca$290 per case detected for non-culture screening and Ca$630 per case for culture test screening. However, this does not mean that we should necessarily choose non-culture tests. The additional cost of detecting one additional case (in this case Ca$3,000) may be considered good value, since the disease is treatable, and successful treatment can help to reduce the spread of HIV and other sexually transmitted diseases. What this illustrates is that we need to be careful in interpreting ratios of costs and effectiveness.

Just as there is no correct level of funding for the health sector (see Chapter 19), there is no particular level of cost-effectiveness that indicates that a service should be provided. As was discussed in Chapter 12, in effect there must be a threshold above which projects are or should be chosen, reflecting the opportunity cost of additional resources in the health sector. If this has been made explicit it is possible for the analyst to present to decision makers the best understanding of what should be done given the available evidence. However, public organisations are often reluctant to be explicit about this. It is sometimes possible to assess what this is from the patterns of past decisions, but such exercises tend to show the diversity rather than the consistency of values in past choices.

13.5 Double counting, muddled thinking and making bad decisions

Economic evaluation can help to ensure that all relevant factors are counted once, and to avoid counting anything twice. It is surprisingly difficult to avoid double counting. There are particular risks of double counting resulting from assessing benefits both as benefits and as lower costs. Sometimes, when policy options are discussed informally, benefits are counted twice (for example, 'there is a reduction in mortality' and 'there is an increase in healthy years of life' are in part the same benefit). Sometimes it is more difficult to detect double counting in the complex descriptions of costs and benefits. An advantage of setting out clearly what are all the flows of costs and benefits is that it makes it easier to detect double counting.

Equally, it is common for important costs not to be taken into account, especially when an asset is already owned. Even where a resource is not marketed, or apparently marketable, the opportunity cost of its use is still the alternative use of the resource by the owning institution. For example, a hospital might build a new wing on a car park, claiming that the land had no value, as it could not easily be sold. However, the land has alternative uses irrespective of its saleability. Where are patients and staff going to park their cars now? Will there be a loss of revenue if car parking is charged for and is therefore a source of revenue? The hospital might find that some time later it has to spend a large sum to buy some adjacent land for car parking. Alternatively, there may be a private company interested in operating a concession using that land and willing to pay rent. The new wing may still provide the best use of resources, but that can only be established by considering the value of the land in alternative uses.

It is often not possible to place a value on, or even to give a clear description of, some costs and benefits, so that additional judgments outside the framework of the analysis may be needed. For example, an option may have more or less desirable consequences for equity, but this may not be integrated into the analysis. It does not mean that the economic evaluation should be taken to be just one argument, since it is in itself a framework within which we present a collection of arguments. When using economic evaluation in such circumstances it is important to remain clear about what is included and what arguments are genuinely additional. Only the latter should be allowed to supplement the economic evaluation in the decision process.

Sometimes the most effective use of economic evaluation is to confront decision makers with the implications of their potential choices. One former British government minister complained that the economic advisers always made him feel uncomfortable about the choices he made. This probably reflects good economic advice.

13.6 Use and abuse of economic evaluation

The aim of these chapters on economic evaluation has been to discuss the theoretical basis for economic evaluation, to outline the methods used and the problems

Box 13.1 Economic evaluation of renal services for older people (IV)

For the first three parts of this case study see Boxes 10.2, 11.2 and 11.4.

Some practical issues in the economic evaluation of renal services for older people
The document inviting tenders for this study asked for an economic evaluation to support the decisions on expansion of dialysis services for older people. This suggests that the answer is already known, and all that is needed is the supporting documents. The evaluation team could not accept that the answers were already known, given the lack of any published studies.

In the first phase of the project it was agreed that it would be important to give more focus in the questions addressed in this report. Three questions have been addressed. First, are there any people for whom additional services would be cost-effective? Second, which groups should be included in the expanded service? Third, which mode of dialysis should be chosen, and for whom?

Question. This is useful – the original documents were unfocused. The doctors were not keen to include peritoneal dialysis – they said that it was already well known that older people do badly on peritoneal dialysis.

Consultant. Yes, it is important to agree the right questions, and to include all relevant ones. The views on peritoneal dialysis are typical – people often do not like analysis of options that seem wrong, especially when there is no evidence to support the feeling. I have often found that people are particularly reluctant to consider options if they think there is a risk that careful analysis will suggest that they are cost-effective. This is probably the case in the inclusion of peritoneal dialysis in this study. We found little evidence comparing the different dialysis modalities, and in this study we found no differences in outcomes for the majority of patients.

The calculations of the costs of dialysis took a societal perspective, including costs to patients and their families, as well as to the funders. Since all those included in the study were retired it was decided not to put in any cost for time off work for patients, but where there was a carer of working age a cost was calculated. Costs for all health services used by patients were included, since these all contribute to the person's survival and quality of life. However, the cost of pensions was not included, since they are a transfer payment.

Question. I don't understand this point at all. You say in the report that you would include the cost of lost wages, but not pension. Surely pensions are just incomes in old age, like wages for younger people?

Consultant. Many people find the distinction between costs and transfer payments difficult, but it is important to understand. Remember we are interested in assessing opportunity cost – that is, the loss to society of using resources for a particular purpose. A pension (or indeed any welfare payments to people who are not working) is really just funds taken from one person and given to another. It is like giving your children pocket money – at the time you do that your family does not get richer or poorer – it just transfers spending power between generations.

The results of this study showed that the lowest cost per year of life gained is for those who are successfully put on to peritoneal dialysis. Costs are higher for those on haemodialysis, and are much higher for those who have generally poor health. The costs do not seem to be related to age itself, although older people in the study generally have more co-morbidity.

Question. Does that mean that we should only provide peritoneal dialysis, since it is more cost-effective than haemodialysis? And should we refuse treatment to those with other health problems? Is it fair to give older people treatment in preference to those less old?

Consultant. All that this study has shown is that peritoneal dialysis is *relatively* more cost-effective than haemodialysis. Remember that we can only ever assess cost-effectiveness relative to other uses of resources. Even though haemodialysiss is shown to be less cost-effective than peritoneal dialysis it may be better value than treating other diseases. The evidence does not suggest that we should never treat people with co-morbidities, but *if* we are setting priorities then there is a case for giving them lower priority, and increasing the overall health gain.

You raise an interesting and controversial question concerning age. There are some advocates of age discrimination on equity grounds that we should all have a chance of the same length of good-quality life, but others fiercely oppose any age discrimination.

encountered in carrying out an evaluation, and to assist with the interpretation of evaluation results. There are thorough and comprehensive guides available (such as Drummond *et al.* 2005) that provide more detailed guidance on methods and techniques.

There are several warning signs to look out for in assessing economic evaluation results. First, it is important to look at the perspective taken by the analyst. If the evaluation is from the point of view of a provider of care or a particular interest group, this should be interpreted as such.

Second, it is important to assess whether the full range of plausible options has been included. It is important to be sure that the best option has not been excluded at an early stage (or never considered at all). In many senses the early stages of an analysis, in which the problem is properly described and the options are identified, is the most important, since the finding of the study will rely heavily on what was initially considered.

Third, some specific questions should always be asked. Are the cost estimates likely to reflect opportunity cost? Has a reasonable approach been taken to the assessment of benefits? Have costs and benefits been expressed in terms of their present value (discounted), and is the discount rate used the one that is recognised as appropriate?

There are other warning signs. It is sometimes clear that the analysis has come after the main decision to proceed with a project, and simply aims to justify existing decisions. It can be very difficult to persuade policy makers to abandon policies based on previous misunderstanding and errors.

Since economic evaluation aims to provide a framework for the inclusion of data on efficacy, effectiveness and costs, it is not 'just like any other argument'. If the premises of the evaluation are accepted it should not be possible to argue against the conclusions that follow. However, it is equally true that economic evaluation is not simply a tool for making decisions, since it is almost never possible to include all important arguments and to measure everything that is relevant to the decision. But when the additional judgements of policy makers are added, it is important to ensure that it is only additional factors that are taken into account, to avoid double counting.

It is useful to understand the limitations of economic evaluation, both in terms of its theoretical foundations and in the practical problems in doing it. It is equally important to understand that decisions made without the help of such evaluation are likely to be worse. Thinking clearly, measuring carefully and interpreting sensibly can increase health gain, improving life expectancy and quality of life.

Part III

Further economics of markets and market intervention

14 Contracting

14.1 Introduction

In Chapter 6 we developed the model of perfect competition and in Chapter 7 we considered some features of health markets which cause the market to fail. One of the key features of the perfect competition model, which we did not yet consider, is that transactions are assumed to take place in a single instant. This assumption seems reasonable for the sale or purchase of a single item in a shop or market stall. However, many goods and services are not bought and sold through such one-off exchanges. Buyers and sellers may undertake an exchange of goods and services over a period of time and develop long-term relationships. Contracts are one method by which these relationships are developed. In this chapter we examine the economic rationale for a contract and issues related to the design of contracts.

For example, each time new drugs are needed, a hospital's purchaser (who may be a member of hospital staff or a purchaser for a larger group of hospitals) is unlikely to visit a pharmacy and make a series of purchases on a one-off basis. It is more likely that a long-term contract is entered into with a pharmaceutical supplier which specifies, among other things, ordering procedures, negotiated prices associated with particular purchased quantities, quality specifications and delivery schedules. A series of purchases over a given time period are likely to be covered by the contract, and the current contract may be the latest in a series, with the expectation on both parts that the contract plays a role in a long-term relationship between the supplier and hospitals. Even this is a relatively straightforward situation compared with the kind of contract that would need to be developed in relation to the maintenance of the hospital's building and equipment. In this case, the services required over a given time period cannot all be specified in advance, since breakdowns are not fully predictable. It may be wise, for reasons we will explore further below, to specify a payment arrangement other than a price per service. Quality specifications are more difficult to write. A contract covering maintenance in hospitals in Bangkok is one of those considered in Box 14.1.

There has recently been interest in the use of contracts to purchase clinical services on behalf of patient populations. For example the National Health Service of the UK has been reorganised so that purchasing groups at district or sub-district level purchase clinical services from public hospitals on behalf of a defined patient population. The Zambian health system has been redesigned on similar lines. While these types of reforms will be addressed more fully in the final chapter of this text, it is worth while at this point, and as you read this chapter, considering the following question. What kinds of contract specifications are feasible and appropriate for the purchase of clinical

Box 14.1 Contracting-out in Bangkok hospitals

The Thai government has directly addressed the 'make or buy' decision in the Thai public sector by mandating that public employment must decrease. As a result, hospitals are increasingly contracting-out both non-clinical services, like cleaning, and clinical services such as diagnostic and treatment technologies.

In comparing the transaction costs associated with employment and contractual relationships, it is clear that the entrenched privileges associated with public employment which are common to many developing countries adversely affect the comparison in favour of contracting-out. For example, difficulties in disciplining or firing civil servants make employment contracts particularly inefficient methods of procuring goods or services. In the Thai case, it was also argued that cultural attitudes to hierarchy compounded the adverse comparison. For example, cleaners would carry out any tasks allocated by their superiors, and consequently neglect the cleaning job for which they had been employed.

In contracting diagnostic and treatment technologies, other apparently inefficient characteristics of the bureaucracy also affected the transaction cost comparison. Procurement rules meant that equipment could take three years from order to installation, by which time it might be out of date. Most of the contractors were reimbursed by nominal monthly rent and an out-of-pocket patient fee. This produced an efficient service from the perspective of its smooth running, very limited 'down time' and hence availability when needed. However, it proved difficult to implement an exemption policy by which those unable to pay could still receive treatment. Contractors faced no incentive to operate such a policy, and hospitals were apparently in a weak position to negotiate, monitor or enforce it.

Contracting-out the whole diagnostic or treatment service proved more successful in terms of maintenance (down time) than contracting-out maintenance alone, which had earlier been tried. It is difficult to specify an efficient reimbursement mechanism for a maintenance contract which embodies appropriate incentives to make effective repairs only when they are needed. An annual payment (for example) might result in the contractor claiming that equipment needed replacement when repair would be possible but expensive. A payment per repair might result in shoddy repair work which would frequently need to be redone. The problem is that the underlying state of equipment (repairable or not) and the quality of repair work are inherently difficult to observe and monitor.

For non-clinical services, contracts were poorly monitored and the quality of services was generally believed to be low, but not as low as those which prevailed under the directly provided services. Costs were slightly lower for the contracted-out service. This emphasises the importance of taking a comparative stance in the 'make or buy' debate. The contractual difficulties associated with the arrangements for non-clinical services (such as the implicit contract between superior and junior employees that orders would always be obeyed no matter how unreasonable) are considerable. In such circumstances even unsatisfactory formal contractual arrangements may be the relatively better option.

Source: Tangcharoensathien *et al.* (1997).

services? Spot contracts[1] are unlikely to be indicated where a third party pays for the transaction, given the difficulty and cost of third-party attendance at every transaction. It should be clear that contracting for clinical services has some features in common with, and probably surpasses the complexity of, the hospital's maintenance contract.

The concepts and ideas described in this chapter derive from the economics literature on contracting. They enable us to structure and categorise the types of complexity involved in contracting in the health sector, and to analyse its implications for appropriate contract specification.

14.2 What is a contract?

The contract contrasts with the market transactions assumed in previous chapters in which:

1   You expect nothing more than exchanging goods at mutually satisfactory prices.
2   There are no long-term relationships between buyers and sellers.
3   All parties have good information.
4   Parties can walk away from the transaction if they want.
5   Transactions are costless.

Where these conditions do not apply, exchange is made possible through the use of contracts. As we have seen above, contracts can be quite simple, presenting few difficulties in their specification, execution and monitoring. However, in this chapter we are most interested in contracts which are not straightforward. Such contracts are at the heart of debates focusing on how to structure exchange in the health sector.

Contracts can be formal and explicit (written and legally binding agreements) but they can also be implicit. Milgrom and Roberts (1992) define implicit contracts as 'Shared understandings that are not legally enforceable but that the parties consider to be binding on one another's conduct'. For example, the type of clothing expected to be worn at work may not be written in a formal employment contract, but may be mutually understood by employer and employee to be part of their implicit contract. Defined this broadly, it is important to recognise that all relationships are governed by contracts. It is often helpful to think about the advantages and disadvantages of more implicit and more explicit contracts in a particular context. If the question is instead framed as *whether* to contract, it is likely that difficulties in the non-contractual (or implicit contractual) relationship will be missed.

From this perspective, the debate as to whether or not to introduce formal contracts between public purchasers and providers, as has been done in the UK and Zambia for example, is a debate about whether formalising the otherwise implicit contract between those who pay for and those who provide public services brings more advantages or disadvantages. The argument for greater explicitness is that formal contracts clarify purchasers' objectives, and more clearly specify distinct roles of purchasers and providers. In contrast it can be argued that flexibility and mutual goodwill are better fostered under more implicit contractual relationships, and the presence of unmeasurable dimensions to the delivery of health care. The idea that contractual difficulties can be avoided if explicit contracts are avoided is naïve.

14.3 Transaction costs

In a seminal article in 1937 Ronald Coase asked the questions 'If markets operate so efficiently, why have firms?' 'Why is everything not bought and sold through a contract?' and their corollary: 'If the organisation of economic activity in firms implies that markets don't work well, why have contracts?' 'Why not make everything in one big firm?'

Within a firm a number of economic activities are organised and exchange between those who carry them out is made under different rules from those operating in markets. Even in a simple firm with an owner and an employee producing a single product, Coase's questions could be rephrased 'Why does the owner choose to employ her labourer rather than to buy the labourer's product on market terms?' An intuitive answer is that the owner owns the means of production and the labourer has insufficient wealth to purchase them, but this does not explain why means of production are not rented out to the labourer, or why an efficient capital market will not be able to lend the labourer resources to purchase his own means of production. In fact the replacement of employment arrangements with market arrangements through the contracting out of services in some health sectors illustrates that this choice is not purely theoretical. In some cases, for example, hospital contracts have been awarded to cleaning firms which have been established using cleaners who were previously directly employed by the health authority or hospital.

Another intuitive answer is that economies of scale may determine the choice. It may be cheaper to purchase a good from a company that is producing in bulk for several purchasers than to try to produce it yourself. However, the firm could decide to produce in bulk to cover more than its own needs, and to sell to other purchasers itself.

Coase's answer to the question is that a firm's decision to 'make or buy' (or to employ cleaners or enter into a formal contract with a cleaning company) depends on an assessment of the transaction costs associated with the two modes of procuring a good or service. At one level this is almost a tautology. Firms will organise the procurement of a good or service in the manner that costs them least. This is not particularly helpful. The value of this insight is rather in the attention that it draws to a category of cost, *transaction cost*, which lies at the centre of the make or buy decision and thereby determines the pattern of economic activity. By implication, transaction costs can be defined as all those costs associated with using a particular type of exchange relationship – for example, in terms of the previous section, formal or informal contracts. This simple idea paved the way for a branch of economics known as transaction cost economics which is associated with the economist Oliver Williamson and has increasingly been informing debates on the use of formal contracts in the health sector.

14.4 Transaction cost economics

Williamson relies on two behavioural assumptions which depart from those of neoclassical economics: opportunism and bounded rationality. Opportunism is defined as a strategy involving guile, intended to further self-interest. The term bounded rationality was coined in 1957 by Herbert Simon, an organisational theorist. It refers to information problems, but adds to that limited cognitive, reasoning and computational abilities on the part of individuals. It is distinct from uncertainty, which is usually an additional assumption of Williamson's models. Given uncertainty, bounded rationality implies that individuals cannot calculate all the possible outcomes and their associated probabilities which would enable the computation of the rational price, or offer of supply. The presence of bounded rationality implies that contracts are incomplete – they cannot specify all relevant possibilities which affect the contracting parties' returns from participating in the contract.

Williamson uses the sort of table shown in Figure 14.1 to explain the importance of these departures. Where neither new behavioural assumption applies, the situation is described as bliss: contracts can be fully specified and followed. Where there is opportunism and no bounded rationality it is possible to specify contracts completely, leaving no scope for opportunistic behaviour. Where there is bounded rationality but no opportunism, contracts can be governed by a general clause such as 'parties to the contract promise to disclose all relevant information candidly and to behave in cooperative fashion during contract execution and at contract renewal intervals'. In the absence of opportunism, parties will adhere honourably to that clause. However, where both behavioural assumptions apply, contractual difficulties arise.

These problems are particularly acute in the context of asset specificity. The distinction between specific and non-specific assets is whether they are redeployable or not. (Notice the distinction between a fixed cost and a specific asset. A building, for example, is fixed but could be redeployed in many uses.) There are four types of asset specificity: site specificity (successive stages of production need to be located in close proximity to each other); physical asset specificity (specificity is related to physical features such as machine parts specific to a given product); human asset specificity (skills and knowledge embedded in the labour force are specific – for example, because of on-the-job learning, or the importance of team configurations) and dedicated asset specificity (for example, expansion of existing plant on behalf of a particular buyer).

Asset specificity causes two types of problems. The first is the fundamental transformation: a situation that starts with competitive bidding *prior* to contract can become one of *ex post* monopoly *after* the contract. The problem is that, once the investment has been made, no alternative supplier will be able to match the prices of the first successful bidder – since each new successful bidder would have to invest *specifically* to fulfil this contract. The second problem is the inherent monopsony in asset specificity – these assets have a single buyer.

The resulting bilateral monopoly means that one or both parties are vulnerable to appropriation. If one party pulls out of the contract, behaves unreasonably, or announces a sudden change of price, the other has the choice of complying or pulling out of the contract. Opportunism implies that such behaviour must be expected. Bounded rationality implies that such behaviour will not always be resolvable by

		Bounded rationality	
		Absent	Admitted
Opportunism	Absent	Bliss	General clause contracting
	Admitted	Comprehensive contracting	Serious contractual difficulties

Figure 14.1 Contractual difficulties under bounded rationality and opportunism.
Source: Williamson (1985).

recourse to a law and the explicit, formal agreement of the written contract. Asset specificity implies that the option of responding by pulling out of the contract is highly costly to the investor in the specific asset.

Suppose a company negotiates with a hospital to build a disposal unit for hospital waste at a hospital convenient site and agrees a contract specifying an annual fee for the disposal of all hospital waste. The waste disposal unit is a specific asset and the company may be exposed to the risk of appropriation of the value of its investment by the hospital. If the hospital increases the volume of waste the company's costs increase but it is in a weak position to renegotiate the contract because it cannot redeploy the asset. It might be argued that the contract was not very well specified at the outset. The example is deliberately crude for simplicity's sake, but bounded rationality implies that there will be holes in contracts which opportunistic contracting parties can exploit.

Another of Williamson's tables addresses the types of solution likely under different conditions (Figure 14.2). As before, if bounded rationality is absent, contracting resembles planning – or is comprehensive. Everything can be specified in advance and the plan simply executed with all parties playing their role. If opportunism is absent, a promise form of contract will function well (general clause). If asset specificity is absent, competitive contracting can function because contracts can be discrete and the market is fully contestable. Opportunism can be punished by withdrawal from contracts. In the example above, the waste disposal unit can be redeployed and the hospital will have to find another willing supplier. However, everything fails when all three are present – a need for governance of contracts is introduced.

Governance implies a retreat from classical contracting which is equivalent to the comprehensive contracting and planning concepts above – it is assumed possible to account for every aspect of the transaction in the contract. However, there are degrees of governance. Neoclassical contracting is characterised by greater flexibility and third-party arbitration of disputes – for example, public purchasers and providers in the UK or Zambian health system can appeal to a government body to settle a dispute. Relational contracting reflects progressively increasing duration and complexity of contract: contracts do not relate to a single discrete purchase but to long-term agreements over many different exchanges. The role of *trust* becomes increasingly important. The last point on this continuum is hierarchy or vertical integration – for the public sector the equivalent is reversion to direct provision. (The classical, neoclassical, relational classification is used by Williamson but originates from the work of Macneil 1978).

Behavioural assumption		Asset specificity	
Bounded rationality	Opportunism		
0	+	+	Planning
+	0	+	Promise
+	+	0	Competition
+	+	+	Governance

Figure 14.2 Contractual difficulties under bounded rationality, opportunism and asset specificity.

Note: + Present in considerable degree, 0 absent; uncertainty is assumed in all cases.

Source: Williamson (1985)

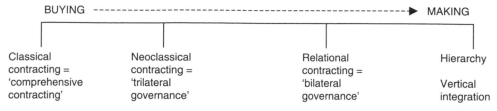

Figure 14.3 Contractual governance, 'making' and 'buying'.

You may have noticed that the movement from classical to neoclassical to relational contracts resembles the movement from formal explicit to informal contracts discussed above. Williamson's framework implies that more complex contractual situations are best governed by a greater degree of informality or the use of implicit contracting.

This is a point of departure for other contributors to contracting debates for whom this appears as more of an assumption than a conclusion. For example, Alchian and Demsetz (1972) and Demsetz (1993) have characterised the firm as a nexus of contracts, implying, as does our section 14.2 above, that contractual difficulties are not avoided, just altered, by greater use of hierarchy than markets. Alchian and Demsetz write about market-like and firm-like contracts, implying that it is the different nature of the two kinds of contract – either of which may be implicit or explicit – that are differently equipped to deal with the contractual difficulties resulting from opportunism, bounded rationality and asset specificity.

A solution which Williamson largely discounts, but which is given substantial attention elsewhere in the literature, is reliance on reputation effects as a constraint on opportunistic behaviour. The argument is that in a multi-period game, participants are constrained from opportunism by the effect of being observed to cheat on future rounds. This suggests that a world of promise or general clause contracting is more feasible than it might otherwise seem. Reputation effects depend on how observable cheating is to those who have not participated in the contract, suggesting that contract performance transparency may usefully be considered another component in a framework categorising the viability of alternative forms of contract. How easy is it, for example, for a hospital to observe the level of performance of its maintenance contractor? This is a different question from how easy it is for the hospital to demonstrate the level of performance to a third party.

14.5 Health sector contracting

14.5.1 *Bounded rationality and opportunism*

The major question addressed in the health contracting literature which immediately responds to an environment of bounded rationality and opportunism is the issue of effective monitoring of contracts. In the bliss of these behavioural assumptions being absent, no monitoring would be necessary.

Health services present notorious monitoring problems in relation to both quantity and quality of services delivered. In most cases it is therefore not only *difficult* to attempt classical contracting, it is probably *inefficient*, since difficulty implies high costs of achieving complete monitoring. Providers can act opportunistically *ex ante* in the development of monitoring mechanisms (for example, proposing measures which conceal the weaknesses of their provision), and *ex post* in their response to the monitoring mechanisms imposed.

For example, in the United States the Diagnosis Related Group (DRG) as the basis of payment became a feature of contracts between insurance companies and health service providers during the 1980s. DRGs categorised patients according to their expected cost profile, based on the initial diagnosis, and co-diagnoses. Patients with higher expected costs claimed higher fees but the intention was that hospitals would face no incentive to over-provide unnecessary services as they had under fee-for-service arrangements. However, in the years following this reform DRG creep became a well acknowledged phenomenon. It was argued that diagnoses were arrived at bearing in mind the fee schedule and patients were increasingly diagnosed as suffering from more expensive to treat conditions (Simborg 1981; Steinwald and Dummit 1989). This diagnostic behaviour on the part of hospital doctors can be interpreted as an opportunistic response to the incompleteness of the hospitals' contracts with insurance companies. In general imperfect indicators of performance imply scope for providers to respond to the letter rather than the spirit of the measure and to distort statistical returns where those are under the provider's control.

In any given context, since classical contracting is excluded, the question to be addressed is the degree of monitoring difficulty and the type of contract most likely to minimise the costs associated with the transaction. This involves consideration of the type of governance appropriate (trilateral, bilateral or hierarchy) and the types of contracts possible within each type of governance. Box 14.2 provides one example of the contract model adopted in Costa Rica that sought to balance these concerns.

Box 14.2 Contracts for health care in Costa Rica

In Costa Rica members of primary health care clinic staff were able to form a health care co-operative, operating under contract and leasing their facilities from the Costa Rican Social Security Institute. These served their pre-existing catchment population and operated in parallel to public clinics that continued to be financed on a historical budget basis. Gauri *et al.* (2004) describe some of the features of the contracts, and these can be seen to be designed to address the difficulties of contracting for health care (see table).

Health care contracts

Contracting problems anticipated	Measures taken to control purchaser or provider behaviours
Poor maintenance of leased equipment	Co-operatives were responsible for maintenance and replacement.
Lack of incentives to contain costs	Capitation based payment (at first) Co-operatives were responsible for purchase of drugs and medical supplies. Identical package of services to public clinics was mandated.

Lack of incentives to promote quality and volume of service	Payment based on management contract (later). Co-operative workers became shareholders in the co-operative. Requirement to evaluate own performance. Monitoring by external auditors.

Because there was a fixed catchment population, capitation-based payment did not provide any incentives to promote quality and service availability – the co-operative could not gain additional revenue by attracting larger numbers of patients to its clinics. It was observed that co-operatives made the same responses to budget shortfalls as public clinics – cutting back on services. The capitation payment was then changed to a payment based on a management contract under which targets for production and coverage were set.

Gauri *et al.* (2004) evaluated the impact of the contracts. They found that the co-operatives provided more general visits and dental visits but fewer specialist visits. They also conducted fewer laboratory tests, and provided fewer medications per visit. There were no differences in non-medical, emergency and first-time visits between co-operatives and public clinics. Overall, co-operatives' total expenditure *per capita* was 14.7–58.9 per cent lower than in public clinics.

Their results suggest that co-operatives may have substituted general for specialist care and taken other expenditure-reducing measures. While it is not clear whether this was an improvement in the appropriateness of care for the patient mix involved, the other results suggest that quality-reducing measures were not adopted across the board: they did not substitute nurses for doctors, or refuse emergency or first attendance care.

The results might be interpreted to imply that this kind of mixed reimbursement system within a health care contract can encourage cost control without seriously compromising quality or volume of services. However, more research on the appropriateness of the resulting care model would be required to conclude that more robustly.

Source: Gauri *et al.* (2004).

In Zambia contracts have been introduced between a central purchaser (the Central Board of Health) and hospitals and district health management teams who manage the provision of primary and secondary level care (see Box 25.2). Contracts stipulate that hospitals will be reimbursed according to a budgetary formula calculated on the basis of bed numbers. Many hospital operating decisions are subject to review by the Ministry of Health. This may be interpreted as the choice of a relational contract mode. The choice of arrangements has been explicitly related to monitoring difficulties by Ministry of Health and Central Board of Health officials. Under more classical contracts, government officials fear the creation of perverse incentives, responses to which they would be unable to monitor. We can interpret these concerns within the frameworks introduced in this chapter, which would also suggest the identification of potential perverse incentives associated with current contractual arrangements and the consideration of the ability to monitor those.

14.5.2 Risk and reimbursement mechanisms

Reimbursement mechanisms govern incentives and also distribute risk between contracting parties. Examples of reimbursement mechanisms are fee-for-service systems that reimburse providers retrospectively for each service provided to the patient, the Diagnostic Related Group system that reimburses providers prospectively according to the diagnosis at admission, at an estimated average cost for patients with that diagnosis, and capitation, which pays a provider prospectively a fixed price for the coverage of a patient's health care costs over a given time period.

Adding bounded rationality to this uncertainty, approaches to using reimbursement mechanisms as a means to shift risk and manipulate incentives can be developed – but not precisely. In the literature on contracting in the UK, the types of contracts are categorised as block contract (treat a defined patient population, for a fixed reimbursement); cost and volume (provide a given number of treatments for a reimbursement set according to the estimated cost of that); and cost per case (provide variable number of treatments and receive a payment related to number provided). These broadly correspond to capitation and fee-per-patient reimbursement mechanisms (of which DRGs are also an example), with number of patients fixed under cost and volume and variable under cost-per-case.

Capitation shifts risk to the organisation paid on this basis. If a higher number of patients than expected seek to use a service, the additional cost must be absorbed by the provider, so must a higher than expected cost per patient. Fee-per-patient mechanisms shift risk back towards the payer, but not as fully as fee-for-service reimbursement. If the average patient imposes a higher cost than expected, that risk still lies with the provider, but the risk of higher than expected patient numbers now lies with the payer.

The principal consideration that is usually applied to this issue is the incentives to cost control. Since the provider is in a better condition to control costs, it is argued that it is appropriate for the risk of excess costs to be felt there. Certainly US experience suggests that failure to address this issue can be expensive. However, Roberts (1993) suggests that the dangers of supplier-reduced demand under capitation have not been adequately considered.

It is also important to understand the implications of alternative reimbursement mechanisms for the distribution of risk between payer and provider. Propper (1995) argues that in the UK, when formal contracts were first introduced, District Health Authorities (DHAs), which purchased care for the population of the district, were likely to be risk-averse, given the political environment. Under arrangements in which DHAs were more exposed to risk (for example, by increased use of cost-per-case contracts), they might make compensating sub-optimal risk-avoiding decisions from society's perspective. For example, they might keep a sub-optimally high financial reserve to cope with emergencies. If the same is not true of providers, there are arguments for maintaining block contracts. Returning to Zambia, an explicit reason for working with block contracts is that purchasers are wary of accepting risk.

Like the monitoring arguments, these considerations may suggest the need to maintain more rather than less governance in health service contracting.

14.5.3 *Asset specificity*

Consider again the different types of asset specificity. The level of physical asset specificity can be seen to be related to market structure. Given the wide range of medical equipment that has no non-medical use, physical asset specificity is likely to be prevalent where there is an *ex ante* monopsony in the health sector – for example in the British NHS. This could lead to reluctance among private sector firms to invest in medical equipment, given the risk of appropriation. In the UK the Private Finance Initiative operates by renting equipment to the NHS. Reputation factors may be important in explaining this – or perhaps the UK government plans to renege on these agreements in the future?

The same market structure point would appear to apply to human asset specificity – since there is clearly a great deal of health sector-specific human assets but mobility between health sector jobs. In any given situation it is worth thinking also about whether there are any other factors causing human asset specificity of the generic type described above. For example, a chief executive of a health authority may have to sacrifice considerable human assets to change job.

Dedicated assets seem to give rise to few generic health sector issues, but could be an important consideration in any specific situation – for example, where a hospital invests in facilities under a contract to cater for the employees of a company.

Note

1 'A spot market contract is a contract for the immediate market exchange of goods or services at current prices' (Milgram and Roberts 1992).

15 Market structures

15.1 Introduction

The role of markets and competition in health care has been brought to prominence in the discussion of health sector reforms all around the world. In many countries there is a large volume of private health care activity. In others, reforms have introduced a greater role for market mechanisms within the public sector, an issue which is further discussed in Chapter 25. Understanding the theory of markets may help government to form appropriate regulatory or incentive-based policies to ensure the appropriate operation of these markets. When a substantial private market exists in parallel with the public sector then forming public sector policies, which ignore the dynamics of the private market, would seem an unwise strategy.

A simple definition of a market is that it is a set of arrangements by which buyers and sellers exchange goods and services. From Part I, we know that the market is the interplay between demand and supply.

In Chapter 6 we compared markets operating under perfect competition and monopoly, and saw that the level of output which a firm selects and the price which it charges for its product depends on the structure of the market. In simple terms, market structure can be thought of as a description of the characteristics of buyers and sellers (for example, size and number). Although pure forms of these structures are uncommon they are useful in showing the range of possible outcomes. This chapter considers the behaviour of firms and markets under intermediate forms of market structure.

15.2 Imperfect competition

Between the two extremes of perfect competition and pure monopoly there are a range of market forms. These can be analysed by combining the features of the perfect competition and monopoly models. Common problems occur when there is a small number of firms providing a service.

Imperfect competition covers a range of market structures from many firms to a few but, in contrast to perfect competition, relies on each firm facing a downward-sloping demand curve. This results from the relaxation of at least one of two perfect competition assumptions – homogeneous product or perfect information. Departure from perfect elasticity of the demand curve results from the firm differentiating its product from those of other firms – on the basis that some consumers will prefer the differentiated product sufficient to pay some higher price than similar products are sold at. Alternatively, if information is imperfect, some consumers will pay a higher price to one seller, rather than incur search costs in finding the lowest-price product on the market. This also means that any one seller will not lose all their sales by pricing above the minimum.

Demand will be more inelastic where there are relatively few sellers who differentiate their products to an extent inducing strong brand loyalty, or where information problems are acute, and search costs therefore high. Imperfect competition is also known as *monopolistic competition* in some texts, and *oligopoly*, a market characterised by a small number of firms, covers the range of cases at relatively demand-inelastic points on the range between perfect competition and monopoly.

The key feature of an oligopoly is that the decision made by one firm depends on the decision made by other firms, i.e. there is a high degree of interdependence between firms. Firms therefore can only decide upon their best strategy in light of what they know about other firms. Many different possible models exist, depending on what assumptions the firm is assumed to make about other firms in the market.

An example of this type of model is the kinked demand curve model under which firms assume that, if they raise their prices, other firms will not follow but will seize the opportunity to gain market share. However, price reductions will be imitated as other firms seek to avoid losing market share. This implies that the firm's demand curve is elastic above the currently prevailing price and inelastic below it (Figure 15.1). The model predicts price stability and that competition will take non-price forms. For example, competition may take the form of increases in quality without corresponding increases in price.

A substantial part of the literature looks at *collusion*, where there is an explicit attempt by the different firms in the industry to co-ordinate their pricing and output strategies so that together they can reap monopolistic profits. By colluding (agreeing on price and output levels) firms can jointly generate the profits which would be associated with monopoly and share them among themselves, rather than competing supranormal profit away. Formal collusion in the form of cartels is usually illegal within national

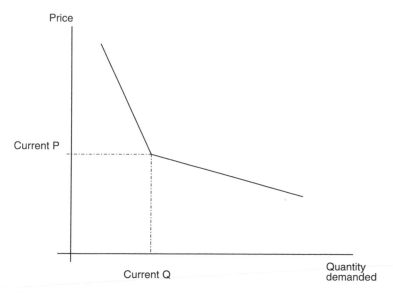

Figure 15.1 The kinked demand curve.

economies. However, international export cartels such as OPEC have been successful in supporting higher prices of commodities through international agreements to restrict export quantities. Such examples also demonstrate the difficulties of maintaining the agreements necessary, since it is in the interest of each to cheat on the rest of the cartel. Consider Figure 15.2, which presents a two-firm case. The cartel may maximise joint profit by producing where total marginal cost (derived by horizontally summing the marginal cost) intersects the marginal revenue curve derived from the market demand. Output is shared, so that MC = MR in each firm and the monopolist's profit is shared between the two firms.

The problem is that both firms have an incentive to increase their share of profit by cutting price and capturing a larger share of total demand. This incentive exists up to the point where each individual firm's marginal cost curves intersect with the market marginal revenue curve. Formal collusion through cartels is very vulnerable to price cutting among members and this has not only at times caused disarray within OPEC, but has undermined the development of similar commodity-based cartels despite some attempts to establish these.

Such collusion can occur in the health sector. Price agreements are quite common. For example, hospitals jointly agree a price schedule for insurers in Brazil, and it is not uncommon for groups of surgeons to agree fee scales for different operations. It is quite difficult to establish whether or not such agreements set prices at monopoly profit levels, have the intention of restricting competition or have another purpose – but at least in some cases it would seem that they are set at a rate judged to be what the market will bear and aim to prevent competitive strategies which involve undercutting on price.

Game theory attempts to model the behaviour of firms by seeing them as players in a game. The classic game is that of the Prisoners' Dilemma. Two prisoners have been taken in for questioning and they are held in separate cells: there is not enough evidence to prosecute them without at least one prisoner confessing. If neither confesses they are both released. If both confess they each get a prison sentence of ten years. But the worst scenario for each is if his fellow prisoner confesses and he does not – a prison sentence of twenty years. What decision would you make under such circumstances? Your answer is probably dependent on your prior relationship with, and knowledge of, your fellow prisoner. Similarly, firms' decisions about outputs in the market are likely to be

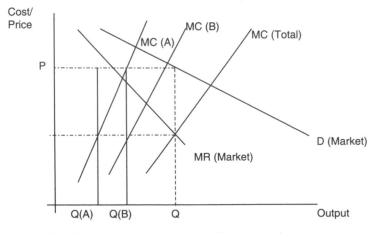

Figure 15.2 The incentive to form a cartel.

affected by the number of times these decision are to be made and firms' beliefs about each other. These become critical factors determining outcome.

The presence of asymmetrical information between producer and consumer may also give rise to forms of imperfect competition. For example, consider a situation where the product is not homogeneous and consumers have preferences over different products. There are likely to be search costs associated with finding their preferred product. Consumers will only invest in search activity up to the point where the expected marginal benefit of search is equal to the marginal cost. Under such conditions, consumers may not search the whole market and hence producers may retain a degree of market power. The smaller the search cost the better informed the consumer will be and the more closely the model will approximate perfect competition.

The presence of asymmetrical information and search costs is pronounced in health markets, as has been discussed in Chapter 7. There are high costs associated with 'shopping around' for the best health care. This has implications for the degree of market power wielded by health service providers.

15.3 Alternative models of provider competition in health care

Traditional theories of competition suggest, crudely speaking, that as the concentration of the market declines and competition becomes more intense, prices will fall. Decreasing degrees of market power, reflected in more elastic demand curves facing the individual firm, are expected to lead to profit levels approaching the normal and prices closer to the minimum points of average cost curves. However, in the health sectors of some countries, there is a commonly observed association between lower market concentration and higher prices. This has led to attempts by health economists to explain this conflict with the predictions of traditional economic theory.

The models discussed below are not mutually exclusive and it is possible that they occur in parallel with price competition. Thus even in health care markets, where lower market concentration (a larger number of firms) is associated with lower prices, one cannot conclude that there is necessarily no simultaneous presence of other forms of competition. The supplier-induced demand model of Chapter 7 is a further example of a possible monopolistic competition explanation of perverse market response.

15.3.1 *Quality competition*

This is perhaps the most straightforward model. It suggests that providers respond to lower concentration (more competition) not by dropping price but by increasing quality. Within a profit-maximising framework, this strategy will be rational if it costs the provider less to gain additional customers by increasing quality than by reducing price. In other words if, per unit of expenditure, quality elasticity of demand is higher than price elasticity of demand, it will be more profitable for the provider to increase quality than to reduce price.

This relationship between quality elasticity and price elasticity may be particularly likely in the health sector if consumers are not very sensitive to price because of extensive insurance coverage and/or because quality dominates in their utility functions.

In addition, the objective functions of actors in the hospital market may differ from those usually assumed. Hospital managers may seek to pursue quality rather than profit-oriented objectives. Physicians may seek to work in hospitals with a good

reputation for high-quality care, implying some rather peculiar features of this particular labour supply curve. Chapter 16 gives more attention to these possibilities and it is
important to note here only that these also provide an explanation of quality competition models.

Quality competition is often (but not always) associated with higher investment in
high-technology equipment and hotel aspects of care. It is less commonly suggested
that quality competition leads to improvements in technical aspects of quality (the
medical appropriateness of the treatment provided). Technical aspects are those patients
are least likely to be able to judge, in comparison with the availability of certain items
of equipment or the luxury of the building. Investing in easily observable aspects of
quality is consistent with profit-maximising explanations, since these aspects play the
most important role in the demand function. It may also be consistent with managerial
theories of hospital motivation (see Chapter 16), if what managers are interested to
maximise is the observable quality of care in their hospital rather than the technical
aspects. According to either explanation, hospitals invest in these aspects in order to
signal to the patient the quality of the service they provide. As more and more facilities
attempt to signal quality, the louder the signal must be in order to be heard against
the background noise. Thus problems of excessive high-tech equipment accumulation
occur. Box 15.1 considers evidence for this kind of competitive behaviour for the
hospital market of Bangkok, and Box 15.2 considers trends in the United States.

15.3.2 *Increasing monopoly model*

Pauly and Satterthwaite 1981 argue that health care is a 'reputation good', meaning
that (1) sellers' products are differentiated and (2) consumers' search among sellers is
conducted by asking friends and relatives for recommendations. The model is thought
to be mainly relevant to primary care. Primary care services are frequently used,
assumed to imply that reputation is a more important factor than for more rarely used
services. Primary care services are also less sophisticated than higher levels of care, and
so patients may feel they are in a better position to judge the service provided. The
argument is as follows:

1   If the number of health care providers within a community increases, the available
    consumer information about each decreases. Therefore consumers find it hard to
    collect information about a new provider.
2   If the search for information becomes more difficult, consumers become less price
    sensitive.
3   Therefore an increase in supply of health care providers makes the consumers'
    search more difficult and may cause the equilibrium fee to rise.

However, the increasing monopoly model makes a number of questionable assumptions about consumer search behaviour. If consumers seek information by asking a
question like 'What do you know about Dr Black?' then indeed as the number of
providers increases the people with knowledge about Dr Black are more thinly spread
and information is harder to find. On the other hand if consumers seek information by
asking questions such as 'Do you know a good physician around here?' it is not clear
that search costs will rise with the number of physicians – they may even fall.

There is no substantial evidence supporting the increasing monopoly model but the

---

Box 15.1 Market structure and competitive strategy in Bangkok

By 1993 there were 105 private and eighty public hospitals in Bangkok. 80 per cent of the private hospitals were 'for profit'. Forty-five per cent of the population were estimated to be covered by some kind of health insurance. An analysis of the hospital market aimed to differentiate between price competition, supplier-induced demand (see Chapter 7) and quality competition by estimating the correlation between measures of competition within areas of 2 km and 5 km radius of Bangkok and measures of price, service intensity and indicators of quality.

Correlations between price levels and measures of competition (numbers of hospitals and Hirschman–Hirfendahl indices based on bed numbers for areas of 2 km and 5 km radius) were insignificant, suggesting that price competition, if present, did not dominate competitive strategy. There was positive correlation between measures of competition, expenditure per bed, and a measure of asset value per bed, providing some evidence of quality competition. However, this result had to be interpreted cautiously. The highest levels of competition were found in central Bangkok, areas where there may have been other reasons for high expenditure and asset levels per bed.

The issue of quality competition was further explored by generating 'quality adjusted prices' (Cowling and Cubbin 1971), which indicate an expected price given quality characteristics. There was no relationship between the actual and quality-adjusted price, suggesting that the Bangkok market would bear 'significant and unjustified' price variation. Further, the difference between the two prices correlated positively with the level of competition, assessed by all measures. This implies that after quality factors were taken into account, prices were higher in hospitals which faced greater competition – possibly explained by the presence of supplier-induced demand.

Privately owned hospitals which were floated on the stock market offered higher quality, charged higher prices and made higher profits. They tended to charge considerably higher prices than were apparently warranted by their quality of care characteristics. There may be a virtuous circle (from the hospital's perspective!) by which hospitals develop their reputation (for example, through quality signals), 'premium price' above the level justified by their quality standards (Cleverly 1992) and in turn signal quality through the act of 'premium pricing'.

This evidence tends to urge caution in advocating or encouraging a greater role for the private sector, as was done in Thailand, where regulatory capacity is weak. Quality competition, described by increasing prices associated with possibly irrelevant quality dimensions used to signal, does not result in better value for money in health services for patients.

Source: Bennett (1997).

---

questions it raises are interesting and relevant. For example, how do different facilities form a reputation? Is it through good reports or avoiding bad ones? We understand little about the processes through which consumer information in health care markets is generated.

Box 15.2 Competition and cost in the US health care system

Meltzer and Chung (2002) examined the impact of higher levels of competition on patterns of cost across different patient groups in California. They compared the years 1983, when retrospective reimbursement dominated hospitals' revenues, and 1993, when prospective reimbursement (using a DRG-based system) had been introduced. (See section 14.5.2 for definitions of these terms.)

Previous research had suggested that competition under retrospective reimbursement increased costs, whereas competition under prospective reimbursement reduced costs. Under retrospective reimbursement this might be explained either by quality competition or supplier-induced demand. Under DRG-based reimbursement quality competition and supplier inducement strategies are muted by the ceiling on reimbursement per patient, but the impetus by which greater competition would lower expenditure per patient is less clear.

Meltzer and Chung considered the differential responses to higher levels of competition for patients of different levels of cost within the twelve largest DRG categories. Markets were defined by county boundaries, and the level of competition measured by the HHI as 'less competitive' (HHI >0.20), 'moderately competitive' (0.20 ≥ HHI > 0.10), 'competitive' (0.10 ≥ HHI > 0.05) and 'very competitive' (HHI ≤ 0.05). Patient cost data were generated from the use of institution-specific ratios of costs to charges, and total charge data.

Consistently, across all twelve DRG categories, Meltzer and Chung found that in 1993 more competitive markets were associated with lower costs, whereas in 1983 more competitive markets were associated with higher costs for all categories of patient. In 1993 lower costs were particularly marked for patients aged over sixty-five years and those in the most expensive expenditure percentiles within each DRG.

This was consistent with their theoretical model. Within each DRG patients will be distributed according to expected cost profiles around the reimbursement level which has been set according to an estimate of the average cost profile. Those with expected costs above the reimbursement level are unprofitable; those with expected costs below the reimbursement level are profitable. Hospitals will seek to compete for the profitable patients – perhaps by offering additional services such as amenities that increase the expenditure per patient – and they may adopt an opposite strategy in relation to unprofitable patients to encourage them to seek care elsewhere. If hospitals in general respond in this way, a hospital that fails to do so will accumulate a higher ratio of unprofitable to profitable patients. Incentives to respond differentially according to patient type may then be exacerbated under higher levels of competition.

This analysis emphasises the importance of understanding institutional arrangements in analysing the role of market structure on performance. While it seems that competition failed to discipline US health markets under retrospective reimbursement, instead promoting cost-inflationary pressures, it may play a different role under prospective reimbursement. Concern about market performance may instead focus on the need to monitor and protect quality of care levels for the most severely ill patients in more competitive environments.

15.4 Monopoly, oligopoly and contestability

We have seen that monopolists and collusive oligopolists can make positive (supra-normal) profits where other firms do not enter the market. It has been suggested that monopolistic and oligopolistic profits may be eroded by the threat of competition even if it remains a threat and no entry in fact takes place (Baumol *et al.* 1982). This idea is referred to as *contestability*. Baumol argues that having one firm does not mean there is no competition, and potential competition (the threat of entry) may serve to discipline the established firm.

Perfect contestability requires only one of the conditions for perfect competition: entry is absolutely free and exit is absolutely costless. This implies that the potential entrant will enter if profit can be made and does not consider entry and exit costs. It further implies that:

1 No entrant can make a supranormal profit, at the market price.
2 If the incumbent producer(s) price(s) above average cost even for a very short period, it is vulnerable to 'hit and run' entry which may result in losses for the incumbent. The incumbent will not therefore price above average cost.
3 Technical inefficiency offers the same opportunity to a potential entrant. By setting up efficient production the entrant can undercut the incumbent and force her out of business. Production must therefore be technically efficient.
4 Price must equal marginal cost, since other choices represent profitable opportunities to potential entrants. Consider Figure 15.3, which assumes normal cost curves. We have already seen that price must not be set above average cost to avoid profitable opportunities for entrants. Suppose the incumbent prices below marginal cost (for example, at point A on Figure 15.3.) The incumbent is producing a number of units of output (Qa–Qx) which are loss-making. This implies that an entrant could sell a smaller amount at a lower price without making a loss. (The lower price can be set so as to compensate for the reduced loss from moving towards Qx.) Suppose,

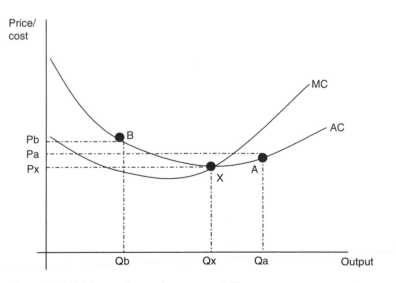

Figure 15.3 Pricing under perfect contestability.

instead, the incumbent sets a price, such as B, above MC. Profitable opportunities exist through increasing production along Qb–Qx and the entrant could cut the incumbent's price by selling a slightly larger output and ensuring that additional profit offsets the lower price. Here there is a condition, however – elasticity of demand must be such that the increased production will be purchased. In a two-incumbent case it is always possible to increase production above the average level of production of each firm by replacing existing production without relying on an increase in total market demand.

At the level of the market, structure is determined by the ratio of Qx to market demand at Px. While excess demand exists, profitable opportunities arise from the replication of the incumbent's activity. In the case of economies of scale, one firm will operate at the point at which demand is exhausted at P = AC. Figure 15.4 describes this case. P*Q* is the price and output decision of an incumbent monopolist. This scenario illustrates the exception to the P = MC rule given above. An entrant is constrained from undercutting P* by being unable to increase demand sufficiently to compensate for the price reduction. Normal profits could be maintained while cutting price by moving to a position further along the AC curve (such as A), but the position and elasticity of the demand curve indicate that this is not possible.

Under perfect contestability the welfare implications are identical to those of perfect competition, since no supranormal profits are made, and outputs are priced at marginal cost, implying efficient consumption and production decisions in own and related markets.

While perfect contestability is likely to be no more prevalent than perfect competition, this theory suggests that markets may be disciplined by potential competition as much as by actual competition. The theory strengthens the arguments of anti-interventionists, suggesting that markets may be getting it more or less right most of

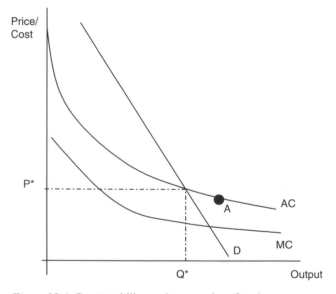

Figure 15.4 Contestability and economies of scale.

the time. Its less restrictive assumptions suggest that conditions may more frequently approximate contestability, and therefore efficiency.

In a health sector context, the theory of contestability has been used to argue that health sector reform which relies on the operation of competitive pressures (such as the creation of an internal market, for example, see Chapter 25) can function even when it is clear that markets are not competitive by conventional definitions.

It is therefore highly relevant to ask to what extent contestability might apply to such markets. How easy is it for firms to enter and exit relevant health service markets? One factor that severely inhibits entry and exit is that of sunk costs. Sunk costs are costs of investment which cannot be transferred to a new industry if that investment fails. (Similar to the concept of asset specificity introduced in the previous chapter.)[1] These kinds of costs are thought to be significant in health service provision at higher levels of technology, and include the specialised nature of hospital buildings and of much medical equipment. In general, barriers to entry are likely to be quite important across the health sector.

The contestability theory may not satisfy us that monopoly will not cause problems for health markets as a whole. However, many specific markets within the health sector look more contestable. For example, the market for the provision of family doctor services may be readily entered by those with medical qualifications who otherwise practise in more specialised health markets. If premises, equipment and ancillary services can be rented or bought in easily, that market may be quite contestable over a range of output levels. The pharmaceutical retailing market may be low-cost to enter and exit if pharmacists can be employed on short contracts, premises are easily convertible to other types of shop and stocks move quickly.

15.5 Measurement of market structure

Most of the market structure models we have described assume that market structure (number of sellers in the market, their degree of product differentiation, the cost structure) determines conduct (such as price, research and development, investment, advertising) and so yields market performance (efficiency, ratio of price to marginal cost, profits). This is commonly known as the structure–conduct–performance paradigm.

It is clear that there are limitations to this perspective. Most important, the paradigm offers no explanation of structure but rather starts with structure given. The contestability model departs from this by also providing an explanation of why a market is structured as it is structured, in terms of the relationship between production functions, cost functions and demand functions – market structure would follow from the least-cost replication of production. In Chapter 14 we saw that transaction cost economics offered a different explanation of market structure – market structure would follow from attempts to minimise transaction costs. There has been further criticism of the structure–conduct–performance paradigm from the perspective that the firm's conduct can be targeted at changing the structure of the industry in pursuit of objectives other than efficiency. For example, advertising strategies may explicitly aim to concentrate market power in the hands of fewer competitors.

From any of these perspectives, attempts to operationalise and test the implications of market models require measurement of market structure. The simplest measure is the *concentration ratio* that is given by

$$CR_n = \sum_{I=1}^{n} S_I$$

where S_I is the share of the ith firm in the market and n represents the number of firms chosen to include. This measure only considers the n largest firms in the industry.

An alternative measure is the Hirschman–Herfindahl index (HHI):

$$HHI = \sum_{I=1}^{N} S_I^2$$

where N is the total number of firms in the industry and S_I is the share of the ith firm. This ranges from close to 0 (large number of competitors all with small market shares) to 1 (single monopoly supplier). Box 15.3 shows an example of the calculation of the HHI within the health care market in New Zealand.

Another problem with empirical work which aims to measure market structure is the question of how to define a market. Definitions can be product or geographically specific. Highly product-specific definitions of markets lead to high concentration ratios (for example, the market for MRI) relative to more industry-specific definitions (for example, diagnostic technologies). This explains part of the rationale for firms to try and differentiate their products through advertising and other marketing strategies. Zwanziger *et al.* (1994), ask the question 'What is the relevant market for hospitals?' They find that this can vary according to the reimbursement scheme, and that there may be less competition than initially appears to be the case. Propper and Bartlett (1997) take a different view of the UK hospital market, suggesting that when viewed from the perspective of individual procedures and specialities, there is more competition than might be imagined. For example, for certain kinds of elective surgery, patients travel quite significant distances for care, implying higher levels of competition than might be expected between hospitals considerable distances apart.

15.6 Markets, hierarchies and networks

As we saw in Chapter 14, a central feature of the analysis of the 'make or buy?' decision is the role of transaction costs in the evolution and interaction between institutions both internally and externally within a market. As it becomes more difficult to contract through market organisation, theory suggests that the firm or organisation may decide to integrate with another firm rather than try to exchange goods by buying and selling. Vertical integration occurs when firms merge with other firms at a different stage of the production process (for example, when a car manufacturer buys the manufacturer of some of its component parts). Horizontal integration occurs when firms merge with others at the same stage of the production process, and produces either greater market concentration (for example, when two brewers merge) or firms with more diversified product ranges (for example, when a manufacturer of chocolate confectionery merges with a firm producing breakfast cereal.) Organising transactions within a firm, in contrast with organisation between firms, has been described as hierarchy. Hierarchical transactions 'are ones for which a single administrative entity spans both sides of the

Box 15.3 Measuring market concentration: secondary services in New Zealand

Ashton and Press (1997) consider the market concentration of a number of services in New Zealand before and after the introduction of health sector reforms to promote competition in 1993. Seven secondary services were selected: tonsillectomies and/or adenoidectomies, prostatectomies, knee joint replacements; hip replacements, cataract removal; angioplasties and coronary artery bypass grafts (CABG).

There were several issues which arose when they tried to define the market, including how to delineate the market area. They calculated the HHI for a number of scenarios. (The HHI is multiplied by 10,000 to make interpretation easier.) When is a market concentrated? The cut-off is arbitrary, but in practice a value of 1,800 has been used. Thus an HHI above 1,800 is considered to indicate a market which is highly concentrated. This value is used as the cut-off for anti-trust cases by the US Department of Justice.

One set of results from Ashton and Press is shown in the table. Since they were looking at a number of different markets carrying out the same procedures, they categorised the procedures according to what proportion of markets were considered to be relatively unconcentrated.

Concentration of market for selected procedures

Procedure	No. of markets	% of markets with HHI < 1800
Angioplasty	7	71.43
Cataract removal	23	64.71
CABG	5	80.00
Hip replacement	23	45.45
Knee replacement	22	42.86
Prostatectomy	19	27.78
Tonsillectomy	21	65.00

The results suggest that the markets for the selected procedures were all highly concentrated. The CABG and the angioplasty were the least concentrated markets. Interestingly, these two procedures also involved the highest degree of specialisation and, one would expect, the highest barriers to entry, and thus relatively more market concentration. One possible explanation is that these services are often not available locally and patients expect to travel to use them, increasing the geographical area that constitutes a market.

Source: Ashton and Press (1997).

transaction' (Williamson 1985). On this understanding as discussed above, one can view market structure as dependent on transaction costs.

The market and hierarchy duality may miss important intermediate forms of relationships. In Chapter 14 we discussed relational contracting (where the contracting relationship is long-term and stable). Developments in new institutional economics emphasise the role of norms and networks as mechanisms to reduce transaction costs, consider more dynamic approaches to institutions and look at how over time they evolve to seize efficiency increasing opportunities. These developments imply that new approaches need to be taken to the understanding of market structure and its implications.

What is a network? In simple terms, it can be thought of as a set of links or relationships between individuals or organisations. A task network refers to a set of organisations involved in the activities needed to accomplish a task. The set of organisations may include, for example, government units, non-governmental organisations or the private sector. Thus outcome or performance is related to how well these networks function in terms of both co-ordination and communication. Primary organisations have a central role in performing the task, while secondary organisations are complementary or supportive of the primary organisation (Grindle and Hilderbrand 1995).

Networks can be seen as an alternative (to markets and hierarchies) way of organising activities, able to represent individuals and activities in the context of a broader system of structures or organisations. In addition to price and governance structures, emphasis is now also placed on factors such as trust and reputation.

The design of the network can emerge from collaboration or inter-firm alliance (e.g. the aligning of airlines in competitive networks). This view of networks as an alternative form of organisation is underpinned by both transaction cost minimisation and oligopolistic market competition strategy.

Given these characteristics, it is difficult to distinguish different forms of organisation. Indeed, Bradach and Eccles (1989) suggest that different forms of institutions (markets, networks and hierarchies) are not mutually exclusive.

Formal networks have become a common feature of more market-oriented health care systems such as those of Taiwan (Lin and Wan 1999) and the United States (Broyles *et al.* 1998). These new perspectives on market structure give us new frameworks with which to evaluate and understand relationships between organisations in the health sector. For example, the introduction of internal markets in health care provision (see Chapter 25 and especially Box 25.2) can be viewed, from a classical perspective, as an attempt to tap the benefits of competition and market forces. However, from a new institutional economics perspective, these reforms can be interpreted as the attempt to move from hierarchical to market modes of transacting in order to economise on transaction costs. However, as new structures emerge, they may not resemble those intended, as organisations manoeuvre to exploit new possibilities in the market. Merger activity is an easily observable response, and has been prevalent among purchasers and hospitals responding to the reforms in the UK, for example. Equally important, if less observable, is the emergence of networks in formal and informal varieties. At the extreme, these may virtually reinstate hierarchical relationships, for example informally reintegrating purchasers and providers through long-term relational contracts, personal relationships and evolving norms of behaviour which govern the parties of the network.

Note

1 Although specific assets constitute sunk costs, not all sunk costs are specific assets. For example, the legal work involved in establishing a new company is a sunk cost, but not a specific asset.

16 Hospital and health provider behaviour and motivation

16.1 Introduction

Throughout our discussions of market models to this point, we have assumed that firms are profit-maximising. As with the other assumptions of the model, it is worth considering the implications of relaxing it. In this chapter we consider the extent to which health care providers may be motivated by factors other than profit maximisation and how this might affect their behaviour.

16.2 Profit maximisation and alternative motivations

The goal of profit maximisation provides the motivation in much of the economic theory of the firm. If firms do not maximise profits, then it follows that they may not minimise costs or maximise revenue. There are reasons to question the realism of profit maximisation in health care provision in many parts of the world. In this section, we explore alternatives to profit maximisation which can be found in the literature of the economic theory of the firm. In the next section, we will explore the insights this literature generates into the motivation and behaviour of health care providers.

16.2.1 Managerial theories of the firm

In many large firms the owners (shareholders) are not the managers. Owners effectively employ managers to act on their behalf. As with the doctor–patient relationship, principal–agent theory provides a useful framework to analyse the implications of this arrangement. Managers may act as imperfect agents for the owners and may pursue objectives other than profit maximisation. One model suggests that managers maximise revenue subject to a profitability constraint imposed by shareholders and possibly by the danger of take-over by another firm. There are several reasons why managers may maximise revenue:

1 The earnings of top managers tend to be related to sales.
2 Large sales give prestige to managers.
3 High revenue avoids having to make staff redundant.

The situation for a firm with some degree of monopoly power is reflected in Figure 16.1. Under profit maximisation managers would choose to produce at point X (where the excess of total revenue over total cost is greatest). If managers are attempting to

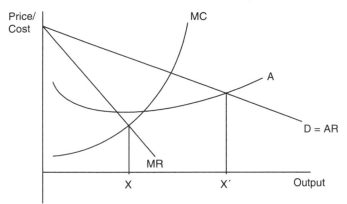

Figure 16.1 The firm under revenue maximisation.

maximise revenue subject to a 'break-even' profit constraint (profits must not fall below zero), then they would choose a rather higher output level at X'. If the profit constraint is binding at some positive level, then the chosen output level will lie between X and X'.

Under perfect competition, managers cannot pursue non-profit-maximising strategies, as they would make losses and would be driven from the market. The degree to which managers are able to pursue objectives other than profit maximisation (i.e. their discretionary power) depends on the nature of the market within which they operate and the strength and nature of competition.

Revenue maximisation (like profit maximisation) may be an oversimplification of the objectives that the manager is likely to have. A less restrictive theory is that managers maximise a managerial utility function (subject to constraints) and this contains a number of arguments. For example:

Managerial utility = f(salary, security, power, status)

Of these variables, only salary is easy to measure. Many economists dislike this kind of model, since it is hard to derive clear predictions about behaviour. It sacrifices ability to predict for realism of assumption (see Box 1.1).

Managerial theories have been applied in the health sector. Some studies have assumed revenue maximisation as the manager's objective, in some cases with a quality constraint. Others have compiled a rather more complex set of objectives. For example, Hornbrook and Goldfarb (1983) consider the following list of dimensions which they consider are important to the managers of US hospitals: level of emergency stand-by capacity, total admissions, the diagnostic mix of admissions and the hospital's 'style of practice' with respect to ancillary services and length of stay. It is suggested that different hospitals may attach different weights to these dimensions, depending on their particular utility function, but will try to maximise utility subject to constraints (such as the community's ability to pay for hospital care and community epidemiology). Health care providers with different types of ownership (public, private for-profit, private non-profit) are likely to put different emphases on these dimensions.

16.2.2 Behavioural theories of the firm

The managerial theories described above assume that the firm/health care provider has a single utility function. In contrast behavioural theories recognise that firms are made up of diverse sets of actors, who may not share the same goals. The firm (or hospital) therefore is not treated as a single decision-making unit, but as one with multiple actors and objectives. There may be conflict between the goals of different individuals and groups within firms. The way in which firms behave depends upon the relative power of different actors and how the institutional arrangements within firms lead to conflict resolution.

The roots of behavioural theory are in the work of Herbert Simon (1957). Simon made a distinction between substantive and procedural rationality. Economic theory is based on substantive or unbounded rationality, that is, rational agents are said to make decisions which maximise the achievement of their own goals, given existing constraints. Procedural rationality occurs when agents may not necessarily succeed in maximising their own goals but, given the relative importance of the decision, give it appropriate deliberation. Procedural rationality allows for the use of rule-of-thumb measures.

In the context of a hospital behaviour theory, this approach has considerable appeal. Managers may have different objective functions from clinicians, different doctors may have different goals. Different types of agents may have control over different elements within the hospital (e.g. doctors may control the use of beds but managers may have control over how many beds can be managed by each doctor). How competing objective functions are reconciled is likely to depend on the internal structure of the organisation.

It was suggested earlier that there may be differences in objectives between provider institutions according to their ownership. Ownership may also affect the internal structure of hospitals and other provider institutions, and this may be another route through which ownership affects the behaviour of different health care providers.

16.3 Models of hospital behaviour

The development of hospital models can be seen to parallel the development of the theory of the firm (McGuire 1985). Some fall within the tradition of the profit-maximising firm. Others parallel the managerial theory of the firm where the hospital pursues managerial objectives. Still others parallel behavioural theories, where the concern of the model is with internal bargaining between rival interest groups within the hospital, rather than with the specification of an objective function for the purpose of predicting behaviour within the market place.

However, more recent models have applied composite objective functions consisting of both profit and managerial (or perhaps even clinical) objectives (for example, Ellis and McGuire 1986; Dranove 1988; Hodgkin and McGuire 1994). Pure profit maximisation and pure managerialism have given way to mixed-objective functions, and duopoly (or bilateral monopoly) models have been applied to doctor–manager bargaining (Custer *et al.* 1990; Muurinen 1986).

16.3.1 The hospital as a physicians' co-operative

Pauly and Redisch (1973) describe the not-for-profit hospital as a 'physicians' co-operative', implying that the objective function consists of the incomes of physicians, who dominate among groups of hospital decision makers. This is the closest a model specifically focusing on hospital behaviour comes to espousing profit maximisation. In this model the full price of care is determined by consumer demand, and the amount of care produced and offered to patients depends in turn on the quantity of inputs chosen by the decision makers (e.g. capital, labour and physician inputs).

In a model where the number of physicians is fixed (the closed staff model) the hospital maximises net average revenue to physicians:

Net average revenue to physicians = $(P.Q - rK - wL)/M$

where P is the total price for care, Q; r and w are the input prices for capital (K) and labour (L) and M is the number of physicians on staff. The hospital is viewed as profit-maximiser, with all the residual profits given to the physicians as income, but the physicians are the decision makers.

The physicians may either follow the co-operative strategy, operating as a cartel, or follow a non-co-operative strategy. Within the co-operative strategy three possible sets of arrangements are considered: (1) the 'closed staff' model in which the physicians regulate their numbers in order to maximise average net revenue and each takes an equal share; (2) the 'discriminatory hiring' model in which some physicians are partners who share equally in the net revenue and other physicians are hired and paid their marginal product; (3) the 'open-staff' model, in which any physician wishing to join the hospital can do so and share equally in the net revenue.

Pauly and Redisch analyse optimal staffing from the point of view of the physicians in each of these sets of arrangements. An interesting result from their model is that an increase in demand could lead to higher price levels, lower output, and fewer physicians, as the cartel seeks to maximise net revenue per physician (a result also found in models of soviet collective farms). Under the non-cooperative strategy, the cartel breaks down (or never forms) if the incentive structure encourages the individual physician to free-ride. Pauly and Redisch suggest non-cooperation is more likely where there are larger numbers of physicians, and it results in a smaller number of physicians working in the hospital. By employing more non-physician labour and utilising other hospital inputs an individual physician may be able to charge a higher price for his/her own services. But this inflates hospital costs, reducing net revenue.

16.3.2 *The quantity/quality non-profit theory*

One prominent theory of hospital behaviour is that proposed by Newhouse (1970) to describe non-profit firms of all kinds. Under this theory, the objective of the hospital is to maximise utility. The hospital's preferences are defined over quantity of output (number of cases, etc.) and quality of output.

This objective function implies that a hospital would be prepared to make sacrifices in terms of quantity (for instance, number of patient days) in order to provide higher quality. This can be represented by an indifference curve. For each level of quality, the hospital faces a given demand curve and a given cost function. Increases in quality from low levels would bring increases in demand, as improved quality attracted patients. There would therefore be no trade-off at these low quality levels. But at higher levels of quality the higher costs of provision would deter those with lower ability to pay, leading to a reduction in the quantity of service provided. The result is the unconventionally shaped budget constraint of Figure 16.2. Chosen quantity–quality level is Ql*Qn*.

The model yields a number of predictions, including: least cost production; a bias towards high-quality services and away from low-quality services, even where the low quality services would be in demand; duplication of equipment and capital intensity.

Newhouse's model is an example of a managerial approach, stressing the role of non-financial objectives and the decision-making influence of the manager rather than the clinician. Other examples of this approach include Feldstein (1968), Reder (1965), Lee (1971) and Joseph (1975). Feldstein assumes an objective of maximum output for a given quality; Rice assumes output maximisation; Reder models clinicians as quality maximisers and administrators as having a combined quality/quantity maximising objective related to prestige and salary; in Lee's model, managers are motivated by the prestige acquired for the institution through high input utilisation; Joseph includes quality, quantity and also the number of patients turned away. What all have in common is that they are based on the specification of a utility function that consists of objectives defined in terms of the quantity and/or quality of care provided. High on the list of human motives in these accounts of hospitals is the prestige felt by managers (and perhaps medical staff also) at working in an institution of high reputation.

16.3.3 *The Harris model*

The Newhouse model maximises the utility function of the managers in the hospital, whereas the Pauly–Redisch model assumes *de facto* control by physicians. The Harris model (Harris 1977) presents the hospital as a scene of continual conflict between two groups.

Harris describes the hospital as composed of two separate firms, rather than as a single firm. One of the firms is made up of medical staff, who comprise a demand division. The hospital administration comprises a second firm, or supply division. Harris views

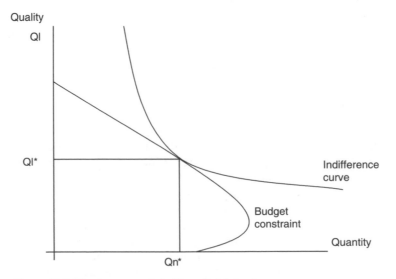

Figure 16.2 Newhouse model of hospital behaviour.

Source: Newhouse (1970).

these two firms as quite separate structures: 'Each half of the organisation has its own managers, objectives, pricing strategies and constraints.' He describes the interaction of these two firms as a 'non-co-operative oligopoly-type game'. The level of spare capacity forms a key battleground. The administration seeks to maximise bed occupancy but the doctors seek bigger defensive margins to minimise the risk of insufficient capacity.

In Harris's discussion the doctors would seem to be the more powerful group. But, despite his emphasis on conflict, his conclusions are in fact similar to those of Newhouse: 'quantity and quality dominate in the objectives which the conflict results in the hospital pursing'. This discussion predicts conflict over the level of spare capacity and a tendency to expand (given a soft budget constraint).

The model offers an explanation of the expansionist tendencies of US health care in the 1970s and 1980s which are a key concern of Part IV. The model also offers some other perspectives which may be useful for policy making and regulation of the hospital sector. First, given the role of physicians, we can expect that the hospitals' preference for technologies will be driven by the preferences of the physician demanders. Second, hospital regulation aimed primarily at the trustee–administrator group may have little effect. Regulation to limit hospital costs must establish incentives for and constraints on the physician–agent as well as the administrator.

Harris's model is an example of a behavioural model which is concerned with the potential for conflict in the objective functions pursued by different decision makers within the organisation. Models of internal bargaining in hospitals described in Muurinen (1986) also fall into this category, as do the models of Custer *et al.* (1990) who describe the relation between hospitals and their medical staffs as variously 'non-co-operative', 'co-operative' or 'dominant–reactive', and consider the implications of prospective and retrospective reimbursement under each characterisation of the relationship.

16.4 The relevance of these models to provider institutions in other health systems

These models all originate in the United States and thus describe the consequences of incentive structures common there. Since these provide a snapshot of provider institutions operating in perhaps the most private sector-oriented health system in the world (see Part IV), it is useful to consider the relevance of these models to different types of hospital environment, taking public hospitals in publicly oriented health systems as the opposite case.

While some of the models focus particularly on the not-for-profit hospital (e.g. Newhouse), in general there are difficulties in applying this body of work to public hospitals operating in public health systems. There are clearly a range of differences which might be considered. For example, in a public system the payment mechanism for the hospital does not usually permit payment to vary with activity levels, in contrast to arrangements on which the models described above are based, where the majority of care is funded through cost-per-case and fee-for-service contracts. Similarly, in contrast to the US situation, salary reimbursement is the more common means of paying individual health professionals. With respect to the internal hospital budgeting process, in traditional public budgeted systems, financial administration is usually centralised. Individual departments have limited control over their allocation or use of resources.

To some extent the models described above can be adapted. For example, in the absence of a payment–activity relation, the upward sloping part of Newhouse's budget constraint (Figure 16.2) is eliminated. An objective function represented by an indifference curve reconciling the trade-off between quantity and quality through tangency with a normally shaped budget constraint could be proposed. However, differences between the two operating environments may have implications for the objective function itself. Might such hospitals maximise quality, subject to the relevant constraints? The other models suggest some alternative possibilities for the objective function which might predict something different. Under fixed physician salaries, the physician income or profit maximisation model of Pauly and Redisch is excluded, but the possibility that doctors' interests are pre-eminent, resulting in maximisation of doctors' objective functions, or factors closely associated with medical promotion criteria are not ruled out. This might translate to the unwarranted selection (for example, judged by cost-effectiveness criteria) of research-valuable patients, for instance. Alternatively, where they work in both public and private sectors, decisions which benefit physicians' parallel private practices might dominate. Where there is conflict between the objective functions of doctors and managers, and both have significant influence on decision making, conflict focusing on resource use within the hospital may ensue, similar to that described by Harris.

However, given the differences in incentive structures, the balance of tension between the two 'firms' is likely to be different. To conclude that the model of Harris applies because some kind of tension is apparent can provide only a starting point to an understanding of hospital behaviour in public systems.

16.5 Models of hospital behaviour and health policy

Why do we want to better understand the motivations and therefore behaviour of hospitals or other health service providers? Much of the content of health policy is designed to influence the behaviour of health service providers. For example, changes in hospital reimbursement mechanisms have usually been designed in order to change the incentives facing hospitals and therefore their behaviour – perhaps on the assumption that provider institutions are profit or revenue-maximising. The introduction of separation between purchasers and providers seems to assume that providers will respond to market forces by trying to improve the quality and efficiency with which they offer services – but why should they, if profit maximisation is not their objective? Even interventions such as in-service training programmes designed to improve the appropriateness of care provided, or attempts to improve management information systems, assume a particular set of motivations. In such cases perhaps the assumption is that hospital decision makers will strive to make the most technically appropriate decisions if only they are provided with the necessary technical skills and information – in other words, that they are the perfect agents of their patients, or even of society. On the basis of the insights provided by the hospital models presented in this chapter, all these assumptions appear rather simplistic. In order to manage incentives, it is important to understand motivation.

One example of the application of the kinds of models discussed in this chapter to these kinds of policy concern is a study by Ellis and McGuire (1986), who use this type of model to explain how hospitals will respond to the introduction by the Medicare programme in the United States in 1983 of prospective reimbursement for hospital services. Their model is set up within a principal–agent framework (see Chapter 18) under which the doctors are considered as agents for two principals, the patient and the hospital. Imperfect agency (in the doctor–patient relationship) results in two adverse outcomes, depending on the payment scheme. Under retrospective hospital reimbursement, there is a danger that doctors will be induced to over-treat in order to boost hospital net revenue. Under prospective payment, the incentive may be to under-treat. The incentives provided by these payment schemes lead to agency costs in the form of inefficiency. They propose a solution in the form of mixed reimbursement comprised of both prospective and retrospective payments. They argue that a mixed reimbursement scheme is more likely to lead to an efficient level of supply, fewer inappropriate admissions, more appropriate competition between hospitals, and less 'DRG creep' (see Chapter 14, section 14.5).

It is useful to view the various models we have reviewed above through the lens of principal–agent theory (also see Chapter 18). Agency relationships between the payer and the hospital, and between the hospital and its employees, are both of interest. The objective of hospital reform may be to reconcile the objective functions of principals, agents and the goals of social welfare. The problem is to align incentives so that the tension between the objective functions of doctors and managers produces hospital behaviour approaching that consistent with maximisation of social welfare as closely as possible.

The Newhouse approach can be seen as one in which there is implicitly a fairly (but not perfectly) successful alignment of incentives of the behaviour of the hospital with social objectives (the hospital aims at balancing quantity and quality, but with over-emphasis on quality relative to the efficient solution). However, under the Harris account of hospitals, where the hospital is essentially split into two firms, the agency problem appears more pronounced, with considerable costs associated with the active conflict between the two groups. Managers find themselves giving way to more powerful doctors, presumably with considerable social welfare costs. The model described by Pauly and Redisch is one in which the hospital, dominated by doctors, who pursue their own ends is likely to be very far from in effective incentive alignment.

Custer *et al.* (1990) argue that the degree of incentive alignment between hospital and doctor determines the efficiency of production. Such an alignment might imply productive efficiency, but this alignment may not necessarily be one that improves social welfare. Internal incentive alignment may be a necessary, but not sufficient, condition for improving social efficiency.

Within public health system structures, there is evidence to suggest that public sector hospitals in the UK, and in other parts of the world (for instance, Zimbabwe: Hongoro 2001) are, and have been, largely controlled by doctors. Strong and Robinson (1990) described the UK reforms of 1974 as institutionalising a system of medical syndicalism, in which contracts between the health service and its medical staff specified very little, and distributed residual power largely to doctors.

Both Sloan (1980) and McGuire (1985) have suggested that hospital behaviour could not be explained by a single model. A focus on the agency relationships and property rights implicit in the contractual arrangements that constitute the hospital helps explain what makes hospitals different from one another and how they might change in response to changes in their environment. Transformation in the hospital sector in the United States brought with it a new set of hospital models in which prospective payment systems replaced retrospective, cost-based reimbursement (Ellis and McGuire 1986; Dranove 1988; Custer *et al.* 1990; Hodgkin and McGuire 1994).

This highlights a key difference between the 'theory of the hospital' and the 'theory of the firm'. While the alternative models of firm behaviour which were used to introduce the chapter are viewed as permanent descriptions which can predict the firms' response to changing conditions (such as price, or level of competition), models of hospital behaviour themselves change in response to changing conditions. For example, prospective reimbursement might better align the objective functions of hospital managers and physicians, and consequently a behavioural model such as that of Harris might give way to a managerial model. Box 16.1 illustrates this possibility, using a study carried out in a Lebanese hospital.

Box 16.1 Changes to decision rights in a Lebanese hospital arising from a corporatisation programme.

Eid (2004) used a 'decision rights' approach (Crémer *et al.* 1995) to explain the behaviour of a hospital in Beirut.

The decision rights approach argues that, given inevitable contractual incompleteness (see Chapter 14), efficient hospital behaviour will result from the allocation of residual decision rights to the party with both the incentive and the information to use those rights productively. It also predicts that willingness to accept risk requires a high-powered incentive environment – or one that rewards individuals and teams in close relation to their level of performance (see Chapter 19).

While these principles are well established in private sector firms, and also intuitive, Eid points out that they are in practice not applied in public sector organisations. For example, although it is common to charge a public hospital manager with responsibility for hospital productivity, it is also common to allocate decision rights over hiring, rewarding and firing people elsewhere. Public hospitals also usually operate in a low-powered incentive environment, employing salaried managers who would then be predicted to avoid risky decisions.

The Beirut hospital's programme of corporatisation involved the decentralisation of decision making from the Ministry of Health to a private sector organisation established as the effective board of the hospital, and the hospital's management. Eid compared the compatibility between the decision rights allocations and economic principles before and after the programme. She found that the features of decision rights that emerged under decentralised arrangements were more compatible with economic principles. For example, the creation of the decision right to raise revenue through charging patients co-located financial responsibility with financial authority to a greater degree, and enabled high-powered incentives to be introduced for employees and the hospital director, whose position was compared to a private sector manager owning part of the firm.

This case illustrates how the appropriate public hospital model may be dependent not just on actors within the hospital but on the larger arrangements that govern the hospital. Post-corporatisation, it is likely that the hospital as a whole acted much more like a profit or revenue maximiser than pre-corporatisation. In Part IV we will further review the case for higher and lower-powered incentives in public sector organisations.

---

17 The economics of regulation

17.1 Introduction

The economic rationale for regulation arises from market failure. As we have seen repeatedly, perfect markets produce efficient outcomes. Therefore, if inefficient outcomes are observed, they must stem from market failure. The aim of regulation is to correct market failure on the understanding that if one market distortion exists, introducing another (regulation), can lead to efficiency improvement – the theory of the second best which was introduced in Chapter 6. Given the extensive failures of health markets as introduced in Chapters 7 and 8, it is unsurprising that health markets are among the most extensively regulated in most economies.

Regulation may also arise to correct inequity, although, as discussed in Chapter 1, it is usually rather difficult to disentangle inequities from inefficiencies in health markets. Most observed inequities (for example, lack of access to care for some part of the population) are also inefficiencies (a failure of the health system to address high priority demands from a social welfare perspective). For this reason we will not separately address efficiency focused regulation and equity focused regulation, although it is clear that some of the regulations we describe below address both kinds of problem.

17.2 What is regulation?

Regulation may be thought to occur when a government/state exerts control over the activities of individuals and firms (Roemer 1993). The exact 'action' is described as the *regulatory intervention* or *regulatory mechanism*. Interventions that are used to affect variables such as price and quantity can be categorised as being either:

1 *Legal restrictions or controls* where participants must conform to legislated requirements. If participants do not abide by these laws, they will face punishment.
2 *Incentives* to which participants change their behaviour and lead to changes in the target variable. These incentives could take both monetary and non-monetary forms, and may be used in the context of both government and non-government roles.
3 *Incentive regulation* is a further extension of the use of incentives. The use of incentive regulation can be thought of as 'rules' which regulate the relationship of verifiable outcomes such as price (Laffont and Tirole 1993). Here rewards or punishments are related to observed behaviour.

These definitions are broad, and include market interventions such as taxes and subsidies as well as rules that are legislated or set by administrative fiat. In this chapter we will largely concern ourselves with the second kind of regulation (legislated or administratively set rules) – though in principal other kinds of market intervention are also 'rules'. For example, a tax is a rule that a particular activity carries a particular penalty, even if the intention is not punitive.

In addition to these formal rules, more informal codes of conduct, guidelines or recommendations may exist. Formal rules mix formal rule setting and explicit contractual agreements. Informal regulation is a system which uses co-operation between parties (e.g. health professionals, the ministry of health, and other interested parties) to achieve outcomes (MacIntosh 1997). Interventions in this case may be the development of good practice norms, for example. These informal rules are not binding on the regulated (Moran and Wood 1993). There may also be 'informal controls' which occur through day-to-day social interaction. People behave in accordance with social rewards such as approval or disapproval of others (Allsop and Mulcahy 1996; Lindbeck 1997).

17.3 Regulation in the health sector

The key roles that regulation can play within the health sector are:

1   Control of market entry and exit.
2   Control of competitive practices.
3   Control of market organisation.
4   Control of remuneration.
5   Control of standards/quality.
6   Ensuring safety.

(Allsop and Mulcahy 1996).

Each of these may be explained in terms of the correction of one or more market failure. The first three respond to concerns regarding the implications of monopolistic market structure (although some kinds of controls over entry may create problems of monopoly – see section 17.5.1 below). The fourth, control of remuneration, may respond to a number of different market failures. This measure may correct for monopoly power, it may aim to motivate providers through rewarding particular desired features of performance, or it may involve the use of monopsonist power to hold wages and health services costs down. These last two – control of standards and quality and ensuring safety – aim to correct for information asymmetry problems. If consumers cannot observe standards, quality and safety features, there is a case for expert inspection or review.

The extensive size of private sector activity and deliberate policies promoting it, especially in low-income countries, have led to the increasing 'marketisation' of the health sector and a concomitant need for stronger regulation (Bennett *et al.* 1994).

Figure 17.1 explores three dimensions related to regulation: what to regulate, who to regulate and how to regulate. The figure shows three levels at which target variables may be addressed by regulation, together with the nature of the instruments used. The 'what to regulate' is reflected by a range of target variables, described in terms of entry, quantity, quality, price, distribution and competitive practices. The choice of 'who to regulate' must encompass successively complex levels in the provision of services,

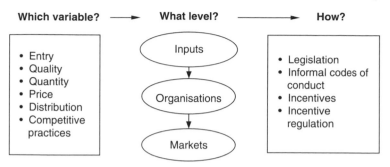

Figure 17.1 The process of regulating.

Source: Kumaranayake *et al.* (2000).

addressing individual inputs such as unqualified drug sellers and licensed pharmaceutical retailers, organisations such as solo physician practices, hospitals, nursing homes, and the market in general. The levels are obviously linked (for example, combinations of inputs create organisations) and a number of organisations coexist in the market. The 'how' to regulate refers to the instruments used to affect these variables, described later in this chapter.

The target variables can apply at different levels and are aimed at different actors within the health sector. Entry refers to initial acceptance into the market. There are issues regarding entry at each level:

1   The entry of individual inputs to the organisation: the selection of personnel, drugs or medical equipment.
2   The entry of organisations to the market: licensing of facilities, clinics and individuals.

Quantity regulation can be used to affect the volume of inputs in health service provision (for example, 'certificate of need' laws restricting the purchase of equipment or facility development); restrictions on the number of organisations (for example a limit on the number of private clinics which will be granted a licence within a given area); or the promotion of an increased number of providers in the market through anti-monopoly legislation. Quality regulation refers to standard setting and quality assurance, and covers such areas as quality control of drugs and approved curricula for the training of health professionals. Price regulation includes the articulation of minimum salary levels of health workers and the setting of fees for the provision of particular services. Regulation of distribution might set quotas so as to locate health professionals in under-served areas. Regulation of competitive practices aims to reduce adverse outcomes from anti-competitive behaviour. In practice, these areas may interact and even conflict – for example, regulations aimed at ensuring a minimum quality of a service or good in a market also work to restrict entry into the market.

The third dimension in Figure 17.1 is the 'how' of regulating and refers to the manner in which regulation is undertaken, i.e. the nature of the regulatory instruments. These instruments range from formal legal controls enacted through legislation, providing for sanctions if the regulations are not followed, to informal codes of practice or policy guidelines. A second way of regulating is through the creation of incentives, both financial (whether a tax or a subsidy) and non-financial, aimed at encouraging participants to change their behaviour.

17.4 Review of regulatory mechanisms

This section reviews the performance of regulatory mechanisms that have been used in the health sector. Most are legislative. Regulatory mechanisms chosen must depend on the structure of the health care system (e.g. the way it is organised, and how health care is produced and distributed). Within a health system there are many markets – for instance, the market for supplies, for medical equipment and for services. The appropriateness of any given regulation is specific to the system and market under consideration.

17.4.1 Entry

The licensing of professionals before they are allowed to be employed in the sector is one of the earliest forms of regulation. (The professional guilds of the Middle Ages served a similar function.) Licensing serves to regulate the labour input into the production of health care services for all professions involved in health care.

The rationale for licensing is that consumers are unable to judge for themselves the quality of the professionals they seek services from. An expert evaluation of competence to practice which can be clearly signalled provides information with public good characteristics (see Chapter 8), since the information is non-rival. There is therefore a rationale for a collectively organised licensing system. In theory, licensing can provide two types of information about quality: it can certify that the licensed person has obtained a sufficient level of knowledge and it can provide information about the performance of individuals. In reality the first type of information is a much more common feature of licensing systems. The second type is usually provided only in relation to extreme cases, in the form of provision to de-register those who underperform grossly. It is also sometimes provided more routinely – for example, where mandatory refresher courses run by professional organisations are a prerequisite of continued registration.

However, licensing also restricts entry to the market. Organised professional groups may use licensing to promote their own interests by limiting entry and reducing competition (e.g. by raising licensing standards for potential entrants). This will allow them to earn economic rent (monetary return which is greater than what is necessary to persuade them to supply their services), as shown in Figure 17.2. In this case, the licensing causes a restriction in supply, and so the wage that physicians who are in the market will earn is higher than if there were no supply restrictions. Leffler (1978) attempts to estimate these rents for American physicians and argues that they are not as high as might be expected. Many countries have a requirement that facilities must be registered before they can open. In order to register, facilities such as hospitals, clinics and nursing homes must meet minimum standards established in the registration legislation.

17.4.2 Prices

One approach to controlling prices or fees charged is through the negotiation of payment schedules between government and professional associations. This approach is

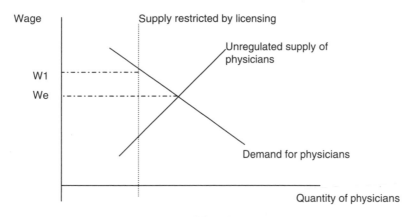

Figure 17.2 The potential impact of licensing requirements on physician incomes.

contingent on the relative power of the negotiating parties. Figure 17.3 shows the impact of price control on the market for nurses. This analysis suggests that shortages or surpluses are likely to arise in the relevant labour market in response to price control, depending on the relationship between the controlled price and the equilibrium. If the equilibrium is at wage We and quantity Qe, if the controlled wage is at W1 a surplus of nurses Q3–Q2 results. However if the controlled wage is at W2 a shortage of nurses Q4–Q1 results.

However, Figure 17.3 relies on the assumption of an underlying competitive market characterised by an upward-sloping supply curve. Suppose instead the input for which price is controlled is supplied through a monopolistic market. Price controls might then be intended to imitate the price that would result from a perfect market. Regulators may aim to set price at the minimum point of the average cost curve or, as is common for regulated utilities, at the marginal cost of production. Since there is no supply curve, this does not necessarily create any shortage or surplus of the input in question. The intended effect is to force the monopolist to price-take, rather than price-set, and

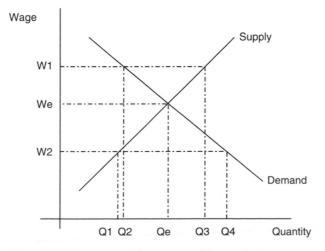

Figure 17.3 Price control in a competitive market.

thereby to induce the monopolist to supply in accordance with the marginal cost curve. In Figure 17.4 a price control which reduces the equilibrium price from Pe to Pc results in the monopolist increasing production of the service or input from Qe to Qc. In the UK, price regulations mandate marginal cost pricing for National Health Service trust hospitals – although the absence of cost information makes this regulation very difficult to enforce.

In insurance-based systems, consumers do not face prices as such but there is extensive rate regulation, which establishes the terms under which public and private insurers pay hospitals and other providers. US physicians are reimbursed under Medicare on the prevailing rates for services in the area. In addition, volume-type standards have been put in place.

17.4.3 *Quantity*

Quantity restrictions are common. Controls have been put on staff levels, operational budgets, equipment, physician training and even on patient numbers. Motivated by the need to reduce costs and to prevent duplication of services, certificate of need (CON), laws have been used to control the construction of new capital facilities, gross investment in new equipment, the expansion of special services and the purchase of expensive equipment such as CT and MRI scanners in the United States. CON laws require state agencies to approve the entry of new hospitals, the expansion or modernisation of hospitals and the provision of services. By 1979 almost all states had enacted some form of CON law.

The rationale for CON laws is that natural market forces lead to excess capacity and cost inflation. One model of competitive behaviour which predicts this is the quality competition model (See Chapter 15). However, an unintended effect of CON laws is that they may reduce competition in the provision of services, leading to increased monopoly power and price increases. Some studies suggest that hospitals favour CON laws on the basis that they protect them from competition (Campbell and Fournier 1993).

Regulation of particular hospital inputs makes those inputs more expensive. For example, a case may need to be prepared to argue for a licence to purchase a particular

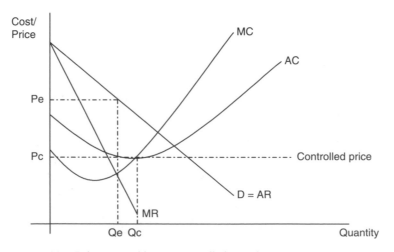

Figure 17.4 Price control in a monopolistic market.

input incurring transaction costs, or other hospitals may need to be 'bought off' from making a competing bid. The impact is to alter the relative prices of different inputs in the production function. Hospitals will therefore substitute non-regulated inputs for regulated ones, again offsetting cost reduction. To the extent that the regulation intends that less use is made of the regulated input, this is the effect desired. However, understanding the mechanisms through which hospitals will respond to regulation highlights the need for regulations to be carefully 'fine-tuned' since inefficient substitutions might also result. If certificates of need are issued on the basis that existing treatment profiles justify replacement or expansion of equipment, there is a danger that perverse incentives to over-treat using the given technology will be reinforced rather than undermined by the regulation (Abbott and Crew 1995).

17.4.4 Quality

Quality is not unidimensional. For example, good quality requires appropriate facilities and equipment, short waiting times, good clinical outcomes, timely and accurate information and good food.

Accreditation is one mechanism which aims to assess and ensure quality. Originating in the United States, accreditation occurs when an independent agency defines and monitors the standards of facilities that voluntarily participate in the scheme (Scrivens *et al.* 1995). Accreditation was originally developed by physicians to support improvements to conditions in hospitals and was seen as an instrument of self-education.

However, accreditation has evolved to serve a control function in the United States while still acting as a process of peer review in other countries. In the United States accreditation became linked with hospitals receiving funds from Medicare. During this process the concept of accreditation based on 'minimal standards' was upgraded to being based on 'achievable optimal standards'. More than 80 per cent of American hospitals are accredited. The Accreditation Committee which assesses the facilities is comprised mainly of health professionals and has a few consumer representatives. Accreditation occurs in a peer review context in Australia, Switzerland, Spain, Italy and Brazil.

Accreditation provides a way for hospitals to 'signal' improved quality based on accepted standards and may thus limit the need for excessive investment in high-technology products in a market characterised by quality competition (see Chapter 15). Accreditation systems could be developed for facilities other than hospitals such as private clinics.

The use of quality registers has also been discussed in terms of quality assurance. In contrast to accreditation which is quite macro in nature, generating a summary statistic for the entire facility, the quality registers operate at a micro level. Their purpose is to help various specialties control quality by comparing their performance with overall specialism averages. Participation is voluntary and the register can be disease or method-oriented. Such 'league table' approaches have been criticised in other contexts, however. Devoid of context they may be as misleading as they are helpful. For example, evidence that a specialist group in a large hospital are particularly heavy users of a technology may not be very helpful if the possible case mix differences are not well understood. Case mix is influenced by the mix of alternative providers and their sub-specialisms and the structure and functioning of referral relationships as well as by the designated role of an institution in the health system.

The approach has characteristics similar to systems of 'performance indicators' which have sometimes been exercised in peer review, sometimes linked with financial rewards and sometimes part of a 'naming and shaming' exercise. There has been interest and experimentation with such systems in the UK, where a set of performance indicators was compiled in the 1980s, and where a system of rating hospital and health authority performance on a league table basis was published in 2000. These tables have been criticised for failing to take account of context, and for showing a close correlation between socio-economic deprivation and poor health service performance.[1]

Complaints mechanisms provide another opportunity for quality regulation. Many countries have provision for recourse in the face of medical malpractice or negligence. However, there has been limited use of this in most countries, in contrast to the litigious environment of the United States. Self-regulating professional bodies are hesitant to impair their professional reputation. In response to this phenomenon, there seems to be a swing towards complaints mechanisms which involve or are controlled by non-professionals, much to the displeasure of the medical professionals (Bartlett 1996). In India the Consumer Protection Act of 1986 attempted to strengthen the rights of consumers and their ability to seek redress through the courts in cases of medical malpractice. Bhat (1996) reviews experience under this legislation but concludes that such measures are not in themselves sufficient to significantly impact poor quality of care in the private sector. For example, 71 per cent of cases filed in the state of Gujarat were decided in favour of the defendant, complainants faced considerable difficulty in getting experts to support their cases, and half of outstanding cases at the time of the review were 'pending'.

All these regulatory mechanisms aim to induce providers to choose higher levels of quality. They aim either to exploit providers' interest in pursuit of profit to do this, or to exploit providers' interest in quality for its own sake, which follows from the identification of motivation in some of the alternative models of hospitals described in Chapter 16. If quality *per se* is the motivation of health service providers, regulation will not be necessary, since providers will anyway maximise quality within the constraints of their market. However, if the quality emphasised in hospital managers' objective functions favours particular dimensions which are observable to outsiders, the attempt to render otherwise unobservable characteristics observable (for example, through accreditation) makes sense.

Operating on the assumption of the profit motive, regulatory mechanisms can focus on the demand side – aiming to increase consumers' willingness to pay for higher-quality providers, for example. Such mechanisms must be successful in shifting the demand curve to the point where it becomes more profitable to provide high quality of care, or they will not succeed in increasing quality care in the market. This is likely to be particularly difficult in low-income economies.

Alternatively, they can focus on the supply side, aiming to make it more expensive to provide poor-quality than good-quality care – by increasing the chances that poor-quality care will result in compensation payments in medical negligence cases, for example. In that case, the average costs associated with making compensation payments must more than account for the difference in cost between offering low and high standards of care.

Different approaches are likely to favour particular features of health markets and address different kinds of quality concern. Increasing the viability of litigation is only likely to influence the worst instances of medical malpractice, while an accreditation system addresses only those aspects of quality it is able to measure through its monitoring system.

17.4.5 Pharmaceuticals

Many countries have agencies that approve whether drugs can enter the market, the purposes for which the drug can be used (for which diseases doctors can prescribe the drug) and even the information contained in the drug package when it is sold. Regulations in most industrialised countries require drug manufactures to establish not only the safety of the new drug but also its efficacy and even its cost-effectiveness. The process of approval is often long and costly.

In contrast to the considerable regulation of drug safety and efficacy, no comparable regulation exists for the entrance of new non-pharmaceutical treatments (like key-hole surgery) and treatments which were standard practice before the introduction of the regulation are not subjected to the same evaluation. Thus while market entry is controlled in the case of drug treatment, there are no constraints on other new interventions. This distorts the economic incentives regarding these alternative forms of therapy, probably tipping us toward 'too much surgery' and not enough 'pharmaceutical treatment'. This is a relevant comparison for many diseases for which either surgical or non-surgical interventions are indicated.

A second type of regulation tries to restrict monopoly profits thought to be enjoyed by the pharmaceutical industry. Price controls are often suggested as a remedy. We have already considered some simple models of the effect of price regulation in section 17.4.2 above. The pharmaceutical industry argues that price controls, by inhibiting profit potential, stifle investment in research and development. Taking the monopoly model used in section 17.4.2, it is reasonable to suggest that applying a marginal cost pricing rule to the pharmaceutical sector would diminish interest in speculative investment in research and development since the normal profits which result, can be achieved without such investment. Patent protection law recognises monopoly profit as a reward for successful research and development and as providing necessary incentives. However, this need not be accepted as an argument against all price control. Drug company profitability is the third highest of any economic sector in the United States, expenditure on advertising and political lobbying is typically higher than on research and development, and much research and development into new drugs is financed publicly (Bond 1999). This may suggest that the failure to regulate to control pharmaceutical prices owes as much to 'public choice' explanations of regulatory practice to which we now turn, as to 'public interest' ones.

17.5 From theory to practice

Up to this point, we have considered regulation through a 'public interest' approach – from the perspective of an enlightened government serving the public interest. Each of the areas of regulation has been addressed from the perspective of its potential to improve on the outcomes of the market.

'Public choice' theory suggests that regulation, as it is practised, is the result of the bargaining, power-play and self-interest of the actors who are involved or involve themselves in the regulatory industry. The theory, first developed by Stigler (1971) and further developed by Peltzmann (1976) and Becker (1983), suggests that regulation is the result of the interaction of special interest groups who provide financial and political support in return for favourable legislation. The cost of securing regulatory change is high, whereas the amount of effort and resources that any group will expend will depend on the probable gains (rents) that group can capture as a result of the legislation.

For the general public the effect of any given regulatory change is very small, whereas for special interest groups it is very high. There will therefore be uneven investment in securing regulatory change by the groups affected. Special interest groups will devote considerable resources while the general public will take little interest. This results in 'regulatory capture'. Those organisations and individuals which a public interest motivation of regulation seeks to regulate take control of the regulatory process. The theory therefore predicts that the impact of regulation is to redistribute wealth away from the general public and towards special interest groups, and that, as the power of special interest groups changes, legislation will change over time.

From this perspective, far from improving on market outcomes, regulation may reduce welfare. This model is an example of a model of government failure that we came across at the end of Chapter 6. The interaction between voters, special interest groups, politicians and bureaucrats leads to public choices which will not improve (and may worsen) efficiency or equity relative to an unregulated market.

From a public choice perspective, doctors can also be seen as economic participants with skills to sell as well as being part of a special interest group with interests to defend or pursue (Moran and Wood 1993). From this perspective regulation can be viewed as a constraint or control but also as an opportunity to secure income or power. Box 17.1 discusses self- and public interest perspectives further.

Even from a public interest perspective, there are a number of reasons why the implementation of regulatory intervention may not lead to the desired gain.

1   *Transaction costs*. The traditional analysis assumes that there are no transaction or other operating costs of implementing, monitoring and enforcing the regulatory intervention. In practice, the regulatory process can become both cumbersome and bureaucratic. In the extreme, parallel state machinery can be created with a large staff, lobby groups emerge to pressure regulators on behalf of interested parties and further groups may emerge to counter the influence of these.

2   *Rent-seeking behaviour*. Much theory assumes that once a regulation is implemented (regardless of the cost) the desired outcome has been achieved. However, this does not take into account the response of those being regulated. In situations where large rents (profits) are being made, providers will attempt to protect those rents and this rent-seeking behaviour may lead to adverse consequences. For example, increasing cigarette taxes may spur the growth of a black market which may ultimately reduce the price of cigarettes to the end user and reduce the revenues from the tax.

3   *Information asymmetries*. The regulator will to a large extent be dependent on the regulated organisation to provide information about the firm. The firm is in a position to delay or mislead the regulator by delaying the transmission of data or by presenting inaccurate information.

It is therefore difficult to predict the impact of regulatory intervention without knowledge of market structure, cost conditions and objectives of firms. 'Deadweight loss due to high profits, rent seekers, transaction costs, asymmetries of information, economies of scale and moral hazard issues represent barriers to creating an efficient health care delivery system through a regulatory model' (Liss 1995).

Box 17.1 Public interest or self-interest?

Studies have attempted to empirically test the relevance of public choice and public interest theories to the health sector. In the United States Paul (1984) looked at the timing of the decision to license physicians by different states. He found a strong negative relationship between the year of licensure and the *per capita* number of physicians in a state, and interpreted this as rejecting the public interest theory. However, the interpretation of this is difficult. The observed relationship could mean that the physician lobby was strong enough to demand licensure.

Moran and Wood (1993) suggest that US doctors lacked power to influence state governments with respect to licensing (which would be in its self-interest because it would restrict entry) due to their lack of social standing and authority. In contrast, UK doctors were organised early (1518) and developed a self-regulatory body which limited entry and dominated the supply of services. Aljunid (1995) suggests that in many low and middle-income countries professional organisations pushed for licensure or registration in order to control entry into the profession.

While the evidence may be mixed, it seems reasonable to suggest that most governments are likely to formulate government policy for both public and self-interest reasons. This suggests that the impact of regulation will in some cases improve efficiency or equity, but in other cases interventions will yield a cost to the public as a whole and lead to inefficient and inequitable allocation of resources. Each case of regulation is worthy of analysis with respect to its impact on social welfare, and may be understood in terms of either public interest or public choice theories.

Note

1 'Warning over hospital ranking system', *Guardian*, 6 December 2000.

18 Incentives and agency

18.1 Introduction

Throughout the book, we have referred extensively to incentives – but we have rather taken their meaning and implications for granted. This chapter takes a closer look at what we mean by incentives, and develops the framework of principal–agent theory through which incentives operate. Sections 18.7 to 18.11 go on to review the difficulties of managing the mix of incentives that are present in any context and some examples of policy measures which can be used to intervene in the incentive environment in the health sector.

18.2 What is an incentive?

For economists, incentives are the driving rationale behind market behaviour. Economic incentives are defined as allowing 'individuals to behave in accordance with expected material rewards or favours that can be traded for such rewards including leisure'. This can be contrasted with social norms where people behave in accordance with social rewards such as approval or disapproval of others (Lindbeck 1997).

Incentives are present in every situation. For example, the market provides a set of incentives to a firm. If the firm is profit-maximising, these incentives result in the firm aiming to minimise its production costs. This argument is by now very familiar. In Chapter 16, we suggested that some firms, including hospitals, might pursue objectives other than profit maximisation. In some of the models examined there, the owners of the firm were still assumed to wish to maximise profits. However, the managers, as the imperfect agents of the owners, might pursue other objectives. This suggests that, in any departure from an owner-operated business without employees, the assumption that the market provides all the relevant incentives is flouted. In most contexts, therefore, incentives can be understood only within a principal–agent framework.

18.3 Further insights from agency theory

We have already encountered the principal–agent idea in the context of doctor–patient relations (Chapter 7). Although the problem there deserves special attention, as it is at the centre of all types of health service provision, in practice principal–agent relationships are ubiquitous. Within the health system, for example, there is an agency relationship between the Ministry of Health and a health authority or local government authority with health responsibilities. There is an agency relationship between a hospital manager and hospital employees. Sometimes agency relationships operate in both directions between two organisations. For example, national medical associations are the agents of doctors who employ them to advance the interests of the profession, but individual doctors are also agents of the associations in upholding standards and the good name of the profession. Wherever there is an agency relationship, there is an explicit or implicit contract (see Chapter 14) and, within that, a set of incentives through which the principal aims to direct the agent to act on her behalf.

Where these contracts and incentives are implicit, it is interesting to consider their nature and effectiveness. For example, how does the Ministry of Health try to direct local health authorities to deliver on its policy measures? Sometimes there are quite explicit measures – for example, financial penalties for failing to deliver against target performance measures. However, the systems are often subtle and may be unobservable to outsiders. They are sometimes hidden in the trading of political favours, or well understood criteria for promotion (or dismissal, or for relegation to a dead-end post) which may not be written down.

The combination of *agency* and *information problems* (information asymmetry combined with uncertainty or risk) produces interesting economic problems. Where information is perfect, principals easily specify the actions required from agents to secure payment. As in the doctor–patient relationship, problems arise when one party is privy to information and the other is not. (We will concern ourselves with problems where information is 'impacted' in the agent, or 'asymmetrical' on the agent's side.)

The standard set-up for principal–agent problems contains the following components (Strong and Waterson 1987):

1   The principal delegates to the agent responsibility for selecting and implementing an action.
2   The agent is compensated by the principal.
3   The principal is the 'residual claimant' to the outcome of the agent's actions.
4   The principal's problem is to negotiate a contract which specifies the agent's remuneration, knowing their interests are not in complete harmony.
5   Both agents and principals select from the alternatives on the basis of their utility functions.

18.4 Moral hazard

Moral hazard arises where there is shared information up to the point of selection of an action. The principal does not observe the action – only the uncertain 'pay-off'. For example, if a doctor carries out a full set of tests, studies the most recent medical journals for the latest evidence on treatment effectiveness, and monitors carefully as the patient responds to treatment and modifies intervention in response to that monitoring, a patient may have a better chance of recovery. Such assiduous medical attention could make a difference to some patients, but not to others.

There could be three types of patients: (1) patients who will get better anyway, (2) patients who will get better only if the doctor is assiduous, and (3) patients who will die anyway. Neither doctor nor patient knows in which category the patient is at the outset – they share the information of these three possibilities, and the lack of information as to which one applies in this case. However, only the doctor knows the level of effort that has been applied to the patient's case (the action). Table 18.1 shows a 'pay-off' table reflecting this situation.

Assume further that this doctor, the only one available, prefers golf to reading medical journals and spending time in the hospital, and both patient and doctor know that. How can the patient (principal) induce the doctor (agent) to make the relevant effort? One solution is an outcome-dependent contract that compensates the doctor for lost time on the golf course so that she chooses to pay assiduous medical attention. Assume that the doctor has a normal utility function: increasing in income at a diminishing rate (Figure 18.1).

Curve Z shows the doctor's utility when she pays minimal medical attention to the patient, Curve Z′, when she pays assiduous medical attention, reflecting the value she places on the lost time on the golf course associated with having to make more effort. Ü is the doctor's 'reservation utility', the minimum the doctor will require to achieve before working for this patient at all. The doctor will work for the patient for a flat rate of a, because she will be free to play golf and will achieve Ü on curve Z that way. The patient could offer the higher rate of b, as compensation for the lost time on the golf course, but the doctor's own best interest is still to choose golf and achieve utility level U′ and, because the patient cannot observe effort, he cannot withhold payment on the grounds that effort has not taken place.

Table 18.1 'Pay-off' table: moral hazard

Medical attention	Patient type		
	1	*2*	*3*
Minimal	Recovers	Dies	Dies
Assiduous	Recovers	Recovers	Dies

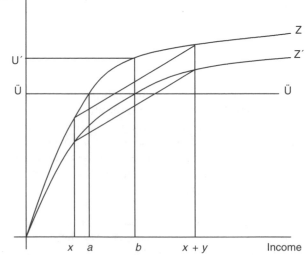

Figure 18.1 Determining an outcome-dependent contract.

The patient's problem is to choose a sum x, at the start of treatment, and a further sum *y*, to be paid in the case of recovery, that will be sufficient to induce the doctor from the golf course in order to increase the chance of recovery.

Assume that there is an equal chance of the patient being in each patient category, so:

1   If the doctor decides to make an effort, there is a one-in-three chance that she will receive sum x only, despite the effort (the patient was actually type 3), and a two-in-three chance that she will receive x + y.
2   If the doctor decides to play golf, there is a two-in-three chance she will receive sum x only, and a one-in-three chance that she will receive x + y.

Suppose the disutility of effort = *z* (the value of the lost golfing time to the doctor). The patient's problem is then to find x and y, such that

$$\{U[1/3x + 2/3(x+y)] - z\} \geq \{U[2/3x + 1/3(x+y)]\} \geq \ddot{U}$$

In Figure 18.1, equality in each of the expressions above can be determined where x and x + y cut the utility functions, such that Ü divides the straight lines joining the two cutting points in 2:1 and 1:2 ratios respectively (i.e. where one-third and two-thirds the value of x; and two-thirds and one-third the value of y equals Ü respectively). These are the levels of x and y for which the doctor achieves her reservation utility, and is indifferent between making an effort and not making an effort. (For the patient to ensure the doctor's attention, he need just add 1 (or an infinitesimal amount) to *y*.)

Notice that *x* is lower than a, and *x* + *y* is higher than b. The patient has to pay more in the case of recovery than if he could observe effort. This is because he has to compensate the doctor for bearing the risk that, even with effort, she will only earn *x* (if the patient is type 3). The expected total payment [1/3x + 2/3(x + y)] is also higher than b. This is because the doctor is risk-averse, owing to the shape of the utility function. A certain income is consequently worth more to the doctor than an equal chance of losing or gaining a given sum in comparison. (The additional sum produces less utility than the lost sum is felt to cost.) We explore the concept of risk aversion further in Chapter 22. Hence the patient (principal) must bear the cost of hidden action and risk in an outcome-dependent contract.

18.5 Adverse selection

In situations of adverse selection, only the agent has the information relevant to the selection of an action. The principal can observe the action and the outcome only.

Assume the same doctor (same utility functions and reservation utility; same preference for golf over effort) and two types of patients: (1) those more likely to benefit from minor treatment; (2) those more likely to benefit from intensive treatment. It costs the doctor less effort (and allows more golf time) to provide minor treatment, but while the doctor knows, the patient does not know whether he is type 1 or type 2.

The pay-off table is shown as Table 18.2. If the patient type is observable to the patient, he can pay for minor treatment, knowing himself to be type 1, or for intensive treatment, knowing himself to be type 2. The difference in the required payment will be equal to the sum required to compensate the doctor for the disutility of making the extra effort to provide intensive treatment. (Assume this is z: the same disutility as

Table 18.2 'Pay-off' table: adverse selection

	Outcome	
Treatment	Recovery	Death
Patient type 1		
Minor	2/3	1/3
Intensive	1/3	2/3
Patient type 2		
Minor	1/3	2/3
Intensive	2/3	1/3

associated with the different effort of the moral hazard problem.) Hence the patient seeks a contract that forces the doctor to reveal her knowledge of his patient type, which can only be an outcome-based contract.

There is no conflict between type 1 patients and doctors: both interests are served by provision of minor treatment. The doctor will maximise her chances of earning her bonus without making extra effort. The patient's problem is to induce the extra effort in case he is a type 2 patient.

As before, the patient seeks to ensure that the increased chance of a bonus on recovery outweighs the disutility of providing intensive treatment in the doctor's utility function, and the relevant formula is the same one as above:

$$\{U[1/3x + 2/3(x + y)] - z\} \geq \{U[2/3x + 1/3(x + y]\} \geq \ddot{U}$$

The solution can be identified in the same manner, on Figure 18.1. As before, the expected payment is higher than b, to compensate the doctor for bearing additional risk.

18.6 Applying these ideas

It is interesting that, in practice, clinical health workers tend not to be paid according to patient outcome. There are a number of possible explanations.

First, we assumed in the example a lazy doctor, uninterested in her patient's recovery. Many doctors we have taught have been uncomfortable with that caricature, and we discussed the idea of 'imperfect agency' in Chapter 7. We do not claim that this is an average real doctor but instead refer the reader to Box 18.1. By emphasising only the self-interest component of the doctor's motivation we can explore the implications of *any* self-interest component playing a role in the doctor's choices. We should not discount the model because we believe doctors are not as venal as in the model, only if we believe that they are instead completely unmotivated by any self-interest. Nevertheless, if patients believe that doctors are largely motivated by patient rather than self-interest, it may explain why performance-dependent contracts are unusual.

Second, if the doctor's role in determining recovery (or the difference made between minimal and assiduous attention) is small, the cost of inducing extra effort becomes large: the certainty of extra effort has to be outweighed by a bonus payment (y) multiplied by a small additional chance of its being earned relative to when only minimal attention is paid. Patients might not consider the increased chance of recovery worth the large price that would be paid whether or not the doctor's effort had been the deciding factor. (The probability of recovery may still be quite large.) Some doctors may also be uncomfortable with an explanation based on their relatively trivial role in many conditions, and this is of course, a condition and context dependent explanation.

Third, given the inefficiency associated with using the outcome-dependent contract (the greater expected payment than certain payment under action observability), it may be that there are other mechanisms for ensuring assiduous medical attention that are more efficient. Clearly, we do observe other mechanisms in medical market places: professional codes of conduct, professional bodies who discipline members whose standards are shown to have fallen short of those codes, legal remedies and ethical principles.

It follows from this discussion that in situations of moral hazard or adverse selection we might expect to see greater use of outcome-dependent contracts where (1) principals believe there is a large gap between their own and agents' objectives (utility functions); (2) the agent plays a large role in determining outcome; and (3) there is an absence of more efficient mechanisms for securing agent effort. Box 18.2 provides a case study from a context in which outcome-dependent contracts are sometimes used in the health sector (of Cameroon) that considers the importance of point 2 above, in that system.

18.7 Moral hazard and adverse selection in insurance markets

The concepts of moral hazard and adverse selection are used extensively in analysis of insurance markets (for example, in Chapter 22). Here, rather counter-intuitively, the agent is the enrolee, and the principal is the insurance company. The agent has to avoid risks on behalf of the insurance company.

Moral hazard arises because the insurance company cannot observe risk avoidance (hidden action). The principal may try to induce risk avoidance by paying differentially according to the outcome. A good example is the 'no claims bonus' typical of car insurance. Such schemes imply less than perfect insurance. The agent may be more risk-averse than the principal because the insurance company has a large number of clients and is therefore most interested in the average outcome, whereas the agent is interested in only one outcome. Perfect insurance and the observation of risk avoidance would therefore likely be Pareto-optimal, because risk would be carried by the less risk-averse party. Information asymmetry therefore induces a Pareto-suboptimal result.

Adverse selection occurs in insurance markets as a result of the hidden information in the underlying health risk of the agent. We assume that enrolees know more about their existing health risks than the insurance company (hidden information). Offering a standard set of insurance benefits at a standard price is the equivalent of offering a fixed salary in the example, and the health insurance company has to solve its problem by offering varying benefits and co-payments (that increase with the enrolee's uptake of health services) in order to force the enrolee to reveal their hidden knowledge in choosing among available contracts. As before, this results in less than perfect insurance, despite the agent's risk aversion indicating that full insurance would be Pareto-optimal under perfect information. We return to applications of moral hazard and adverse selection in insurance markets in Chapter 22.

18.8 Incentive compatibility

Outcome-dependent contracts aim to reconcile the incentives of principals and agents, and are an example of incentive compatibility-based intervention. This has been a main thrust in the design of a range of interventions, including contracts and regulation within the health sector. Incentive compatibility was first used as a concept to identify the range of actions for which participants in the market would not find it advantageous to break the rules or behave opportunistically. The concept of incentive compatibility can be thought of as the process of designing mechanisms to restructure the incentives or rewards facing individuals in order to achieve a desirable outcome.

As suggested above, agents, information asymmetry, risk and uncertainty are pervasive in the health sector as elsewhere. They imply that the information deficit has costs, in Paretian terms, and leaves principals with the options of seeking missing information (which may be costly), tolerating agent 'opportunism' (defined, as before, as any strategy involving guile intended to further self-interest – here meaning the agent's maximising her own utility function by concealing information) or seeking, through contract specifications, to induce appropriate action on the part of the agent. Here we have focused on comparison of the last two options. In real contexts, 'pay-offs' are more likely to be uncertain than risky as described here (i.e. the probability distributions are not known), thereby making attempts to use strategies to induce agent behaviour in line with principal utility functions an approximate science.

It is worth exploring the concept of incentive compatibility because its application to economics has been widespread and 'getting the incentives right' has been a main thrust in the design of a range of interventions, including contracts and regulation within the health sector. In this chapter we consider in detail two areas where the issues of incentives and incentive compatibility have become prominent in the health sector: regulation and contracts. Within these sections we explore the role of incentives and the design of mechanisms.

18.9 Incentive management

Whether or not explicitly and deliberately, all organisational structures embody sets of incentives (encouraging people to work with or against the organisation). In Chapter 17, we recognised that institutional, informational and capacity constraints limited the implementation and impact of legislated mechanisms. Given these informational, transaction, administrative and political constraints, interest has now turned to examining whether incentive management (defined as deliberate attempts to manipulate incentives to achieve desired objectives) may better accomplish the objectives of regulation. In Chapter 17, we recognised 'incentive regulation' as a form of regulation. Here we consider this type of regulation in more detail.

Incentive management may take two forms. First, the government can subsidise or tax regulated firms. Subsidies can take several forms: direct subsidies (which may be paid as a lump sum or as a 'price subsidy' which is effectively a subsidy per unit of output sold), government loans at low interest, or government guarantees for borrowing on private markets (Laffont and Tirole 1993).

Figure 18.2 shows the effect of a government price subsidy on a competitive market (with upward-sloping supply curve). The price subsidy implies that a fixed amount (ab) is paid for each unit of production sold. This is equivalent to each firm receiving a

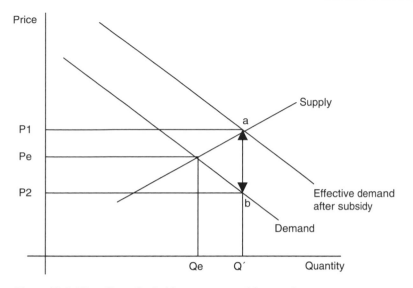

Figure 18.2 The effect of subsidy on a competitive market.

higher price for each unit of the good – which is equivalent to a shift of the demand curve outwards, from each firm's perspective. Firms respond so that the market reaches a new equilibrium (at a) where production is higher. Firms receive price P1 for each unit sold, whereas consumers pay only P2. The effect of the subsidy is therefore to lower the price paid by the consumer (but not by the full extent of the subsidy paid – compare Pe – P2 and ab), and to increase output. The extent to which these two effects occur depends on the relative elasticities of supply and demand curves.

The effect of a unit tax is the opposite – it can be viewed as the opposite shift in the demand curve and will reduce output and increase price (but not by the full extent of the tax).

However, many subsidies in the health sector are not of a price subsidy nature, but rather flat-rate subsidies to specific institutions. A flat-rate subsidy would not affect the decision making of a profit-maximising firm – it would be received as a windfall payment, and profit-maximising decisions would be made regardless. It follows that flat-rate subsidies can work only in the context of non-profit-maximising behaviour on the part of the firms subsidised. For example, if the firm is a revenue maximiser subject to a 'break-even' constraint (like the firm of Figure 16.1), the flat-rate subsidy has the effect of reducing average cost (for example to AC'), and reduces price and increases output as might be expected (Figure 18.3).

Financing health service provision through a public provider and a budget mechanism is analytically similar to a flat-rate subsidy – although the assumed objective function of the provider is apparently neither profit maximising nor revenue maximising. Rather, the provider's interest in delivering appropriate services to the population covered as efficiently as possible seems to be assumed. It is worth considering whether such altruistic motivation seems reasonable in any given context, and which other mechanisms are used for the principal (the provider of finance) to achieve the behaviour intended by the agent (the providing institution).

Combining user fees with a flat-rate public subsidy – perhaps the most common set of arrangements for public provision in low-income countries – provides an odd-looking

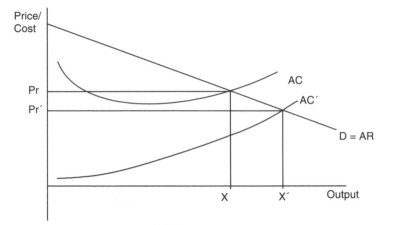

Figure 18.3 The effect of a flat-rate subsidy on a revenue-maximising firm.

mix of incentives to provider institutions. Countries with this set of arrangements need to consider carefully their assumptions about the objective functions of provider institutions, and the contractual arrangements (implicit or explicit) which govern providers' use of subsidy.

The second form which incentive management can take is that the government can make transfers to participants through its purchasing function. This is no different from subsidy in analytic terms but is associated with a greater explicitness of contractual arrangements. For example, in the UK, contractual arrangements between health authorities and hospitals have been classified as 'block', 'cost and volume' and 'cost per case'. Block contracts are equivalent to fixed rate subsidies whereas 'cost per case' contracts are equivalent to price subsidies. 'Cost and volume' contracts agree a specific price–quantity point in the terms of Figures 18.2 and 18.3. In the UK case, additional user fees are ruled out by regulation, however.

Incentive management is practised actively in low-income countries too. For example, in Malaysia and Thailand allowances are paid to encourage physicians to forgo private practice, a form of subsidy to the services provided by those physicians. Why might this be a good way to solve the problem of 'dual practice' whereby salaried public sector doctors spend a substantial share of their time in the private sector? Figure 18.4 looks at the situation from the perspective of a doctor who chooses how to spend an eight-hour working day (the time budget). The analysis assumes that there is a flat-rate wage in the public sector, and a diminishing marginal wage in the private sector. (The doctor can choose to work the most profitable opening hours in her private clinic.) This produces a curved 'iso-income' line (with slope equal to the relative wage rate across the two sectors) that holds the doctor's income constant. At the point of tangency between the iso-income line and the budget line, the doctor will choose to divide her working time.

If the time offered to the public sector is thought to leave the public sector short-staffed, the government might increase wages to alter the physician's decision. This would alter the iso-income line – for example, to the dashed one in Figure 18.4 – and increase the number of hours offered. However, this would be quite costly, and to secure all eight working hours the government would have to pay at the rate of the most profitable hour of operation of the physician's private clinic. A non-private practice

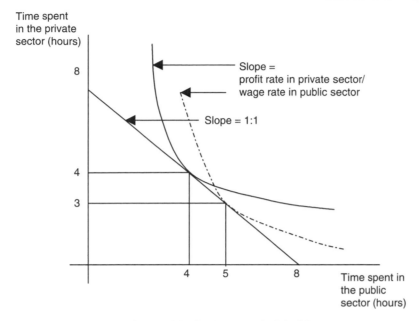

Figure 18.4 A model of a physician's 'dual practice' decision.

allowance can instead attract the full working day of the doctor by at least matching the total income she would have earned from private sector work in the part of the day allocated to that. Suppose that the schedule of earnings possible in both sectors is as in Table 18.3. In order to attract all eight hours of the doctor's working day to the public sector, the government would have to pay a wage of 10,000 shillings per hour, or a total of 80,000 shillings per day. However, the same could also be achieved by paying a non-private practice allowance of 10,000 shillings per day and maintaining the hourly wage at 6,000 shillings – a total wage of 58,000 shillings per day, equal to the income the doctor would have earned by dividing her time as in Figure 18.4.

In practice, non-practice allowances may be more expensive, since doctors who operate dual practice often continue to earn as if they were working a full day in the public

Table 18.3 Possible schedule of earnings in public and private sectors (shillings)

Hours	Profit in private sector	Wage in public sector
1	10,000	6,000
2	9,000	6,000
3	8,000	6,000
4	7,000	6,000
5	6,000	6,000
6	5,000	6,000
7	4,000	6,000
8	3,000	6,000

sector despite spending a significant proportion of that time in the private sector. That would imply that the full extent of private sector earnings would have to be compensated, but would still be cheaper than trying to induce full-time public sector work through the wage rate. Alternatively, measures to monitor public sector work and pay only for hours worked might be considered.

18.10 Incentive regulation

Incentive regulation can be thought of as rules which regulate verifiable outcomes such as price (Laffont and Tirole 1993). Rather than attempting to micro-manage an individual participant's behaviour, incentive regulation can adopt market-based criteria. For example, in the regulation of telecommunications in the UK, a price-cap incentive scheme has been put into place, replacing the rate-type regulation. Price-cap regulation attempts to address the same problems as rate regulation but breaks the link between revenue and costs. The firm or market price is based on last year's price, corrected for inflation and then decreased by some percentage X. This X factor means that the real price falls over the period of the price cap. There is some incentive to lower quality and so the regulator must monitor this. There is also an incentive problem. Since this year's regulated prices are based on last year's achieved efficiencies, there is certainly no incentive to achieve efficiency gains higher than the X per cent required. Such achievement will only drive further efficiency demands the following year. Depending on the penalties for failing to meet the X per cent efficiency gain, firms may try to game the system by using failure to meet targets this year as a means to negotiate a less stringent target the following year. Much depends on the regulator's ability to monitor the firm's costs and effort in seeking efficiency improvement.

Other incentive regulation schemes are based on the government and regulated firm sharing costs or profits. For instance, firms may be allowed to charge higher prices, but some proportion of their profit is taxed. Alternatively if X is constant, then firms are allowed to keep cost improvements that are greater than X per cent (Propper 1995). The advantage of such schemes is that if the variables are well specified and easily observable, the monitoring and implementing costs of such regulation are relatively low.

In comparison with other approaches to regulation, mechanisms based on incentives seem to be associated with much lower transaction costs. However, monitoring is still important. Both incentive management and incentive regulation can be implemented through contractual obligations, rather than legal requirements, and an example of incentive regulation in the health sector is considered in Box 18.1.

18.11 Contract design: the incentive compatibility constraint

Different contract types are seen in the health sector, both between and within organisations. In order to restructure incentives there are two important constraints: first, within the design of a contract each person would be willing to participate – the participation constraint. Second, the contract needs to structure incentives in order to meet the desired objectives: the incentive compatibility constraint. In section 18.4 we encountered the participation constraint in the form of the 'reservation utility' of the agent, and the incentive compatibility constraint required that the contract be structured so that the agent took the action that furthered the principal's objectives.

In contrast to the precisely solvable problems of sections 18.4 and 18.5, real contract

Box 18.1 Incentive regulation in the health sector

In a US social experiment on incentive regulation of nursing homes, Norton (1992) looked at whether monetary incentives can improve the access and health of Medicaid residents in nursing homes while saving money. Nursing homes were given three kinds of financial incentives:

1   Tied to admission (daily reimbursement rate to depend on case mix in order to increase the admission of sick patients).
2   Tied to case outcomes (a lump sum bonus was awarded when a resident improved her health).
3   Tied to discharges (a lump sum bonus was awarded when a resident was promptly discharged to home or to an intermediate care facility to encourage nursing homes to fill their beds with people who could most benefit from their care).

Norton found that the incentive regulation had beneficial effects on access, quality and costs of care. The admission incentives induced the nursing home to take in people with severe disabilities. Nevertheless the need to have independent confirmation of discharges was emphasised. Incentive mechanisms seem to have much lower transaction costs associated with them. However, the Norton experiment suggests that monitoring is still important, particularly to see if the incentive is having the desired effect on behaviour.

Source: Norton (1992).

design raises a number of difficulties for which there is no solution but which require the development of carefully judged strategies. As we saw in sections 18.4 and 18.5, the problem of designing incentives arises because there are unobserved hidden actions or asymmetrically observed factors relevant to the choice of action. There are many examples of both kinds of problem in the health sector. For example, there are difficulties for payer organisations in verifying exactly what treatments have been administered to each patient (hidden action); and there are difficulties in verifying the symptoms of disease and the appropriateness of diagnoses recorded (asymmetrically observable information).

In any payment system, rewards must be linked to some aspect of performance that is observable. Under incentive management and regulation, the objective is that the aspect chosen should also be that which is intended to be encouraged. In the examples of sections 18.4 and 18.5 the pay-offs were observable (financial returns) and the solution was therefore calculable. However, in situations including many found in the health sector, the observable aspects of performance may have very little relation to unobservable actions or underlying objectives. The equivalent of pay-off in the health sector might be health outcome, but contract reimbursement is almost never linked to health outcome. An exception can be found among traditional practitioners in some countries – see Box 18.2. One reason why health outcome is not usually used as a basis for payment is that in many situations it is not primarily dependent on health service

---

Box 18.2 Traditional healers and incentives in rural Cameroon

Traditional healers in Cameroon are paid according to a 'contingent payment scheme' under which payment increases according to the success of the treatment. Leonard (2000) argues that this payment scheme will induce effort on the part of the traditional healers in cases where the condition of the patient implies that success of treatment is dependent on the healer's effort. It also implies that, where patient effort is an important determinant of outcome, healers will be very interested in mechanisms to induce patient effort in order to secure higher payment.

In contrast, employers of those working in clinics and hospitals within the public and mission systems use a 'penalty-based' scheme to manage incentives. Records are kept of activities, and if these indicate inappropriate practices, sanctions can be applied. Possible sanctions are more serious in the mission system, where dismissal and demotion are options, than in the public system, where relocation is the most serious credible sanction. Since this reward system is not directly related to outcome, patient effort is predicted to be of little interest to workers in these two systems.

Medical skills also differ among the three systems, with untrained personnel available in the traditional system and semi- and fully trained personnel in the public and mission systems. (Note that Leonard's comparative analysis of the three systems does not rely on the existence of *different* skills in the traditional sector.)

Leonard argues that 'These combinations of skill and incentives lead people rationally to choose different types of practitioners depending on the disease from which they suffer'. He develops a scale which quantifies three dimensions – medical effort, patient effort and medical skill – with respect to common conditions experienced by the population of rural Cameroon. It was predicted that traditional healers would be most likely chosen where the combination of patient and medical effort was high, mission hospitals (and to a lesser extent clinics) where medical effort and medical skill were most important, and public hospitals or clinics where medical skill was important but effort less so.

On this basis, a utilisation decision was predicted for each of 537 episodes of care and compared with the actual patient utilisation decision. The model generated correct predictions for 50 per cent of cases over the five provider types (whereas a model with no predictive power would be expected to predict correctly for about 20 per cent of cases).

These results suggest that not only does the characterisation of incentives capture the key features of the incentives operating in the different provider institutions, but that incentive characteristics are well understood – at least implicitly – by those making decisions regarding where to seek care.

Source: Leonard (2000).

---

inputs. An outcome-dependent contract would not provide incentives for health workers to make heroic efforts to revive patients with a poor chance of recovery. Yet we may want to ensure our contracts contain such incentives. Health outcome is also not easily observable by third-party payers – and may be opportunistically concealed even in the case of a direct transaction (see Box 18.2 for more discussion of this).

The design of incentive management or regulation depends on how participants respond to incentives and the clarity of the formula or rule linking rewards to actions. If there exists some vagueness about the formula or 'rule' that is used, then individuals will also respond to these incentives in ways that are not desirable. For example, if lecturers' salaries are geared to the number of new courses designed or to innovations in teaching, then individuals can try and respond by corrupting the related outcome measures (Kreps 1997). For example, teachers might re-label existing course or teaching techniques, so that they are counted as new.

Hughes (1993) discusses different types of financial payments used to increase the preventive activities of family doctors in the UK. The contract by which the private family doctors are paid by the National Health Service was substantially revised in 1990. New initiatives included the introduction of target payments for immunisation and cervical cytology paid only if specific coverage levels were achieved which replaced per-service payments; and sessional payments of a lump sum for provision of health promotion clinics. Hughes suggests that target payments may fail to induce appropriate behaviour, since they do not reward the targeting of the service to the patients most likely to benefit or effort to increase coverage levels if targets are not believed attainable. Sessional payments might reward the reorganisation of health promotion activity from a routine component of doctor–patient interactions to special clinic activity – not self-evidently a positive change.

Further design issues arise when tasks or outcomes are multi-faceted (Holmstrom and Milgrom 1990). Individuals can more easily alter behaviour that is perverse to the original intention of the incentive where outcomes are multi-characteristic or multi-task dependent. When the organisation performs several tasks or outputs, which vary in the degree to which they can be observed, tasks or characteristics that are observable would have a higher-powered incentive effect relative to other outcomes.

If rewards are related to observable tasks or characteristics, there is an incentive for regulated firms and individuals to neglect other tasks or characteristics. The contractor has the incentive to increase production or manage production in such a way as to skew observed characteristics to meet the target. In Uganda there has been a change from reimbursing hospitals on the basis of bed numbers to bed occupancy (Ssengooba *et al.* 2002). While both bases of reimbursement can present problems, the switch to bed occupancy is likely to result in longer lengths of stay – unless these are monitored and credible penalties are attached to gaming the system in this way. It is tempting to judge evidence of an existing association between an indicator such as bed occupancy and desired activity characteristics as a basis on which to manage incentives, but the act of using the indicator as a basis for reimbursement may well undermine the relationship.

Propper (1995) suggests that this has also occurred in the UK, where hospitals are assessed on the basis of an efficiency index that is heavily weighted in favour of in-patient activity. Then there is both an incentive to over-emphasise inpatient activity in the hospital's service mix, and to over-record in-patient activity – and evidence that both have been occurring.

The designers of contracts have to weigh the advantages and disadvantages of relying on incentives related to tasks and characteristics which are observed with more certainty, but with less impact on performance, and those tasks and characteristics which are observed with less certainty but are more likely to impact behaviour.

A further design issue arises in the use of relative or group targets – and where outputs involved rely on teamwork. There has been extensive work in the area of labour economics which looks at comparative pay schemes such as tournaments by which the firm ranks competing agents in terms of relative performance and allocates remuneration according to the ranking. For example, Nalbantian and Schotter (1997) present evidence from an experiment involving different group incentive programmes between workers and firms. Their findings suggest (1) history matters: how a group of individuals perform under one incentive scheme depends on its previous experience under a different one and (2) relative performance schemes outperform target-based schemes. However, again this result is mitigated by the context of larger groups performing multiple tasks. Holmstrom (1989) argues that larger firms perform more tasks, therefore have weaker incentives and suffer a relative disadvantage in performance because of the multi-faceted nature of the judgments required.

What is the possibility of adjustment in the design of contracts? In the private sector owners or managers can devote substantial effort and resources to maintaining and perfecting reward systems and adjusting the schemes as they receive information about dysfunctional or opportunistic behaviour. To what degree can adjustments occur when there is an interaction between the state and individuals in the private or public sectors? Courty and Marschke (1997) examine a reward scheme within a bureaucracy. They find that this process is much slower in government due to the absence of well defined goals (like profit) and because bureaucracies are controlled by multiple principals with potentially conflicting interests and differing understanding of the impact of incentives. The conflict between bureaucratic discretion and objective measurement imposes moral hazard costs and reduces any efficiency gains from implementing market-based measures. This is particular the case when output is difficult to measure – specific goals may focus effort the wrong way (Heckman *et al.* 1997).

We saw in section 18.2 that reorganisation of incentives could not avoid simultaneously redistributing risk. The various forms of incentive management and regulation discussed here therefore have differing implications for risk distribution that have efficiency implications. For example, if a payer organisation faces significant risk associated with the reimbursement mechanism, it may respond by conserving inefficient levels of reserve to ensure that crisis is avoided under all possible scenarios. If a provider organisation faces high levels of risk it may also devise inefficient measures to protect itself. For example, under capitation, providers must offer services as required for a fixed payment that does not respond to the level of demand. Providers may use alternative mechanisms to deter demand or 'cost shift' – such as referring patients to higher-level providers, failing to recommend appropriate treatments or using waiting lists or queues to cope with excess demand. Further consideration is given to the efficiency of such rationing mechanisms in Chapter 21.

Part IV

The economics of
health systems

19 Health systems: a framework for analysis

19.1 Introduction

Markets are arrangements through which people exchange goods and services, giving up those things they value less, and gaining those they value more. When people work, they exchange leisure time and effort for food, housing, clothing and other goods they value. By converting their leisure time and effort assets into money, they can exchange for other things of value. In this way we can see money as a device that allows easier use of the market to exchange things we have for things we would value more. As the first three parts of this book have described, in simple markets, such as those for fruit and vegetables, the buyers and sellers are easily identifiable, and are generally well informed. The market can work well with little in the way of rules and regulation. But understanding markets becomes more difficult as the products become more complex and when actors start to include people acting as agents for the consumer or seller.

Well functioning markets are a common part of most of our lives, and most access to goods and services uses at least elements of market processes. Within health systems, markets exist widely but tend to be complex and regulated. As we have seen, analysis has to take into account agency, regulation, oligopolistic or monopolistic arrangement of suppliers, monopsonistic organisation of purchasing by agents on behalf of the ultimate consumers, compulsion of payment through taxation or social insurance arrangements. At times, we can hardly recognise what we see as a 'market' at all. Yet through viewing a health system as a series of complex markets, and by focusing on elements of exchange, incentives, rationing mechanisms and underlying demand and supply curves, cost and production functions, important insights can be gained into the strengths and weaknesses and likely effects of alternative forms of organisation.

This part of the book aims to introduce the reader to this approach to viewing health systems. There are two major sets of issues that will be addressed. The first is the implications of alternative ways of organising financing for funding levels and rationing. How much in total will be spent; what services will be provided; and who will get them? The second concerns the institutional structures of alternative health systems and focuses particularly on arguments about the incentives to efficiency implicit in these.

19.2 Alternative health systems, funding levels and rationing

There are several approaches to the question 'What is the right level of funding?' A common starting point in the political debate about health care funding is to assert that all health care needs should be met. Defining what we mean by need is more complicated (Culyer 1976). One starting point (Matthew 1971) defines need not in terms of the size of the health problem an individual faces, but rather in terms of the feasibility of intervening to remove or reduce that problem. A need is therefore defined as the capacity to benefit from a service. Taking this approach, someone with serious and incurable disease may have great need for care and palliative services, but no need of curative health care (see Box 19.1). But even on this more restrictive definition of need, economists seldom accept that all needs should be met. Rather they argue that needs should be met if the benefits of doing so exceed the costs (in other words exceed the forgone benefits if resources are used for this purpose). This approach is considered in more detail in Part II.

Box 19.1 Normand and McPake disagree on need

Normand.   I really feel quite strongly about the 'capacity to benefit' definition. Too many people talk about 'needs' when they really mean problems. Unless there's something that can be done about it, a problem isn't a need.

McPake.   Yes, but I think that 'capacity to benefit' trivialises important distinctions. My three-year-old never 'wants' an ice cream, she always 'needs' one. According to your definition, she's right.

Normand.   Yes, she needs an ice cream, but we can't meet all needs.

McPake.   She doesn't need an ice cream! I prefer a framework that accepts that different claims on uses of resources – whether we call them wants or needs – have an order of importance. Our non-technical language has different words for my grandfather's need for heart surgery and my daughter's desire for an ice cream for good reason.

Normand.   Obviously, we can acknowledge an order of importance without trying to draw arbitrary distinctions that inevitably leave grey areas. Is aesthetic plastic surgery a 'need', a 'want' or a 'desire'? A cost–benefit framework enables that ordering, without requiring arbitrary distinctions.

McPake.   I accept that drawing a hard line between needs and wants is difficult, and that really we have a continuum of more important and less important claims on resources. There are grey areas between needs and wants, but towards the ends of the continuum the terminology is clear, and that is often all that is needed. A 'need' is a more important claim on resources, a 'want' or 'desire' is a less important one.

Normand.   I see no reason for economists to join in the use of imprecise language. At these ends, we have high and low benefit–cost ratios – that tells us what we need to know and keeps the importance of *our ability to tackle the problem* centre-stage. My definitions are much clearer and more precise than yours. The cost–benefit framework takes account of the extent to which serious problems can be alleviated. If we consider all opportunities to achieve benefits as 'needs' then we can leave the cost–benefit framework to decide which ones should be met.

McPake.   I think we should separate the issue of what is a 'need' from how efficiently we can tackle it. The definition of a need – that it is a more important claim on resources – *is* messier than capacity to benefit. I think that's a necessary evil.

Normand.   Your proposal leaves those problems for which we can do nothing, like curing untreatable conditions that threaten survival, within the range – possibly at the high end. I thought we both agreed that these were not needs. We waste our time even allowing them into the debate.

McPake.   I agree that problems with no effective intervention are not needs for intervention, and that 'capacity to benefit' is a necessary condition for 'need'. I'm not convinced that it is sufficient, though I think it is the most viable definition for the purposes of our textbook. What I'd like to highlight in the book, though, is that using benefit–cost ratios as our sole guide to importance won't bring out the greater seriousness of the problem addressed by heart surgery than by ice cream. The ice cream is cheap, and very satisfying for my daughter – if we accept her as a sovereign consumer, the benefit–cost ratio is high. The heart surgery is expensive, and may have quite a low benefit–cost ratio. We may well agree that it has a low priority for resource allocation, given that benefit–cost ratio, but to rank it as a less important 'need' than my daughter's ice cream ignores the acuteness of the resource allocation issues we are talking about. No wonder economists are viewed from the outside as callous pennypinchers! Apparently we think ice cream is more important than heart surgery.

As we have seen, individuals' own valuations (willingness to pay) of goods and services can be charted by a demand curve. Those who value the benefits most highly are willing to pay the most – these demands can be found on the left end of the demand curve. Those who place a relatively low value on the benefits to themselves are willing to pay less – these demands can be found at the right-hand, lower end of the demand curve.

If we accept consumer sovereignty – that is, that consumers are the best judge of their own interests – and also accept the current distribution of income and wealth, the appropriate level of provision (and by implication funding) can be defined at Q* in Figure 19.1. Q* is easily achieved by setting price at marginal cost. The simplest way to ensure that resources are allocated to those who value their own demands most highly is also via the price mechanism. The 'invisible hand' will direct resources to high-value demands, away from low-value demands and, at the margin, allocate the last unit of a resource to a demand with a value equal to the price.

Q* could also be achieved in a public system by setting funding levels such that Q* can be provided. However, a public system also has to develop a rationing mechanism that allocates resources to high-value and away from low-value demands. If the values derived from demand curves were satisfactory to society and policy makers, the idea would be ludicrous. Why take the trouble to estimate Q* and aim to develop a rationing mechanism which would exactly mimic the price mechanism when prices already perform the function perfectly and without effort? We have already encountered a response to this question in our analysis of market failure in Chapter 8, and the fact

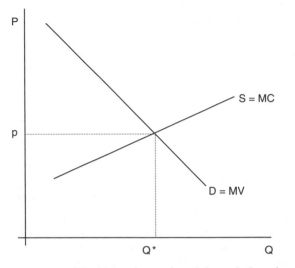

Figure 19.1 Health services rationed through the price mechanism.

that no society leaves delivery of health services to be determined by an unregulated price mechanism suggests that no society and no policy makers consider that values derived from demand curves are at all satisfactory.

There are three important sources of divergence between private and social demand. First, values derived from demand curves are determined not only by willingness but also by ability to pay. Richer people's demands are weighted more heavily than the demands of poorer people. If society or policy makers believe that demands should be weighted equally in health sector resource allocation, values derived from demand evidence alone cannot be relied upon. Second, lack of information influences the way individuals order and value their own demands. They may place high value on interventions with limited effectiveness because they have been misled by product claims, or may believe that only an injection will cure an illness best treated by a tablet. They may not value simple preventive measures through ignorance of the risk of disease, or of the relative risks of rare side-effects.[1] This limits the extent to which the demand curve can be interpreted as the individual's true valuation of health interventions available. Third, there are important externalities in the health sector: individuals' valuations of their own benefits will not usually take account of the benefits, for example of reduced risk of disease transmission, received by others.

We can hypothesise a social demand curve which would perform the same function as the private demand curve in valuing and ordering demands for the use of resources from a social perspective (see Box 19.2). The balance of considerations could lead to any relative positioning of the private and social demand curves, and different sub-health markets are likely to balance the three sources of divergence differently. For example, private demand for immunisation is likely to lie to the left of the social demand curve owing to substantial externalities. In addition, lack of information may lead the average patient to under-value immunisation. Furthermore, the highest relative valuation of it is among the poorest populations who suffer most from communicable disease but whose low ability to pay means that they express only a low level of demand in the market. In a market the demands expressed reflect the relative valuation of goods

Box 19.2 A social demand curve?

We have seen that demand curves measure the marginal valuations of the individuals making up a market for the good or service being traded. They slope downwards for each individual because we expect 'diminishing marginal utility' to be associated with any good under consideration. Summing the demand curves of all individuals then also gives a downward-sloping curve (see Chapter 2).

The concept of a social demand curve is a graphical representation of the same idea for social marginal valuations. We also expect diminishing social marginal value. Consider the case of a measles vaccination. We've argued that individuals' values of immunisation are likely to be quite low and the private market demand curve might be drawn as curve PD in the diagram. The higher values (to the left of the graph) are likely to be associated with the better educated, who understand the value of immunisation, and the rich, who can easily pay for it. A social demand curve gives a value to the immunisation of each individual equal to society's total value for that immunisation. This includes (1) full understanding of the likely benefits of immunisation for the individual concerned (correcting for imperfect information); (2) the value of immunisation for others whose risks are affected (taking account of externalities); and (3) removing wealth-related weights associated with individuals' preferences. Some people would argue for a more radical weighting favouring the poorest (see Box 9.6). On the basis that all these adjustments for social value from private values are likely to increase value, we can argue that the social demand curve (SD in the graph) for this service lies to the right of the private demand curve. The social demand curve will still slope downwards. Highest values will be placed on immunising individuals at highest risk of contracting and passing on the disease – those who live in the most cramped conditions, for example, and the marginal value of immunising the next individual will fall to zero at the point when herd immunity is reached. The ordering of priorities within the social demand curve will therefore be quite different from those within the private demand curve. Efficiency requires the equation of social demand with social marginal cost (which may also differ from social private cost in various ways). This concept of efficiency includes the concept of equity in whatever form it has been encompassed in social demand.

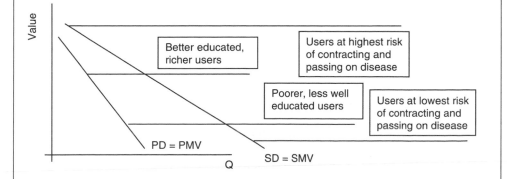

Demand and social value of immunisation.

Social demand curves are concepts rather than measurable entities – we cannot observe social values, although we might expect them to be closely related to concepts such as 'benefit', 'QALYs' and 'DALYs', which have been discussed in Part II. In fact, cost–benefit analysis, and certain types of cost-effectiveness analysis, can be seen as aiming to achieve the equivalent of the equation of social demand with social marginal cost.

Abstracting further, we can compare different types of intervention by constructing curves of 'marginal social value minus marginal social cost', similar to what has been done in Figure 21.1. This enables the widely varying costs of different types of interventions to be taken into account in contrasting social and private optima. Instead of creating an optimum where marginal social value equals marginal social cost, the optimum is found where marginal social value minus marginal social cost equals zero – an exactly equivalent position. Roughly speaking 'QALY league tables' locate points on this curve (though see the discussion of the relationship between QALYs and utility – or welfare – in Chapter 11, especially section 11.4)

and services by different individuals, but these are effectively weighted by their ability to pay (wealth). Together these factors mean that the social demand for immunisation is likely to lie to the right of the private demand. On the reverse logic, the opposite may be true of the services of CT scanners.

A better definition of optimum provision and funding is therefore where the marginal social value of the application of a unit of resources equates with its marginal social cost. Since marginal social cost is defined in terms of opportunities forgone, as explained in Chapter 10, comparing marginal social cost and marginal social value is equivalent to asking the question 'Does society place a higher value on the unit of resource used this way, or used another way?' Figure 19.2 shows that where the social demand curve lies to the right of the private demand curve, a new Q* higher than that suggested by the use of private valuations (Q1) applies, a higher level of funding must now be defined as optimum, and levels below that defined as 'under-funding'.

Alternative ways of financing and allocating health services have implications for the

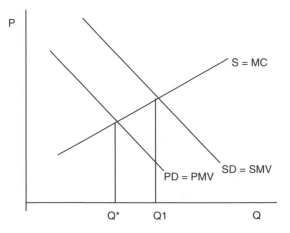

Figure 19.2 The impact of the social demand curve on optimal provision level.

total level of finance, the types of health services that will and will not be financed, and the distribution of those services among individuals (or groups of individuals in the case of services with wider application). The following chapters consider the likely implications of different ways of organising the system for each.

19.3 Alternative health systems: institutional structures and incentives

Alternative ways of organising health systems have implications for the ownership of health-providing and financing institutions, the internal governance structures of each, the flows of resources within and between institutions and hence the incentives that actors within the system face to pursue the objectives of both *allocative* and *internal* efficiency. (See Chapter 6 for explanation of these efficiency terms.)

A simple framework suggests that incentives to pursue efficiency strengthen as institutions become more private – for example, some literature refers to 'high-powered incentives', operating in markets, and 'low-powered incentives', operating within hierarchical organisations such as large companies and public agencies. The argument is that the owner-operator of a one-person business fully internalises the results of her efforts while, under other arrangements, the results of efforts will at least be shared by others. The strength of incentive is then defined as the responsiveness of reward to individual effort, and varies from 100 per cent in the single owner-manager case to 0 per cent under a fixed salary that does not respond at all to the level of effort or performance of the employee, even in the long term (through career prospects, for example).

This argument tends to emphasise the financial component of incentives. Those who find rewards in work well done, knowing that they have alleviated suffering, or in social respect may be more highly motivated by knowing that their services, produced in a public organisation, are distributed on the basis of need, than by being paid more money for their good performance. Nevertheless, there are probably limits to the reimbursement levels consistent with that outlook across a sufficient proportion of employees, as the deteriorated salary levels, motivation and performance of health workers in some public systems seems to attest.

Few cases correspond to the extremes of the high-powered and low-powered incentive continuum. In practice, even small businesses are taxed and may be subsidised, indicating a degree to which investments and returns are shared rather than individual. It is also difficult to conceive of a situation in which there is absolutely no return to making a greater effort to deliver a service. In practice, analysis of the incentives in institutional arrangements involves a qualitative assessment of the balance of incentives, and of the degree of their strength.

There is also limited identification of higher-powered incentives with more private forms of organisation and lower-powered incentives with more public ones. A well-tuned-to-performance promotion system with a steeply graduated pay structure, which exists in some public sector organisations, aims to reward performance financially, and may do so as effectively as a profit-sharing system in a private organisation. Where teamwork is practised, inevitably it is difficult to match pay to performance. This applies as much in private sector as in public sector organisations. Fixed salaries and poor career structures and promotion incentives can be found in both public and private organisations.

Incentives are sometimes discussed as if they could only direct people to appropriate activity – harder work, more focused effort, improved performance. However, incentives can also be perverse. Perversity is in the eye of the beholder, to the extent that an incentive may be judged perverse if it serves to encourage activity that in the judge's opinion is undesirable. Perverse incentives stem from a conflict between activity generating a reward and activity desirable from some other standpoint, for example activity promoting health. Hence the challenge is to get incentives 'right', rather than always stronger. Where perverse incentives are likely to arise, it may on balance be better to attenuate incentives as a whole (allow lower-powered incentives to prevail), even though incentives to appropriate activity may also be weakened.

Some of the belief in the strength and value of private sector incentives is based on faith in the perfect competition model (see Chapter 6) The underlying idea that profit seeking implies concern with cost minimising (internal efficiency) and seeking to meet the demands that consumers express (allocative efficiency) may have some validity, despite the problems with the model as a normative guide discussed in Chapter 6. More market exposure means stronger pressures to perform efficiently than where there is less market exposure. These kinds of pressures may be helpful in a range of contexts – but they can also prove perverse from a social welfare perspective. This is particularly the case in more complex situations in which several market imperfections apply – the divergence between private and social demand discussed in section 19.2 may become a source of perverse allocative efficiency incentives, viewed through this lens.

For example, it may benefit a hospital financially to under-invest (from a social value perspective) in preventing hospital-acquired infection (HAI) if there are no financial penalties for the hospital when HAI occurs. A hospital with no stake in its end-of-year financial performance may invest more in preventing HAI than one with a strong incentive to break even or generate a surplus. However, reducing a hospital's stake in its financial performance might achieve the gain of reduced levels of HAI at the expense of desired cost control in other areas of hospital activity. Alternative approaches might be to create a ring-fenced budget for HAI control while maintaining incentives for hospitals to control costs in other areas of its operation (where financial penalties for poor performance can be used more effectively). A mix of incentives for different types of transactions in different parts of the health system is therefore advisable, and needs to be judged according to the specific characteristics of those transactions.

Hence transaction costs economics, which was introduced in Chapter 14, can be a useful lens through which to view the appropriateness of institutional arrangements. Given its argument that different transactions will be most appropriately governed by different institutional arrangements, the existence of small firms, large firms, public and private organisations, centralised and decentralised structures need not be interpreted as evidence of health systems in chaos, but of efficient response to the different transaction characteristics those institutions manage.

As we saw in Chapter 14, it will be useful to consider the transaction characteristics of the business of specific types of institutions and the match between those and the governance arrangements in place. To return to the example above, transactions for HAI have specific information characteristics. Most notably, it is difficult to identify the source of an HAI and therefore to apply penalties to the organisation in the health system in which it arose (Allen *et al.* 2002). This characteristic might argue for more integrated governance, or other means of attenuating high-powered incentives applying to investment decisions in HAI prevention. Other transaction characteristics that this framework highlights are the asset specificities in transactions, and the frequency with which transactions take place.

It is also sometimes helpful to apply the agency ideas introduced in Chapter 18 to better understand the incentives in a given set of arrangements. This seeks insights from looking at the relationship between the principal (for example the owner of a firm) and the agent (for example the manager). Another factor that is likely to reduce the power of incentives as organisations get larger is that the difficulties of aligning incentives between multiple layers of principals and agents increase. In the public sector, the ultimate principal is the public, which elects policy makers. These are in turn the principals of senior government officials; in turn the principals of managers of the institutions that make up the public health system; in turn the principals of front-line service providers. At each link of that chain of principals and agents, issues of aligning incentives so that the agent serves the objectives of the principal arise, and at each stage it is likely that the result is at best approximate, while welfare losses are incurred, as was explained in Chapter 18. This provides some explanation as to why health systems may not closely reflect public preferences or achieve social efficiency.

In applying a qualitative agency analysis (individuals' real objective functions are not liable to quantification in the manner hypothesised in Chapter 18), there are a number of questions that it is helpful to ask of a given situation:

1   *Where are the agency relationships in the system?* These will be multiple, and analysable from different standpoints. For example, under insurance the enrolee is the agent in the sense that the insurance company wants the enrolee to avoid risk on its behalf. However, there are other, more obvious respects in which the insurance company is the agent of the enrolee, most notably in carrying risk. Agency relationships are often, but not always, reflected in financial flows to the extent that where money is transferred there is an associated expectation that goods and services will be provided, according to the direction of the payer. Money need not be involved, however – for example, in regulatory transactions.

2   *What are the possible and likely differences in the objective functions of agents and principals?* If objective functions are identical there is no need to consider the situation in agency terms. It can be assumed instead that the supposed agent will act identically as the principal would in pursuing their common objectives. Such a situation is likely to be rare, however. Even where there is apparent agreement on broad objectives, differences in detail will affect the outcome of the transaction between principal and agent. For example, both a Director of Public Health and her agent, a director of a TB control programme, might agree that the health of the public is the main objective, but the agent is more aware of the need for resources for TB than for other diseases. Where he benefits from information asymmetry and acts opportunistically he may misrepresent the data to which only he is privy, in order to secure those resources. Considering the detail of difference in objective function is likely to be insightful.

3   *What are the information asymmetries in the relationships, and where are the common uncertainties?* In the doctor–patient (agent–principal) relationship the doctor has more information than the patient about the appropriate course of treatment for the patient's condition, but there are common uncertainties regarding the effectiveness of any course of treatment. These prevent the patient from knowing, even *ex post*, whether or not the doctor acted in her best interests. These characteristics

set up an agency problem similar to the one treated theoretically in Chapter 18, but not typically addressed by the type of incentive compatible contract which solved that problem. It is interesting to ask why, in almost all health systems, other institutions such as medical ethics seek to address the same problem instead.

4   *How do principals try to control agents?* Wherever there are divergences of objectives, information asymmetries and uncertainties in agency relationships, measures can be identified to be in place to resolve the resulting problems, that can be interpreted as measures to increase the incentive compatibility of the contracts (which are sometimes implicit) between agents and principals. Identifying the measures in place and considering their effectiveness will often explain outcomes, and suggest areas in which policy could be developed with the objective of improving them.

Note

1   It is important here to distinguish between mis-valuation, which can be attributed to lack of information, and judgment of mis-valuation, where the underlying difference is of opinion. A medical professional may judge an intervention as advisable on the basis of its capacity to prolong life while a patient may judge its detrimental effects on quality of life too high a price to pay. In the case of underlying differences of opinion, economics emphasises the sovereignty of the consumer as best judge of her own interests while paternalist approaches might emphasise the superiority of professional values. In practice it is almost always impossible to distinguish between alternative causes of differing judgments and the dilemmas for medical professionals can be acute. Here, we need concern ourselves only with the theoretical implications of lack of information, for the interpretation of demand evidence.

20 Health systems around the world
An introduction to variation and performance

20.1 Introduction

A health system is made up of users, payers, providers and regulators, and can be defined by the relations between them. Governments can play a number of different roles as financers, regulators and/or providers of services. In some health systems the government is the dominant actor, providing and financing most services. Tax revenues pay for building and equipping facilities for service provision, for employment of the people who work within them, and the supply of drugs and other non-durable inputs. Patients receive services free at the time they use them. Some countries have even outlawed private practice, although it is doubtful that it has ever anywhere been possible to prevent all private transactions involving health related services or commodities. At the other extreme, government can be a more minor actor, although there is always some government subsidy or tax on components of the health system, regulation of some service transaction (such as minimum standards for the qualification 'medical doctor' or for hospitals) or public ownership or employment of some of the resources used to produce health services. Particular components or sub-systems, within a national system, can have almost wholly public or private characteristics. For example, public services may involve no private transactions at all, and some sectors, for example unregulated pharmaceutical markets, can operate entirely without government intervention. It is probably the case though, that even at the sub-system level, purity of public or private characteristics is rare – mixtures of public and private characteristics are the norm.

Health systems are typically characterised by *insurance*. This is broadly defined to mean that users pay regularly towards health system expenses in order to avoid bills that would levy an unacceptable burden on household budgets at the time of use, and in order to share risk between larger population groups to avoid catastrophic costs associated with health care.[1] Broadly defined, public systems can be considered a form of insurance, with the relevant share of tax effectively equivalent to a health insurance premium. More commonly, the term health insurance is restricted to arrangements where separate premiums and a separate *earmarked* fund for health services are created. Even with this narrower definition of insurance a wide variety of arrangements is found. *Social* insurance implies compulsory membership and usually a public or *quasi-*public insurance agent. *Private* insurance is offered by private insurance companies and is usually voluntary but is nonetheless usually subject to substantial regulation.

The fact that most health systems have a number of sub-components, characterised by different mixes of public and private characteristics and different levels and types of insurance coverage, makes a whole national health system difficult to categorise. This has been increasingly the case since the widespread adoption of health sector reforms which started at the end of the 1980s and has involved innovations in mixing public and private roles in the health system and in some cases (with notable exceptions) a greater degree of segmentation within national health systems. Before this wave of reforms, health systems tended to be dominated by characteristics that could be associated with ideal types. It is still useful to delineate these because they are still helpful in characterising sub-components of health systems, because they form the baseline from which different national health systems have more recently evolved, and because an analysis of the performance associated with those more ideal types still provides us with an understanding of the strengths and weaknesses of these particular combinations of characteristics that continues to inform innovations in health system development.

In the mid 1980s, health systems at national level could largely be characterised along a public–private spectrum. At the extreme public end of the spectrum was the *Semashko* system, typical of the former Communist countries of Central and Eastern Europe. One example of this was the health system of the former German Democratic Republic. In principle, it was centrally and publicly financed and provided almost all services free of charge to patients. All health staff were salaried and the private sector was extremely small (OECD 1992). However, in practice in Semashko systems divergence from these characteristics was reported, even before the reforms associated with transition to more market-oriented economies and societies began. While services were intended to be free, substantial 'under the counter' payments seem to have been made by patients in order to secure services, a form of default privatisation.

Until it was reformed in the late 1980s, the UK health system was dominated by the largely publicly provided and financed National Health Service (NHS), but included some user charges (for example, for dental and optical services, and for prescriptions) and also contained a small private insurance sector outside the NHS. Most of the resources used within the NHS were owned or employed publicly, but primary care doctors known as general practitioners (GPs) were contracted private individuals or firms. Examples of other countries whose systems were dominated by public provision and finance, but which had more private components than the former Communist countries, included Denmark, Sweden and New Zealand (OECD 1992, 1994). This system is known as the *Bevanite* health system, after Aneurin Bevan, one of its designers.

A number of poorer countries modelled their health systems on either the Bevanite or Semashko model. Taking Uganda as an example, the health system was designed to be dominated by public finance and provision. A range of publicly owned health facilities from small aid posts in most remote regions, intended to provide services for minor illnesses, through health centres, district and regional hospitals and two teaching hospitals in the two largest cities are all publicly equipped, directly employ all health personnel, and are publicly supplied with drugs and other items. However, problems of inadequate resources and poor management of resources in the public sector ensured that the public system was not as dominant in health services provision as intended. Within the public system, substantial default privatisation was reported, as in the former Communist countries. In addition, pure private practice filled the gaps the public sector had left, and covered a high, if difficult to document, proportion of primary care provision. This included some of the purest private sector arrangements to be found, with unregulated providers selling unsubsidised or taxed services directly to health service users. Private not-for-profit providers (mainly religious organisation-run facilities) played a substantial role. Examples of countries in which similar descriptions apply include India, Pakistan, Bangladesh, Kenya, Tanzania and Ghana, although the extent of default privatisation within the public system varies considerably (Berman *et al.* 1995a; Bennett *et al.* 1997). Waves of reform in these countries have not had the effect of changing the pluralistic nature of their health systems, viewed from the national level.

Social insurance dominated the health systems of most of the remaining industrialised countries. The *Bismarck* model of social insurance, developed in Germany, has often been considered the standard model of social insurance. In the former Federal Republic of Germany 75 per cent of the population was insured compulsorily, about 13 per cent voluntarily with the same (*quasi*-public) sickness funds, while 10 per cent of the population was insured privately. There were both public and private providers (51 per cent of hospital beds were public; ambulatory care physicians and pharmacies were largely private). Both types mainly operated on contract to the statutory sickness funds, although investment costs were usually directly funded by state governments), and there were only minor co-payments paid by patients at the time of use. Examples of countries in which similar system models operated included Belgium (where co-payments were more substantial and a higher proportion of health service costs were met through tax-based finance), France (with 99 per cent insurance with statutory sickness funds but a reimbursement model for many health sector transactions whereby health service users paid and were later reimbursed), the Netherlands and Austria (OECD 1992, 1994).

The majority of Latin American countries (defined henceforth as Mexico and the countries of Central and South America, excluding the Caribbean island nations) contained three important sub-systems: public, social insurance and private (insurance and out-of-pocket financed). Taking Peru as an example, about 30 per cent of health sector expenditure went to public sector providers, 35 per cent to separate social insurance providers and about 35 per cent to private providers. About 20 per cent of this last 35 per cent flowed through private insurance funds and 80 per cent through out-of-pocket payments. Theoretically, the public sector covered over 70 per cent of the population, the social security sector over 20 per cent and the private sector about 2 per cent. However, this overstated the difference in coverage levels. In practice, as in other poor countries, the public sector achieved less than intended and public documents admitted that about one-third of the population had no access to services while the private sector served a much larger population who sought alternatives to both public and social insurance provided services – about 20 per cent of the population (Ministry of Health, Peru 1997a, b). Although distributions varied between the three major sectors, this segmented health system applied to almost all Latin American countries at one time (IADB 1996).

Private, voluntary insurance played an important role in a limited number of countries and always coexisted with some form of cover or compulsory arrangements for those it excluded or would otherwise exclude. The United States was the most prominent country that relied on this set of arrangements, with employers expected to provide cover to their employees and dependants (about 60 per cent of the population insured that way) or individuals to insure themselves (13 per cent). Public finance directly covered only the elderly, disabled and poor (23 per cent) and military veterans (4 per cent). Fourteen per cent of the population were officially 'uninsured', although this group was indirectly able to access some services.[2] The majority of providers were private, although there were some public health institutions established in areas the private sector failed to serve, such as inner cities. Private insurance covered 99 per cent of the population of Switzerland. Other countries had also relatively high levels, at least in the mid-1990s, including South Africa (20 per cent of the population; 50 per cent of expenditure) and Brazil (25 per cent of the population) (OECD 1994; van den Heever 1997; Chollet and Lewis 1997).

This categorisation of national health systems started to break down after the mid-1980s when a series of innovations in health system design started to be introduced. The Semashko systems underwent fundamental reform in response to the market-oriented transition of their societies and economies. Many sought to emulate the Bismarck model of social insurance, with varying degrees of success. For example in the Czech Republic the health care system adopted a social insurance model in 1991, with a number of insurers financing health care providers on the basis of contracts (Rokosová and Háva 2005). A number of Bevanite systems introduced contracts between public purchasers and public providers of services, in some cases increasing the opportunities for private providers to participate in the system, and the role of private investment funding. For example, in the UK responsibility for purchasing services was separated from responsibility for providing them in 1991. This separation largely remains, although emphasis on co-operation rather than competition between providers has increased in the intervening period, and the purchasing role has been increasingly delegated to primary level (Robinson and Dixon 1999). Poorer countries whose systems were modelled on Semashko or Bevanite systems have also introduced reforms which have sought to improve the performance of the public sector and to better regulate the private sector, sometimes also using contracts. New forms of partnership between public and private sectors have been introduced. Prominent examples include partnerships in pharmaceutical and vaccine distribution, technology diffusion and in seeking to extend the availability of HIV/AIDS treatment. These reforms have not changed the plural nature of these health systems and in some respects may have increased their diversity. Some Bismarckian health systems have introduced greater roles for public regulation and in some cases provision, but also new and larger co-payments (direct payment of a share of health service costs by users). In France, user charges for primary and hospital care increased after the Plan Juppé of 1995, and the role of public regulators in setting national expenditure targets, and regulating practice guidelines, quality controls (hospital accreditation) and access to specialist care, increased (Lancry and Sandier 1999). A number of Latin American countries have sought to achieve greater universality and to lower the boundaries between the segments of their systems. For example, Brazil introduced the Unified Health System (SUS) in 1988 and Colombia started to integrate its public and social insurance systems through reforms which came into effect in 1996. Switzerland moved to compulsory insurance in 1996, bringing its system closer to a Bismarckian one. There have been a large number of innovations in the health system of the United States. In particular, enthusiasm for a variety of managed care arrangements aimed at controlling costs waxed in the late 1980s and early 1990s but had waned by the late 1990s. There has been no one national health reform programme that has significantly affected the overall characteristics of the system in the United States.

These reforms were prompted at least in part by an analysis of the performance of health systems that suggested that the ideal types had particular advantages and disadvantages and the argument that better mixing of health system characteristics could capture advantages and avoid disadvantages so as to achieve improved outcomes for all. The effects of these reforms have been argued by some to represent a convergence of health system characteristics (Ham 1997). The following sections of this chapter consider the evolving performance of health systems since the 1970s, showing how performance diverged in the era of the ideal types and the degree to which it has converged or otherwise changed in the subsequent period.

20.2 Health sector expenditure patterns

Table 20.1 shows expenditure performance for a selection of OECD countries presented in three groups. (The non-OECD countries have substantially lower GDP *per capita* and health expenditure and less reliable data collection systems making comparison difficult.) The table suggests that those health systems originally categorised as more public in character spent less, as a share of GDP, in 1982, having apparently experienced lower health sector inflation between 1972 and 1982. The exceptions to this pattern in the countries shown over that period are that Sweden, in the Bevanite group, spent a comparable share of its GDP on health to the highest-spending countries in 1982, although its health expenditure inflation was relatively low, and New Zealand's expenditure grew as rapidly as Bismarckian countries' although its overall level as a percentage of GDP was relatively low.

Between 1982 and 1992 the tendency of Bevanite countries to experience less health expenditure inflation was no longer discernible. While Denmark and Sweden experienced negative growth rates (in share of GDP terms), the UK experienced the fastest growth of all countries in the group except the United States, and New Zealand's growth was also relatively fast. In the 1992–2002 period health expenditure inflation was faster in the selected Bevanite than Bismarckian countries. Throughout the 1972 to 1992 period, health expenditure in the United States was higher and grew faster than in any other country. Between 1992 and 2002 its rate of growth slowed to among the lowest of all the countries selected, although its overall level of expenditure in 2002 was still about double the typical level of other OECD countries and its share of GDP nearly double. Despite the absence of comparable data for the middle period, the Swiss health system appears also to have grown rapidly throughout the period. In 1972 the Swiss spent a similar proportion of GDP on health care as other European countries but by 2002 their expenditure was markedly higher in absolute and share of GDP terms.

The data seem to tell the story that differences in expenditure performance that were associated with ideal types of health system in the mid-1980s started to disappear as reforms to those systems that moved them away from those ideal types were introduced. Caution should be exercised in considering that causative relationships between health system characteristics and performance are well established. The countries have been selected rather arbitrarily, for illustrative purposes. The simple categorisation of countries misses important differences in health systems and obscures important similarities that exist across groups. Important possible confounding factors have not been controlled. Nevertheless, there are grounds to accept this broad explanation of trends. There are good theoretical grounds for expecting public expenditure to be more easily controlled than private and social insurance expenditure. Cost control was a major impetus for reforms to Bismarckian health systems in the 1990s and those countries sought to emulate measures used in public health systems that were thought to be

Table 20.1 Health expenditure, 1972–2002

Country	2002 per capita expenditure (1995 US$)	As % GDP				% change in health expenditure share		
		1972	1982	1992	2002	1972–82	1982–92	1992–2002
Originally Bevanite								
UK	2,031	4.7	5.9	7.1	7.7	26	20	8
Denmark	2,835	6.3	6.8	6.5	8.8	8	–3	35
Sweden	2,489	7.5	9.6	7.9	9.2	28	–18	16
New Zealand	1,255	5.3	6.9	7.7	8.5	30	12	10
Originally Bismarckian								
Germany	2,631	6.5	8.6	8.7	10.9	32	1	25
Belgium	2,159	4.3	7.4	8.2	9.1	65	11	11
France	2,348	6.2	8.0	9.4	9.7	29	17	3
Netherlands	2,298	6.7	8.4	8.6	8.8	25	2	2
Originally private insurance								
Switzerland	4,219	5.5	7.5	9.3[a]	11.2	36	–[a]	20
United States	5,274	7.6	10.3	14.0	14.6	36	36	4

Note:
a Swiss accounts were revised in 1985 and the two data series cannot be linked.

Sources: OECD (1994) (1972–1992 data) and World Bank Health Nutrition and Population statistics (2002 data).

Equity

associated with their slower health expenditure growth. This was not the concern driving reform in Bevanite health systems, in some of which the health services were under-financed was prevalent. Rather, poor-quality se did not respond to users' choices and preferences were expected to improve in for example, to the introduction of contracts between purchasers and pro existed in insurance-based systems. It might be expected that this emphasi .ould support, rather than dampen, rising expenditures.

It is not easy to interpret the trends represented by these data normatively. They do not identify which health systems are more efficient. Higher-spending health systems could be technically less efficient – spending more for an equivalent level of achieve-ment – or allocatively inefficient – spending more for a higher level of achievement that would not be judged by society worth the sacrifice of expenditure in other sectors. Alternatively, lower-spending health systems could be technically or allocatively ineffi-cient. They may under-perform in outcome terms, even taking account the lower level of expenditure, or they may fail to spend where the increased level of achievement associated with more spending would be judged worth the sacrifice of expenditure in other sectors.

20.3 Performance in terms of equity

Van Doorslaer and Masseria (2004) analysed inequality and inequity in utilisation of health services in twenty-one OECD countries. Table 20.2 shows their results for those countries that we have been considering. The table shows the utilisation data for the quintiles (20 per cent of the population) at the top and bottom of the income distribu-tion in each country. It also shows concentration and health inequity indices that sum-marise the distribution of utilisation across all five quintiles of the population. Both indices range from 0 to 1 in absolute terms (0 equates with perfect equality or equity; numbers close to 1 imply that utilisation is highly concentrated at the upper end of the income distribution; close to -1, highly concentrated at the lower end of the income distribution). The calculation of the concentration index that measures distribution of income (the Gini coefficient) is explained in Chapter 24. The same principles apply to the calculation of any concentration index.

The horizontal equity index attempts to measure the extent to which it appears that there is equal utilisation of the service for equal need. Need was estimated by identify-ing those demographic and morbidity variables that predict utilisation on average across the population, using regression analysis. For each population group, actual utilisation could be compared with that predicted on the basis of need. Given the concentration of need-related variables in the lowest income quintile of the population, a distribution of utilisation that is equal (CI = 0) will be inequitable (HI > 0). A degree of pro-poor inequality (CI < 0) will be required to produce an equitable result (HI = 0).

Overall, there is a tendency across the countries for utilisation of specialist doctors to be inequitably distributed in favour of high-income groups, for utilisation of general practitioners to be inequitably distributed in favour of low-income groups, and for hospital care utilisation to be approximately equitably distributed (few significant results). In Sweden and the United States, where it was not possible to separate general practitioner and specialist doctor utilisation, the pattern accorded with that for special-ists (inequitable in favour of high-income groups), and this was the case for total physician utilisation across most countries.

Table 20.2 Inequality and inequity in utilisation, selected OECD countries: need-standardised utilisation of income quintiles 1 and 5 of the population, concentration index (CI) and horizontal inequity index (HI)

Country	General practitioner utilisation (visits in twelve months)				Specialist utilisation (visits in twelve months)				Hospital care utilisation (days' in-patient stay in twelve months)			
	Poorest	Richest	CI	HI	Poorest	Richest	CI	HI	Poorest	Richest	CI	HI
Originally Bevanite												
UK	4.351	3.564	**-0.119**[c]	**-0.042**	1.437	1.562	**-0.062**	0.017	0.907	0.893	**-0.181**	0.013
Denmark	2.579	2.411	**-0.104**	**-0.028**	0.752	1.049	**0.009**	**0.093**	1.636	1.054	**-0.205**	-0.093
Sweden[a]	3.248	3.928	0.012	**0.042**	–	–	–	–	0.714	0.906	**-0.122**	-0.006
Originally Bismarckian												
Germany	4.978	4.491	**-0.075**	-0.021	2.599	3.719	**-0.003**	**0.045**	2.053	1.376	**-0.059**	-0.029
Belgium	5.745	4.468	**-0.144**	**-0.057**	1.713	2.072	**-0.031**	**0.038**	1.369	1.079	**-0.222**	-0.048
France	4.597	4.665	**-0.027**	-0.005	1.969	2.653	0.037	**0.063**	0.794	1.039	-0.019	0.035
Netherlands	3.180	2.710	**-0.098**	**-0.038**	1.558	1.739	**-0.051**	0.019	0.825	0.690	**-0.158**	-0.040
Originally private insurance												
Switzerland	2.208	1.956	**-0.062**	-0.024	1.174	1.724	**0.051**	**0.074**	1.158	0.099	**-0.128**	-0.063
United States[b]	2.982	4.223	**-0.020**	**0.068**	–	–	–	–	0.088	0.072	**-0.167**	**-0.038**

Notes:
a Data entered in general practitioner columns for Sweden are for total physician utilisation (general practitioner and specialist utilisation) and have been adjusted for the shorter length of recall period (three months) in the Swedish than in other (twelve month) country surveys.
b Data entered in general practitioner columns for the United States are for total physician utilisation (general practitioner and specialist utilisation).
c Indices in **bold** indicate that there are significant differences in utilisation between population income groups, and that the index can be said to be significantly different from 0.

Source: Masseria and van Doorslaer (2004).

In contrast to the health expenditure data, there appears to be no clear grouping of equity and equality indices associated with the health system types. This is not very surprising, given the unavailability of these data for earlier periods when the systems groups were more distinct. However, Masseria and van Doorslaer's analysis was able to estimate the importance of different determinants of inequality and inequity and for our purposes, it is particularly interesting to look at what they found to be the role of private insurance in seven countries in which that analysis was possible. Private insurance means different things in different countries – for example, in the United States, as we have seen, it distinguishes the insured from the uninsured, whereas in other countries it is complementary to public or social insurance, covering the costs of co-payments in France, for example, and enabling quicker access to certain hospital services in the UK. In general, private insurance is judged to contribute a small amount to pro-rich inequity. In France, both private and public insurance increase GP use to a similar degree but private insurance is associated with 1.6 extra visits to a specialist whereas public insurance adds only an extra 0.3 visits. In the United States the insurance coverage gap accounts for nearly 30 per cent of the total degree of inequity found in doctor utilisation and increases the inequity in the number of nights spent in hospital, but not the probability of admission (for which data are not shown in Table 20.2). In Switzerland people must insure themselves but can choose what type of insurance to buy. The rich tend to favour insurance policies with high deductibles, and this may explain their using less health care, and contribute to pro-poor inequity (Van Doorslaer and Masseria 2004).

Table 20.3 summarises a similar analysis carried out for low and middle-income countries, where different types of health service utilisation are most relevant. In this analysis the types of service use compared are naturally need-adjusted (on the assumption that all children should be immunised, all births supervised by a trained person and all those with infections treated medically), and so the concentration indices can be considered as measures of degrees of inequity. Almost all the indices are positive, indicating that pro-rich inequity applies across this group of countries to all these services. The two exceptions are pro-poor inequities for full basic immunisation coverage in Uzbekistan, and medical treatment of diarrhoeal disease in the Kyrgyz Republic. Since the second and third of these are the only measurements available of medical treatments for these conditions in Semashko countries, it may be that pro-poor inequities in these countries are more general.

Pro-rich inequity levels are highest for the percentage of births attended by a medically trained person in the low-income countries that were modelled on Bevanite or Semashko systems. Low levels of use of this service among the lowest income quintile (only 3.5 per cent of the poorest Bangladeshi women and 4.6 per cent of the poorest Pakistani women give birth under medically trained supervision) are associated with these high levels of inequity.

On average, this group of countries has higher levels of inequity than the segmented health systems of Latin America, which in turn have higher levels of inequity than the Semashko health systems. There are important exceptions, however. Medical treatment in Ghana and Kenya exhibits relatively small degrees of pro-rich inequity compared with Colombia and Bolivia.

The first group of countries has the lowest incomes and the lowest overall use of most services (immunisation is an exception), with the implication that it is difficult to attribute the relatively poor performance in equity terms to health system structures *per se*.

Table 20.3 Inequity in utilisation: selected low and middle-income countries

Country	Full basic immunisation coverage			% births attended by medically trained person			% seen medically if ill: diarrhoea			Acute respiratory infection		
	Poorest	Richest	CI	Poorest	Richest	CI	Poorest	Richest	CI	Poorest	Richest	CI
Modelled on Bevani/el												
Semashko												
Bangladesh 2000	50.3	74.9	0.0852	3.5	42.1	0.6174	16.4	41.2	0.2346	_b	_b	_b
Ghana 1998	49.6	79.3	0.0868	17.9	86.1	0.2979	26.2	(32.3)[a]	0.0090	24.3	(46.7)	0.0713
India 1999	21.3	63.8	0.2546	16.4	84.4	0.3220	54.6	81.5	0.0880	53.3	82.2	0.1007
Kenya 1998	48.1	59.9	0.0577	23.2	79.6	0.2419	41.4	48.5	0.0434	54.9	78.5	0.0210
Pakistan 1990	22.5	54.7	0.2064	4.6	55.2	0.5989	36.6	66.4	0.1534	49.4	85.4	0.0996
Uganda 2000	26.5	42.6	0.0898	19.7	77.3	0.2972	33.0	57.7	0.0986	61.3	89.0	0.0450
Segmented												
Bolivia 1998	21.8	30.6	0.0607	19.8	97.9	0.2966	29.6	46.0	0.0920	2706	69.5	0.1870
Colombia 1995	57.7	77.3	0.0677	60.6	98.1	0.1028	22.4	39.0	0.1346	34.3	68.0	0.1159
Nicaragua 2001	63.6	71.0	0.0439	77.5	99.3	0.0567	37.6	41.9	0.0490	45.0	74.5	0.0956
Peru 2000	57.9	81.1	0.0766	13.0	87.5	0.3176	35.1	57.3	0.0437	47.9	78.9	0.0965
Semashko												
Kazakhstan 1999	68.7	(62.3)	0.0080	99.2	98.5	0.0011	_b	_b	_b	_b	_b	_b
Kyrgyz Republic 1997	69.3	73.1	0.0007	96.0	100.0	0.0045	44.6	(53.7)	0.0993	_b	_b	_b
Uzbekistan 1996	80.9	77.5	0.0124	91.7	100.0	0.0150	_b	_b	_b	_b	_b	_b

Notes:
a Figures in parentheses are based on small samples and should be treated with caution.
b Data unavailable.

Source: C. Watkin *et al.* (forthcoming).

It is more reasonable to compare the segmented and Semashko health systems where income levels are similar. Semashko systems seem to be associated with higher overall use of services across the board, smaller degrees of inequity, and pro-poor inequity in some cases.

20.4 Performance in terms of health outcomes

Table 20.4 shows life expectancy and infant mortality rates for countries in each of the old health system categories. The data show far more association with the income level of countries than with health system categorisation. Health status is well understood to be affected by a wide range of social and economic variables and it would be surprising,

Table 20.4 Health status performance, 2003

Country	Life expectancy[a]	Infant morality[b]	Child mortality[c]
Originally Bevanite			
UK	77.6	5.3	6.5[d]
Denmark	77.1	4.4	5.9[d]
Sweden	80.1	2.8	3.9[d]
Originally Bismarckian			
Germany	78.3	4.2	5[d]
Belgium	78.3	4	5
France	79.3	4.4[d]	5.5[d]
Netherlands	78.5	4.8	5.7
Originally private insurance			
Switzerland	80.5	4.3	5.7[d]
United States	77.4[d]	7[d]	8[d]
Modelled on Bevanite/Semashko			
Bangladesh 2000	62.4	46	69
Ghana 1998	54.4	59	95
India 1999	63.4	63	87
Kenya 1998	45.4	79	123
Pakistan 1990	64.0	74	98
Uganda 2000	43.2	81	140
Segmented			
Bolivia 1998	64.1	53	66
Colombia 1995	71.9	18	21
Nicaragua 2001	68.8	30	38
Peru 2000	70.0	26	34
Semashko			
Kazakhstan 1999	61.3	63	73
Kyrgyz Republic 1997	65.0	59	68
Uzbekistan 1996	66.7	57	69

Notes:
a Life expectancy at birth, total (years).
b Mortality rate, under one year, per 1,000 live births.
c Mortality rate, under five years, per 1,000 live births.
d Data relate to the year 2002.

Source: World Bank: World Development Indicators (http://devdata.worldbank.org (accessed 16 March 2006).

on the basis of this type of analysis, if health systems could be shown to be critically determinant of health status outcomes. A more promising approach may be to consider the role of specific components of health systems in promoting health status.

Health expenditure is also strongly correlated with income, so a direct comparison of health expenditure and health outcome variables is also not very helpful. In Figure 20.1, instead, the extent to which a country spends more or less on health than it would be predicted to do, given its income level, is compared with its life expectancy compared with that predicted by its income level. The figure suggests that spending more or less than expected is not the dominant explanation of life expectancy performance. Countries in the top left quadrant spend more but achieve less in life expectancy terms than would be predicted. Besides the United States, these countries are largely low-income ones, initially modelled on Bevanite or Semashko systems, but now characterised by high levels of default privatisation. Expenditure in these systems appears on average less effective than in others. In contrast, in the bottom right-hand quadrant are countries with above expected life expectancy and below expected expenditure. These include two Latin American countries, one of which (Colombia) has reformed its segmented health system more fundamentally than the other (Peru), a social insurance-based European country (France) and a Bevanite system that has reformed by separating purchasing from provision (Sweden).

Anand and Barnighausen (2004) have examined the impact of numbers of doctors and nurses on maternal, infant and child mortality rates using multiple regression analysis. The overall density of human resources for health (HRH: the total of the doctor and nurse work force expressed *per capita*) has the greatest impact on maternal mortality of the three types of outcome (elasticity = 0.474: a 1 per cent increase in the workforce density is associated with a 0.47 per cent decrease in maternal mortality),

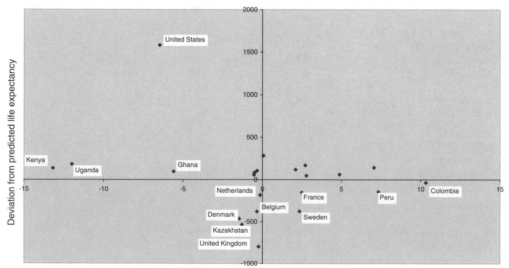

Figure 20.1 Expenditure and health gaps in four sub-regions of Latin America and the Caribbean.

Note: The health gap compares observed life expectancy with the expectation based on *per capita* income.

Source: Interamerican Development Bank (1996)

and Anand and Barnighausen speculate that this may be because qualified medical personnel can better address the illnesses that put mothers at risk. Nevertheless, the effects on infant and child mortality are still significant (elasticities 0.235 and 0.260 for higher income countries; 0.212 and 0.231 for lower income countries respectively).

This suggests that differential investment in human resources across health systems is likely to affect health outcomes. Health system types cluster in their infant mortality (as in Table 20.4) and in their investment in human resources, in ways that would be predicted (broadly) by income levels. Figure 20.2(a) and (b) therefore takes the same

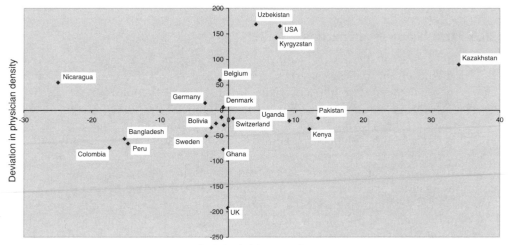

Figure 20.2 (*a*) Physician density and infant mortality, 2001 or near year.

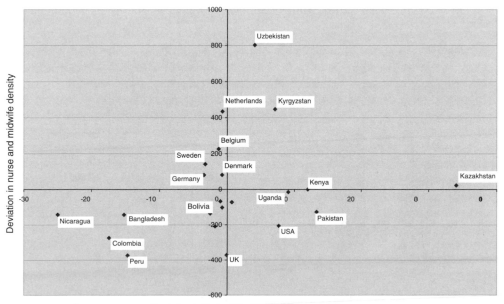

Figure 20.2 (*b*) Nurse and midwife density and infant mortality, 2001 or near year.

approach as Figure 20.1: how does deviation from expected deviation in investment in HRH (physician and nurse density respectively) relate to deviation in expected health outcome, in this case infant mortality? Figure 20.2(a) shows that a cluster of countries, mixed in their system types – four Latin American countries, Bangladesh and Sweden – obtain relatively good IMR results for relatively small investment in physicians, whereas the United States and three former Semashko systems, use a relatively high number of physicians but obtain relatively poor IMR outcome. The outlying countries are largely similar in relation to nurse density (Figure 20.2b) although the United States makes relatively low use of nurses for its income level.

20.5 Health system satisfaction

A few international surveys of health system satisfaction have been undertaken by Robert Blendon and colleagues. These have focused on OECD countries. The first survey conducted in 1988 and covering Canada, the Netherlands, West Germany, France, Australia, Sweden, Japan, Great Britain, Italy and the United States suggested that Bismarck-type systems produced the most satisfaction, public health systems less, and the private health system of the United States the least. However, already by 1994, when a further survey was conducted, these distinctions seemed to have diminished. While still relatively low compared with satisfaction in the original survey, and the other countries included in this one, satisfaction had grown in the United States (from 10 per cent to 18 per cent agreeing with the statement 'On the whole, the health care system works pretty well, and only minor changes are needed') and had fallen significantly in Canada and West Germany (from 56 per cent and 41 per cent to 29 per cent and 30 per cent respectively) (Blendon *et al.* 1990, 1995).

Convergence in satisfaction seems also to emerge from a comparison of a different five countries for which comparable data have now been collected on three occasions (Figure 20.3). There is now little difference between the views of citizens in Canada and

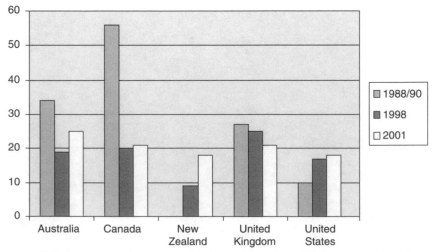

Figure 20.3 Citizens' overall views about their health care system in five countries, selected years 1988–2001.

Source: Blendon *et al.* (2002)

the United States, and there are no statistically significant differences across the group. Data from the European Value Survey (1999/2000) suggest that differences in those reporting themselves as having a great deal or quite a lot of confidence in their health care system among European countries are not now grouped by old health system type, although differences are larger than those in the last year of Figure 20.3, and those in former Semashko systems in general report less satisfaction with their health system.

It would appear that as health system structures have converged, so have satisfaction levels. However, the explanation may be more complex. Satisfaction in countries such as Canada and Germany seems to have declined as resource limits have been encountered and cost control mechanisms have started to be introduced. More recent and more detailed work by Blendon and his colleagues suggest a mix of factors that affect overall satisfaction levels, affecting population groups differentially. These suggest continued distinct differences between public perceptions of health systems and new comparative patterns among countries. Comparing quality and access perceptions across the five countries in Figure 20.3, citizens in the UK and Canada report the least constraint to access posed by cost or difficulties paying medical bills, whereas Australia and New Zealand report the greatest satisfaction with the quality of care they receive. While citizens in the United States are most likely to report that cost factors have deterred their use of care, or that they had difficulties paying medical bills, they were not significantly more likely to report their medical care as excellent, were least likely, after the UK, to consider that the care they received from their physician was excellent or very good, and reported the greatest difficulties in accessing specialist care, or care at night or at weekends (Blendon *et al.* 2002).

Notes

1 Catastrophic costs have been defined as costs greater than 40 per cent of annual income after basic expenses have been covered (Xu *et al.* 2003).
2 Percentages sum to more than 100 per cent because of duplicate coverage.

21 Reliance on the state

Public health service systems

21.1 Introduction

Chapter 20 suggested that public health service systems had better controlled cost inflation than other types of system. Conversely, it is often argued that they are 'under-funded', leading to more rationing of essential care and poor quality services. Evidence of any direct effects of rationing and service quality on health outcomes is hard to assemble. There are many factors determining health status, and these are not precisely understood. Furthermore, health status improvement is not the only valued outcome of a health system – others that may be considered important include freedom from anxiety, and comfort during illness. Palliative care may be valued for its own sake. Achievements of this sort should be added to health status improvement to reflect population satisfaction. Satisfaction levels may prove to be highly sensitive to levels of health system adequacy.

In the archetypal public health service system, simplified and stylised for the purpose of this chapter, funding is provided through general taxation and the system is charac-terised by public ownership, providers of care are given fixed annual budgets, and health workers are direct employees. Health services are free to users at the point of use.

21.2 'Under-funding' and rationing of services?

Where the source of all funding for the health sector is public, policy makers should aim to ensure that the funding provided equals their estimate of the optimal level of provision (Q** on Figure 19.2).

Getting the funding level right is a necessary condition for ensuring that resources are rationed to the highest priority uses. In place of the price mechanism, public systems must use alternative measures to decide who gets how much of what. There are four means to ration in a pure public system: setting the pattern of supply; gatekeeping; waiting lists; and queues. A fifth means – applying user charges – has been ruled out in our characterisation of an archetypal public system. Issues relating to user charges will be considered in Chapter 25.

No matter how well funded, all public systems must set the pattern of supply, and in so doing enable some demands on the health system and disallow others. The pattern of supply determines access costs and the level at which other rationing mechanisms have to be applied. A new hospital can always be built and will always reduce access costs for someone. In the situation of most public systems, where resources fall short of the ability to meet a wide range of legitimate demands facing them, setting the pattern of supply involves making more critical choices. Limiting the growth of premature baby units implies higher gatekeeping thresholds (see below) and increases the probability that a baby capable of survival is denied treatment. Despite this, the level of funding may be appropriate given the opportunity cost of resources for this purpose. Costs per QALY reach high levels in this area (Rogowski 1998). In the public systems of poor countries, routine and unquestionably high-priority health services, such as caesarean section capacity in the case of complicated births, are out of reach of millions of women at the time of need. Even this does not necessarily imply poor rationing through poor planning of the pattern of supply. All uses of resources have extremely high opportunity costs in poor countries and even in an ideally allocatively efficient context, it is difficult to see where resources could be found to staff and equip operating theatres in remote and sparsely populated regions.

It is easy – and common – to assume that such problems indicate the failure of public decision making, both in ensuring optimal funding levels and in setting patterns of supply appropriately. Decisions on setting the pattern of public supply should, at least in principle, attempt to order demands for health resources according to marginal social value. By using the results of economic evaluations where they are available, and by attempting to apply social values more generally where they are not, public systems have the opportunity to improve on the pattern of supply which would result from a price-rationed system. In practice, there is wide variation in the extent to which supply planning achieves its potential (for example, see Box 21.1).

In England and Wales, the National Institute for Clinical Excellence has the role of advising on marginal changes in supply setting, in the sense of interventions to be added to, or withdrawn from, those to be provided by the National Health Service. Dawson (2000) has conceptualised NICE's problem as in Figure 21.1. The model takes the example of a new urology service (Viagra) approved by NICE. At the outset, the fixed budget is being spent according to marginal health gain (which accords with our framework if the social welfare function equates to the health gain function). Before the new technology, the fixed budget (yz – about £450 million) is being spent by allocating about £150 million to urology services and about £300 million to other services in such

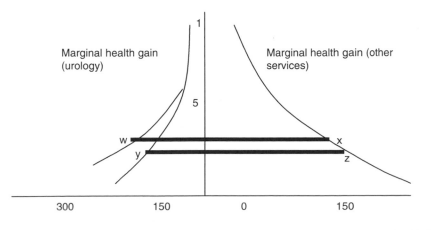

Figure 21.1 The NICE problem with Viagra.

Box 21.1 Setting the pattern of supply in public systems: geographical resource allocation

Pattern of supply is determined in public systems directly by public decision making. This usually has more centralised and decentralised components. Building a hospital will seldom be an option for a local health authority, but decisions to increase levels of equipment or to develop a new service may be.

From a central perspective, one major question is how to distribute resources among local health authorities. Typically, public health systems have developed rather inequitable and allocatively inefficient financial distribution among local areas. In many countries this resulted from funding criteria being facility rather than population-based. Inequitable facility distribution from a population perspective was commonly the result of historical factors: the facilities and their distribution existed prior to the development of the public system.

South Africa's health sector resource distribution reflects the peculiar history of that country. Zwarenstein and Price (1990) document the disparities in the availability of hospitals and hospital beds to urban and rural populations and by 'race'. For example, bed ratios varied from 130 people per bed for the urban white population to 460 people per bed for the rural black/Asian/coloured population outside the 'homelands'. McIntyre *et al.* (1991) propose a formula which would allow these inequities to be addressed. The formula would determine the resource allocation to each region or 'homeland' on the basis of an estimate of needs for curative and preventive services and population size and structure. Comparing the results of the formula with the existing allocation of resources suggests that one region, Western Cape, receives 183 per cent of the estimated appropriate allocation while another, KwaNdebele, receives only 10 per cent. Including an allocation for teaching, the estimates change to 141 per cent and 12 per cent respectively.

Some countries already apply a formula such as is proposed by McIntyre *et al.* (1991). In England such a formula was first introduced in 1977. It adjusted population numbers for standardised mortality ratios weighted by their importance in bed use and patterns of use of facilities. At the introduction of the formula the most over-provided region received about 15 per cent in excess of its fair share of resources and the most under-provided region about 11 per cent less. After ten years the formula had achieved a narrowing of that range from +7 per cent to −4 per cent (Mays 1995). Such formulas have the advantage over traditional resource allocation mechanisms of transparency, and almost certainly move health systems in a more equitable direction in resource allocation, but cannot be perfectly objective. Since 'need' cannot be directly measured, debate remains as to the variables which best proxy for need and how they should be combined – for example, mortality or indicators of social deprivation (Mays 1995; Sheldon *et al.* 1993).

a way that the services producing the highest marginal health gain receive funding up to a cut-off point (about two units of health gain per £1,000 spent) after which services are not funded. A range of applications of Viagra pass this cost-effectiveness test, offering marginal health gain per £1,000 of greater than two units. This affects the marginal health gain curve for urology services. If there is no increase in health service funding to accommodate the greater productivity of investments in health, the appropriate response is to reallocate the same budget, increasing urology's share (to about £160 million) and reducing that for other services (to about £290 million): budget line wx. The effect of this is to increase the cut-off point for inclusion in health service supply to about two-and-a-half units of marginal health gain per £1,000 spent.

A key question to which this analysis gives rise is: what is the mechanism by which other services will contract? Maynard and Street (2006) argue that NICE has inflated NHS spending by approving technologies of marginal cost-effectiveness that are providing small health gains for the population, but failing to identify redundant technologies for removal. While new proposed interventions can be considered from this marginal perspective, there is no means to identify those technologies that should be candidates for removal without periodic appraisal of everything – infeasible, given the resource requirements of appraisal.

The Dawson model is an ideal – it requires a comprehensive review of everything before the marginal health gain curves can be drawn and any initial budget line set so that only interventions with a health gain per £1,000 of two units are funded, and continued comprehensive appraisal of every technology, to identify which should fall out as new technologies are approved. In practice, even when NICE guidance is available, it is not always implemented (Sheldon *et al.* 2004), and a health-maximisation objective, consistent with the cost-effectiveness framework of Part II, or even a broader social welfare objective consistent with the framework of this part, captures only part of decision makers' concerns (Towse and Pritchard 2002; Bryan *et al.* 2006). We are unlikely to find supply setting is quite as rational as the model describes.

Most public systems attempt to use 'gatekeeping' (or a referral system) to ration services to those with the highest-priority demands. In the UK, it is intended that the whole population should be registered on the list of a general practitioner, who should act, in all cases other than emergencies, as the first point of contact with the health system. Whenever a case falls outside the general practitioner's areas of competence, or requires specialist facilities, the general practitioner should refer the patient to an appropriate provider. In theory, this process should ensure that specialist and referral services are rationed towards those patients whose demands have been sanctioned as appropriate, or as 'needs that should be met' (see Box 19.1). In practice, the mechanism works imperfectly, general practitioners have widely varying rates of referral (Wilkin *et al.* 1989) and large numbers of patients directly attend accident and emergency departments for minor complaints that could be dealt with by the GP. In some cases this is because it is more convenient and in others because they have not been able to register with a GP (Lowy *et al.* 1994). Direct use of hospital out-patient departments is a common problem in developing countries (for example, in Zimbabwe: Hongoro and Musonza 1995), where mechanisms to enforce referral systems are not or cannot be applied. However, if the price mechanism were used to ration between levels of care, reliance would be placed on the patient's own assessment of need for specialist services weighed against their higher price, and assessment of the risk of paying twice by paying a generalist for advice as to whether specialist services are necessary and then paying for those services recommended. In practice, countries which do not use gatekeeping systems encounter problems of inappropriate use of specialists for generalist advice and sometimes an absolute lack of a source of generalist advice for patients as to the appropriate type of specialist to consult (Rosenblatt *et al.* 1998; Franks and Fiscella 1998).

The third rationing mechanism in public systems is waiting lists. Waiting lists are administered queues by which patients referred to departments where an out-patient appointment, day case appointment or hospital bed is not available are listed and allocated the resource as it becomes available in order of registration on the list. In principle, the waiting list mechanism does not prioritise higher-value demands. There is no reason to suppose that the highest value should be placed on the demand of the potential patient who has waited longest. In practice, however, waiting lists do adopt prioritising mechanisms – emergencies are prioritised and sometimes a numerical scaling of priority is proposed (Culyer and Cullis 1975; Gudex *et al.* 1990). The underlying assumption is that all cases receiving the same weight on the list have the same priority and that waiting is a fair means of rationing among cases of equal social value. Again, it is easy, and common, to assume that evidence of long waiting lists is in itself evidence of inadequate resource allocation to the health sector, and poor rationing within it, whereas it is at least plausible that the opportunity costs of increasing provision of services with long waiting lists are higher than the social values placed on shortening the lists (see Box 21.2).

There is, however, inevitable inefficiency in using waiting lists, especially in the case of chronic diseases. The 'output' of cataract surgery is years of improved vision,

---

Box 21.2 The dynamics of waiting lists

Street and Duckett (1996) divide typical approaches to waiting lists into demand and supply-side approaches. A large literature supports the view that supply-side approaches are misguided. If expected waiting time is understood to be acting as the price of the service concerned, it follows that supply-side approaches, by reducing that price, will increase demand, and a number of UK studies of waiting lists in practice support that view. It would follow that mechanisms to restrict low-value demands prior to their registration on waiting lists would have more potential to reduce lists. These include prioritisation mechanisms, about which there is a growing body of evidence: Meiland *et al.* (1996) in the Netherlands; Langham *et al.* (1997) in the UK provide two examples.

Demand has largely been viewed as originating from general practitioners and patients, but a number of authors have focused on the role of hospital doctors in the system. According to one argument, conditions for which long waiting lists develop are of low scientific interest – a factor discussed in this chapter as capable of distorting incentive structures in public systems). According to another, consultants use waiting lists as a signal of their reputation with patients and general practitioners, creating the incentive to maintain them unnecessarily. Whatever the underlying explanation, consultants who control the rationing of hospital resources may face perverse incentives, and these can be further entrenched if hospitals are rewarded for long waiting lists by receiving additional resources – as is implied by supply-side approaches.

Street and Duckett (1996) explain how politically motivated approaches to solve the problem in the UK have been misguided from the perspective of the social demand value framework we are using in this book. For example, setting targets for the number of patients waiting over a given period, reallocates resources between patients on the list towards those who would have waited longest – precisely those deemed low priority according to previous weighting decisions. They argue (after Iversen 1993) that the solution is to introduce enforceable contracts between funders and providers; and to ensure that funding is linked to work load. Arrangements in Victoria, Australia, which follow these guidelines are shown to have dramatically reduced lists.

and of hip surgery, years of pain-free mobility. By making elderly people wait for treatment we may be reducing the overall benefits associated with a given operation or treatment.

The final rationing mechanism in public systems to be considered is the queue, in which patients physically wait to receive services. Queues ration on the basis of the patient's willingness to allocate time in order to receive a service. There is no reason to believe that there will be a strong relationship between such willingness and the social value of the service. Although controversial, it is sometimes argued that higher social value should be placed on the receipt of services by breadwinners and mothers on whom the rest of the family rely – such people are likely to place a high value on time and be least able to spend long hours queuing. The system of 'triage' by which a nurse or doctor quickly assesses the emergency status of patients attending accident and emergency departments attempts to impose a prioritisation on the basis of social value. In general, queuing is an inefficient and inappropriate rationing mechanism – its use is often a means of maximising the efficiency with which health professionals' time is used (which may or may not be justifiable) rather than as a means to ration services.

In extreme emergencies, waiting cannot be used as a rationing mechanism – the patient will die before they reach the top of a waiting list or the front of a queue, supply constraints are absolute, and gatekeeping assumes critical importance. The case of premature baby units has been mentioned above. Organ transplant is another example of critical and time limited demand, but absolute supply constraints that in this case are not largely determined by the funding level of the system. In such cases there is likely to be explicit consideration of gatekeeping thresholds – days of gestation which warrant admission to a premature baby unit, the age and health condition of a candidate for organ transplant. These explicitly ration on the basis of social value and are unsurprisingly controversial.

21.3 Provider behaviour in a public system

Public health services systems have traditionally owned the physical resources necessary to provide services and directly employed the health professionals working in them. Under public ownership, provider institutions have traditionally been reimbursed by budget, which may be global, or may be made up of separate expenditure 'votes' for different types of expenditures (such as salaries and drugs) between which limited virement (reallocation of expenditures between votes) is permitted. This situation is criticised as providing little incentive to the provider institutions for improvements in either efficiency or quality of care.

Chapter 19 proposed a series of questions that would allow the incentive environment to be further explored. These were:

1   Where are the agency relationships in the system?
2   What are the possible and likely differences in the objective functions between agents and principals?
3   What are the information asymmetries in the relationships?
4   How do principals try to control agents?

Figure 21.2 depicts a typical public health system, using the example of Zambia before it was reformed by the separation of purchaser and provider functions in the early 1990s. Ignoring the private and informal components of the system for now, direct public ownership and direct public employment prevailed, public institutions were reimbursed by line-item budget and employees within those institutions were paid by salary.

To a certain extent, principal–agent relationships are traced out by the financing flows that are indicated there. The central government is the agent of the population and is in turn (implicitly) contracting with district health teams and hospitals who then become agents of central government. Health teams and hospitals are then principals with respect to managers of health facilities and departments and so on. At the end of this series of principal–agent relationships are individual health workers in health facilities. However, to equate a principal–agent relationship with a financial flow is simplistic. There are other duties felt by individuals and institutions than to those who pay them – for example, a direct duty of care to patients, which implies that the health

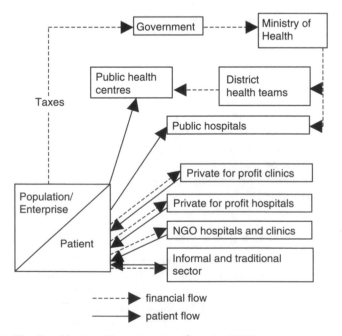

Figure 21.2 The Zambian health sector pre-reform (*c.* 1990).

worker is also the agent of the patient even when not directly (or even very indirectly) paid by the patient; and there are claims on individuals and institutions in the system which are made on other grounds than payment. For example, community health groups may play a role in directing the activities of a health facility – or acting as its principal – where they are not the paying institutions. Regulators including those professional associations responsible for 'self-regulation' are also aiming to achieve principal status with respect to those regulated. Where there is more than one principal aiming to control the agent, unless objectives are compatible, it will be impossible for the agent to be 'perfect' with respect to both, because there is bound to be some conflict between the objective functions of the two principals. This is a problem most pronounced in the public sector because a straightforward relationship between a provider and her customer is replaced by complex governance and regulatory structures.

A number of perverse incentives are commonly attributed to such a public institutional structure. Those institutions which succeed in reducing their costs may be penalised by reductions in their budget for the following year – hence the infamous end-of-year spending sprees which ensure that an institution does not appear to have excess resources. Efficiency improvements that imply a higher rate of patient 'throughput', such as switching from in-patient to day surgery, may increase expenditure over a given period of time, causing budget shortfall. Measurable improvements in quality such as improvements in survival rates will not automatically attract new resources and, if costly, are unlikely to be pursued.

These can be understood by reference to a degree of conflict between the objective functions of the providing and paying institutions (question 2). They suggest that the paying institution has the greater interest in operation at minimum cost – it would like to redistribute resources that seem to be unused at year-end, whereas providing institutions would like to retain those resources, even for rather marginally useful purposes. In using this year's expenditure as a guide to next year's the paying institution is trying to reallocate resources that seem to be in surplus, but in doing so passes the risk on to the provider institution that next year's work load will require a larger budget. To deflect this allocation of risk, the provider institution spends unnecessarily to signal to the payer greater need for resources than this year's expenditure will otherwise signal.

This use of signals also identifies information asymmetries (question 3). The provider institution understands better its need or not for the items purchased in the last period of the year. Much-needed replacement of computers in a department might await the end of year to make sure resources allowed, or a budget surplus might be used to purchase new computers to replace machines with years of life left. It is costly (if feasible at all) for the paying institution to find this out, and this information asymmetry is the source of the ability of the provider institution to send false signals.

In this scenario, the principal (the payer) controls the agent (the provider) by limiting expenditure to the level of the previous year (question 4). It is this control mechanism that generates the perverse incentives. Before moving on to considering alternative control mechanisms, however, it is worth considering why such institutional structures are so common. This set of arrangements has quite low administrative costs and is relatively transparent – the basis of this year's decision making is very clear. It protects payers against allegations of favouritism that can arise when the payer is forced to make qualitative judgments about the relative needs of different bidders for resources. It follows that more sophisticated control mechanisms are likely to require investment in their administration, including in monitoring and reporting mechanisms that render the basis for more sophisticated decision making more transparent.

Crude attempts to measure and reward performance within a budget-governed system, benefiting from limited investment of this type, are capable of inappropriate manipulation. Mullen (1985), for example, argued that the use of 'performance indicators' in the UK was likely to produce behaviour aimed at improving the indicator rather than improving performance. A crude example would be the unnecessary increasing of length of stay to increase a bed occupancy performance indicator. The problem is that the monitoring of the indicator does little to assuage the underlying information asymmetry in performance itself.

When health professionals are directly employed, the most common form of reimbursement is by salary. Salaries are also criticised for providing little incentive to performance as they are fixed and paid regardless of performance. In some Central and Eastern European countries, a salary system seemed to be associated with poor performance and motivation on the part of health professionals. This scenario implies (1) a principal employer and an agent employee; (2) conflict in objective functions, with effort entering negatively for the employee and positively for the employer (as in the theoretical agency case of Chapter 18); (3) asymmetry in information concerning the employee's effort (not strictly required for the mechanism to function but rather explains the choice of mechanism); and (4) an inadequate mechanism of control that fails to respond to level of effort.

However, this may be an excessively harsh view of the potential of a salary system. Arguably the problem in those countries characterised by poor employee motivation arose from the demotivating impact of inadequate salaries combined with failure to relate promotion and career prospects to fair judgments of performance. The fair judgment of performance will always pose difficulties arising from information asymmetry, similar to those that arise in the reimbursement of provider institutions. In practice, whatever people think is to be measured and used in the promotion process will be encouraged within that salary system. For example, if research and publication ensure the fastest route to promotion, it is likely that junior doctors will prioritise them at the expense of patient care. To the extent that salary reimbursement systems fail to promote good performance, the cause is probably the difficulty of measuring good performance (information asymmetry) and perverse institutional incentives to recognise other types of merit (or demerit) that are easier to measure.

21.4 The political efficiency of transactions

All the above presumes an underlying economic rationale at the beginning of the principal–agent chain. If the ultimate principal – in the case of public action, the electorate – is somewhat effective, that would capture adequately the issues involved. To the extent that this is not the case, it has been argued, an underlying political rationale dominates instead. In other words, understanding the imperfections in the relationship between the electorate and elected politicians explains the nature of the incentives that permeate public institutional structures.

According to Frant (1996), factors which affect the likelihood of a politician being re-elected are the 'high-powered' incentives of the public system. In this context the behaviour of concern is political opportunism – or the politician operating in her own best interest rather than that of her constituents. In general, as with high-powered financial incentives, high-powered political incentives are helpful – they increase the allocative efficiency of activity by forcing politicians to do things valued by their constituents. But they can also be too high-powered in contexts in which it is difficult for the electorate to monitor the behaviour of politicians. In these cases, political opportunism can result from politicians choosing to spend money on visible things when fully informed voters would prefer less visible things. The solution would then be to substitute low-powered political incentives by putting the activity out of reach of the normal political process. Frant reviews three ways of achieving this: (1) the creation of independent public authorities (governed by a board; in charge of a linked set of functions and with access to an independent revenue stream); (2) earmarking funds and (3) using the mechanism of an independent civil service.

Health services fall into a category in which it is difficult for voters to judge quality and in which visible investments may be made at the expense of more important less visible ones. What insights does Frant's analysis provide? It suggests that the rationale for creating independent public authorities (for example, granting greater managerial and financial autonomy to hospitals) is to remove the threat of inappropriate political interference.

Earmarking funds for health is often supported on the basis that it seems to make increased funding for the health sector possible (Le Grand 2002) – or enables health service transactions that otherwise won't take place. Earmarking funds for specific purposes has been used or proposed as a means of protecting activities of high public health importance but low political visibility from local-level political decision making in both the UK and Uganda (Terence Higgins Trust 2007; Jeppson 2001).

De-linking health staff from public service commissions has been a common measure in developing countries – for example, in Zambia and Uganda. However, in systems in which health workers have not been part of the civil service there do not seem to be particular problems associated with the presence of high-powered political incentives. Perhaps health is 'special' here, because health workers are protected by relatively scarce skills, or perhaps the professional associations play an intermediary role which protects health workers from the dangers of political opportunism.

Politicians are clearly lynchpins in the structured set of principal–agent relationships with which we started the section, and Frant raises interesting questions about their incentives which seem to provide useful insights into why some public institutions are structured the way they are. He may over-state the case that financial incentives are everywhere low-powered in the public sector, and therefore ignore interesting questions about the interface between financial and political incentives which surface in the area of autonomous hospitals, for example.

21.5 Conclusion

Figure 21.3 attempts to characterise the relative positions of different types of health services on curves of marginal private and social value that are standardised for marginal cost (as explained in Box 19.2). While the characterisation may be accused of verging on caricature, the underlying point – that health service priorities are likely to be completely reordered from a social rather than private perspective is difficult to contest. It follows that the price mechanism is a poor allocator of resources in the health sector. This is recognised in virtually all health systems around the world. Most

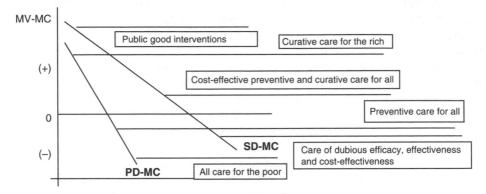

Figure 21.3 Ordering priorities on the basis of marginal social value compared with marginal private value.

countries use elements of service planning, gatekeeping, waiting lists and queues in place of prices for rationing at least for some parts of the sector. They also intervene in the market to support delivery of priority services – to the poor and of preventive and public health services that are not prioritised by price rationing.

The principal problems of public systems are the lack of mechanisms to push funding toward appropriate levels; weakness in the application of rationing mechanisms; and difficulties in managing incentives that promote performance improvement, especially where public sector capacity is weak. In the worst cases, results may even be inferior to what would arise from price mechanisms. Populations of neglected areas might be better off if their taxes were not collected and used to provide services to the élite in teaching hospitals in capital cities. Nevertheless, evidence from lower, middle and upper-income countries – that better solutions to geographical and service pattern resource allocation questions can be found using the available rationing mechanisms, and that better performance out of public systems can be achieved through investment in transparency and fairness – suggest that where policy makers support distribution of health sector resources on the basis of social values, pure public systems are more likely to deliver than reliance on the price mechanism.

Nevertheless, real debates are not about choosing between pure public and pure private systems, but about configuring systems with the most useful components of each. We will continue to build the foundations of this debate throughout the rest of Part IV.

22 Voluntary insurance-based systems

22.1 Risk aversion

Insurance companies will sell insurance only if the premiums are sufficient to pay for claims and the costs of administration, and they normally aim also to make a profit. The policies offered will therefore be (on average), actuarially unfair; that is to say, on average policy holders get back less than they pay in. People will voluntarily choose to purchase such insurance only if they are *risk-averse*, in other words, they are willing to pay more than the *actuarially fair premium* (the probability of an event multiplied by its cost). The extent to which individuals are risk-averse determines the viability of insurance markets.

Risk aversion can partially be explained in terms of diminishing marginal utility of wealth. If individuals are *risk-neutral* with respect to utility (that is to say, they are willing to sacrifice only the amount of utility equal to the probability of an event multiplied by its utility cost), they will still be risk-averse with respect to income, since the actuarial premium would have a lower utility value than the utility cost of the event multiplied by its probability.

Figure 22.1 demonstrates this point. The graph shows the relationship between wealth levels and utility measured in imaginary 'utils' for a skier. The skier considers the

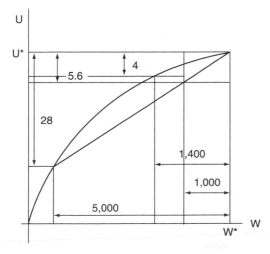

Figure 22.1 The decision to purchase insurance.

purchase of insurance against a risk of accident on the slopes. An accident would cost her £5,000 and there is a 20 per cent chance of an accident occurring. The actuarial premium is £1,000. The utility loss associated with paying the premium is shown on the graph to be four utils, while the utility cost associated with the risk is twenty-eight utils. If the skier is risk-neutral with respect to utility, she will be willing to sacrifice up to 5.6 utils (28×20 per cent) for insurance, an amount which can be identified graphically on a straight line between the starting point and the point associated with the risky outcome. She will therefore be willing to pay up to about £1,400 according to the graph. It follows that the more utility of wealth diminishes (the more the utility of wealth curve bends), the more an individual will be willing to pay for insurance, for any given level of risk aversion with respect to utility.

It is expected that risk aversion with respect to utility varies from individual to individual and is an argument of his or her preference function (see Chapter 2). The extent of risk aversion with respect to wealth determines the viability of insurance markets. This varies according to individuals' diminishing marginal utility of wealth, and level of risk aversion with respect to utility. In the example above, insurance will be exchanged only if transaction costs and profits can be contained within the £400 slack between the actuarially fair premium and the maximum the skier is willing to pay.

22.2 Adverse selection: the Rothschild–Stiglitz model

A major problem associated with private insurance markets is adverse selection, defined as in Chapter 18 as a situation in which only the agent (in this case the insured person) has information relevant to the selection of a given action. Individuals' risks vary and their own knowledge of some of their particular risks is better than that of the insurance agency.

In Figure 22.2(a) neither of those factors is taken into account. Risks are homogeneous across the population (the risk of an adverse event occurring is a), and known by the insurance agency. The axes of Figure 22.1 represent the wealth levels of the individual in the case that the event does not occur (W1), or does occur (W2). The line X is drawn with slope of the (negative of the) odds ratio of the event occurring and not occurring. The line represents certainty equivalent points to the individual's expected wealth in the presence of the risk. (That is, for every euro loss of wealth in the case that the event does not occur, there is a $(1-a)/a$ increase in wealth in the case that it does, along line X.) It also represents the range of actuarially fair contracts that can be offered to this individual, equivalent to the range of zero profit (and zero administrative cost) insurance contracts, which is similar to the budget constraint concept in Chapter 2 and later. While insurance companies will aim to make a profit, they are assumed to be constrained to make no less than zero profit. The 45° line drawn on the figure represents full insurance: the individual's expected wealth is equal in the case of the event occurring or not.

On the assumption that individuals are risk-averse, as suggested by section 22.1, they will prefer situations where their expected wealth is more certain, whether or not the event occurs, to those where it is less certain. Hence their indifference curves will have the normal shape in W1–W2 space, and will be closest to the origin at the 45° line. Point B (fully insured) will be preferred to a point such as A (less than fully insured) where zero profit insurance options are available (along line X).

In Figure 22.2b, heterogeneous risk and asymmetrical information are introduced in

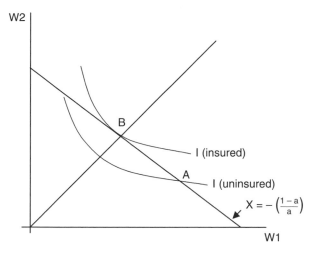

Figure 22.2 (a) Insurance market with homogenous risk and perfect information.

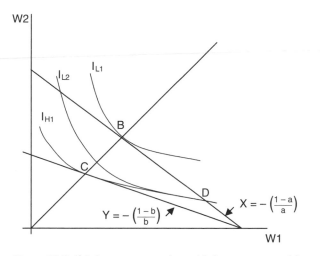

Figure 22.2 (b) Insurance market with heterogenous risk and asymmetric information.

a stylised manner. Assume that there are now two individuals, L and H, whose risks are a and b respectively (with b > a). The negative odds ratio line for individual H is drawn as Y. In the presence of information about the individuals' risks, the insurance company could offer zero-profit contract C to the high-risk individual where her indifference curve (I_{H1}) reaches tangent with line Y, while continuing to offer contract B to the low-risk individual. In the absence of that information, if both contracts are offered, high-risk individuals will opt for contract B, at which they can reach a higher indifference curve but at which insurance companies make negative profit. Insurance contract B will therefore not be offered. The availability of only the more expensive insurance contract C represents a welfare loss for low-risk individuals: only indifference curves lower than the one that intersects B are available at contract C, or at no insurance.

  There is a zero profit insurance contract that this or another insurance company could offer low-risk individuals that would not attract the high-risk individuals, however, at D. This is preferred to contract C by low-risk individuals but not by high-risk individuals. The emergence of contract D represents the finding of a *separating equilibrium*. Individuals reveal their risk status by the insurance contract they select.[1]

Nevertheless, low-risk individuals are significantly under-insured at point D: their wealth in the event of the risky event occurring is lower than in the event of it not occurring, despite their risk aversion and willingness to purchase insurance at the actuarial rate, and they achieve a lower indifference curve (I_{L2}) than at B (I_{L1}). The presence of high-risk individuals thus causes a welfare loss for low-risk individuals, even in the case of the separating equilibrium being achievable.

22.3 Applying the model

In health insurance markets, information is not wholly asymmetrical. In addition to providing an explanation of the range of insurance contracts available, offering different degrees of protection, and the rationale for individuals to select different contracts depending on the degree of their risk aversion and the degree of their risk, the model shows the incentive for insurance companies to acquire information about individual risks and to use it in structuring their offer of insurance protection. There are significant profitable opportunities apparent in offering contracts with improved terms to lower-risk individuals in comparison with the contract that can be offered to unscreened populations who have effectively to be assumed to be high-risk. Detailed health checks, screening questions and penalty clauses should those questions be later proved to have been answered incorrectly are predicted and observed in health insurance markets.

The result of these efforts to improve the balance of information between the two parties is that both high- and low-risk individuals may find themselves under-insured. Those screened as high-risk may find the only contract available prohibitively expensive while low-risk individuals may not be able to demonstrate their status as such to insurance companies. Evidence from the US insurance market suggests that the uninsured include both groups (see Box 22.1) and evidence from the South African market suggests a growing problem of adverse selection (Box 22.2).

22.4 Moral hazard

A second problem affecting all types of insurance parallels the rationing problem considered in the previous chapter. Since full insurance implies that the price will not be paid by the consumer of services at the point of use, price will not serve the function of a rationing mechanism. The extent to which the insured, when not faced with the price at the point of use, increase their use of services is known as *moral hazard*. In the terms of Chapter 18, the principal (the insurance company) cannot observe the actions the insured person takes to avoid risks or unnecessary use of health care; it can only observe the resulting level of use which might have arisen from unavoidable risk and necessary use.

If we assume (as discussed in Chapter 19) that the values derived from demand curves and prices represent social values of benefit and cost, the optimal point of consumption and provision of services can be defined as the point at which demand equals price (Q* on Figure 22.2). Under full insurance, demands will be expressed

Box 22.1 The long-term uninsured in the United States and adverse selection

Some 17.9 per cent of non-elderly Americans were uninsured in 2005 (Holahan and Cook 2006). Rhoades and Cohen (2006) analysed the characteristics of the long-term uninsured: those who were continually uninsured between 2001 and 2004, 6.6 per cent of the population under sixty-five (see the diagram). The data show that the uninsured are likely to be younger and healthier as well as poorer, suggesting that adverse selection is an important explanation. Under-eighteens mainly have access to free or highly subsidised health insurance, explaining their high level of cover. Nevertheless, being poor is a better predictor of uninsured status than having poor health status or being in the young adult age group.

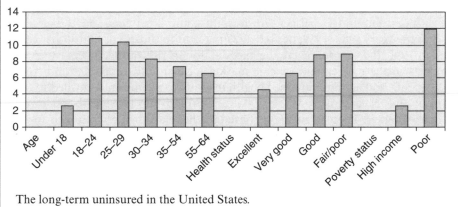

The long-term uninsured in the United States.
Source: Rhoades and Cohen (2006)

The proportion of uninsured in the non-elderly population continues to increase. Holahan and Cook (2006) considered the factors leading to this trend. Between 2000 and 2003 the US economy was slowing down, and insurance premiums increased faster than wages and incomes. Between 2003 and 2005 employer-sponsored insurance continued to decline, despite an improving economy. Factors implicated by this analysis were changing employment patterns towards small-scale employers who are less likely to offer health insurance. This implies that more people are making individual health insurance purchase decisions, increasing the importance of adverse selection in the market. However, low-income households had the fastest growth in the uninsured rate, accounting for 1.1 million of the 1.3 million increase in the number of uninsured in 2005.

It would seem that both affordability and adverse selection explanations of low coverage of health insurance in the United States are prevalent and increasing.

Source: Holahan and Cook (2006); Rhoades and Cohen (2006).

Box 22.2 South Africa's private insurance market

South Africa is one of a small group of countries which has a significant private insurance market. Van den Heever (1997) reported that highly regulated 'medical aid schemes' and actuarially based health insurance cover 17.2 per cent and 4.4 per cent of the population respectively, and consume 43 per cent and 4 per cent of resources respectively.

Medical aid schemes are non-profit trusts that were prohibited from applying underwriting principles in setting premiums. More recently they have been administered by contractors working on a for-profit basis, and paid as a percentage of income. Their behaviour has become indistinguishable from for-profit agencies and they have succeeded in changing the law to allow a degree of risk rating in the determination of premiums. The situation has evolved to a classic 'third-party payer' model and inflation in the medical aid scheme market, which averaged between 7 per cent and 11 per cent for hospitals, and 2 per cent and 10 per cent overall in the years 1983–1989, peaked at 27 per cent for hospitals and 17 per cent overall in 1990, the year following the introduction of risk rating.

As costs in the medical aid scheme market have spiralled, competition from pure for-profit and actuarially based health insurance, which is not entitled to tax exemption, has become more viable and more attractive to those with the lowest risks in the market. These are also purchased by the relatively rich, but their lower risks are apparent from their consumption of a less than proportionate share of resources. Adverse selection out of the more community-rated medical schemes further threatens the latter's viability, as predicted by the Rothschild and Stiglitz model (see main text).

Söderlund and Hansl (2000) investigated two hypotheses in relation to developments between 1985 and 1995 in the South African insurance market:

1   The risk of ill health is not equally distributed between health insurers, and the differences are increasing with time.

They found increasing separation of risk types over the period since 1985, although they could not associate it with the 1989 reform and suggested that the process of risk separation may have started earlier – consistent with Heever's view that change began with the privatisation of management arrangements and an earlier report of Söderlund and Hansl that it had previously been possible to select according to easily identifiable risk factors such as age and disability.

2   Risk selection is associated with health care cost escalation.

They found that risk-rating did seem to be associated with increased premium inflation, as positive adjustments to premiums were associated with high risks without compensating negative adjustments for low risks.

Source: van den Heever (1997) and Söderlund and Hansl (2000).

up to point a, where the demand curve intersects the horizontal axis. 'Excess demand' can be defined as Q*a. Insurance agencies are also faced with the need to devise rationing mechanisms. In Figure 22.3, we have replaced our usual stylised straight line demand curve with a more realistic curved one, to emphasise that a large proportion of excess demand ab/aQ* can be rationed by using prices that are a relatively small proportion of the marginal cost-based price (xO/PO).

Common rationing mechanisms used by insurance agencies are price-based: deductibles that require the insured to pay the first fixed amount of any bill, and co-payment that requires the insured to pay a fixed proportion of the bill. A deductible of x reduces demand from a to b, and also has an important effect on proportionate transaction costs, since they are likely to be relatively high for small bills. Co-payments swivel the effective demand curve upward from the point of intersection with the deductible, or from the horizontal axis if there is no deductible (D'D). At price p, demand will be further reduced to c. It is worth noting that only the removal of insurance altogether is capable of rationing demand back to Q*. Thus these price-based rationing mechanisms are capable of reducing but not eliminating moral hazard.

Returning to the conceptual framework of Chapter 19, we are concerned with the extent to which voluntary insurance-based health markets provide the optimal amount of health services, and ration in such a way as to allocate health sector resources towards uses with the highest social values. Dropping what we have argued to be the highly unrealistic assumption that values derived from demand curves can be deemed even to approximate social value, we find little in voluntary insurance markets that promotes social objectives. In the price rationing of insurance itself, 'uninsurable' demands are eliminated by adverse selection, without any likely relationship between insurable demands and social value of demands. Indeed, we can identify a number of demands likely to prove uninsurable or uninsured for which there is reason to believe that private demand values understate social values – diseases of the poor, especially where communicable, and palliative care of chronic but incurable diseases such as cancer and AIDS. In the rationing of services to the insured, price-based rationing mechanisms reinforce the ordering of private valuations in determining which services will be offered and received and which not. In the absence of other intervention,

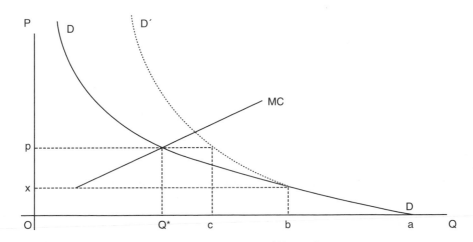

Figure 22.3 Moral hazard under full insurance, deductibles and co-payments.

ineffective but popular treatments will be promoted while effective but unpopular treatments will not.

Insurance agencies use a further rationing mechanism that is not price-based, that is, disease and service exclusion lists. These usually exclude high-cost diseases and interventions, and uses of health services that can be considered optional rather than risks, such as cosmetic surgery. Some of these exclusions may imply social value-based rationing – cosmetic surgery in many of its applications is unlikely to be a high social priority – while others may imply the reverse. In any case, at least to some extent, such exclusion lists are likely to 'shift' costs within the health system, rather than change the pattern of provision of the whole system, an issue which will be considered at more length in Chapter 24, where health systems delivered through multiple, parallel sub-systems are considered.

22.5 Institutional structures and incentives

In the framework of analysis presented in Chapter 19, the simple theory was discussed that incentives for efficiency strengthen as institutions become more private – owing to the profit motive, the threat of being driven out of business and the closer relationship between the individual's rewards and the individual's effort. To what extent can such a theory be sustained with reference to health systems characterised by voluntary health insurance?

In the archetypal system we are considering in this chapter, provider institutions are privately owned, though they may be for-profit or not-for-profit. In the case of hospitals, they are large institutions with multiple decision makers and workers, distant from the one-man business in which rewards equate with the business's performance.

In Chapter 16 we discussed the various models of motivation and behaviour of private hospitals, looking at managerial and behavioural theories, and in Chapter 18 we discussed incentives.

These models have differing implications for the nature of incentives in hospitals. For example, if the 'physicians' co-operative' model applies, and fee-for-service reimbursement pertains, incentives to effort will make themselves felt. Physicians will likely be interested in doing more work – but incentives to economise on costs incurred by the hospital, patients or third party payer will be absent (see below). If Newhouse's quantity and quality model applies, there are incentives for technical efficiency (in the sense of aiming to eliminate X-inefficiency for any given quality of care – see Chapter 9), but the quantity and quality objective may conflict with allocative efficiency (if a lower quantity and quality are allocatively efficient). In Harris's model, the 'trustee administrators' are likely to have some concern with technical if not allocative efficiency; but the physician group may succeed in frustrating this.

The above suggests that even technical efficiency incentives are likely to be weak in this setting, and it is not surprising that evidence of greater technical efficiency in the private health sector is equally weak. For example, Valdmanis (1990) found that public hospitals in Michigan (United States) were technically more efficient than non-profit private hospitals. Studies in other countries comparing private and public hospitals generally fail to find the efficiency effect predicted by the simple theory (for example, in Thailand: Pannarunothai and Mills 1997, and in South Africa: Naylor 1988).

If technical incentives are weak, allocative efficiency incentives are likely to be almost absent. The combination of the lack of allocative efficiency incentives arising from the motivations and behaviour attributed to private hospitals and 'third-party' payment (separation between the insurer and the provider of services: the 'contract' model) is likely to be the more important source of the cost control problems in private systems discussed in Chapter 20. At least until recently, reimbursement of providers has usually been in the form of fee for service for both hospitals and doctors, which may encourage both types of provider to maximise the number of services offered to each patient. Furthermore, since the number of patients referred to a hospital or doctor is less under their control than the volume of services provided to each patient, it is argued that fee-for-service reimbursement mechanisms produce high service intensity per patient, possibly associated with a highly technological approach to patient care. It is certainly unlikely that fee-for-service reimbursement will encourage careful consideration of the necessity of marginally helpful diagnostic tests or dubiously effective procedures (see Box 7.2).

The combination of third-party payment and fee-for-service reimbursement has often been classified as inherently inflationary. Under such conditions, moral hazard occurs on both demand and supply sides of the market, since both providers and patients pass their costs on to a third party and do not have to take them into account in deciding the services to provide and use. Under private insurance, patients usually have a free choice of providers (again recent reforms and new models such as Preferred Provider Organisations may restrict this). Where neither providers nor patients bear costs, the most likely form of competition between providers is *quality competition.* Providers compete using *quality signals* (which often take advantage of the consumer's relative ignorance) such as high levels of amenity (for example, private rooms, telephone, fax and television facilities), and availability of specialist facilities on the basis that consumers may associate these characteristics with high-quality clinical care (see Chapter 15 and Boxes 15.1 and 15.2).

However, it is likely that a further element in this mix is required for inevitable inflation – lack of constraints on the demand side. The health insurance inflation of the 1970s and 1980s in the United States was grounded in this mix of factors, and South Africa has undergone a similar experience (see Box 22.2). In the United States, it is probable that the introduction of a range of reforms focused on cost control and the rapid development of various forms of insurance organisation known collectively as Managed Care resulted from a perceived need to introduce demand constraints. The experience of recession and current widespread concern about international competitiveness seemed to have imposed limits on the extent to which US industry was able and willing to absorb further health insurance inflation. Nevertheless, these innovations in the US system seem to be on the wane in 2006, despite relatively poor US economic performance.

22.6 Conclusion

In the archetypal voluntary insurance system, there is little to promote rationing on the basis of need, and much to promote both technical and allocative inefficiency, and an inflationary spiral. The finding in Chapter 20 that systems coming closest to the archetype described have the most serious cost control problems and little to show for their higher spending levels in the form of better health status indicators would seem to be consistent. This is clearest in the case of the United States, but

Switzerland too appeared to achieve very little marginal health status for its high level of expenditure.

Note

1 A profit-maximising monopoly insurer would not offer contract D because any adoption of contract C by low-risk individuals represents profit for the company, whereas contract D offers zero profit.

23 Social insurance systems

23.1 Introduction

The development of formal systems of health care finance in the nineteenth and twentieth centuries centred mainly on employment and the workplace. There are several reasons why this path was followed. First, to an extent it is in the financial interest of employers to have a healthy work force, with low absence for sickness, so that an employer-sponsored health service may be a rational profit-maximising strategy. Second, there are advantages for risk management to have large numbers in a health plan. The large number employed in large firms could be provided with medical insurance efficiently and with low transaction costs. An additional advantage of involving employers in the health system finance is to use their financial and bargaining skills to improve the quality and cost of the services.

From the viewpoint of the workers there may also be a percieved advantage in that the employer pays all or part of the cost of the health insurance. In some cases this is an illusion. The extent to which the employer actually pays depends on characteristics of the labour market. In a highly competitive labour market the money paid by the employer (including wages and all other emoluments such as health insurance and pension contributions) is determined by market forces, and any increase in the health insurance premiums will be reflected in lower take-home pay for the workers. If the labour market is characterised by monopoly buyers or sellers the position is more complicated, and who actually pays the health insurance premium will depend on the shapes of the demand and marginal cost curves. The range of possibilities is for all to be paid by employers or all to be paid by employees.

Figure 23.1 shows a range of options. In all of these the simplifying assumption is made that provision of insurance does not affect the supply of labour. Whether conditions are competitive (in which case labour demand and supply curves intersect to provide equilibrium wage and employment levels), monopsonistic (under which employers set wage and employment levels subject to the constraint of the labour supply curve from which a marginal cost of labour curve can be derived) or monopolistic (for example, in the case of an effective union which can dictate wage and employment levels subject only to the constraint of normal profit: average productivity of labour equals average cost of labour), mandated provision of insurance results in a reduced wage rate (equal to less than the cost of the insurance) and a reduced employment rate. Under the more realistic assumption of a positive effect of the provision of insurance on the supply of labour, in each case the effect is to reduce the impact of the provision of insurance on both wage and employment variables. Where the full cost of

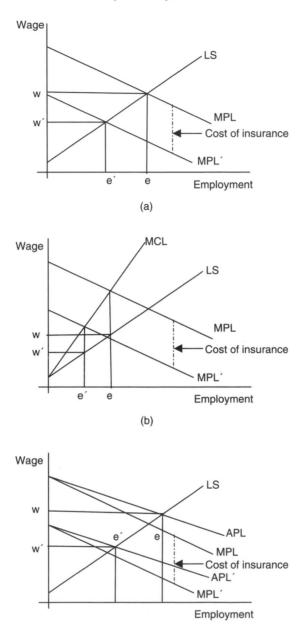

Figure 23.1 The effect of insurance provision on labour market equilibria.
   (*a*) Competitive demand and supply.
   (*b*) The supply of labour, monopsonistic demand.
   (*c*) Competitive demand and monopolistic supply.

insurance is valued to its equivalent in wage increase, employment remains the same and the wage is reduced by the cost of insurance exactly.

Whereas the system in the United States developed on a *quasi*-actuarial basis, in Central Europe the model that emerged involved deliberate solidarity, with contributions based on income and access to care depending on need. In order to achieve this, governments replaced employers as the regulators of the system. As a legal framework for these schemes was put in place, and the income-based health insurance contributions became compulsory, in certain respects 'social insurance' health systems became similar to systems of 'tax-based finance'. Conversely, tax-based financing can be considered to be government-operated social health insurance.

One way to distinguish social insurance from tax-based finance is whether the revenues gathered are earmarked for health care (i.e. a fund is established that can be used only for that specified purpose). Earmarked insurance funds can be contrasted with general taxation funding in which health must compete with all other priorities for government expenditure. In addition to the degree of certainty and stability that can be associated with earmarked funds there is some evidence that there is a higher willingness to pay when the use of the funds is known. There is indirect evidence of this in the finding that, in general, spending *per capita* on health services is higher in countries with social insurance than in tax-funded systems, *ceteris paribus* (Normand and Busse 2001). Possibly because of higher levels of funding (and the associated better package of services) it also tends to be more popular than tax financing (Mossialos 1998)

Health service revenues may be earmarked jointly under social insurance with pensions and unemployment benefits. It is worth pointing out that the terminology used to describe different financing models can be confusing. The term 'insurance' is sometimes used even when the funding comes through general taxation, as is the case in all but two Canadian provinces (OECD 1994), and the UK's 'National Insurance', which is really just a payroll tax that goes into general government funds.

It has become common to consider both tax-based funding and social insurance as 'public insurance' models which can use either 'integrated' or 'contract' forms (OECD 1992). 'Integrated' forms imply ownership and direct management of provider institutions by the insurer (in the case of tax-based funding, the government), while 'contract' models imply separation of the two and the purchase of services from provider institutions by insurers or government. This type of model is equivalent to the 'third-party payer' model in voluntary health insurance discussed above. Until recently tax-based financing mainly used 'integrated' models and social insurance 'contract' models. This section will consider the 'archetype' social insurance model as one in which an earmarked fund is created and ownership of provider institutions is separate from the provision of insurance, just as in Chapter 2 'archetype' tax-based finance was considered to imply direct ownership and management of provider institutions by government. Chapter 25 will consider the implications of mixing these characteristics, as is becoming increasingly common.

A second difference (which is usual rather than required) between social insurance and tax-based finance is that social insurance contributions are usually collected by a *quasi*-autonomous body (or bodies) which is regulated rather than directly controlled by government. There may be other differences that arise from political interpretation of the distinctive features of the two arrangements. For example, there may be more focus on 'entitlement' under a social insurance system. There may also be greater willingness to pay higher social insurance premiums because the greater transparency in collection and spending of funds enjoyed is valued. In contrast, when paying higher tax, the distribution of any increase between alternative uses is not known, and some possible uses such as defence and industrial subsidy may enjoy much less support in the population.

A third usual rather than required difference is that patients tend to have greater choice of providers under social insurance than under tax-based financing. Of course there is no necessary reason for this. The fact that it is seen as a feature of social insurance demonstrates the significant extent to which the traditions of insurance have been retained in this model. It is also worth noting that measures to reduce costs in contract models often restrict the choice of provider.

This chapter considers only health systems in which social insurance can broadly be considered 'universal', covering 100 per cent or very close to 100 per cent of the population. Chapter 24 considers the quite common situation (characterising most of the Americas and a number of South East Asian countries, for example) in which some social insurance coexists with public and private sub-sectors covering different sections of the population. The implications of competition and movement of population groups between sub-systems create significant complications and issues, sufficient to suggest that these systems can only be analysed separately.

The principles a government should apply in setting social insurance premiums should be the same as those used to determine how much tax revenue to allocate to the health system. However, the mechanism for setting the contribution rate may be outside the direct control of government, and the resulting decisions may reflect the opinions of other interested parties. As we have seen in Chapter 20, social insurance systems have tended to allocate a larger proportion of GNP to health services, and to have experienced faster expenditure growth over recent years than tax-funded systems. There are a number of reasons why we might expect greater pressures on health system expenditures under social insurance than under tax-based financing, which might explain this phenomenon. We have already suggested that there may be greater political acceptability of premium increases than of tax increases. Combined with a *quasi*-autonomous insurance agency which may see itself as representing 'consumers' as much as planning health services for the population as a whole, a greater influence of private demand pressures than under tax-based financing models would be expected. Additionally, as discussed above, a 'contract', or third-party payer, model may contain more pressures for higher costs than an integrated one, both to provide more care per patient and to allow the prices of health sector resources to increase. In most cases social insurance organisations have some role at least in suggesting increases in premium rates, and in the absence of competition for customers they have little incentive to keep rates low.

However, there are also reasons why contract models might reduce costs. A shift from providing budgets to hospitals to funding them on the basis of work load might be expected to introduce more explicitly information on costs and efficiency, and this could reduce costs. This is the thinking behind 'new public management' reforms, where the provision of services is separated from funding and commissioning. An important question is the extent to which social insurance systems operate in this way. Over the years the relationships between the SHI organisations and the providers may become close, and any theoretical advantages of funding mechanisms may be lost.

It is difficult to conclude from a theoretical perspective whether or not the higher level of resources allocated to the health sector as a whole that is typical in social insurance systems is more or less allocatively efficient than the lower level associated with tax-based funding. It is important to be clear about the extent to which higher levels of resources are really allocated to health, since some visible differences may in fact be higher prices for the same volume of care. This changes distribution of surplus between providers and users of services, but does not represent a different allocation of resources (and does not affect economic efficiency). However, higher prices also encourage more resources to be applied to health sector ends, and this does have efficiency implications that are context-specific. For example, where doctors are highly paid relative to other professions, more young people may be expected to train as doctors, and an over-supply of doctors could develop. Doctors may carry out activities undertaken by nurses in other countries, suggesting a sub-optimal skill mix in the sector. Comparison of the ratio of doctors to nurses in different countries suggests that their roles are very different in different settings.

As we have seen in Chapter 21, it is possible to argue that tax-based funding is unlikely to meet the level of funding which would be achieved under a private demand-driven system. In contrast, private demand is likely to over-allocate resources to health, since those demands towards which it is biased (high technology, curative care) are likely to consume higher levels of resources than those which it is biased against (preventive and public health measures) both per intervention and in terms of the total resources required by feasible levels of provision.

We can compare the performance of social insurance in terms of its ability to allocate resources according to the priorities of the social demand curve introduced in Chapter 19. Under social insurance, at least in principle, access to services is the same for rich and poor, in contrast to the case where prices are used to ration access to care. However, it is important to look carefully at how characteristics of the system can impose barriers (see Box 23.1). Additionally, social insurance avoids the problem of 'adverse selection' discussed above in relation to private insurance. By enforcing membership of an insurance scheme the drop-out of lower risks which is central to the adverse selection problem is avoided, and as a result, population groups for whom private demand is insufficient but social demand may be high will receive services. This is an important rationale for social insurance. Its 'social' nature is determined by the solidarity created by the inability to drop out. However, to the extent that the population's demands as a whole play a greater role in determining the allocation of resources, we would still expect the problem of information shortages to result in bias towards high-technology curative services and against preventive services. Services known to generate externalities are also likely to be well provided under this system, since the link between receipt of treatment by an individual and payment has been removed. In practice there is a high degree of overlap between externality and prevention, and if prevention is poorly understood these services are likely to be under-provided relative to a tax-based system.

Rationing mechanisms available to social insurance systems include the full range of those available to tax-based finance systems and private insurance systems. Analysis of the likely implications of social insurance for the nature of rationing depends on the balance struck between price-based rationing mechanisms (co-payments and deductibles) and planning mechanisms based on assessment of social demand. This varies widely between social insurance systems. For example, in Germany planning mechanisms are dominant in the setting of a 'benefit package' that all sickness funds (social insurance institutions) are required by government to provide, although this is possibly changing with recent reforms (Normand and Busse 2001; Figueras *et al.* 2004; Busse *et al.* 2004). This package is amended on the basis of 'benefit', 'medical necessity' and 'efficiency', consistent with a social value framework. Further planning mechanisms include the development of hospital services according to hospital plans, and controls over contribution levels and budgets. Market mechanisms are present but controlled

Box 23.1 Access to health services under universal health insurance in South Korea

Yang (1991) described the Korean national health insurance system in the late 1980s. Membership was compulsory and insurance societies covered 90 per cent of the population, with the remaining 10 per cent entitled to health services through public assistance programmes.

However, access to health services was constrained by two major factors. First, effective co-payment rates were extremely high – up to 65 per cent for hospital out-patient services (see the first table). Second, the geographical distribution of health resources was extremely uneven (see the second table).

Effective co-insurance rates for out-patient services

Service	1985	1986	1987
General hospital	50	60.1	62
Hospital	50	62.1	65
Clinic	30	40.3	41.2

Source: Yang (1991).

Distribution of health resources: hospital beds and physicians

Variable	Seoul	Three major cities	All other cities	Rural areas	Total
Population (000) (%)	9,639 (23.8)	6,932 (17.1)	9,872 (24.4)	14,006 (34.6)	40,448
No. of physicians	8,817 (40.8)	4,431 (20.5)	6,691 (30.9)	1,697 (7.8)	21,626
Physicians per 100,000 population	91.47	63.92	67.67	12.12	53.47
No. of hospital beds (%)	27,721 (30.5)	17,026 (19.0)	–	–	89,463
Beds per 100,000 population	282.9	245.6	–	–	221.2

Source: Yang (1991).

The result was substantial remaining inequity. Both factors had important implications for access to any services, and for the resultant 'two-tier' system of high-quality services for the rich and low-quality for the poor. Worse, if compulsory premiums were paid by those who could not afford to use health services, owing to co-payments or lack of geographical access, the result may even have been a cross-subsidy from poor to rich. The premiums of low-income families could have subsidised the services received only by those who had the financial resources to pay high co-payments or the geographical luck.

Reforms of the system took place in 1999 (financing), 2000 (pharmaceuticals) and 2001 (provider payment) (Kwon and Reich 2005). These have changed the public private shares in health expenditure (Jeong 2005). A study has measured the extent to which three different Asian countries achieve equal treatment for equal need and concludes that Korea is now the most successful (Lu *et al.* 2007).

It can be concluded that Korea has resolved the worst inequities of its health system structure.

Such high co-payments as Korea once operated are probably found in only a few countries. However, geographical access issues are relevant to all theoretically universal systems. In an ideal health system the distribution of hospital and specialist resources would favour more population-dense areas, and average distances to all types of health provider would decrease with increased density. These arrangements minimise the average geographical access costs of the population as a whole but inequity of access is then inevitable. In real health systems, health professionals' preference for the amenities in urban areas (especially in poorer countries), historical patterns of health service provision and the location of prestige health facilities in larger cities exacerbate these even in a universal financing system.

and muted in the setting of physician reimbursement. A point system determined by a joint committee of sickness funds and physicians is used to pay doctors and there are relatively small co-payments for pharmaceuticals – until recently only approximately 5 per cent of sickness fund pharmaceutical expenditure (Busse 1999). In contrast, in France, price-based rationing plays a much greater role. Patients pay 10.6 per cent of health service expenses out of pocket (Caussat *et al.* 2003, cited in Turquet 2004), patients pay at the time of use and are reimbursed later, and financial factors are a commonly stated reason for not seeking care. Increasing co-payments has been the principal response to cost-control concerns alongside decisions to exclude some services from social insurance cover altogether. Only recently have policy makers started to pay more attention to planning mechanisms beyond constraining the number of doctors and hospital beds, for example in trying to encourage a 'gatekeeper' system to emerge (Lancry and Sandier 1999; Turquet 2004). In general, social insurance systems tend to make greater use of co-payments than do tax-funded systems, thereby relatively emphasising private rather than social demand.

23.2 Institutional incentives

Contract models in social insurance have typically varied widely and ranged from the salary- and budget-based reimbursement of public systems to the fee-for-service mechanisms of private voluntary insurance systems. For example, under the French system, public hospital doctors are paid by salary whereas private hospital doctors are paid on a fee-for-service basis. General practitioners' fees are strictly regulated (Rochaix and Wislford 2005). In German hospitals, capital expenditure was directly funded according to the state government's hospital plan while operating expenditure was traditionally reimbursed on a *per diem* basis, with a diagnosis-related group system being introduced in 1993 (Kamke 1998).

Social insurance systems normally have a combination of highly regulated financing, and provision by publicly owned hospitals, or providers working to highly regulated contracts. Along with other characteristics of social insurance systems, the incentives are between those in budget/salary systems and the incentives to over-provide services of a fee-for-service system. These arrangements in the hospital sector prompt questions about the underlying 'objective function' of hospitals, since they cannot be assumed to maximise profit (see Chapter 16). Only by understanding what hospitals are aiming to achieve can we assess how the incentives they face may impact on their performance. Revenues are a key component of the objective function of most conceivable types of hospital, since revenues determine the resources hospitals can mobilise, the ability to meet managerial objectives, the extent to which services can be offered and their quality. Revenue-related objectives are therefore likely to appeal to profit-motivated, managerial, professional satisfaction-oriented and public service-motivated hospitals alike. However, attitudes to costs are likely to vary, with profit-motivated hospitals being more likely to seek to minimise costs and others less interested in the control of at least some cost components.

Stepan and Sommersgutter-Reichmann (1999) considered the situation of Austrian hospitals. In Austria hospitals were funded partly by the public sector, via the federal government, and partly through the national insurance companies. Reimbursement rates through this system were such that the margin between cost and revenue was negative or zero in the case of out-patients, and slightly positive in the case of in-patients. However, patients with supplementary insurance could be charged higher prices for in-patient care to include payments to both physicians and the hospital for superior hotel services. Stepan and Sommersgutter-Reichmann commented that the incentives in this situation would appear to promote emphasis on in-patient care at the cost of out-patient care, especially since supplementary insurance did not cover out-patients. This was compounded by the number of beds devoted to supplementary care being limited to 25 per cent of the hospital's total beds – another reason for hospitals to seek to increase their bed numbers.

These unintended incentives generated by organisational and financing structures are likely to contribute to the allocation of health sector resources to services with the highest collective private demand, especially where optional additional insurance offers the most significant additional revenue-generating activities.

23.3 Conclusion

The archetypal health systems we have considered so far can be located on a 'continuum' producing outcomes dominated by private demand considerations at one extreme and by social demand considerations at the other. Providing institutions in these archetypal systems can be characterised as over-providing services and over-emphasising expensive high-technology intervention in the service mix at one extreme and as lacking incentives to internal efficiency and public responsiveness at the other. The continuum ranges from private insurance (private demand, over-supply) through social insurance to tax-based systems (social demand, efficiency incentive-deficient).

By 'archetyping' health systems a number of distinctions may have been overdrawn, and pure versions of the health system types described may be difficult to find, especially as the types of reforms discussed in Chapter 25 are increasingly being adopted.

However, by developing simplified models, we have been able to demonstrate the use of the economic principles developed in the preceding chapters to the building of models that help to explain health system performance. The rest of Part IV will further develop the models to debate highly complex health systems resulting from the coexistence of parallel systems and the implications of combining health system characteristics in less conventional ways – the thrust of health sector reforms around the world.

24 Parallel systems

24.1 Introduction

In Chapter 23 a comparison was made of the main archetypes of systems of health sector finance and provision. It was pointed out in this comparison that in reality the health system in almost all countries is more complicated than models imply, and in many cases a wide range of systems coexist.

The 'segmented' health system of many Latin American countries has been described in brief in Chapter 20. In these countries the system is composed of a series of sub-components: tax-financed services, social insurance, private insurance and out-of-pocket private health care markets for rich and poor. Population groups with no access to any of these coexist. Box 24.1 presents more detail on the range of patterns of provision within this group of countries. Chapter 20 also discussed the parallel coexistence of a range of 'sub-systems' within the overall system of a number of other poorer countries. This tends to occur where the public system has failed to play the role originally envisaged for it. In these countries, the configuration of 'sub-systems' is different from those of the 'segmented' Latin American countries, in particular containing a much less important, if any, social insurance component. Finally, the United States, while discussed substantially in Chapter 23 as a private health system, can also be considered as a parallel health system which includes a more extensive private voluntary insurance sector than other countries, but also includes important components of public finance and public provision, as explained in Chapter 20.

To some extent, each sub-system presents the characteristic issues of its equivalent archetype system, as discussed in Chapters 20 to 23. Nevertheless, interaction between sub-sectors produces further issues, problems and opportunities that are characteristic only of parallel health systems. We start this chapter, however, with a discussion of the general characteristics of the 'out-of-pocket' sub-system that nowhere approaches universality and has therefore not been discussed as a system in its own right.

24.2 The out-of-pocket sub-system

There are many manifestations of 'out-of-pocket' health system components. A market for drugs for which prescriptions are not required operates in almost all countries, often, but not always, in a highly regulated environment. 'Out of pocket' financed consultation with primary care doctors, formally registered, exists in almost all countries (other than those few which formally ban private practice) from the Harley Street practitioners in London to the medical practitioners of the slums of Karachi.

Box 24.1 The 'segmented' health systems of Latin America

The countries in the table have 'segmented' health systems, meaning that they all have public, social insurance and private sub-systems. The shares of each segment vary markedly, with private shares ranging from 75 per cent in Uruguay to 15 per cent in Colombia (almost halved since 1998 following a reform programme there which was partially successful in universalising the social security system and moving Colombia away from segmentation). The median countries' private sector share is high, at 52 per cent, comparable to the US share at 55 per cent.

   ECLAC (2006) find that where countries' public expenditure is better targeted on low-income groups, out-of-pocket spending among those groups is smaller. The figure reproduced from their analysis in the table shows that public spending is not equally well targeted towards those groups in Latin American countries, and suggests that the countries whose public expenditure tends to benefit richer groups (Peru, Ecuador and Guatemala) are among the countries with highly segmented health systems.

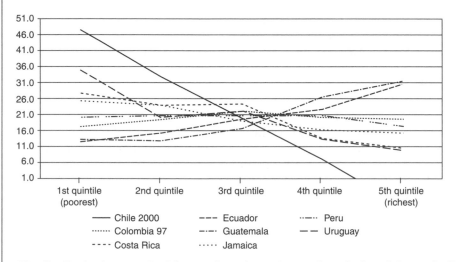

The distributive impact of public spending, share of expenditure by beneficiary quintile, Chile, Colombia, Costa Rica, Ecuador, Guatemala, Jamaica, Peru and Uruguay.

Source: Pan-American Health Organisation, Strategic Health Development Areas (SHD/HP) database

Health expenditure in selected countries, 2004

Country	Total health expenditure per capita (international dollar)	Total health expenditure (THE) (% GDP)	Expenditure (% THE)		
			Public	Private	Social security
Uruguay	914	9.5	24.9	75.1	11.3
Mexico	636	6.3	47.9	52.1	29.7
Panama	593	7.6	65.4	34.6	34.9

Colombia	568	7.8	85.3	14.7	50.8
El Salvador	389	8.1	45.8	54.2	16.0
Paraguay	323	7.5	33.7	66.3	12.6
Venezuela	294	4.8	7.7	52.3	9.4
Peru	263	4.6	49.4	50.6	21.4
Guatemala	254	5.7	40.2	59.8	19.3
Ecuador	234	5.1	37.8	62.2	11.6
Nicaragua	216	7.6	48.0	52.0	12.8
Bolivia	187	6.8	60.7	39.3	7.7

Source: WHO, National Health Accounts, http://www.who.int/nha/country/en/ (consulted 4 January 2007)

Source: ECLAC (2006).

The model that most closely resembles a simple 'free' market is where out-of-pocket fees are charged for services provided by for-profit operators, especially in the informal sector in poor countries, where supply factors are not subject to restriction by regulation. Prices and quantities bought and sold are determined by the interaction of demand and supply. Rationing is strictly on the basis of willingness and ability to pay, and problems of 'moral hazard' do not apply. The implication is that private demand-based values are not challenged in any way: services are not offered to those with inadequate ability to pay and users are not protected from 'catastrophic' illness costs (Box 24.2) Most evident, however are the implications of information asymmetry in a context in which the financial incentives associated with maximising sales of whatever treatments are available seem often to outweigh the incentives to ethical practice (see Box 24.3). The restricted access of the poor to this sub-sector is consequently a mixed blessing. These markets do not exhibit the type of cost escalation associated with a stronger role for the private sector in the health systems of other countries, simply because they are absolutely demand-constrained. The poverty of the populations makes demand price elastic, even for services considered essential by those making utilisation choices. (For many poor populations in poor countries, elasticities of demand for health care greater than one have been measured – see, for example, Box 3.1.)

These free markets also provide evidence of externality problems. Unrestricted use of drugs is allowing resistant organisms to develop. Resistance to antibiotics and chloroquine is commonly reported in such settings. There is too little use of other services whose effectiveness is increased at critical coverage levels and 'public goods' such as vector control of malaria and schistosomiasis are, of course, not provided at all by this type of market. In the first two cases, it is difficult to separate the problems of information asymmetry and externality.

Consider the position of the demand curve in this market in relation to the social marginal value curve. For at least some products, dominant externalities are negative, and lack of information causes people to demand poor-quality and inappropriate drugs that they would not demand in the presence of full information. For these products, the social marginal value curve lies to the left of the demand curve – the optimal production level is exceeded. For other products, the reverse might be the case, the valuations which the relatively poor consumers can place on appropriate and effective drugs may be low relative to those implied by a weighting system more

Box 24.2 Out-of pocket health expenditure and catastrophic payments

National Health Accounts (NHA) data are enabling new understandings of patterns of health financing at the global level, and the role of out-of-pocket payments in them. Poullier *et al.* (2002) calculate the relationship between out-of-pocket expenditures and GDP *per capita*, shown in the scattergraph.

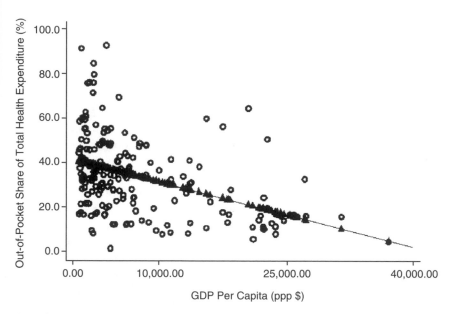

Out-of-pocket share of health spending, by income.

Source: Pouillier *et al.* (2002)

Within countries, the shares of income spent on health care across income quintiles do not follow a uniform pattern. Nandakumar *et al.* (2004) show this pattern for four countries, noting that the poorest of the four (Malawi) was the one in which health care expenditure was progressive: the poorest spent a smaller proportion of their income on health care (see table). This is consistent with the received wisdom that health care is a luxury good with a high income elasticity of demand. However, in the other three, the poorest quintiles spent proportionately more on health care

Percentage of household income spent of health care

Country	Egypt	Jordan	Lebanon	Malawi
Poorest quintile	9.9	12	18.5	15.5
Second income quintile	8.7	7	16	17.9
Third income quintile	7.6	6	15	18.4
Fourth income quintile	7.1	5	14	27.9
Richest quintile	7.4	4	13	20.4

Source: Nandakumar *et al.* (2004) based on national NHA surveys.

than the richest. It is possible that the reason for this is that insurance arrangements limit the expenditure of progressively richer groups while excluding poorer groups in those countries. If so, it suggests the potential for out-of-pocket payments to inflate health care costs overall relative to pooled financing arrangements.

Xu *et al.* (2003) report patterns of expenditure deemed 'catastrophic' defined as expenditure exceeding 40 per cent of effective income (income surplus to basic subsistence needs). Defined this way, the authors show an association, over the fifty-nine countries included in their study between the proportion of households making catastrophic payments and the share of out-of-pocket payments in total health expenditure (see second scattergraph).

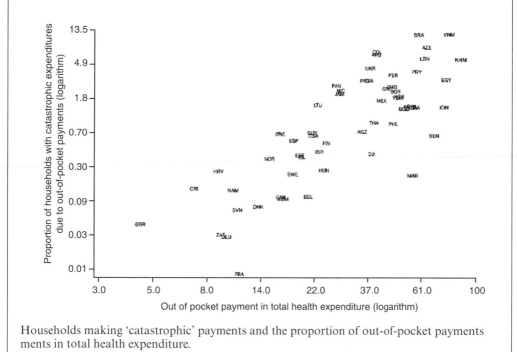

Households making 'catastrophic' payments and the proportion of out-of-pocket payments ments in total health expenditure.

equitable than disposable income. Can regulation of the market address any of these problems?

More regulated out-of-pocket markets may be capable of controlling some, but not all, of the problems of this market. Common forms of regulation of over-the-counter pharmaceuticals include licensing of products; qualification standards for pharmacists; and restrictions on allowed activities of unqualified personnel in pharmacy shops.

Figure 24.1 considers the implications of the regulations for an extreme example of an over-valued product – a drug with few effective applications, and potentially harmful effects if inappropriately prescribed, past its use-by date or poorly stored prior to sale. Assume that the free market operates with a high level of demand due to widespread belief in the drug as a cure-all, and there is a supply curve equal to the marginal cost

---

Box 24.3 The private sector in India

Yesudian (2001) documents a range of allegations directed at private health care providers in India and the responses of professional associations, consumer courts and regulatory bodies to the perceived problems.

A committee of experts surveyed Bombay's nursing homes (private hospitals) and reached a series of findings:

1   Sub-standard and crowded facilities, several in sheds or lofts in slums.
2   Failure to disinfect operating theatres after each operation.
3   Dumping of infectious waste material in municipal bins.
4   Lack of labour rooms, despite claims to offer maternity services.
5   Dirty and poorly lit facilities.
6   Failure to register notifiable diseases.

Bhat (1999) attempted to quantify the prevalence of these and other malpractices by asking providers' opinions about their frequency. According to the responses, most prevalent are over-prescription of drugs, inadequate measures for the disposal of waste and fee-splitting practices by which, for example, a referring doctor shares the fee with the doctor or ancillary service s/he refers a patient to.

These accounts suggest that there are elements of private sector activity which come quite close to an unregulated free market, and that ethical behaviour cannot always be relied upon to resolve potential contradictions between profit-maximising and public health in the presence of significant information asymmetries.

---

curve because firms are 'price takers' (see Chapter 6). Price is determined at p, and quantity bought and sold at q.

Along the left of the MSV curve are the few effective applications of the drug, and underneath the quantity axis are the negative social values for the many harmful applications. The shaded area abc shows the welfare loss associated with the free-market solution in comparison with the perfect solution (where quantity Q* of the drug is provided in cases where application is most effective). One regulatory option is to refuse the drug a licence. Assuming this is fully implemented, quantity 0 is bought and sold. In comparison with the perfect solution, area (ade) is the welfare loss. In the absence of alternative interventions, the analyst might conclude that since area ade is smaller than abc, the regulation is appropriate – in other words the costs associated with the unavailability of the drug for effective cases are smaller than the costs associated with the unregulated availability of the drug.

Increasing the qualification levels of those who prescribe and dispense (which is the result of the effective implementation of higher qualification standards and control of activities of the unqualified in pharmacy shops) is intended to push the market solution towards the optimum point a. The policy assumes that a qualified pharmacist will not prescribe and dispense dangerous drugs, or inappropriate drugs. Point a might be achieved – but there are two problems. First, like public policy makers, in most cases the

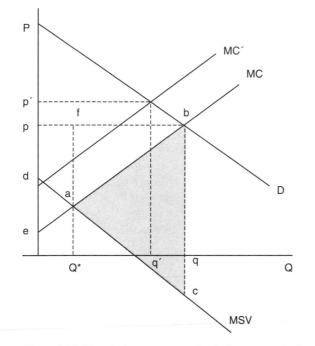

Figure 24.1 Regulating an over-valued pharmaceutical product.

pharmacist will not have the necessary data to pinpoint a. However, if they ask the right question when they prescribe, 'Is this patient likely to benefit to an extent which makes the price worth paying for him?' they may get as close as possible given the available information. Second, pharmacy training must be assumed to instil ethical behaviour as well as knowledge in the pharmacist, since the pharmacist must be willing to forgo profits of abf in order to behave ethically. Alternatively, sanctions against unethical behaviour must be effective.

Imposing qualification standards will also increase the cost (and therefore supply) curve (for example to MC′), which will also have the effect of reducing the quantity bought and sold (to q′) – but this alone will not select appropriate uses of the drug over inappropriate and harmful ones. If we assume that price remains the rationing mechanism (i.e. that pharmacists are not ethically motivated to ration according to MSVs), price rises to p′, and the effect is to restrict use of the drug to a smaller number of those willing and able to pay a higher price who are not necessarily those for whom use of the drug is appropriate.

24.3 Rationing of the public system, social insurance and private insurance in a parallel systems context

When public sub-systems are compared with their social insurance sub-system counterparts and those in turn are compared with their private sub-system counterparts, they generally exhibit lower *per capita* expenditure. This pattern matches the results of comparisons of universal systems, but some of the suggested causes of higher and lower expenditure are even greater in this context. If there appears to be reluctance among voters in a democracy to increase tax-based funding in line with health sector cost and technology growth in a universal system, this is likely to be even greater when a significant proportion of voters are not direct beneficiaries of expenditure in the public health sector. Extensive public subsidy of the social insurance sector will not create a more universal interest in public health expenditure if the expenditure votes are separate and competitive rather than jointly determined. The users of the three sub-systems are differentiated by increasing wealth and social status. As the sub-system becomes more privatised, this effect is reinforced, since poor and low social status populations are likely to secure a less effective voice in even the most democratic societies.

Arguments about the overall extent of 'under-' or 'over-funding' closely parallel those of their universal system counterparts. From a societal perspective, funding within the public system may be more appropriately spent than that in the private one. The public good measures implemented in the country are usually in the public sector, and sometimes in the social insurance sector. A system aiming to prioritise primary health care and offer limited access to higher levels of care through referral usually operates. The coexistence of other sub-sectors serving the needs of urban, middle and upper-income groups may even allow the public sub-sector to concentrate more effectively on an appropriate mix of care for poor rural populations than is possible in more universal systems, especially where private and social insurance systems are well developed and extensively provide referral hospital level services.

At the same time, private demand considerations evidently dominate in the private insurance sector, where high levels of technology are present and specialist consultations dominate ambulatory services. Latin American countries are renowned for their high rate of caesarean births, which probably reflects both private demand dominance and the level of specialist involvement. Within countries, there is an association between location of birth and type of delivery (see Box 24.4). As was discussed in Chapter 23, rationing to control moral hazard largely depends on co-payments, but the implications for the failure to provide particular types of services – undervalued ones because of externality and information asymmetry, and services to the poor – may be less important if the sector is defined as serving the rich and providing them with curative services. However, the use of disease exclusion as a rationing mechanism, which aims to control adverse selection rather than moral hazard, is effectively a 'cost-shifting' strategy in a parallel system context. The high levels of ability to pay of the rich and relatively healthy can be exploited to offer luxurious services to patients and substantial profit to insurers with a high concentration of elective surgery cases that have predictable prognoses and limited costs. The extent of risk sharing is limited, and the most expensive cases are returned to the public or social security sub-sectors. These sub-sectors effectively cover nearly the whole population for the most catastrophically expensive risks whatever proportion of the population is considered to be covered by the private sector. Adverse selection, cost shifting and cream skimming are closely related in this context. The incentives to cost shifting can be shown graphically in Figure 24.2.

The figure shows the potential profitability of different types of insurance to a monopolist private insurer, and the potential surplus to be shared in an oligopolistic insurance industry (see Chapter 15). Assume, for simplicity, that comprehensive insurance is the combination of insurance for elective surgery and insurance for chronic illness care only. The demand for elective surgery and treatment of chronic illness are assumed to be somewhat lower than for comprehensive insurance, but demand for elective

Box 24.4 Caesarean births in Latin American countries

Latin American countries' caesarean section rates are among the highest in the world, with a median of 33 per cent for selected institutions in eight countries included in a study in this region (Villar *et al.* 2006). The medically indicated rate may be as low as 1 per cent and is unlikely to be higher than 15 per cent (*Lancet* 2006).

Villar *et al.* (2006) show that the rate of caesarean delivery is associated with the type of institution at which women give birth, with the highest rates at private facilities, the lowest at public facilities, and social security facilities carrying out this procedure at an intermediate rate. The highest proportions of caesareans are 'elective', i.e. not responding to an emergency situation for which the procedure is indicated.

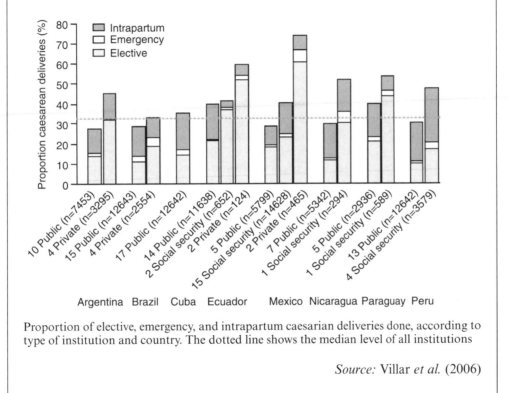

Proportion of elective, emergency, and intrapartum caesarian deliveries done, according to type of institution and country. The dotted line shows the median level of all institutions

Source: Villar *et al.* (2006)

surgery insurance is the higher of the two. Cost is assumed to be lower for elective surgery, and higher for chronic illness care. The hatched areas in each diagram show potential profitability. Since it is more profitable to the insurer to offer insurance for elective surgery only, it will not offer comprehensive insurance. Assuming there is some demand for chronic care insurance above its cost, an insurer may offer this separately, but it will represent a relatively minor activity. The public or social security sector is left with the responsibility to offer chronic care to all who are deemed to need it at a cost potentially as large as the larger shaded area in the third figure. (The size of

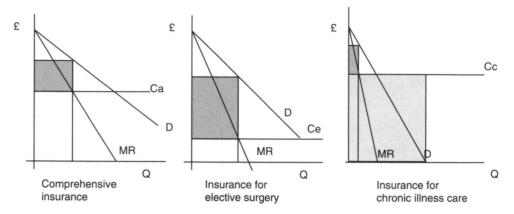

Figure 24.2 Cost-shifting incentives in private insurance.

this area depends on the volume of care the public or social security sectors decide to offer.)

Where a social insurance sub-sector exists, it usually exhibits intermediate characteristics with respect to the trade-off between private and social demand factors (for example, in its caesarean birth rates – see Box 24.4), although in some countries it is effectively integrated with the public sub-sector. In contrast to the typical social insurance model considered in Chapter 23, the social insurance model in many segmented Latin American systems is integrated, with no competition between social insurance agencies. The characteristics of this social insurance model leave it more likely to lie further towards the public end of the spectrum than the model of Chapter 22. There are fewer incentives on the part of providers, who are not competing with each other to provide services responsive to consumer demand or to maximise performance from a social value perspective. There are also weaker incentives for insurance agencies that are statutorily entitled to their revenues whatever the views of their enrolees, to steer providers towards private demand responsiveness. In some countries this leads to little distinction between public and social security sub-sectors. Both are considered poor-quality, resource-inadequate and with poorly motivated staff more interested in parallel private sector income generation.

24.4 The interaction of the four sub-systems: equity

The most evident deficiency of these parallel sub-systems is the levels of inequity implicit in the data presented in Box 24.1. Levels of funding *per capita* have a steep and positive gradient as the population served becomes richer and healthier. While those who can afford private insurance and whose condition does not exclude them receive services comparable to the most luxurious and well resourced available anywhere in the world; at the other extreme, large population segments are denied access to services at times of need. The characteristics of the different groups vary.

Lorenz curves are a useful technique for measuring inequity in the distribution of any resource. The standard form of the Lorenz curve depicts percentage of population against percentage of income, ordering the population from the lowest to highest income earners, moving from left to right (see Figure 24.3). For example, point a on

Figure 24.3(a) shows that the poorest 30 per cent of the population earn only 10 per cent of total income. A 45° line represents perfect equality in income distribution. The greater the curvature of the Lorenz curve the more unequal the distribution. The information on the Lorenz curve can be summarised by the Gini coefficient, which expresses the area between the Lorenz curve and the 45° line as a proportion of the triangle 0AB in Figure 24.3(a). Musgrove (1986) has depicted the inequity of health sector resource distribution in Peru by adapting the technique (Figure 24.3(b)). The figure shows that inequities in the distribution of physicians *per capita* and in the distribution of expenditure per person with illness symptoms are marked. The Gini coefficient for the distribution of physicians is 0.51 – for income distribution this level would be interpreted as extremely inequitable (Todaro 1989). Musgrove's data are based on geographical inequity only – the data used are based on health regions rather than individuals. Further disaggregation by groups of individuals with access to different sub-systems could increase the measure.

In the United States, the well served group of the population constitute the majority and those without insurance cover will not be denied emergency and some other forms of care but can find themselves with no access to expensive treatment for chronic or incurable conditions. The poorest in the United States are covered by social insurance. The uncovered group is made up of those whose health status excludes them from cover, those who are irregularly employed or self-employed, or work for small employers who do not provide cover or pay sufficiently to cover its cost, or those who exclude themselves as part of the adverse selection process (see Box 22.1). In poor countries without a social insurance sector, those whom the public sector does not

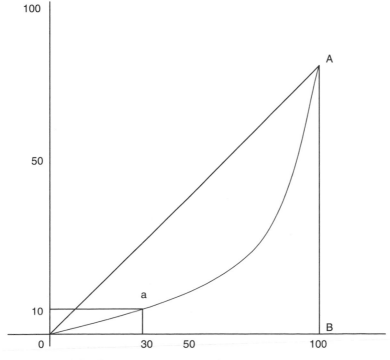

Figure 24.3 (a) The Lorenz curve.

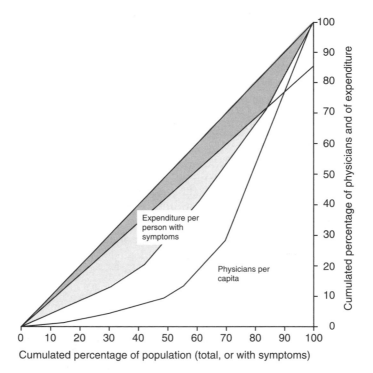

Figure 24.3 (b) Health sector resource distribution in Peru. Lorenz curves showing the inequity of the distribution of physicians relative to population and of Ministry of Health patient-related expenditure relative to population with symptoms, Peru, 1982.

Source: World Bank data.

reach at all are remote rural dwellers, often coincidental with the poorest population groups in the country. Use of unregulated out-of-pocket reimbursed private providers is the option available to that proportion of the population who can raise the necessary money. Also effectively uncovered in many countries are population groups who use poor-quality and public providers that fail to provide appropriate care – because drugs are out of stock, staff absent or other necessary components of care are unavailable. Those with a little more money or geographical luck have access to moderately priced services in the NGO sector (reputedly but not always demonstrably better than in the public sector), and the formally employed may have access to employer-sponsored services where these have been organised. For a small urban élite, expensive private services can be purchased, or privileged access to public services may be obtained. For example, senior civil servants may use their authority to command a greater than equitable use of public services, or a private ward system may give higher public subsidy for those paying a higher fee, as has been documented in Indonesia (Gani 1996).

In the segmented Latin American parallel systems, the main difference is the additional recourse to a social security sector of variable quality for the formally employed and the slightly more extensive private insurance system. Maceira (see Box 24.5) has charted the way that coverage patterns have typically developed over recent decades in Latin American countries. The analysis highlights the way that external economic shocks can dramatically change the extent and type of cover of large population groups, and is relevant to any parallel health system.

24.5 The interaction of the four sub-systems: efficiency

These patent inequities are also important inefficiencies – in themselves and in what they reflect. Allocative efficiency is achieved where the marginal value of expenditure is equated across the range of health interventions available. There are several reasons to suppose that this will be less the case in a parallel health system than in a universal one. Figure 24.4 shows how the three sub-sectors – public, social security and private – might increasingly diverge from a social welfare potential curve. According to this analysis, reallocating resources from the private sub-sector to the public one could increase the total social value generated through the health sector.

This analysis relates to allocative efficiency alone. Arguments that technical efficiency is likely to be greater in the private sector imply that the value of marginal activity in the

---

Box 24.5 Population movement between sub-systems in parallel health systems

Maceria (reported in IADB 1996) describes movement in population coverage by different sub-sectors in response to external pressures. In the representations of the diagram, the population is ordered by income level along the horizontal axis, and its distribution is shown on the vertical axis. Sector 1 of the diagram shows the initial distribution of the population between the three sub-sectors, public, social security and private. Sector 2 shows the effect of crisis in the public system – quality and quantity of services offered there decline and a proportion of those initially covered by the public sector turn to the private sector. Sector 3 shows the effect of falling incomes in the social security sector, for example as a result of declining formal sector employment, or as a result of lower formal sector incomes. In the latter case the number affiliated to social security does not fall but the quality and quantity of services do and the effect is the same – people previously covered by social security services start to seek care in the public sector, placing more pressure there. Sector 4 shows the combination of the effects of the changes of the previous two stages – public sector services are even further stretched, more private sector services are sought by both ex-public service users and ex-social security service users and a group unable to access private services – for example, because of inability to pay or lost access to social security services – become excluded from all services. In sector 5 the existence of large excluded groups and the stress on public services creates conditions for expansion of activities of non-governmental organisations.

The details of the analysis – for example, whether the 'initial' situation ever pertained, or the order of events – are less important than the message of this analysis, that the sub-systems making up a parallel health system are highly interdependent. Population groups move between sub-systems and pressures on one part of the system have knock-on effects on other sub-systems. Public sector adequacy has a major impact on the development of the private sector. While the richest members of society remain protected from this process, the poorest suffer the most extreme effects.

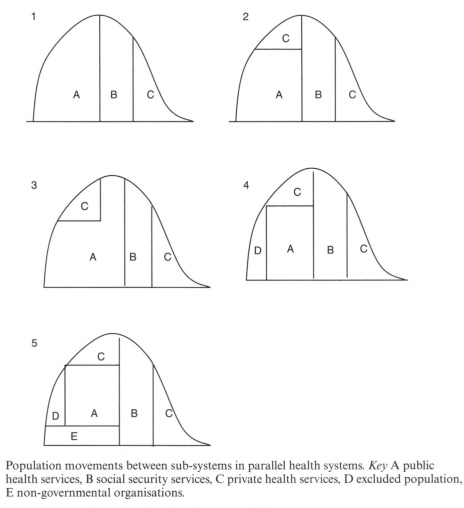

Population movements between sub-systems in parallel health systems. *Key* A public health services, B social security services, C private health services, D excluded population, E non-governmental organisations.

Source Adapted from Maceira, cited in IADB (1996).

three sub-sectors might be closer. The public sector may be trying to allocate resources to higher-priority activities but it is so inefficient that the net value of its output per unit of resource is no higher than in the technically efficient but allocatively inefficient private sector. The shortage of evidence with respect to the hypothesis that the private sector exhibits higher levels of technical efficiency has been discussed in Chapter 22.

To the extent that the social insurance system and even the private system is subsidised with resources originating in general taxation (often in the form of tax breaks in the private sector), the inequities and inefficiencies are compounded. Trying to prevent the rich from spending their money inappropriately is likely to be a futile pursuit and some people would consider it to be an inappropriate extension of the role of the state. The same argument does not apply to the spending of the tax dollar, shilling or peso. Spending these less rather than more efficiently and equitably is difficult to defend.

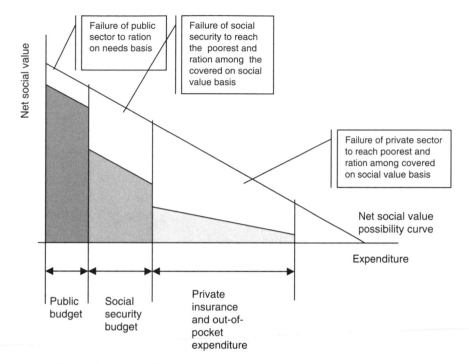

Figure 24.4 The achievement of social welfare potential in three sub-sectors of a segmented health care system.

Inefficiency also arises from duplication between the various parallel sub-systems. On the financing side, there are several administration, information and collection systems. On the provision side, each system has to contain separate slack to deal with occasional demand surges. Each system has to start from zero in planning geographical access, resulting in phenomena like public, social security and private hospitals sitting side by side in a capital city, while within the same country there may be no formal health services at all covering a wide geographical area.

24.6 Conclusion

From a social welfare perspective the principal problem of parallel health systems is the loss of solidarity provided in more universal systems. The lack of risk sharing, especially between social groups, reduces the availability of some of the most effective and needed services. Segmentation ensures the weighting of demands according to wealth by separating groups within which risks are pooled on the basis of economic power. The higher the proportion of the population using the out-of-pocket sub-sector, the more access to health resources depends on ability to pay. Within the sub-systems with insurance characteristics (in the broad sense: including public finance and provision), some market failures are avoided. For example, the provision of public goods at some level is enabled; patterns of supply are to some extent planned according to need (increasingly as the type of insurance is more public); 'catastrophic' costs are avoided at least by some groups. At the same time, rationing according to ability to pay is broadly maintained.

Choices about the degree of equity, solidarity and universality of health systems are fundamental political choices and reflect the culture and social values of societies. At stake is whether or not health services should properly be placed among the rewards for economic success, or whether they must be treated separately and distributed according to a commonly specified social welfare function. In the language of the political left, this involves the choice between treatment of health services and health as a 'commodity' or as a 'right'.[1]

This choice is not ultimately a technical one. However, the extent to which different policies move health systems towards social or private demand-based values is, as we have seen, capable of technical assessment. The final chapter of Part IV assesses the changes that have occurred in the reform of health sectors in the last decade, in the context of this and other types of market failure.

Note

1 Up to this point, we have been assuming that what we have termed 'social values' are shared by policy makers globally. However, it is at this stage necessary to acknowledge that the implicit values of many systems and sub-systems contradict social values so greatly that we have to modify this assumption. Those divergences between private and social demand-based values classically included among 'market failures' are probably almost universally accepted as problems. In contrast, the relative weights which private demand-based values place on service delivered to the poor and the rich implicitly at least are accepted in systems which take very limited measures to redistribute them. Nevertheless, few governments explicitly acknowledge sympathy with the implications of those weights in the health sector.

25 The economics of health sector reform

25.1 Using economic principles to analyse health system reforms

Health system reform involves the changing of health system features with the intention of improving health system outcomes. Chapters 19 to 24, and earlier chapters, have suggested how health systems features can vary, and how outcomes might respond to that variation. The distinctive perspective of economics on the relationship between health system features and outcomes is that it is driven by an understanding of how health system features create incentives, and how actors within the health system respond to those incentives in ways that affect outcomes.

On that basis, we have already discussed relevant arguments over a number of topics in health system reform – usually categorised by the types of feature changes involved. This chapter is organised according to such a categorisation, and combines review of previous with new material to address each of these topics.

25.2 Financing reforms

25.2.1 User fees in tax-financed systems

Many tax-financed systems introduced user charges during the 1990s. More recently, a few have removed them.

There were two broad justifications for introducing the fees. One was the need to reduce moral hazard in contexts where prices are otherwise zero. The second was the wish to increase the funding level of the health system without resorting to higher levels of taxation, or reallocating resources from other types of public expenditure.

We have already encountered much of the analysis relevant to the moral hazard argument in the analysis of co-payment within an insurance system. It was concluded that co-payment rationed according to private demand, and could fully control moral hazard as defined by reference to private demand based values only if co-payment levels were set at 100 per cent of the marginal cost of the services provided (see Chapter 22). The same applies to user charges. If they were to be set at 100 per cent of marginal cost, public subsidy would be restricted to covering the deficit where downward-sloping cost curves apply, which might be roughly equivalent to providing for fixed costs.

We have seen that public health service systems have superior rationing methods from a social demand perspective and it is therefore likely that the need to raise revenues dominates moral hazard arguments in most of the cases in which user charges have been introduced. There may, however, be some exceptions. Much of the support from

UK family doctors for proposed introduction of user charges for their services seems to arise from their perceptions of high levels of 'wasteful' use of their services.[1]

There is no costless source of revenues, and there is little difference to society in paying the same amount of resources directly to health providers, or via the taxation system. Furthermore, a single administrative system for the raising of revenues for health services has potential efficiency advantages over a multiplicity of systems.

However, we have seen that particular constraints apply to tax-based funding. Democracies operate imperfectly in allocating the levels of funding that populations want to be spent on particular types of publicly funded services. It is also important to consider the macroeconomic effects of higher taxation. If higher tax leads to people choosing to work less or take fewer risks, then the effect is to lower incomes, and thereby to lower tax revenue. The phenomenon of 'capital flight' by which businesses and people transfer their savings and transactions to other economies imposes macroeconomic cost on increasing tax rates. However, it is also possible that higher taxes will lower people's disposable income, and thereby encourage them to work harder. This is a classic economic question – there is an income effect, in which lower income leads to more work, and a substitution effect, where we would expect people to choose more leisure, since higher income tax effectively makes leisure cheaper. Although much of the observed tax policy in the 1980s and 1990s suggests that governments believe higher taxes generate work disincentives, the empirical evidence is mixed, and many studies suggest that modest changes in tax have little effect on work effort and risk taking.

The implications of a user charge (which might also be considered a health service sales tax) are likely to be quite different from the implication of higher levels of general taxation. The greater willingness to pay for health services than for other components of public expenditure implies that they may be more acceptable to the majority of the population than general taxation increases. The fact that it is an individual's rather than general access to health services that is taxed changes the likely incentive effects on individuals' work effort and risk-taking choices, and therefore the supply-side macroeconomic implications.

Figure 25.1 explains the role user charges might play in enabling an improved total funding level of health services in a situation where public subsidy is constrained to

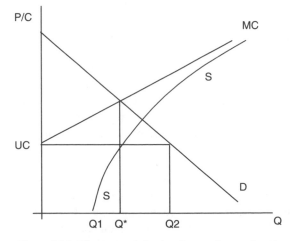

Figure 25.1 The potential role of user charges in a tax-constrained economy.

below the optimal. Assuming (temporarily) that the demand curve measures social marginal value, Q* can be defined as in Chapters 21 to 23 as the optimal level of provision. However, the subsidy curve SS, which denotes possible combinations of user charges and provision consistent with a given level of subsidy, shows that, without user charges, the maximum level of provision the public sector is capable of meeting is Q1. By introducing user charges, public expenditure can be increased along SS, so that at a user charge of UC the optimal total funding level can be achieved. This is consistent with a substantially subsidised price, depending on the level of the fixed public subsidy.

The important problem with this analysis, in common with the analysis of co-payments in Chapter 22, is that the demand curve cannot be assumed to represent marginal social value. Under the circumstances of Figure 25.1, demand will still have to be rationed using non-price methods, since demand at price UC is Q2. To this extent, those demands that are rendered effective will have to be sanctioned by a non-price rationing method. This may or may not effectively select only relatively high values of social demand. In either case, those needs which are not backed by ability to pay at least the subsidised price will be excluded irrespective of further rationing criteria.

As before, we would be likely to find that demands of high social value such as the demands for immunisation of the poorest lay in the 'rationed out' section of the private demand curve. In some settings it may also be possible to exempt from charges the utilisation of the poorest groups, but in low-income countries these are difficult to devise and implement. However, it is possible to levy user charges only on lower-priority health services and achieve effective cross-subsidy of higher-priority services. In principle both these measures could mitigate or remove the problems identified by this analysis. Consequently, much of the debate about user charges considers the extent to which these two measures are in place and succeed. In poor countries, the highest priority services are often excluded from charges but the extent to which other high social demands are rationed is contested. There is evidence that the poor are most likely to reduce their utilisation and that at least some of those services excluded are those for which high costs of delayed treatment and communication apply (for example, Moses *et al.* 1992). Box 25.1 describes a case where user charges were removed, and evidence that the poorest households in particular responded by increasing their use of services and losing fewer work days, suggestive of an improvement of their health. In richer countries, exemption policy is more easily administered and the problems posed by charges are consequently less severe. Nevertheless, there is evidence that many people are deterred from appropriate use of services as a result of charges (for example, Beck and Horne 1980).

25.2.2 *Introducing and reforming insurance mechanisms*

In Chapter 24, out-of-pocket payments were suggested, by several arguments, to be a problem for health systems – increasing the extent to which household payments for health care could be classed as 'catastrophic', for example, and often reflecting a significant role being played by failing free markets for health care.

Catastrophic payment may result from two mechanisms: (1) the absence of pooling of health financing arrangements so that the poorest are in proportion to their means and the sickest, in absolute terms, exposed to higher levels of health care cost, and (2) the absence of pre-payment, which allows for saving in advance of medical need. New insurance arrangements are proposed in these circumstances, as a means to solve both problems.[2]

Box 25.1 The removal of user fees in Uganda

User fees were introduced in Uganda in 1993, set at varying levels by different district health authorities. Although the poor were intended to be exempt, exemption was rarely implemented, leading to the concern that the poor were being excluded from health services by the fees.

In March 2001, during the presidential elections, fees were withdrawn. Deininger and Mpuga (2004) analysed the impact of this change. They used data from two household surveys conducted before and after the removal of the charges. Both surveys contained data about socio-economic status, the reporting of ill health, and the use of health services. The table shows the main findings from comparative descriptive statistics.

Main findings of before-and-after surveys

	1999–2000	*2002–2003*
Share of those who used health care when sick: all (%)	69	79
Lower two income quintiles (%)	61	74
Upper two income quintiles (%)	77	83
Share of households not using health services when ill, citing high cost as the reason (%)	50	35
Number of workdays lost due to illness per episode	8.3	7.0

These findings suggest that after, compared with before the removal of charges people had a higher propensity to seek health care when they were ill, that this was particularly pronounced among the lower income quintiles and was associated with a reduced number of days' work lost due to sickness. Of those that did not use health care when ill, there was a marked reduction in the use of the high cost of services as the explanation. However, a simple time comparison cannot rule out other explanations of the changes, such as the growing prosperity of the population between the two surveys.

Regression analysis was used to evaluate the determinants of being rationed: citing high cost or long distance as the reason for not using health services. Taking other plausible determinants into account, the removal of user fees was estimated to have resulted in a reduction of 8 per cent in the probability of being rationed for adults, and 11.5 per cent for children. The results also seem to confirm the pro-poor impact of the change, indicating a reduction in the pro-rich inequity of the utilisation pattern overall, although rural areas benefited less than more urban ones.

These analyses are convincing that utilisation patterns changed in the ways described between 1999 and 2002 and not as a consequence of changes within households. However, user fees were not the only change to take place in the health system over this period, with changes also taking place in drug logistics systems, resource allocation mechanisms, the public funding of the not-for-profit (religious mission) providers and other potential system improvements (Kirunga-Tashobya *et al.* 2006). Proxies of the impacts of these changes were not included in the regression analysis. While user charge removal may be the dominant explanation of the impacts observed, other measures that ensure that quality of care is maintained in the face of increasing utilisation are likely also to be needed (James *et al.* 2006).

Source: Deininger and Mpuga (2004).

Despite market failure (in the form of information asymmetries with related supplier-induced demand, monopoly power and services of poor quality) there can be apparently thriving markets for health care, with many small buyers paying out-of-pocket. It may be possible to remove some of this market failure with consolidation on the demand side with one or a few insurance agencies that can in principle exert more oversight over quality standards, control over supplier-induced demand and downward pressure on price.

In Chapters 22 and 23 our analysis of insurance markets suggested potential failure arising from adverse selection and moral hazard (for voluntary insurance), or from a lack of incentives for monopolist social insurers to achieve price and quality improvements for the population. Design of new insurance mechanisms seeks to minimise these problems.

Design encompasses the setting of premium levels and co-payments, structuring of the supply side of the insurance market (number of insurance agencies), eligibility criteria and coverage benefits.

The desire for pooling indicates the desirability of a high ratio of pre- and pooled payment to the total cost of the benefit package (Carrin and James 2004). Under voluntary insurance, co-payments to control adverse selection may be necessary (as discussed in Chapter 22). Under social insurance, adverse selection problems that may be associated with a high ratio are avoided, but moral hazard may still be considered a rationale for co-payments, as may the macroeconomic burden imposed by setting compulsory insurance payments at higher rather than lower levels. The issue is the same in its essentials as charging user charges in a tax-financed system, and has been discussed in the previous section.

Similarly, from this perspective, fragmentation of the insurance system is a feature to be avoided, with maximum risk coverage achieved by a single pool (WHO 2000). Similarly, however, where insurance is voluntary, Chapter 22 provides a rationale for the fragmentation of policies by risk group to mitigate adverse selection. Under social insurance, risk equalisation mechanisms can be used to pool the risks and resources of multiple pools where, for example, there are regional insurance agencies (such as in Taiwan: Carrin and James 2004) or where multiple insurers have been mandated in order to create competition among insurers and provide agencies with incentives to achieve price and quality improvements for the enrolled populations (as in Colombia). Risk equalisation mechanisms assess the risk level of each insurer's enrolled population and compensate those with more risky populations from a shared fund. They seek to ensure an equal availability of resources for equal risk, and to negate incentives that insurers would otherwise face to avoid enrolling high-risk individuals.

Clearly, the schemes that best protect against risk maximise eligibility and benefit coverage, and minimise pre-paid contributions and co-payments, while affordability concerns at the macro-level constrain the extent of both. Figure 25.2 provides a

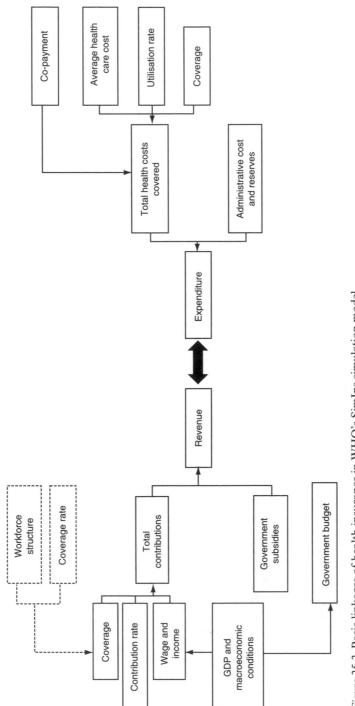

Figure 25.2 Basic linkages of health insurance in WHO's SimIns simulation model.

Source: Chamchan and Carrin (2006).

schematic illustration of the linkages between the relevant variables used by WHO's SimIns, a simulation program that models the impact of insurance design character-istics on outcomes, and Figure 25.3 provides an example of one trade-off that was modelled using this program in Thailand (Chamchan and Carrin 2006). The choice for Thai policy makers is to choose a point on one of the lines in the figure: lower contribu-tion rates and co-payments imply a higher rate of growth of the government subsidy.

In the United States, macro-economic constraints have affected the ability to extend social insurance coverage to low-income children (see Box 25.2).

25.3 Reforms to governance arrangements of provider institutions

25.3.1 Increasing the managerial autonomy of public hospitals

We have already encountered the idea that public, hierarchically organised bureaucra-cies provide weak incentives for efficiency and responsiveness to consumer demands (see Chapter 21). Further analysis of public sector organisations from this perspective has suggested that they are characterised by multiple goals (for example, in-patient, out-patient, ambulance service delivery, health promotion, disease surveillance) and, as agents, have multiple principals (patients, health system managers, departments of health and education, universities, politicians). It is predicted that hospitals will emphasise those activities that are observable and verifiable (Holmstrom and Milgrom 1991), and that principals will 'free-ride' on each others' investments in incentives to performance (Bernheim and Whinston 1986).

Frant (1996) translates the concepts of high- and low-powered incentives from an economic to a political dimension. High-powered political incentives motivate politi-cians to invest public resources in activities that have high visibility to their electorates – not necessarily those that have the greatest capacity to improve the health of populations. For example, the building of a new hospital may have high political visibility; the regular testing of water quality may not. In order to attenuate these perverse incentives,

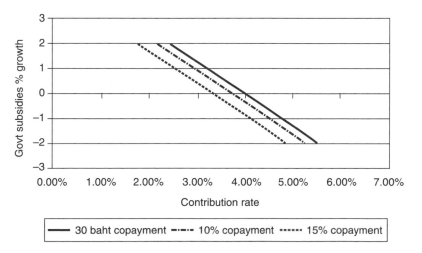

Figure 25.3 Example of a policy trade-off between subsidy growth, pre-paid contribution rate and co-payment, simulated for Thailand, using SimIns.

Source: Chamchan and Carrin (2006).

Box 25.2 Constraints on extending social insurance to low-income children in the United States

Rosenbaum *et al.* (2004) analysed the impact of the introduction of the State Children's Health Insurance Programme (SCHIP) to extend social health insurance to children living in families with lower-middle incomes. This group is more likely than average to be uninsured, failing to qualify for Medicaid, which covers those on the lowest income, but facing difficulty in paying for voluntary health insurance (see Box 22.1).

Rosenbaum and colleagues compared the benefit packages available to children covered by SCHIP and Medicaid. Under Medicaid, children have a legal entitlement to a broad package of services, and exclusions from the package can and have been challenged in the courts. The services covered are extensive, including, for example, early intervention to ameliorate the long-term effects of chronic illness and disability where there may be no prospect of recovery or improvement relative to current function. Such services are usually not provided through voluntary insurance and it is suggested that the cover goes beyond what would normally be thought of as insurance, and is better described as 'a legal entitlement among eligible children to comprehensive health care financing' (p. 15).

Rosenbaum and colleagues note that such extensive coverage has proved unpopular with those charged with financing the benefits. Medicaid officials are said to have pointed to cover of interventions of dubious efficacy and potential abuse such as horseback riding therapy. Rosenbaum *et al.* (2004) point out that data fail to support widespread use of Medicaid for such purposes.

Nevertheless, in seeking to extend coverage to a further group of lower-income children, SCHIP has been much more conservative in the range of benefits provided. Benefit packages covered by SCHIP are based on benchmarks provided by the Federal Employee Health Benefit Plan, the health benefit plan offered state employees, or the best-selling Health Maintenance Organisation (see main text) product in the state. Unlike under Medicaid, these packages may involve co-payments.

Rosenbaum and colleagues argue that while SCHIP has achieved an extension of insurance cover to an important under-insured population, there is a long-term possibility that it will pave the way for a downgrading of Medicaid benefits to the poorest children. While this would have cost-reducing advantages, it would also reduce the services available to the poorest and most vulnerable children whose families will unlikely be able to provide those services through other mechanisms.

Source: Rosenbaum *et al.* (2004).

---

public institutions may be set up so as to minimise political interference and enable low-visibility but high-value investments in public resources to take place.

Many of the characteristics of archetypal public sector organisations may be explained in this light. The job security of public officials may be protected in order that they can make technically appropriate decisions without undue influence of politicians who are subject to high-powered political incentives. This suggests that the cost of low-powered economic incentives is worth paying for protection from the costs of high-powered political incentives.

One approach that responds to both critiques is to increase the autonomy and, along with it, the exposure to market forces of public institutions, and this strategy has most commonly been recommended for hospitals. For example, in Colombia, public hospitals were transformed into 'state social enterprises' in the mid 1990s. They were converted from administrative units of the National Health System, and part of the Ministry of Health, to organisations with their own boards of directors and managerial autonomy. At the same time their finances were transferred (to some extent) from a supply-side basis (transferred by central or local authorities, as budgets for the financing of inputs) to a demand-side basis (transferred by insurance agencies, as payments for services received) (Castaño 2007). Similarly, in Norway in 2002 hospitals became separate legal entities and their management was transferred to a 'decentralised enterprise model' and in the mid 1990s, they had become subjected to market forces by the introduction of free choice of public hospital by patients, and a Diagnostic Related Group activity-based funding system (Laegrid *et al.* 2005).

This combination of measures removes hospitals from direct management through a hierarchy ultimately presided over by the Minister of Health, thus in principle protecting hospitals from high-powered political incentives. At the same time, the element of increased market exposure introduces an element of high-powered economic incentives, in principle motivating internal efficiency (cost minimisation with a view to maximising surplus generation) and responsiveness to patients' preferences.

In order for economic incentives to be effective, the hospital must transform its behaviour towards a more 'firm-like' pattern. Chapter 16 reviewed models of hospital behaviour and concluded that changing the structures of governance might change the effective objective function of the organisation by changing the relationships between the various actor groups within the hospital. Propper (1995) has argued that firm-like behaviour is unlikely to emerge where the hospital is not the residual claimant to any surplus generated. In many cases in which autonomy and revenue-generating responsibility have been passed to hospitals, the financial régime has been such that reserves cannot be carried over the end of the financial year and profit-maximising pricing strategies are ruled out. Under these circumstances there is likely to be some attenuation of high-powered economic incentives.

Nevertheless, across a range of settings, it appears that the opportunity to generate revenue proves a powerful influence over hospital behaviour. One common hospital response is to introduce tiers of services at higher than standard prices. In Zambia, for example, such services are termed 'high-cost' services (McPake *et al.* 2004), and in Indonesia a range of options from 'class III' to 'VIP' and 'super-VIP' are available (Bossert *et al.* 1997). In the UK it is possible to opt to use a 'pay bed' with a higher level of amenities and shorter waiting time (Keene *et al.* 2001). While in Indonesia and the UK, these arrangements pre-dated reforms of hospital governance that introduced greater autonomy and market exposure, prices for the higher tiers of services increased markedly with greater autonomy in Indonesia (Bossert *et al.* 1997), and the availability of pay beds seems to have expanded with greater autonomy in the UK (Williams and Nicholl 1994; Keene *et al.* 2001).

The incentives associated with these arrangements are complex. The demand function of patients for the premium service is dependent not only on the quality and price characteristics of that service but also on the quality and price characteristics of the basic service, its substitute. The unusual feature of this scenario is that the same provider controls the quality and price characteristics of both. Under certain conditions, a profit-maximising hospital will transfer part of its public subsidy to support development of the higher-priced service (McPake *et al.* 2007).

The underlying problem is that contracts for hospital services are inevitably incomplete. Changing the governance arrangements does not really alter the multiple-principal, multiple-goal problem associated with public institutional arrangements. Even if the hospital's own objective function becomes more straightforward (surplus maximisation), those of its principals remain multiple – cost containment, social function and political visibility. The capacity of principals to manage the potentially perverse incentives of a high-powered economic incentive environment is critical for this type of reform to result in better hospital performance in any of these dimensions.

25.3.2 Decentralisation

Hurley *et al.* (1995) provide a useful starting point for thinking about the implications of decentralisation for institutional structures and incentives. The authors look at the role of information and its distribution in determining appropriate allocations of authority, and argue that:

1   centralized planning structures are characterised by hierarchical authority relationships and a concentration of authority whereas decentralised planning structures disperse decision-making authority among smaller organisational units with autonomy of function.
2   information has three relevant characteristics: distribution, communicability and technicality.
3   health planners need three types of information: expert technical information (positive); information regarding health care needs, values and preferences among the population (normative) and information regarding external circumstances affecting the health sector.

Table 25.1 summarises their main arguments with regard to the types of information; and the characteristics of information.

The authors conclude that since most of the information requirements are either dispersed or readily communicable, decentralised structures have informational advantages. A major advantage of decentralised structures is their management of the 'tacit' component of the circumstances affecting the delivery of care. Examples are the local political dimensions of the implementation of an intervention, and even the personalities of those who will be relied upon to play key roles in implementation. Such factors as these are difficult to communicate between one local authority and the centre, and impossible for the centre to process and take into account across many local authorities.

However, Hurley *et al.* pay much less attention to the centralised distribution of technical skills to interpret information. They rather assume this constraint can be managed by increased training and dispersion of those with relevant skills. In low-income countries difficulties in decentralising the skills base have been encountered, for example Tang and Bloom (2000) suggest that the devolution of finance and manage-

Table 25.1 Summary of main arguments regarding information and decentralisation from Hurley *et al.* (1995)

Criterion	Distribution	Communicability	Technicality
Effectiveness of interventions	Concentrated	Accessible to experts	Technical, and skills of interpretation also concentrated
Needs, values and preferences	Widely dispersed	Quantitative needs data can be summarised and meaningfully transmitted. Value data more difficult but Oregon represents example of attempt	Some quite technical (e.g. relationship between morbidity patterns and capacity to benefit); much quite accessible
Circumstances affecting the delivery of care	Dispersed	Much readily transmissible, important components tacit	Mix of technical and less technical elements

ment of basic health services to rural townships in China was too rapid to allow the development of the relevant technical skills. This suggests that a balance between the advantages of ability to use local tacit information and loss of skilled technical input to the planning process is what is being negotiated in decentralisation policy. Nevertheless, such a concentration of technical skills may provide less of an advantage to centralised structures if technical solutions are highly dependent on local circumstances, or on local needs, values and preferences. Problems in the generalisability of technical analysis suggest that the decisions of technically unskilled local administrators may not be inferior to those of technically skilled central experts who are not able to take account of local circumstances.

25.4 Conclusion

There are no recipes for health system structure that will guarantee cost containment, universal access to high quality care, efficiency or equity. The variety of health systems that exist in the world, and the range of reforms that have been introduced in recent decades are evidence of the multiplicity of strategies that different countries have put into place in the pursuit of these goals. The factors that cause health markets to fail, and most critically, the information problem result in health sector outcomes that are far from perfect everywhere.

So no general principles can obviate the need for skilled managers of purchasing and provision in any structure. Certain organisational features may make the job easier or more difficult but these features are likely to vary between contexts. The task of reforming the health sector is also a complex and skilled one. It requires a sound grasp of the principles expounded in this text, as well as inputs from other disciplines, and it requires the ability to apply all that to the specific characteristics of the setting in question.

Notes

1 The argument has to be weighed carefully from a social demand perspective. GPs are likely to sanction uses of their services which they consider medically justified, whereas a social justification which is not necessarily of low priority – the benefits of discussing an irresolvable problem, or valued reassurance – may have motivated the patient in seeking care. Nevertheless, this does not imply that all demands placed on GPs must necessarily be high-priority either. There is no gatekeeping prior to the GP visit, and the important rationing mechanism at this level is time (distance and waiting). This was not judged particularly effective in Chapter 21 at rationing provision towards high social demands.
2 Note that while the two features pooling and pre-payment are usually found together in a financing system in the form of insurance, they are both conceptually and practically separable. Reliance on extended family and friend networks to contribute financially to one member's care in the case of need is an example of pooling without prepayment, while medical savings schemes by which instead of tax, the population is encouraged or instructed to pay into an individual health care account to be used in the case of illness are examples of prepayment without pooling.

References

Abbott, T. A. and Crew, M. A. (1995) 'Lessons from public utility regulation for the economic regulation of health care markets: an overview', in T. A. Abbott III (ed.) *Health Care Policy and Regulation*, Boston MA: Kluwer.

Alchian, A. A. and Demsetz, H. (1972) 'Production, information costs, and economic organization', *American Economic Review* 6 (5): 777–95.

Aljunid, S. (1995) 'The role of private practitioners in a rural district of Malaysia and their interactions with public health services', Ph.D. thesis, University of London.

Allen, P., Croxson, B., Roberts, J. A., Archibald, K., Crawshaw, S. and Taylor, L. (2002) 'The use of contracts in the management of infectious disease-related risk in the NHS internal market', *Health Policy* 59 (3): 257–81.

Allsop, J. and Mulcahy, L. (1996) *Regulating Medical Work: Formal and Informal Controls*, Buckingham: Open University Press.

Anand, S. and Barnighausen, T. (2004) 'Human resources and health outcomes: cross-country econometric study', *Lancet* 364 (9445): 1603–9.

Ashton, T. and Press, D. (1997) 'Market concentration in secondary health services', *Health Economics* 6: 43–56.

Barber, J. A. and Thompson, S. G. (1998) 'Analysis and interpretation of cost data in randomised controlled trials: review of published studies', *British Medical Journal* 317: 1195–200.

Bartlett, W. (1996) 'The regulation of general practice in the UK', *International Journal of Health Planning and Management* 11: 3–18.

Baumol, W. J. (1995) *Health Care as a Handicraft Industry*, London: Office of Health Economics.

Baumol, W. J., Panzar, J. C. and Willig, R. D. (1982) *Contestable Markets and the Theory of Industry Structure*, New York: Harcourt Brace.

Beck, R. G. and Horne, J. M. (1980) 'Utilization of publicly insured health services in Saskatchewan before, during and after co-payment', *Medical Care* 1 (8): 787–806.

Becker, G. S. (1983) 'A theory of competition among pressure groups for political influence', *Quarterly Journal of Economics* 93: 371–400.

Bennett, S. (1991) *The Mystique of Markets: Public and Private Health Care in Developing Countries*, PHP Departmental Publication 4, London: London School of Hygiene and Tropical Medicine.

—— (1997) 'The nature of competition among private hospitals in Bangkok', in S. Bennett, B. McPake and A. Mills (eds) *Private Health Providers in Developing Countries: Serving the Public Interest?* London: Zed Press.

Bennett, S., Dakpallah, G., Garner, P., Gilson, L., Nittayaramphong, S., Zurita, B. and Zwi, A. (1994) 'Carrot and stick: state mechanisms to influence private provider behaviour', *Health Policy and Planning* (1): 1–13.

Bennett, S., McPake, B. and Mills, A. (eds) (1997) *Private Health Providers in Developing Countries: Serving the Public Interest?* London: Zed Press.

Berman, P., Nwuke, K., Rannan-Ehya, R. and Mwanza, A. (1995b) *Zambia: Non-governmental*

Health Care Provision: Data for Decision Making Project, Cambridge MA: Department of Population and International Health, Harvard School of Public Health.

Berman, P., Nwuke, K., Hanson, K., Kariuki, M., Mbugua, K., Ngugi, J., Omurwa, T. and Ong'ayo, S. (1995a) *Kenya: Non-governmental Health Care Provision: Data for Decision Making Project*, Cambridge MA: Department of Population and International Health, Harvard School of Public Health.

Bernheim, B. D. and Whinston, M. D. (1986) 'Common Agency', *Econometrica* 54 (4): 923–42.

Bhat, R. (1996) 'Regulating the private health care sector: the case of the Indian Consumer Protection Act', *Health Policy and Planning* 1 (3): 265–79.

—— (1999) 'Characteristics of private medical practice in India: a provider perspective', *Health Policy and Planning* 14, 1: 26-37.

Birch, S. (1988) 'Item of service remuneration in general practice in the UK: what can we learn from dentists?' *Family Practice* (4): 265–70.

Blendon, R. J., Leitman, R., Morrison, I. and Donelan, K. (1990) 'Satisfaction with health systems in ten nations', *Health Affairs* (Millwood) 9 (2): 185–92.

Blendon, R. J., Benson, J., Donelan, K., Leitman, R., Taylor, H., Koeck, C. and Gitterman, D. (1995) 'Who has the best health care system? A second look', *Health Affairs* (Millwood) 14 (4): 220–30.

Blendon, R. J., Schoen, C., Des Roches, C. M., Osborn, R., Kimberly L., Scoles, K. L. and Zapert, K. (2002) 'Inequities in health care: a five-country survey', *Health Affairs* 21 (3).

Bond, P. (1999) 'Globalization, pharmaceutical pricing, and South African health policy: managing confrontation with US firms and politicians', *International Journal of Health Services* 29 (4): 765–92.

Bossert, T., Kosen, S. *et al.* (1997) 'Hospital Autonomy in Indonesia', Data for Decision Making project, Boston MA: Harvard School of Public Health.

Bowden, A. (2001) 'Variation in health-related quality of life: a case study of an Akamba population', Ph.D. thesis, University of Manchester.

Bowling, A., Jacobson, B. and Southgate, L. (1993) 'Health service priorities: explorations in consultation of the public and health professionals on priority setting in an inner London health district', *Social Science and Medicine* 37 (7): 851–7.

Bradach, J. L. and Eccles, R. G. (1989) 'Price, authority and trust: from ideal types to plural forms', *Annual Review of Sociology* 15: 97–118.

Brazier, J. E., Harper, R., Thomas, K., Jones, N. and Underwood, T. (1998) 'Deriving a preference-based single index measure from the SF-36', *Journal of Clinical Epidemiology* 51 (11): 1115–29.

Briggs, A. H. (2001) 'A Bayesian approach to stochastic cost-effectiveness analysis', *International Journal of Technology Assessment in Health Care* 17 (1): 69–82.

Briggs, A. H. and Gray, A. M. (2000) 'Handling uncertainty in economic evaluations of health care interventions', *British Medical Journal* 319: 635–8.

Broyles, R. W., Brandt, E. N., Jr and Biard-Holmes, D. (1998) 'Networks and the fiscal performance of rural hospitals in Oklahoma: are they associated?' *Journal of Rural Health* 14 (4): 327–37.

Bryan, S., Williams, I. and McIver, S. (2006) 'Seeing the NICE side of cost-effectiveness analysis: a qualitative investigation of the use of CEA in NICE technology appraisals', *Health Economics*, 7 September (e-publication ahead of print, accessed 11 September 2006).

Busse, R. (1999) 'Priority setting and rationing in German health care', *Health Policy* 50: 71–90.

Busse, R., Saltman, R. B. and Dubois, H. F. W. (2004) 'Organization and financing of social health insurance systems: current status and recent policy developments', in Richard B. Saltman, Reinhard Busse and Josep Figueras (eds) *Social Health Insurance Systems in Western Europe*, Maidenhead: Open University Press.

Cairns, J. (1992) 'Discounting and health benefits: another perspective', *Health Economics* 1: 76–9.

Campbell, E. S. and Fournier, G. M. (1993) 'Certificate-of-need deregulation and indigent hospital care', *Health Politics, Policy and Law* 18 (4): 905–25.

Carr-Hill, R. A. (1991) 'Allocating resources to health care: is the QALY a technical solution to a political problem?' *International Journal of Health Services* 21 (3): 351–63.

Carrin, G. and James, C. (2004) *Reaching Universal Coverage via Social Health Insurance: Key Design Features in the Transition Period*, FER/EIP Discussion Paper No. 2, Geneva: World Health Organisation.

Castaño Yepes, R. (2007) 'Hospital Autonomization in Bogotá, Colombia: a transaction cost economic analysis', PhD thesis, London: London School of Hygiene and Tropical Medicine, University of London.

Chamchan, C. and Carrin, G. (2006) 'A macroeconomic view of cost containment: simulation experiments in Thailand', *Thammasat Economic Journal*, 24 (2), and at http://www.who.int/health_financing/countries/thaisim.pdf (accessed 9 August 2007).

Chambers, R. (1983) *Rural Development: Putting the Last First*, London: Longman.

Chollet, D. J. and Lewis, M. (1997) 'Private insurance: principles and practice', in *Innovations in Health Care Financing: Proceedings of a World Bank Conference*, 10–11 March, Washington DC: World Bank.

Chow, G. C. (1997) 'Challenges of China's economic system for economic theory', *American Economic Review* 87 (2): 321.

Claxton, K. P. and Sculpher, M. J. (2006) 'Using value of information analysis to prioritise health research: some lessons from recent UK experience', *Pharmacoeconomics* 24 (11): 1055–68.

Cleverly, W. O. (1992) 'Competitive strategy for successful hospital management', *Hospital and Health Services Administration* 37: 53–69.

Coase, R. H. (1937) 'The nature of the firm', *Economica* 4: 386–405.

Courty, P. and Marschke, G. (1997) 'Measuring government performance: lessons from a federal job-training program', *American Economic Review* 87 (2): 383.

Cowling, K. and Cubbin, J. (1971) 'Price, quality and advertising competition: an econometric investigation of the UK car market', *Economica* 38: 378–94.

Creese, A. L. (1991) 'User charges for health care: a review of the recent experience', *Health Policy and Planning* 6 (4): 309–19.

Creese, A. and Parker, D. (1994) *Cost Analysis in Primary Health Care: A Training Manual for Programme Managers*, Geneva: World Health Organisation.

Crémer, J., Estache, A. and Seabright, P. (1995) 'The decentralization of public services: lessons from the theory of the firm', in A. Estache (ed.) *Decentralizing Infrastructure: Advantages and Limitations*, World Bank Discussion Paper 290, Washington DC.: World Bank.

Cronin, E., Normand, C, Henthorn, J. S., Hickman, M. and Davies, S. C. (1998) 'Costing model for neonatal screening and diagnosis of haemoglobinopathies', *Archives of Disease in Childhood*, Fetal and Neonatal edition, 79 (3): F161–7.

Cullis, J. and West, P. (1979) *The Economics of Health: An Introduction*, Oxford: Martin Robertson (reprinted Aldershot: Gregg, 1991).

Culyer, A. J. (1976) *Need and the National Health Service*, Oxford: Martin Robertson.

—— (1989) 'The normative economics of health care finance and provision', *Oxford Review of Economic Policy* 5: 34–58.

Culyer, A. J. and Cullis, J. G. (1975) 'Hospital waiting lists and the supply and demand of in-patient care', *Social and Economic Administration* 9: 13–25.

Custer, W. S., Moser, J. W., Musacchio, R. A. and Willke, R. J. (1990) 'The production of health care services and changing hospital reimbursement: the role of hospital–medical staff relationships', *Journal of Health Economics* 9 (2): 167–92.

Dawson, D. (2000) 'Some Law and Economics of a NICE Rationing Problem', paper presented to Health Economists' Study Group, July.

Deininger, K., and Mpuga, P. (2004) 'Economic and Welfare Effects of the Abolition of Health User Fees: Evidence from Uganda', World Bank Policy Research Working Paper 3267, Washington DC: World Bank (http://papers.ssrn.com/sol3/papers.cfm?abstract_id=610321 (accessed 14 February 2007).

Demsetz, H. (1993) The theory of the firm revisited', in O. E. Williamson and S. G. Winter (eds) *The Nature of the Firm: Origins, Evolution and Development*, Oxford and New York: Oxford University Press.

Donaldson, C, Shackley, P., Abdalla, M. and Miedzybrodzka, Z. (1995) 'Willing to pay for antenatal carrier screening for cystic fibrosis', *Health Economics* 4: 439–52.

Dranove, D. (1988) Tricing by non-profit institutions: the case of hospital cost-shifting', *Journal of Health Economics* 7 (1): 47–57.

Drummond, M. F., Stoddart, G. L. and Torrance, G. W. (1997) *Methods for the Economic Evaluation of Health Care Programmes*, Oxford: Oxford University Press.

Drummond, M. F., Sculpher, M. J., Torrance, G. W., O'Brien, B. J. and Stoddart, G. L. (2005) *Methods for the Economic Evaluation of Health Care Programmes*, third edition, Oxford: Oxford University Press.

ECLAC (Economic Commission for Latin America and the Caribbean) (2006) The Right to Health and the Millennium Development goals, thirty-first session, Montevideo, Uruguay, 20–4 March.

Eid, F. (2004) 'Designing institutions and incentives in hospitals: an organization economics methodology', *Journal of Health Care Finance* 31, 2: 1–15.

Ellis, R. P. and McGuire, T. G. (1986) 'Provider behavior under prospective reimbursement: cost sharing and supply', *Journal of Health Economics* 5 (2): 129–51.

Enthoven, A. (1985) *Reflections on the Management of the NHS*, London: Nuffield Provincial Hospitals Trust.

European Values Survey (1999/2000) integrated data set, https://info1.za.gesis.org/cei (accessed 7 September 2006).

Feldstein, M. S. (1967) *Economic Analysis for Health Service Efficiency: Econometric Studies of the British National Health Service*, Contributions to Economic Analysis 51, Amsterdam: North Holland.

—— (1968) 'Applying economic concepts to hospital care', *Hospital Administration* 13: 68–9.

Figueras, J., Saltman, R. B., Busse, R. and Dubois, H. F.W. (2004) 'Patterns and performance in social health insurance systems', in Richard B. Saltman, Reinhard Busse and Josep Figueras (eds) *Social Health Insurance Systems in Western Europe*, Maidenhead: Open University Press.

Folland, S., Goodman, A. C. and Stano, M. (1993) *The Economics of Health and Health Care*, Basingstoke: Macmillan.

—— (1997) *The Economics of Health and Health Care*, second edition, Englewood Cliffs NJ: Prentice-Hall.

Fox-Rushby, J., for the Kenqol Group (2000) 'Operationalising conceptions of "health" amongst the Wakamba and Maragoli of Kenya: the basis of the Kenqol instrument', *Quality of Life Research* 9 (3): 316.

Franks, P. and Fiscella, K. (1998) 'Primary care physicians and specialists as personal physicians: health care expenditure and mortality experience', *Journal of Family Practice* 47 (2): 103–4.

Frant, H. (1996) 'High-powered and low-powered incentives in the public sector', *Journal of Public Administration Research and Theory* 6 (3): 365–81.

Friedman, M. (1953) 'The methodology of positive economies', in *Essays in Positive Economics*, Chicago: University of Chicago Press.

Gafni, A. and Birch, S. (1997) QALYs and HYEs: spotting the differences', *Journal of Health Economics* 16: 601–8.

Gani, A. (1996) 'Improving quality in public sector hospitals in Indonesia', *International Journal of Health Planning and Management* 11 (3): 275–96.

Gauri, V., Cercone, J. and Briceño, R (2004) 'Separating financing from provision: evidence from ten years of partnership with health cooperatives in Costa Rica', *Health Policy and Planning* 19 (5): 292–301.

Gertler, P., Locay, L. and Sanderson, W. (1987) 'Are user fees regressive? The welfare implications of health care financing proposals in Peru', *Journal of Econometrics* 36: 67–88.

Gold, M. R., Seigel, J. E., Russell, L. B. and Weinstein, M. C. (1996) *Cost-effectiveness in Health and Medicine*, New York: Oxford University Press.

Gray, A. M., Marshall, M., Lockwood, A. and Morris, J. (1997) 'Problems in conducting economic evaluations alongside clinical trials', *British Journal of Psychiatry* 170: 47–52.

Grieve, R., Nixon, R., Thompson. S. and Normand, C. (2005) 'Using multilevel models for assessing the variability of multinational resource use and cost data', *Health Economics* 14 (2): 185–96.

Grindle, M. S. and Hilderbrand, M. E. (1995) 'Building sustainable capacity in the public sector: what can be done?' *Public Administration Development* 15 (5): 441–63.

Grossman, M. (1972a) *The Demand for Health: A Theoretical and Empirical Investigation*, Occasional Paper 119, New York: National Bureau of Economic Research.

—— (1972b) 'On the concept of health capital and the demand for health', *Journal of Political Economy* 80 (2): 223-55

Grytten, J., Carlsen, F. and Skau, I. (2001) 'The income effect and supplier-induced demand': evidence from primary physician services in Norway', *Applied Economics* 33: 1455–467.

Gudex, C, Williams, A., Jourdan, M., Mason, R., Maynard, J., O'Flynn, R. and Rendall, M. (1990) 'Prioritising waiting lists', *Health Trends* 22 (3): 103–8.

Gwatkin, Davidson R., Shea, Rutstein, Kiersten Johnson, Eldaw Abdalla Suliman, Wagstaff, Adam and Amouzou, Agbessi (forthcoming), *Socioeconomic Differences in Health, Nutrition, and Population*, second edition, Washington DC: World Bank.

Hackey, S. (1993a) 'Regulatory regimes and state cost containment programs: commentary', *Journal of Health Politics, Policy and Law* 18 (2): 491–502.

Ham, C. (1997) *Management and Competition in the NHS*, Abingdon: Ratcliffe Medical Press.

Harris, J. (1977) 'The internal organization of hospitals: some economic implications', *Bell Journal of Economics and Management Science* 8: 467–82.

Hart, O. (1995) *Firms, Contracts and Financial Structure*, Oxford: Oxford University Press.

Heckman, J., Heinrich, C. and Smith, J. (1997) 'Assessing the performance of performance standards in public bureaucracies', *American Economic Review* 87 (2): 389.

Hodgkin, D. and McGuire, T. G. (1994) 'Payment levels and hospital response to prospective payment', *Journal of Health Economics* 13 (1): 1–29. (Review.)

Hodgson, G. (1988) *Economics and Institutions*, Cambridge: Polity Press.

Holahan, J. and Cook, A. (2006) 'Why did the number of uninsured continue to increase in 2005?' Kaiser Commission on Medicaid and the Uninsured, Henry J. Kaiser Family Foundation, at http://www.kff.org/uninsured/upload/7571.pdf (accessed 16 February 2007).

Holmstrom, B. (1989) 'Agency costs and innovation', *Journal of Economic Behaviour and Organisation* 12 (3): 305.

Holmstrom, B. and Milgrom, P. (1990) 'Multitask principal-agent analyses: incentive contracts, asset ownership, and job design', *Journal of Law, Economics and Organization* 7 (special issue: papers from conference on the New Science of Organization, January): 24–52.

Hongoro, C. (2001) 'Costs and quality of services in public hospitals in Zimbabwe: implications for hospital reform', Ph.D. thesis, University of London.

Hongoro, C. and Musonza, T. G. (1995) 'Analysis of the referral system in Zimbabwe's health care system, Harare: Blair Research Institute'. (Unpublished.)

Hornbrook, M. C. and Goldfarb, M. G. (1983) 'A partial test of a hospital behavioral model', *Social Science and Medicine* 17 (10): 667–80.

Huang, P. (1995) 'An overview of hospital accreditation in Taiwan, Republic of China', *International Journal of Health Planning and Management* 10 (3): 183–92.

Hughes, D. (1993) 'General practitioners and the new contract: promoting better health through financial incentives', *Health Policy* 25: 39.

Hurley, J. (1998) 'Welfarism, extra-welfarism and evaluative economic analysis in the health sector', in M. L. Barer, T. E. Getzen and G. L. Stoddart (eds) *Health, Health Care and Health Economics: Perspectives on Distribution*, Chichester: Wiley.

Hurley, J., Birch, S., and Eyles, J. (1995) 'Geographically-decentralized planning and management in health care: some informational issues and their implications for efficiency', *Social Science and Medicine* 41 (1): 3–11.

IADB (1996) *Economic and Social Progress in Latin America, 1996. Report: Making Social Services Work*, Baltimore MD: Johns Hopkins University Press.

Iverson, T. (1993) 'A theory of hospital waiting lists', *Journal of Health Economics* 12: 55–71.

James, Chris D., Hanson, Kara, McPake, Barbara, Balabanova, Dina, Gwatkin, Davidson, Hopwood, Ian, Kirunga, Christina, Knippenberg, Rudolph, Meessen, Bruno, Morris, Saul S., Preker, Alexander, Souteyrand, Yves, Tibouti, Abdelmajid, Villeneuve, Pascal, Xu, Ke (2006) 'To retain or remove user fees? Reflections on the current debate in low- and middle-income countries', *Applied Heath Economics & Health Policy* 5 (3):137–153.

Jeong, H. S. (2005) 'Health care reform and change in public–private mix of financing: a Korean case', *Health Policy* 74 (2): 133–45 (e-publication 25 January 2005).

Jeppson, A. (2001) 'Financial priorities under decentralisation in Uganda', *Health Policy and Planning* 16 (2): 187–92.

Joseph, H. (1975) 'On economic theories of hospital behaviour', *Journal of Economics and Business* 27: 69–74.

Kamke, K. (1998) 'The German health care system and health care reform', *Health Policy* 43 (2): 171–94.

Kamwanga, J., Hanson, K., McPake, B. and Mungule, O. (1999) *Autonomous Hospitals in Zambia and the Equity Implications of the Market for Hospital Services*, Phase 1 report, *A description of the current state of hospital autonomy policy*, London: London School of Hygiene and Tropical Medicine. (Unpublished.)

Keeler, E. B., Melnick, G. and Zwanziger, J. (1999) 'The changing effects of competition on nonprofit and for-profit hospital pricing behavior', *Journal of Health Economics* 18: 69–86.

Keene, J., Light, D. *et al.* (2001) *Public–Private Relations in Health Care*, London: King's Fund.

Kirunga-Tashobya, C., Ssengooba, F. and Oliveira-Cruz, V. (2006) *Health Systems Reforms in Uganda: Processes and Outputs*, Kampala: Institute of Public Health, Makerere University, and London: London School of Hygiene and Tropical Medicine.

Knapp, M. (1984) *The Economics of Social Care*, Basingstoke: Macmillan.

Kreps, D. M. (1997) 'Intrinsic motivation and extrinsic incentives', *American Economic Review* 87(2): 359.

Kumaranayake, L. (1997) 'The role of regulation: influencing private sector activity within health sector reform', *Journal of International Development* 9 (4): 641.

Kumaranayake, L., Lake, S., Mujinja, P., Hongoro, C. and Mpembeni, R. (2000) 'How do countries regulate the health sector? Evidence from Tanzania and Zimbabwe', *Health Policy and Planning* 15 (4): 357–67.

Kwon, S. and Reich, M. R. (2005) 'The changing process and politics of health policy in Korea', *Journal of Health Politics, Policy and Law* 30 (6): 1003–25.

Laegrid, P., Opedal, S. and Stigen, I. M. (2005) 'The Norwegian hospital reform: balancing political control and enterprise autonomy', *Journal of Health Politics, Policy and Law*, 30 (6): 1027–64.

Laffont, J-J. and Tirole, J. (1993) *A Theory of Incentives in Procurement and Regulation*, Cambridge MA: MIT Press.

Lancaster, K. J. (1966) 'A new approach to consumer theory', *Journal of Political Economy* 74: 159–74.

Lancet, The (2006) 'Caesarean section: the paradox' (comment), *The Lancet* 368, 9546: 1472–3.

Lancry, P. J. and Sandier, S. (1999) 'Rationing health care in France', *Health Policy* 50: 23–38.

Langham, S., Soljak, M., Keogh, B., Gill, M., Thorogood, M. and Normand, C. (1997) 'The cardiac waiting game: are patients prioritised on the basis of clinical need?' *Health Services Management Research* 10 (4): 216–24.

Lee, L. (1971) 'Conspicuous production theory of hospital behaviour', *Southern Economics Journal* 38: 48–58.

Leffler, K. B. (1978) 'Physician licensure: competition and monopoly in American medicine', *Journal of Law and Economics* 21 (1): 165–8.

Le Grand, J. (2002) 'How to Save the NHS – again', presentation at launch conference, LSE Health and Social Care, http://www.lse.ac.uk/collections/LSEHealthAndSocialCare/pdf/ eventsAndSeminars/julianLegrandPresentation.pdf#search=%22Julian-Le-Grand%20hy- pothecate%20health%22 (accessed 12 September 2006).

Le Grand, J., Mays, N. and Mulligan, J. (1998) *Learning from the NHS Internal Market: a Review of the Evidence*, London: King's Fund.

Leibenstein, H. (1966) 'Allocative efficiency versus X-efficiency', *American Economic Review* 56: 397–409.

Leonard, K. (2000) 'Incentives and rural health care delivery, Cameroon', in D. K. Leonard (ed.) *Africa's Changing Markets for Health and Veterinary Services: The New Institutional Issues*, London: Macmillan.

Lin, B. Y. and Wan, T. T. (1999) 'Analysis of integrated health care networks' performance: a contingency–strategic management perspective', *Journal of Medical Systems* 23 (6): 467–85.

Lindbeck, A. (1997) 'Incentives and social norms in household behaviour', *American Economic Review* 87 (2): 370.

Liss, G. (1995) 'Comment', in T. A. Abbott III (ed.) *Health Care Policy and Regulation*, Boston MA: Kluwer.

Lowy, A., Kohler, B. and Nicholl, J. (1994) 'Attendance at Accident and Emergency departments: unnecessary or inappropriate?' *Journal of Public Health Medicine* 16 (2): 134–40.

Lu, J. F., Leung, G. M., Kwon, S., Tin, K. Y., Van Doorslaer, E. and O'Donnell, O. (2007) 'Horizontal equity in health care utilization evidence from three high-income Asian econ- omies', *Social Science and Medicine* 64 (1): 199–212.

Lynk, W. J. (1995) 'Nonprofit hospital mergers and the exercise of market power', *Journal of Law and Economics* 38: 437–61.

Maceira, Daniel (1996) *Fragmentación e incentivos en los sistemas de atención en salud en América Latina y el Caribe*, Washington DC: International Development Bank.

McGuire, A. (1985) 'The theory of the hospital: a review of the models', *Social Science and Medicine* 20 (11): 1177–84.

McGuire, A., Henderson, J. and Mooney, G. (1988) *The Economics of Health Care: An Introduc- tory Text*, London: Routledge.

McIntyre, D. E., Bourne, D. E., Klopper, J. M. L., Taylor, S. P. and Pick, W. M. (1991) 'A methodology for resource allocation in health care for South Africa', *South African Medical Journal* 80: 139–45.

Mackintosh, M. (1997) 'Informal regulation: a conceptual framework and application to decentralised mixed finance in health care', Conference on Public Sector Management for the next Century, Manchester: Institute of Development Policy and Management, 29 June–2 July.

Macneil, I. R. (1978) 'Contracts: adjustments of long-term economic relations under classi- cal, neoclassical and relational contract law', *Northwestern University Law Review* 72: 854–906.

McPake, B. (1993) 'User charges for health services in developing countries: a review of the economic literature', *Social Science and Medicine* 36 (11): 1397–405.

McPake, B., Hanson, K. and Adam, C. (2007) 'Two-tier charging strategies in public hospitals: implications for intra-hospital resource allocation and equity of access to hospital services', *Journal of Health Economics* (forthcoming).

McPake, B., Nakamba, P. *et al.* (2004) 'Private wards in public hospitals: two-tier charging and the allocation of resources in tertiary hospitals in Zambia', London School of Hygiene and

Tropical Medicine, http://www.hefp.lshtm.ac.uk/publications/downloads/working_papers/05_04.pdf.

Marmor, T. R. (1999) 'The rage for reform: sense and nonsense in health policy', in D. Daniel and T. Sullivan (eds) *Market Limits in Health Reform*, London: Routledge.

Marshall, A. (1920) *Principles of Economics*, eighth edition, London: Macmillan. Reprinted Palgrave, 1960.

Masseria, C. and van Doorslaer, E. (2004) *Income-related Inequality in the Use of Medical Care in Twenty-one OECD Countries*, OECD Health Working Papers 14, Paris: OECD, doi:10.1787/687501760705.

Matthew, G. K. (1971) 'Measuring need and evaluating services', in G. McLachlan (ed.) *Portfolio for Health*, London: Oxford University Press.

Maynard, A. and Bloor, K. (1995) 'Health care reform: informing difficult choices', *International Journal of Health Planning and Management* 10: 247–64.

Maynard, A. and Street, A. (2006) 'Seven years of feast, seven years of famine: boom to bust in the NHS?' *British Medical Journal* 332: 906–8 (accessed at www/bmj.com, 11 September 2006).

Mays, N. (1995) 'Geographical resource allocation in the English National Health Service, 1971–94: the tension between normative and empirical approaches', *International Journal of Epidemiology* 24 (930), supplement 1: S96–102.

Meiland, F. J., Danse, J. A., Hoos, A. M., Wendte, J. F. and Gunning-Schepers, L. J. (1996) 'The use of the waiting list in a fair selection of patients for nursing home care', *Health Policy* 38 (1): 1–11.

Meltzer, D. and Chung, J. (2002) 'Effects of competition under prospective payment on hospital costs among high-cost and low-cost admissions: evidence from California, 1983 and 1993', *Forum for Health Economics and Policy* 5 (Frontiers in Health Policy Research) 4, http://www.bepress.com/fhep/5/4.

Milgrom, P. and Roberts, J. (1992) *Economics, Organization and Management*, London: Prentice-Hall.

Ministry of Health, Peru (1997a) *Analisis de la demanda por servicios de salud*, Seminario 'Modernization del sistema de financiamiento de salud', Lima: Ministerio de Salud.

—— (1997b) *Analisis del financiamiento del sector salud*, Seminario 'Modernization del sistema de financiamiento de salud', Lima: Ministerio de Salud.

Mooney, G. H. (1983) 'Equity in health care: confronting the confusion', *Effective Health Care* 1 (4): 179–85.

—— (1994) *Key Issues in Health Economics*, Hemel Hempstead: Harvester Wheatsheaf.

Moran, M. and Wood, B. (1993) *States, Regulation and the Medical Profession*, Buckingham: Open University Press.

Morrison, G. C. (1997) 'HYE and TTO: what is the difference?' *Journal of Health Economics* 16: 563–78.

Moses, S., Manji, F., Bradley, J. E., Nagelkerke, N. J. D., Malisa, M. A. and Plummer, F. A. (1992) 'Impact of user fees on attendance at a referral centre for sexually transmitted diseases in Kenya', *Lancet* 340: 463–6.

Mossialos, E. (1998) *Citizens and Health Systems: Main Results from a Eurobarometer Survey*, Brussels: European Commission Directorate General of Health and Consumer Protection.

Mullen, P. M. (1985) 'Performance indicators: is anything new?' *Hospital and Health Service Review* 81 (4): 165–7.

Murray, C. J. (1994) 'Quantifying the burden of disease: the technical basis for disability-adjusted life years', *Bulletin of the World Health Organization* 72 (3): 429–45.

Murray, C. J. L. and Acharya, A. K. (1997) 'Understanding DALYs', *Journal of Health Economics* 16 (6): 703–30.

Musgrove, P. (1986) 'Measurement of equity in health', *World Health Statistics Quarterly* 39: 325–35.

Muurinen, J. M. (1986) 'Modelling non-profit firms in medicine', in A. Culyer and B. Jonsson (eds) *Public and Private Health Services: Complementarities and Conflicts*, Oxford: Blackwell.

Nalbantian, H. R. and Schotter, A. (1997) 'Productivity under group incentives: an experimental study', *American Economic Review* 87 (3): 314.

Nandakumar, A. K., Bhawalkar, M., Tien, M., Ramos, R. and Susna, D. (2004) Synthesis of findings from NHA studies in twenty-six countries, July, PHRplus, Abt Associates, Bethesda MD, at http://www.phrplus.org/Pubs/Tech046_fin.pdf (accessed 16 February 2007).

Naylor, C. D. (1988) 'Private medicine and the privatisation of health care in South Africa', *Social Science and Medicine* 27 (11): 1153–70.

Neumann, J. von and Morgenstern, O. (1947) *The Theory of Games and Economic Behavior*, second edition, Princeton NJ: Princeton University Press.

Newhouse, J. (1970) 'Theory of non-profit institutions: an economic model of a hospital', *American Economic Review* 60: 64–74.

—— (1993) *Free for all? Lessons from the RAND Health Insurance Experiment*, Cambridge MA: Harvard University Press.

Ng, Y. K. (1983) *Welfare Economics: Introduction and Development of Basic Concepts*, Basingstoke: Macmillan.

Ngalande-Banda, E. and Walt, G. (1995) 'The private health sector in Malawi: opening Pandora's box?' *Journal of International Development* 7 (3): 403–22.

Normand, C. and Busse, R. (2001) 'Social health insurance financing', in E. Mossialos, A. Dixon, J. Figueras and J. Kutzin (eds) *Funding Health Care: Options for Europe*, Buckingham: Open University Press.

Norton, E. C. (1992) 'Incentive regulation of nursing homes', *Journal of Health Economics* 11: 105.

OECD (1992) *The Reform of Health Care: a Comparative Analysis of Seven OECD Countries*, Health Policy Studies 2, Paris: Organisation for Economic Co-operation and Development.

—— (1994) *The Reform of Health Systems: A Review of Seventeen OECD Countries*, Health Policy Studies 5, Paris: Organisation for Economic Co-operation and Development.

Ogus, A. (1994) *Regulation: Legal Form and Economic Theory*, Oxford: Clarendon Press.

O'Hagan, A. and Stevens, J. W. (2002) 'The probability of cost-effectiveness', *BMC Medical Research Methodology* 2: 5.

Olsen, J. A., Donaldson, C. and Shackley, P. (2005) 'Euro will group implicit versus explicit ranking: on inferring ordinal preferences for health care programmes based on differences in willingness-to-pay', *Journal of Health Economics* 24 (5): 990–6.

O'Neill, C, Malek, M., Mugford, M., Normand, C, Tarnow-Mordi, W., Hey, E. and Halliday, H. (ECSURF Study Group) (2000) 'A cost analysis of neonatal care in the UK: results from a multi-centre study', *Journal of Public Health Medicine* 22 (1): 108–15.

Pannarunothai, S. and Mills, A. (1997) 'Characteristics of public and private health-care providers in a Thai urban setting', in S. Bennett, B. McPake and A. Mills (eds) *Private Health Providers in Developing Countries: Serving the Public Interest?* London: Zed Press.

Parsonage, M. and Neuberger, H. (1992) 'Discounting and health benefits', *Health Economics* 1 (1): 71–9.

Paul, C. (1984) 'Physician licensure and the quality of medical care', *Atlantic Economic Journal* 12: 18–30.

Pauly, M. and Redisch, M. (1973) 'The not-for-profit hospital as a physicians' cooperative', *American Economic Review* 63: 87–100.

Pauly, M. V. and Satterthwaite, M. A. (1981) 'The pricing of primary care physicians' services: a test of the role of consumer information', *Bell Journal of Economics and Management Science* 12 (2): 488–506.

Peltzman, S. (1976) 'Toward a more general theory of regulation', *Journal of Law and Economics* 19: 211–40.

Posner, R. A. (1974) 'Theories of economic regulation', *Bell Journal of Economics and Management Science* 5 (2): 335–58.

Propper, C. (1993) 'Quasi-markets, contracts, and quality in health and social care: the US experience', in J. Le Grand and W. Bartlett (eds) *Quasi-markets and Social Policy*, Basingstoke: Macmillan.

—— (1995) 'Agency and incentives in the NHS internal market', *Social Science and Medicine* 40 (1): 1683–90.

Propper, C. and Bartlett, W. (1997) 'The impact of competition on the behaviour of NHS trusts', in R. Flynn and G. Williams (eds) *Contracting for Health: Quasi-markets and the National Health Service*, Oxford: Oxford University Press.

Pouillier, J. P., Hernandez, P., Kawabata, K. and Savedoff, W. D. (2002) *Patterns of Global Health Expenditures: Results for 191 Countries*, EIP/HFS/FAR Discussion Paper 51, World Health Organisation, Geneva, November, at http://www.who.int/healthinfo/paper51.pdf (accessed 16 February 2007).

Quirk, J. and Saposnik, R. (1968) *Introduction to General Equilibrium Theory and Welfare Economics*, New York: McGraw-Hill.

Rawls, John (1971) *A Theory of Justice*, Cambridge MA: Belknap Press of Harvard University Press.

Reder, M. (1965) 'Some problems in the economics of hospitals', *American Economic Review* 55: 472–80.

Reich, M.R. (1995) 'The politics of health sector reform in developing countries: three cases of pharmaceutical policy', in P. Berman (ed.) *Health Sector Reform in Developing Countries*, Boston MA: Harvard School of Public Health.

Reinhardt, U. (1978) 'Comment on competition and physicians by F.A. Sloan and R. Feldman', in W. Greenberg (ed.) *Competition in the Health Care Sector: Proceedings of a Conference Sponsored by the Bureau of Economics, Federal Trade Commission*, Germantown MD: Aspen Systems.

Rhoades, J. A. and Cohen, S. N. (2006) 'The long-term uninsured in America, 2001–2004: estimates for the US population under age 65', Medical Expenditure Panel Survey, Agency for Healthcare Research and Quality, Statistical Brief 136, at http://www.meps.ahrq.gov/mepsweb/data_files/publications/st136/stat136.pdf (accessed 16 February 2006).

Roberts, J.A. (1993) 'Managing markets', *Journal of Public Health Medicine* 14 (4): 305–10.

Robinson, R. and Dixon, A. (1999) 'Health care systems in transition: the United Kingdom', World Health Organisation, Europe, http://www.who.dk/InformationSources/Evidence/20011015_2 (accessed 6 September 2006).

Rochaix, L. and Wilsford, D. (2005) 'State autonomy, policy paralysis: paradoxes of institutions and culture in the French health care system', *Journal of Health Politics, Policy and Law* 30 (1–2): 97–119.

Roemer, M. I. (1961) 'Bed supply and hospital utilization: a natural experiment', *Hospitals* Nov 1 (35): 36–42.

—— (1993) *National Health Systems of the World, II*, Oxford: Oxford University Press.

Rogowski, J. (1998) 'Cost-effectiveness of care for very low birth weight infants', *Pediatrics* 102 (2): 35–43.

Rokosová, M. and Háva, P. (2005) 'Health care systems in transition: the Czech Republic, World Health Organisation, Europe, http://www.who.dk/InformationSources/Evidence/20011015_2 (accessed 6 September 2006).

Rosenbaum, S., Markus, A. and Sonosky, C. (2004) 'Public health insurance design for children: the evolution from Medicaid to SCHIP', *Journal of Health and Biomedical Law* 1: 1–47.

Rosenblatt, R. A., Hart, L. G., Baldwin, L. M., Chan, L. and Scheweiss, R. (1998) 'The generalist role of specialty physicians: is there a hidden system of primary care?' *Journal of the American Medical Association* 279 (19): 1364–70.

Rosko, M. D. and Proenca J. (2005) 'Impact of network and system use on hospital X-inefficiency', *Health Care Management Review* 30 (1): 69–79.

Ryan, M., Netten, A., Skatun, D. and Smith, P. (2006) 'Using discrete choice experiments to estimate a preference-based measure of outcome – an application to social care for older people', *Journal of Health Economics* 25 (5): 927–44.

Samuelson, P. (1938) 'A note on the pure theory of consumers' behaviour', *Econometrica* 5: 61–71.

Scitovsky, T. (1941) 'A note on welfare propositions in economics', *Review of Economic Studies* 9: 77–88.

Scrivens, E. E., Klein, R. and Steiner, A. (1995) 'Accreditation: what can we learn from the Anglophone model?' *Health Policy* 34 (3): 193–204.

Sen, A. (1979) 'Personal utilities and public judgements, or what's wrong with welfare economics?' *Economic Journal* 89: 537–58.

Sepehri, A., Chernomas, R. and Akram-Lodhi, H. (2005) 'Penalizing patients and rewarding providers: user charges and health care utilization in Vietnam', *Health Policy and Planning* 20 (2): 90–9.

Sheldon, T., Davey-Smith, G. and Bevan, G. (1993) 'Weighting in the dark: resource allocation in the new NHS', *British Medical Journal* 306: 835–9.

Sheldon, T. A., Cullum, N., Dawson, D., Lankshear, A., Lowson, K., Watt, I., West, P., Wright, D. and Wright, J. (2004) 'What's the evidence that NICE guidance has been implemented? Results from a national evaluation using time series analysis, audit of patients' notes, and interviews', *British Medical Journal*, 329: 999–1004.

Simon, H. (1957) *Models of Man, Social and Rational: Mathematical Essays on Rational Human Behavior in a Social Setting*, London: Wiley.

Söderlund, N. and Hansl, B. (2000) 'Health insurance in South Africa: an empirical analysis of trends in risk pooling and efficiency following deregulation', *Health Policy and Planning* 15 (4): 378–85.

Ssengooba, F., Atuyambe, L., McPake, B., Hanson, K. and Okuonzi, S. (2002) 'What could be achieved with greater public hospital autonomy? Comparison of public and PNFP hospitals in Uganda', *Public Administration and Development* 22: 415–28.

Stebbins, K. R. (1991) 'Tobacco, politics and economics: implications for global health', *Social Science and Medicine* 33 (12): 1317–26.

Stepan, A. and Sommersguter-Reichmann, M. (1999) 'Priority setting in Austria', *Health Policy* 50: 91–104.

Stewart, F. (1975) 'A note on social cost–benefit analysis and class conflict in LDCs', *World Development* 3 (1): 31–45.

Street, A. and Duckett, S. (1996) 'Are waiting lists inevitable?' *Health Policy* 36 (1): 1–15.

Strong, N. and Waterson, M. (1987) 'Agents and information', in R. Clarke and T. McGuiness (eds) *Economics of the Firm*, Oxford: Blackwell.

Strong, P. and Robinson, J. (1990) *The NHS-Under New Management,* Buckingham: Open University Press.

Suarez, R., Henderson, P., Barillas, E. and Vieira, C. (1994) *Gasto national y financiamiento del sector de la salud en America Latina y el Caribe: desafios para la decada de los noventa*, Serie informes tecnicos 30, Proyecto de Economia y Financiamiento de la Salud, Washington DC: Organisation Panamericana de la Salud.

Tang, S. and Bloom, G. (2000) 'Decentralising rural health services: a case study in China', *International Journal of Health Planning and Management* 15 (3): 189–200.

Tangcharoensathien, V., Nitayarumphong, S. and Khongsawatt, S. (1997) 'Private sector involvement in public hospitals: case studies in Bangkok', in S. Bennett, B. McPake and A. Mills (eds) *Private Health Providers in Developing Countries: serving the Public Interest?* London: Zed Press.

Terence Higgins Trust (2007) *Disturbing Symptoms 5, How Primary Care Trusts Managed Sexual Health and HIV in 2006 and how Specialist Clinicians viewed their Progress: A Research Report*, London: Terrence Higgins Trust, http://www.tht.org.uk/informationresources/publications/policyreports/disturbingsymptoms5.pdf (accessed 16 February 2007).

Thompson, S. G., Nixon, R. M. and Grieve, R. (2006) 'Addressing the issues that arise in analysing multicentre cost data, with application to a multinational study', *Journal of Health Economics*

Todaro, M. P. (1989) *Economic Development in the Third World*, fourth edition, Harlow: Longman.

Townsend, J. (1987) 'Cigarette tax, economic welfare and social class patterns of smoking', *Applied Economics* 19: 355–65.

Towse, A., and Pritchard, C. (2002) National Institute for Clinical Excellence (NICE): is economic appraisal working? *Pharmacoeconomics*, 20 suppl. 3: 95–105.

Trigg, A. B. and Bosanquet, N. (1992) 'Tax harmonisation and the reduction of European smoking rates', *Journal of Health Economics* 11: 329–46.

Turquet, P. (2004) 'A stronger role for the private sector in France's health insurance?' *International Social Security Review* 57 (4): 67–89.

UN Development Programme (1999) *Human Development Report, 1999: Globalization with a Human Face*, New York: United Nations Development Programme.

Valdmanis, V. G. (1990) 'Ownership and technical efficiency of hospitals', *Medical Care* 28 (6): 552–61.

van den Heever, A. (1997) 'Regulating the funding of private health care: the South African experience', in S. Bennett, B. McPake and A. Mills (eds) *Private Health Providers in Developing Countries: Serving the Public Interest?* London: Zed Press.

Van Doorslaer, E. and Masseria, C. (OECD Health Equity Research Group) (2004) 'Income-related inequality in the use of medical care in twenty-one OECD countries', in *Towards High-performing Health Systems: Policy Studies*. Paris: Organisation for Eeconomic Co-operation and Development.

Villar, J., Valladares, E. *et al.* (2006) 'Caesarean delivery rates and pregnancy outcomes: the 2005 global survey on maternal and perinatal health in Latin America', *The Lancet* 367: 1819-29.

Vitaliano, D. F. and Toren, M. (1994) 'Cost and efficiency in nursing homes: a stochastic frontier approach', *Journal of Health Economics* 13: 281–300.

Ware, J. E. and Sherbourne, C. D. (1992) 'The SF-36 short-form health status survey' I, 'Conceptual framework and item selection', *Medical Care* 30: 473–83.

Wennberg, J. E. and Gittelsohn, A. (1973) 'Small area variations in health care delivery: a population-based health information system can guide planning and regulatory decision making', *Science 1S2: 1102–1.*

—— (1982) 'Professional uncertainty and the problem of supplier-induced demand', *Social Science and Medicine* 16 (7): 811–24.

West, P. A. (1997) *Understanding the NHS Reforms: The Creation of Incentives?* Buckingham: Open University Press.

Wilensky, G. R. and Rossiter, L. F. (1983) 'The relative importance of physician-induced demand in the demand for medical care', *Millbank Memorial Fund Quarterly* 61 (2): 252–77.

Wilkin, D., Metcalfe, D. H. and Marinker, M. (1989) 'The meaning of information on GP referral rates to hospitals', *Community Medicine* 11 (1): 65–70.

Willan, A. R. and Briggs, A. H. (2006) *Statistical Analysis of Cost–Effectiveness Data*, Chichester: Wiley.

Williams, A. (1991) 'Allocating resources to health care: is the QALY a technical solution to a political problem? Of course not', *International Journal of Health Services* 21 (3): 365–9.

Williams, B. J. and Nicholl, J. P. (1994) 'Patient characteristics and clinical caseload of short-stay independent hospitals in England and Wales, 1992–1993', *British Medical Journal* 308: 1699–1701 (25 June).

Williamson, C. (1985) 'Consulting consumers: a managers' guide to consumers', *Health Services Journal* 105 (5481): 28–9.

Williamson, O. E. (1975) *Markets and Hierarchies: Analysis and Antitrust Implications*, New York: Free Press.

—— (1985) *The Economic Institutions of Capitalism: Firms, Markets, Relational Contracting*, New York: Free Press.

World Bank (1993) *World Development Report 1993: Investing in Health*, New York: Oxford University Press.

WHO (2000) *The World Health Report 2000: Health Systems: Improving Performance*, Geneva: World Health Organisation.

Xu, K., Evans, D. B., Kawabata, K., Zeramdini, R., Klavus, J. and Murray, C. J. L. (2003) 'Household catastrophic health expenditure: a multi-country analysis', *The Lancet*, 362 (9378): 111–17.

Yang, B. (1991) 'Health insurance in Korea: opportunities and challenges', *Health Policy and Planning* 6 (2): 119–29.

Yepes, F. J. and Sanchez, L. H. (1998) 'Reforming pluralist systems: the case of Colombia', in A. Mills (ed.) *Reforming Health Sectors*, London: Kegan Paul.

Yesudian, C. A. K. (1994) 'Behaviour of the private sector in the health market in Bombay', *Health Policy and Planning* 9 (1): 72–81.

—— (2001) *Policy Research India: the Regulating of Private Health Providers*, Alliance for Health Policy and Systems Research paper15, at http://www2.alliance-hpsr.org/jahia/webdav/site/myjahiasite/shared/case_studies/15-India-final-aug02.pdf (accessed 8 January 2007).

Zwanziger, J., Melnick, G. and Eyre, K. M. (1994) 'Hospitals and anti-trust: defining markets and setting standards', *Journal of Health Politics, Policy and Law* 19 (2): 423–47.

Zwarenstein, M. F. and Price, M. R. (1990) 'The 1983 distribution of hospitals and hospital beds in RSA by area, race, ownership and type', *South African Medical Journal* 77: 448–52.

Index

Note: *italic* page numbers denote references to Figures/Tables.